Ross Penster

3-7-13

"SIXTY YEARS & SIXTY HEROES"

A Celebration of Minnesota Sports

By
Ross Bernstein

For Sara & Campbell...

"SIXTY YEARS & SIXTY HEROES
A Celebration of Minnesota Sports"

by Ross Bernstein

(WWW.BERNSTEINBOOKS.COM)

BERNSTEIN BOOKS PUBLISHING

A portion of the proceeds from the sale of this book will benefit the Herb Brooks Foundation. Thank you for your support!

ISBN: 0-9787809-2-2

Printed by Printing Enterprises, New Brighton, MN

PHOTO CREDITS
Cover Photos: (Bruce Kluckhohn: Mauer & Gaborik), (Vikings: Grant, Peterson),
(Twins: Hrbek) (U of M: Whalen, Mariucci & Mayasich) (Pioneer Press: Mikan)

University of Minnesota: 6,9,11,15-18,21-26,28,29,31,33,36-41,43,45,49,51,59,64,65,67,
69,71,73,74,76,77,79-81,83,86-89,91,94-97,101,103,105,107,109,110,111,113,115,117-120,123-127,131,134,135
Pioneer Press: 10,12,15,27,32,51-55,58,66,67,68,78,79,92,93,98-101,105,106
Minnesota Twins: 8,27,33,41,44-49,51,55,56,57,70,71,75,87,90,91,105,121,129
Minnesota Vikings: 11,41,57,59,62,63,65,69,71,73,82,91,101,117,119,130,131
Bruce Kluckhohn: 8,116,117,122,123,128,129,131-133
Don Clark Collection: 19,25,35,39,45,53,65,69,75,89
Dick Jonckowski Collection: 13,16,35
Minnesota Historical Society: 13,17,19,20,21,30,33,34
U.S. Hockey Hall of Fame: 18,27,37,41,50,55,59,61,63,75,77,81,83,121
Tim Cortes: 4,121, (Cover Painting)
TPG Sports: 99
Eric Miller: 95,107,115,125
Vince Muzik: 112-115
Sandy Thompson: 108
Rick A. Kolodziej: 104
Minnesota State High School League: 111
University of Minnesota Duluth: 84,85,87,119,123,133
St. John's University: 42
St. Cloud State University: 89
Minnesota State University, Mankato: 47
Winona State University: 133
Bemidji State University: 85
Hamline University: 15
Augsburg College: 103
Gustavus Adolphus: 81
Duluth Dukes: 113
Tim Herron: 129
Janet Karvonen: 72,73
Patty Berg: 31
Jill Trenary: 93
Duane Baglien: 53
Hazeltine International: 57
Cindy Nelson: 67
Tracy Caulkins: 85
Scott LeDoux: 77
Briana Scurry: 109
Greg LeMond: 97
Dick Beardsley: 79
Amy Peterson: 93
David Wheaton: 99

COVER PAINTING by TIM CORTES

One of the nation's premier photo realism artists, Tim Cortes uses colored pencils as his preferred medium. Hundreds of his collectible lithographs have been sold throughout North America and his clients are a venerable who's-who of American sports. From Shaquille O'Neal to Mark McGwire and from Wayne Gretzky to Troy Aikman, Cortes has been commissioned to create countless commemorative works of art over the past two decades.

Cortes' paintings have been featured in numerous venus around the world, including: the U.S. Hockey Hall of Fame, Franklin Mint, Kelly Russell Studios and Beckett's Magazine, as well as on trading cards, pro sports teams' game-day programs, and in various publications. Known for his impeccable detail, Cortes has dedicated his life to the pursuit of celebrating the life and times of many of the world's most famous athletes and the sporting events in which they play.

Cortes grew up in Duluth, where he later starred as a hockey goaltender at Duluth East High School. After a brief stint in the United States Hockey League, Cortes went on to play between the pipes for two seasons in the mid-1980s for the University of Minnesota's Golden Gophers. Cortes then decided to pursue his passion of art and sports full-time, and enrolled at the prestigious Minneapolis College of Art and Design. He has been painting ever since.

Presently, Tim lives in Duluth with his wife Kathy and their two children. He continues to play senior hockey and also gives back by coaching both youth football and hockey. In addition, he also served as the goalie coach for the three-time NCAA champion University of Minnesota-Duluth Women's Hockey program in the mid-2000s.

TIM CORTES STUDIO

Tim Cortes has created literally hundreds of different pieces of sports art over his illustrious 20-year career in the business, and tries to keep his print edition sizes low to ensure sell-outs and collectability. His latest success, personalized sporting prints, has proven to be extremely popular among his dedicated clientele. From parents, to fans, to the athletes themselves, the concept of putting your own child's name, painted right on the piece itself, is truly all the rage. With the print "Prized Possessions" (see below), which features a collection of vintage hockey equipment, the last name of the client can be remarqued onto the front of the hockey helmet — making the ultimate gift for the sports fan in your life.

If you would like to purchase a signed, limited edition print of any of Tim's works of art,
please check out his web-site or contact his studio in Duluth — where you too can own a piece of sports history.

TIM CORTES STUDIO
921 NORTH 40TH AVE. EAST
DULUTH, MN 55804
(218) 525-4953

WWW.TIMCORTESART.COM

TABLE OF CONTENTS

INTRODUCTION BY ROSS BERNSTEIN

Welcome to "60 Years & 60 Heroes: A Celebration of Minnesota Sports," the new, expanded and updated version of the 1997 regional best-seller, "50 Years • 50 Heroes." The continued popularity of this book has led me to revisit it a decade later and I am proud to say that it is now bigger and better than ever. It has been completely redone with updated "where-are-they-now" bios, interviews, stories, as well as all sorts of new historical information. If you are into sports history and enjoy reading about our state's greatest teams and athletes, then this book is for you.

Here is how the book is laid out: Each chapter represents a year, going back 60 years, and featured in it is, arguably, the greatest moment from the world of Minnesota sports that year. That event is then tied into an interview and biography of a hometown or home-grown hero who played a key role in it. In addition, gone are the old "Cliff Claven" trivia tid-bit sidebars from the old version of the book, and in their place is something much, much better — the No. 2 and No. 3 ranked sporting events from that year — which are also tied into hometown heroes. In a sense, the book tripled in content, going from one to three top headline stories. So, take a year such as 1976, a great one in Minnesota sports history. There was so much stuff going on that year, it was a tough call. Well, I chose Ahmad Rashad and the Vikings losing to the Raiders in Super Bowl XI for the main chapter. Reed Larson and the Gopher Hockey team beating Michigan Tech to win the national championship was No. 2; while Allen Merrick and the Kicks making it all the way to the NASL Finals before losing to Toronto came in at No. 3. Is this open to debate? Absolutely. And that is what makes the book so much fun.

It is important to note, however, that this book is not a list of the 60 greatest heroes in Minnesota sports. Rather, it is a fun way to celebrate 60 great events, tied into 60 great men and women. While some chapters feature detailed accounts, extensive quotes and game summaries, others focus on different aspects of that particular event or person. No two chapters are alike, and hopefully that will add to the uniqueness of the book. Basically, I tried to have fun with it and pick interesting people and events to feature. Many times it was like trying to fit a square peg into a round hole, but overall I would like to think that it all worked out. There are hundreds of individuals who have either been born and raised in Minnesota, or have played here on either a professional or collegiate team that definitely could've been featured in this book. Obviously I couldn't accommodate all of those people, so I chose to celebrate a sampling of men and women who have made a difference in the world of Minnesota sports. For those left out, I am truly sorry.

OK, here are my 10 ground rules for my book. Rule No. 1: I get to make the rules. For starters, there are actually 61 heroes (going from 1948-2008), with Mark Parrish and the Minnesota Wild winning their first ever Northwest Division crown in 2008 being the extra bonus chapter. Hey, the book went to press in the Fall of 2008, and I felt like I had to include this year in it. As long as I am making the rules, I can do crazy things from time to time, such as featuring 61 heroes in a book about 60 Heroes.

Rule No. 2: I tried to pick native Minnesotans as much as I could, whenever I could. Case in point, in 2001 I chose Darby Hendrickson to represent the Wild's first season. Was Darby the best player on that team? Probably not. But, he is from Richfield and he was a Gopher. And, he is my buddy. Hey, I'm a homer.

Rule No. 3: There is a ton of information in the book about the Gophers. Yes, way more so than other schools. I am a huge Gopher fan and a complete and unabashed homer in that regard, for

which I make no apologies. I will say this though, I root for all Minnesota teams come playoff time... just as long as they aren't playing my Gophers. There is a lot of hockey stuff in the book too. Deal with it.

Rule No. 4: I chose not to dwell on the bad deals which were a buzz-kill, such has the Herschell Walker trade in 1989. Sure, that might have been the top story in the local sports world that year, but it makes me want to vomit every time I think about it — so I left it out. In addition, I tried not to focus on the sad stuff either, such as the tragic bus crash that claimed the lives of four Duluth Dukes baseball players en route to a game in St. Cloud on July 24, 1948. I wanted to stay positive and have fun.

Rule No. 5: There is some repetition in the book. It wasn't necessarily laid out to be read "cover-to-cover," but rather picked up and put down. While this book might appear to be a fancy coffee-table book, deep down it is really a bathroom-book in disguise. As such, I wrote each chapter with the understanding that the reader might not have read the previous pages which may have had led into the next chapter. For instance, the 1985 and 1986 chapters are both about the Gopher football team making it to back-to-back bowl games. There are some things repeated in 1986 that were also in 1985 in order to allow for readers to be able to jump around from chapter to chapter. If you read the book straight through, you may read the same fact twice.

Rule No. 6: Because some sports, such as football, go into two seasons — Super Bowls are listed in the year of the season, not the actual game. Case in point, while the 1969 Vikings lost to the Chiefs in Super Bowl IV, the actual game was played in January of 1970.

Rule No. 7: This is my caveat of sorts that says if you find a misspelled name or an error of some sort, please accept my humble apologies. Between the hundreds of sources of information, coupled with the more than 100 hundred interviews that I was able to conduct, occasionally facts became convoluted. I want to get it right though and regard this project as a "work in progress" that will continue to grow and expand over the years to come.

Rule No. 8: There are a boat load of men and women who should absolutely be in this book, that aren't. Because I couldn't write a book that was 14,000 pages long, I chose to have fun with it and do it this way. Having said that, I do feel bad about so many of the folks who were on the bubble. From the 2004 NCAA Final Four Gopher Volleyball team; to the 2003 U.S. Women's Open champion Hilary Lunke; to our three Heisman Trophy winners: Pine River's Terry Baker at Oregon State in 1962 and St. Paul's Chris Weinke at Florida State in 2000. (Yeah, I know, Faribault's Bruce Smith won it in 1941, but the book only goes back to 1948 — so he didn't make the cut.)

Rule No. 9: I added a final chapter at the end about Bronko Nagurski. Even though the Bronk didn't play in the 60 aforementioned years, I put a chapter in there about him just out of pure respect. The way I see it, you can't write a book about Minnesota sports history without including the big lug.

Rule No. 10: Relax. Undoubtedly, whenever a book such as this is written, people tend to get bent out of shape when they realize that so-and-so wasn't mentioned, or that he or she got more ink than so and so. I guess that is just the nature of the beast with something like this, and all I can say is that I tried to be arbitrary and objective in my research, and hopefully the vast majority of people who "should be in here," are in here. Believe me, it was a difficult process to have to eliminate so many wonderful biographies and funny stories because I simply did not have the space.

Rule No. 11: (Just like in the movie *"Spinal Tap,"* my list also goes to 11.) Have fun. This isn't rocket science. I am not winning any Pulitzer Prizes here, so chill out — you just learn something!

Overall, this book is about celebrating the wonderful sports achievements that have made our great state what it is today. Time and again you'll hear Minnesota's native sons in the national media talking about how they are willing to take a lesser salary in order for them to come home again — guys like Kent Hrbek, Jack Morris, Terry Steinbach, Paul Molitor and Dave Winfield.

The common denominator in almost all of those instances seems to be our amazing quality of life that we have here. I think that as Minnesotans we are proud of our own, and equally as proud of those who represent us on the playing field. Something that I have always liked is the fact that Minnesota's pro sports teams are all named after the state, and not after a particular city — like most other professional teams are. I think we all enjoy when our teams do well, and we all whine when they don't. But win or lose, sports is an integral part of the fabric of our lives here.

I think it is also important to note that the word hero is a very subjective word and can mean a lot of different things to a lot of different people — particularly after the tragic events of September 11th, when the word hero took on a meaning that shouldn't even be mentioned in the same collective breath with anything that has to do with sports. In my opinion, sports heroes are people that we looked up to when we were kids. These relationships are fostered early on in life and grow from there. As a kid growing up, my heroes were guys like Fran Tarkenton, Neal Broten and Kirby Puckett. But, I think that at a certain age, people become painfully aware of the fact that sports is a business, and at that point they no longer view athletes as heroes, but as businessmen. They get jaded from time to time. Let's face it. Some of these guys are jerks, and that is about as good as you can sugar-coat it. But, I have chosen to take the high-road in this book and tried to celebrate the achievements that these people have accomplished while they were on the field, not off of it. Translation: Yeah, Randy Moss is in here, and despite what he may or may not have done in his past, he is still a hero/idol/role-model to a lot of little kids who dream of catching touchdowns the way that only he can. Enough said.

With that, I would hope that the readers of this book will be able to reflect back, reminisce, and remember a team, a player or even a special day at the ballpark that he or she might have spent a long time ago just hanging out with someone special. Sports are constantly changing today and I think it is important that we not only look to the future with optimism, but remember and celebrate our past, which is full of great history and wonderful memories. This is OUR history, and we need to embrace it and celebrate it. We need to teach our kids about it and know this stuff, it is really important to who we are as Minnesotans. I take great pride in that and hope that I have succeeded in my mission to both educate and entertain you.

As for me, and my passion for Minnesota sports... you may be wondering just where the heck it comes from. Well, I grew up in the small southern Minnesota town of Fairmont, and after graduating in 1987 I went on to attend the University of Minnesota. There, I wound up becoming buddies with some Gopher hockey players and before long they convinced me that I should try to walk-on to the team. I figured why not? I grew up dreaming of wearing the Maroon and Gold and thought I would go for it. Well, after a brief "cup of coffee," (as a practice pylon nonetheless), Coach Woog politely informed me that it just wasn't going to work out. It turned out that there was another position available on the team though, as the team mascot "Goldy the Gopher." There were two basic criteria for the job: first, you had to be a hockey player; and secondly, you had to be a complete idiot. I apparently fit on both accounts and got the gig.

From there I began wearing a giant rodent costume and making a fool out of myself in front of thousands of people at old Mariucci Arena. Two older brothers with Ivy League MBA's and I aspired to become a giant rodent. Needless to say, mom and dad were not too thrilled about my career aspirations at this point in my life.

There was one story that was particularly hilarious that I will never forget. You see, I used to live in a frat house just a half a block away from the arena and would literally walk over to the game all dressed in my costume, ready to go. Coincidentally, most Friday and Saturday afternoons, our fraternity had kegs tapped for all the brothers to get a jump-start on the evenings' festivities. So, once in a while I would partake in the social goings-on before a game, which sometimes made for some interesting fodder. Anyway, one time after a few cocktails, I came over to entertain the masses at the arena. No sooner than I had gotten my skates off after the first intermission to climb back up onto my perch under the scoreboard, nature called. So, I climbed down and went out into the hall to use the bathroom. Luckily, because the game was going on, it was empty. The coast was clear,

and I could now take off my head to take care of the business at hand. No pun intended. I had to be very careful that no little kids saw me though, otherwise it could mean big trouble. You see, little kids believe in Goldy the same way they believe in Santa Clause and the Easter Bunny, so Rule No. 1 of mascoting is and always will be: "NEVER BE SEEN WITHOUT YOUR HEAD ON!"

Now, for those of you who may not remember the posh lavatory facilities at the old barn, let me refresh your memories... they were a dump. I had to choose between the ever-popular urinal trough, or the more private, luxurious stalls in the rear. I chose the latter. Realizing that my giant head would not fit in the stall with me, however, I took it off and put it on the toilet in the next stall over, closing the door behind me. I then went back into my stall and started to undo my breezers so that I could relieve myself.

It was at that moment that I heard a sound. Someone had come in. I quickly jumped up on top of the stool so that I wouldn't blow my cover. That's when I heard it, a noise I will never forget. It was a horrifying, blood-curdling scream that could set off car alarms and drive dogs mad. As I peered through a crack in the stall door, I saw a little boy just standing there horrified, perplexed, and confused — pointing at the Gopher-less head which was sitting on the potty before him. Figuring that the rest of Goldy had been whooshed away like so many poo-poos before, he yelled out in sheer terror: "Daddy, Daddy, help, quick! Goldy's flushed down the toilet!"

I nearly fell off the can at this point, trying not to laugh. As dad came over and saw the situation, I knew that young junior had been emotionally traumatized. Daddy just shuttled his son away and tried to reason with the little fella, but to no avail. I could hear him screaming "GOLDEEEEEEE!" out the door and all the way down the hall. I only wish I could've heard the conversation that took place in the wagoneer family truckster on the way home from the game. That kid may wind up as a serial killer one day, and it will probably be my fault. Oh well, we'll never know.

Anyway, after three glorious years as a giant rodent, I was approached by a publisher after a game one night who told me that he wanted to write a book about all of the trouble I had gotten into over the years. I told him I was flattered that he enjoyed my shtick, but that other than my mother, I wasn't sure anybody would ever want to read his book. So, I politely said thanks but no thanks. Now, at the time I was a senior and wasn't really sure what I wanted to be when I grew up. So, I got to thinking. What if I wrote a book about the history of Gopher Hockey, but with a twist — what if it featured interviews and stories from hundreds of former players, coaches and media personalities? And, most importantly, what if it was ghost-written with an inside slant from Goldy's perspective? Hey, that's not bad. I thought this could be pretty fun. And, it would certainly help divert my attention away from the scary specter of entering the real world for at least one more year while dad's cash was drying up.

With that, I jumped in head first and started interviewing anybody and everybody who had ties to Gopher Hockey. I was buzzing around the Twin Cities in my little Plymouth Horizon, meeting up with the likes of everybody from Herb Brooks to Lou Nanne to Neal Broten to Stanley Hubbard to Glen Sonmor. It was a riot. If they had stories to tell, I was going to record them and put them in my book. What started as a "neat" project, completely took off. Soon, guys were looking me up and taking me to lunch, just to make sure that they got in the book. It was amazing. They were thrilled that Gopher Hockey was finally going to be chronicled, and they were even more thrilled that if somebody was going to be doing it, that it was one of their own. The book, appropriately titled "Gopher Hockey by the Hockey Gopher," came out in the Fall of 1993 and was an instant regional best-seller. Who knew?

From those humble beginnings, I am proud to say that I have now written more than 40 sports books. Go figure. My passion is sports and I feel truly blessed to be able to make my career doing what I love — chronicling the history and heroes of the Land of 10,000 Lakes. Sports is such a part of our fabric of life here and seems to touch nearly everyone in some way or another. I am truly honored and humbled to be able to share this wealth of information with you in my new book. Hopefully you will have half as much fun reading about and celebrating this amazing tradition as I did in getting the opportunity to bring it all to life. *Cheers!*

FOREWORD BY JOE MAUER

Twins catcher Joe Mauer is without a doubt one of Minnesota's greatest athletes. Mauer grew up in St. Paul and went on to earn all-state honors in football, basketball and baseball at Cretin-Derham Hall High School. As a quarterback on the gridiron, Mauer was named as the USA Today and Gatorade national player of the year in 2000, but he turned down a scholarship from Florida State University to enter the Major League Baseball draft instead. Shortly thereafter Mauer was selected by the Twins with the first overall pick of the 2001 draft. He would go on to spend the next couple of years in the minor leagues, alongside his two brothers Jake and Billy, before making his Major League debut with the Twins in 2004. Taking over for the newly departed All-Star catcher A.J. Pierzynski behind the plate, Mauer played well out of the gates, but struggled with a knee injury that wound up sidelining him or much of his rookie campaign. He rehabbed that off-season, however, and then came back strong in 2005, where he notched 144 hits in 131 games while hitting a solid .294.

Joe burst onto the national scene in 2006, earning American League Player of the Month honors in June, and following it up with his first ever selection to the All-Star Game. He appeared on the cover of Sports Illustrated in August and with that, officially garnered superstar status. He stayed humble though and focused on the fundamentals, ultimately winning the American League batting crown with a .347 average, even becoming the first catcher in history to lead the Major Leagues in hitting. Mauer hit .293 in 2007, All-Star numbers for most hitters, but sub-par for the man most baseball pundits consider to have the best swing in baseball. He roared back in 2008, however, sitting atop the league's batting average leader board for much of the season and earning the starting catching job for the American League at the All-Star Game. One of the most popular players in Twins history, Joe Mauer is, as they say, the "face of the franchise."

"To be a Minnesota Twin is truly a dream come true," said Joe. It's awesome. I mean, I have played in the Big Leagues for five years now and my grandparents have never missed a home game. How cool is that? I have so much support here from friends and family and I couldn't be happier. I am just very, very lucky to be in this situation. I am so proud to be a part of the Twins organization, they are just great, great people. There have been so many great players who have played for the Twins over the years. So, to be a part of that great tradition and history is pretty special. It is not just great players either, it is great people. I feel a tremendous responsibility to wear that uniform with pride and to represent my community the right way."

"As a kid I loved to watch the Twins. My heroes, like so many other kids at the time, were Kirby Puckett and Kent Hrbek. I just loved those guys, they were awesome. It has been so great to get to know Kent over the years too. I see him quite a bit and we have become friends, which is really neat. He is a great guy. Sometimes I have to pinch myself when I am around him. I mean, I WAS Kent Hrbek in the back yard growing up, he was THE guy. I was a lefty, so he was MY guy. My two brothers fought it out over who could be Kirby, but I always got to be Kent Hrbek. As kids, we won a whole bunch of World Series' in that back yard in St. Paul. I never would have imagined in a million years that I would someday get to play for the Twins when I grew up. So, yes, dreams really can come true.

"I feel so blessed to be in this situation and never want to take it for granted. The fans have been great to me and I really appreciate that. To them, I just want to say thanks. Thanks for coming out and supporting us and thanks for always being there. We have such great fans here and that makes our jobs a lot easier. We really appreciate what they do for us. I have been pretty lucky to have been embraced the way that I have been over the years by them. There has been so much support for me and for my family and I can't thank the fans enough for that.

"One of the biggest things I am looking forward to is the new stadium. I, like all of my teammates, am so excited to play in it. Believe it or not, I never got to see a big league ballgame outdoors until I was actually playing in the big leagues. So, I am thrilled about our new stadium and about being able to play in there for a long, long time. Thank you to all of those people who helped to make it happen, we appreciate it so much. Hopefully, it will help us win a whole bunch of World Series titles for our fans in the years to come. Sure, there will be some rain delays and it will be cold in April, but who cares? We will be outside and I can't wait.

"As for life after baseball, I enjoy working with kids quite a bit. In fact, if I wasn't playing baseball I would probably be a teacher and a coach. I still may pursue that when my career is over down the line, who knows? I was lucky. Growing up, I had really supportive parents who let me play all sorts of sports and just let me have fun. I also had a bunch of great coaches too, which I am so grateful for. I would not be where I am today without all of their help and support, that is for sure. I do a lot of clinics for kids during the off-season and I enjoy that quite a bit. It is neat to see the same kids come back year after year and watch their progress. That's a pretty cool feeling.

"I really enjoy giving back too. That is so important. I remember when I was a kid in like sixth grade and going to a Summer camp at Cretin Derham Hall. Paul Molitor came and spoke to us about baseball and about life. We got to ask him questions and hang out with him. I still remember that like it was yesterday. Paul was such a hero to everyone at Cretin and really a great role model for all of us who went there. Now that I play for the Twins, I have so much more appreciation for what he did and how he was so giving of his time. It is hard sometimes to juggle all of the demands that are put on you, but I try my best to do whatever I can. I remember how excited I was to meet Paul all those years ago and it is pretty neat to think that I might be able to have the same kind of impact on a kid today. You know, there have been a lot of guys over the years from this organization who have given back so much and I am just trying to do my part as well. It is so important to give back to your community, however you can. It is a big responsibility being in the public eye and I always try my best to make the right choices. I want to represent myself, my family, my team and my community as best as I can. I take that stuff pretty seriously.

"I guess when it is all said and done, I would hope to be remembered as somebody who tried his best; who was a good teammate; and who played the game the right way. Most importantly though, I hope to be remembered as a world champion."

— Joe Mauer —

FOREWORD BY LINDSAY WHALEN

Lindsay Whalen is by far and away the most popular women's basketball player ever to hail from Minnesota. Born and raised in Hutchinson, Whalen starred in basketball, tennis, and ran track at Hutchinson High School – earning All-Missota honors in each sport. The hard-court was her passion, however, and it was there that the four-time all-conference selection led her Tigers to three consecutive conference championships. From there, Whalen went on to fulfill her childhood dream of playing for the University of Minnesota. In fact, the speedy guard would become the first three time All-American and four time team MVP in Gopher history. The 2002 Big Ten Player of the Year earned All-Big Ten honors in 2002 and 2003, followed by academic and athletic All-American honors as well. In 2004 she took all of Minnesota on a magical ride, leading the Lady Gophers to their first ever Final Four. And, although they came up just short in the semifinals to the University of Connecticut, the Gophers had made the leap from college basketball obscurity to college basketball national contender.

In the end, Whalen had rewritten the record books on campus, ending up as the school's all-time leading scorer (male or female), with 2,285 career points – good for 20.3 points per game. Among her many honors and accolades, in 2004 Whalen was the first woman to be named as the Minneapolis Star Tribune's Sportsperson of the Year, beating out Twins' Cy Young Award winner Johan Santana and NBA MVP Kevin Garnett. She was even the first athlete in U of M history to have her own bobble-head doll. Further, on January 3, 2005, her No. 13 jersey was retired by the University on what was officially declared as "Lindsay Whalen Day" in Minnesota.

Whalen graduated from the University of Minnesota in 2004 with a degree in sports management and then went on to play professionally in the WNBA, where she was selected the first round of the draft (4th overall) by the Connecticut Sun. Legions of Minnesota basketball fans were hoping that some how, some way, the Minnesota Lynx could find a way to draft the hometown hero. They tied, making a pre-draft trade with the Seattle Storm to move up and acquire the 6th pick in the draft, but Connecticut swooped in and picked Whalen before Minnesota had a chance. Lindsay quickly won over the Connecticut fans over with her energy, attitude and talent. She led the Sun to the WNBA Finals in her first and second seasons and has even emerged as the team's all-time assists leader.

Lindsay, now a WNBA All-Star, continues to play for the Sun as of 2008, while also playing for an elite team in Prague, Czech Republic, during the off-season. She and her husband, former Gopher golfer Ben Greve, who were married in 2007, live in Connecticut and Minnesota.

"I am just a huge Minnesota sports fan," said Whalen. "I grew up following the Vikings, Twins, Gophers, North Stars and Timberwolves — I followed them all. I just loved sports, both playing them and watching them on TV. I will never forget the Twins winning it all in 1987 and 1991, that was so amazing. I was a huge Kirby Puckett fan too, he was the best. I also enjoyed watching Kevin Garnett, with the Wolves, as well as Randy Moss and Anthony Carter with the Vikings. Sports has always been a big part of my life, whether playing it or watching it, I just love

everything about it."

"Growing up in a town like Hutchinson was so much fun. When you grow up in a small town like that you can play sports all year round, it is great. The whole community rallies behind you and really gets into it. Sports was a big part of our identity, so letting down our fans was almost harder than losing. I remember losing to Winona in the sectionals my senior year of basketball and being so disappointed. It was always a dream of mine to make it to the state tourney and to come up short was tough.

"From there, I was so blessed to be able to play at the University of Minnesota. I had dreamed of playing for the Gophers, so when it finally happened it was a real dream come true for me. The entire experience was just so wonderful. Williams Arena was such a special place too. The highlight for sure was our amazing run to the Final Four back in 2004. What an incredible season that was. I remember it like it was yesterday. I was blessed to be on that team with such great people. We worked hard and had a common goal, which was probably why we had so much success. Everyone stepped up that year and it was magical. I would have loved to have won the national title, but it was a wonderful experience getting to the Final Four and being able to represent my school and my community in such a positive way. I just love the Gophers and will always wear the Maroon and Gold proudly.

"Then, to get drafted in the WNBA, that was almost surreal. I have really enjoyed my time with the Sun for the past five seasons. Being able to play professional basketball is something I never could have dreamed of when I was a kid, so to be out on the court doing what I love, and, getting paid for it — sometimes I have to pinch myself. I just want to do my part to make sure the league grows in popularity, and that starts with giving back and working with all of our young fans who support us. Girls youth basketball has taken off since the league's inception 12 years ago and that has been great to see. It is pretty neat to think that my daughter could one day grow up dreaming of playing professional basketball, because I know that when I was growing up that was not even in my wildest dreams.

"As for the Fans in Minnesota, first and foremost, just thanks for all your support. Our fans are awesome. They were there for us no matter what and we really appreciated that. Hopefully our run to the tournament in 2004 not only entertained our current fans, but also created a whole bunch of new ones as well. We all felt a sense of responsibility to help grow the game and to get more and more young girls playing basketball, so hopefully we accomplished that in doing what we did.

"As for the future, I enjoy living in Connecticut, but I miss Minnesota quite a bit too. It is a lot of fun to see the world through basketball though. My husband and I enjoy this lifestyle for now and will just see where it takes us. Who knows? Down the road when basketball isn't in the picture anymore, we may wind up back in Minnesota close to our families. I would like to get into coaching someday too, so we'll have to see what happens.

"When it is all said and done, I just want to be remembered as someone who was a good teammate, who worked hard, was reliable, and could always be counted on to do her best for her team."

— Lindsay Whalen —

FOREWORD BY KENT HRBEK

As a child growing up, literally, in the shadows of Bloomington's Metropolitan Stadium, Kent Hrbek often fell asleep to the sounds of cheering Twins and Vikings fans. It's no wonder then, that he grew up as a die-hard Minnesota sports fan. From his days of rounding the bases on the T-ball field with his big No. 6 jersey (in honor of his hero, Tony Oliva), to "touching em' all" in the Dome years later, Hrbek went on to become one of Minnesota's biggest stars. Hrbek played his entire 14-year Major League career with the Twins, leading the team to a pair of World Series titles in 1987 and 1991, while hitting .282 and belting out 293 career homers. Currently, Kent can be seen hosting his own TV show called "Kent Hrbek Outdoors." So, who better to talk about the state-of-the-state of the next century of Minnesota sports, than our favorite home-town hero, "Herbie."

"It's kind of weird, but I've come full-circle in my life. I started out as a huge Minnesota sports fan, playing and loving sports, and just wanting to be around the ballpark. Then, I was fortunate to have become an athlete who was considered as an idol to a lot of people and had a successful career in my home town. Now, today, I'm a huge Minnesota sports fan again. It's hard to believe that it's been so long since I hung it up. I guess you don't realize that you're a fan again until you go back to the ballpark and see your mug hanging from a banner out in right field."

"Sports is a really important thing for a lot of people in Minnesota. And, with regard to the fans and athletes of Minnesota, I think we've always been known as a state of underdogs. I don't care if it was the North Stars, the Twins, the Vikings, the Timberwolves, or the Gophers, we've never been favored to win anything. I know that no one expected us to win the World Series in 1987 and 1991, and when we did it, it just made it all that much more special.

"Minnesota fans are great. Not only are they knowledgeable about our local sports teams, but they stick by them. But, that doesn't mean that they're not fickle. They definitely need a winner for them to show up at the ballpark, I found that out first-hand! I think it's hard today for a lot of people to follow a team that's not winning. It's also tough for a fan to go sit in a ballpark during the summer after the hard winters up here. When the sun shines, people want to enjoy the outdoors while they can. They appreciate it and feel that they've earned it. It seems that everyone has a cabin on a lake somewhere that they can go to, and if they don't, they probably have a relative who does. But when they are in those cabins, hunting and fishing, you can bet that they have their TVs and radios on — and are tuned in to a ballgame.

"I think that a lot of the sentiment against sports that is going on today has to do with money and free-agency. It's a big issue nowadays and it makes it kind of scary to think about what's in store for small markets like us. Back when I was a kid, we followed the Twins and Vikings season after season and got to know them it seemed, as if they were family. Today, with free agency, the fans feel burned when players that they rooted for leave to go somewhere else. And, it's hard for teams to keep a strong nucleus together for any length of time to be successful. So, it's tough for the fans to make an emotional investment in a team and its players when they know that it might change the next year.

"I also think that sports have become a competitive business where people nowadays can follow not only the local players but their heroes from all over the country. When I was a kid, we hardly ever saw Mickey Mantle play on TV. But today, kids can see stars like Ken Griffey Jr. every other night. So, the media has made it easier for people to still be close to their heroes without actually going out to the ballpark. And, I think that has hurt the attendance, which affects the economics of the sport. Because of the big salaries in the game today, professional sports have moved from being a family affair to a corporate one. And that's too bad. The evolution of sports has turned a simple game into more about selling tickets, advertising, naming stadiums, and big corporations. But, if franchises want to survive, that's what has to happen I guess. Everyone seems to be upset at the players and the salaries today, but it's hard to fault them if the owners are willing to give them the money.

"Salaries have gotten out of control too, like Kevin Garnett's contract situation a few years ago. I don't know, is it anyone's business? I mean it never used to be. I never had any idea what the heck Tony Oliva or Rod Carew's salaries were every year. I just loved them for what they did on the field and the joy they brought me when they hit one over the fence. I could give a crap what the heck they did off the field or how much money they made. But, today that's all different. Who knows what's in store for the next 50 years? It will definitely be very interesting. It's scary to think that football and baseball might be a thing of the past here in the future, and thank goodness we got hockey back. I don't know, it's a tough call. A lot of people would rather see our tax dollars go toward education, which I would have to agree is a very valid argument.

"But I think everything goes hand in hand, and by that I mean that in order to have kids doing well in school, they need positive role models and idols to follow, and who better than sports heroes. As a kid, the only opportunities that I had were all somehow related to sports — little league baseball, football, hockey, soccer, basketball, and what have you. Kids need sports because it's a positive influence in their lives that builds teamwork, a positive attitude, and self esteem. I think it goes right along with education, because they learn a lot of things out there that they wouldn't otherwise learn in the classroom.

"This book is about heroes, and it's too bad that Ross couldn't go into the countless other unsung heroes on all the teams that weren't always in the limelight, because they were just as important. I think too that as a kid grows up and gets older and wiser, they realize that their childhood heroes were just athletes, and it was their moms and dads who were the real heroes — making them the people that they are. I'm optimistic about our future, and am glad that we can celebrate out past. I think that the concept for this book was really neat, and it was an idea that was long overdue. I really enjoyed reading about our rich sports heritage that we have here. It was a fun read and it brought back a lot of great memories of when I was a kid, and I think that's what sports is all about — great memories."

— Kent Hrbek —

FOREWORD BY BUD GRANT

Without question, Bud Grant is one of the greatest athletes and sports icons to ever play and coach in Minnesota. Grant was born and raised in Superior, Wis., and came to the University of Minnesota in 1946 after serving in the Navy at the Great Lakes Naval Station outside Chicago. As a Gopher, Grant was a legend, excelling in three sports and earning nine letters from 1946-49. He was a two-time All-Big Ten end on the gridiron under Coach Bernie Bierman; he starred as a forward and was the team MVP on the basketball team; and also played centerfield and pitched for the baseball team — where he led the team in hitting as a freshman. He would go on to graduate as one of Gold Country's best ever. In fact, he would later beat out Bronko Nagurski and Bruce Smith to be named as the "Top Athlete at the U of M for the First 50 Years of the Century."

From there, he joined the Minneapolis Lakers' dynasty where he averaged 2.6 points per game in each of the two years he played for the club, both of which were NBA championship teams. Anxious to try something different, Bud then joined the NFL's Philadelphia Eagles, who had made him their No. 1 draft pick that year. So talented was Grant, that in 1952, after switching from linebacker, where he led the team in sacks, to wide receiver, he finished second in the league in receiving and was voted to the Pro Bowl. After two years in Philly, he headed north of the border to play for the Winnipeg Blue Bombers of the Canadian Football League. Then, in 1957, after only four years in the league, and at the prime of his career, the front-office offered the 29-year-old the teams' head-coaching position. He accepted and proceeded to lead his Bombers to six Grey Cups over the next 10 years, winning four of them.

Ten years later, Grant came home to take over as the head coach of the NFL's Minnesota Vikings. It would be the beginning of one of the greatest coaching sagas in all of sports as he went on to coach for 28 years, winning a total of 290 regular season and post-season games, 122 as coach of the Winnipeg Blue Bombers of the CFL from 1957-66, and 168 as coach of the Vikings from 1967-83 and 1985. At Minnesota his teams made the playoffs 12 times, and won 15 championships: 11 Central Division (1968-71, 1973-78, and 1980), one NFL (1969) and three NFC (1973, 1974 and 1976). They also made four Super Bowl appearances as well.

In 1994 Bud was inducted into the Pro Football Hall of Fame in Canton, OH. With it, he became the first person ever to be elected to both the NFL and the Canadian Football League Hall of Fames. A zealous outdoorsman and activist, today Grant is a champion of preserving the environment for future generations. But, just because he is retired, don't think for a second that he has slowed down. Nope. When he is not consulting for his beloved Vikings, he is either out in a duck blind, deer stand or watering hole — bagging a trophy or reeling in a lunker. Modest as ever, Bud is truly a part of our fabric of life here in the Land of 10,000 Lakes.

"When Ross first called to interview me for a book he was writing about the history and heroes of Minnesota sports, I was skeptical 'How could someone possibly do justice to so many people and events?' I wondered. But he has done a fine job. Anyone who is interested in Minnesota sports will undoubtedly relate to someone or something in it."

"I am proud to have played a part in contributing to the wonderful history of Minnesota sports. Having been a member of the Gophers, Lakers, and Vikings, I have a unique perspective on sports in Minnesota. Sports has come a long way in this state. I remember always playing in front of capacity crowds at Williams Arena and Memorial Stadium at the University of Minnesota. But, today there is more competition for people's interests, especially with sports.

"Like myself, people enjoy the outdoors here. Whether it's boating, fishing, hunting, camping, golfing, or anything else, outdoor activities are precious to Minnesotans. These people like to participate in sporting activities, but they still find time to watch them as well. Sports fans here are knowledgeable and they appreciate good competition as well as good sportsmanship.

"Fans in places like New York, Philadelphia, and Chicago are fanatics about their local teams, but it's a narrow band of people. Our state has a broader group of fans. Sports in Minnesota encompass more of the mainstream, from casual observers to the die-hards, who will check to see how the Twins, Vikings, Timberwolves, or Gophers did, even if they didn't watch or listen to the game. It doesn't matter if they're from International Falls or Pipestone: people love and follow our teams here because they're interested, and they genuinely care.

"Traveling throughout Minnesota over the years, it has always amazed me at just how insightful our fans are and how closely they follow Minnesota's athletes and teams. And, they are proud of their accomplishments and exploits.

"In addition to following what's happening in Minnesota sports, it's nice to sit back and reflect on what's happened — to reminisce about our past and allow it to conjure up fond memories. This book will help sports fans do just that. There's something for everyone in it. If you enjoy reading about sports, history, biographies and funny stories, then you'll love this book because it's all in there. This is history, and it's significant that it has finally been captured on paper for all to see.

"We have a wonderful sports heritage to be proud of here in Minnesota, and it's all brought to life in the book."

— Bud Grant —

In 1947 a group of Twin Cities businessmen which included the likes of Ben Berger, Morris Chalfen and a young newspaper reporter by the name of Sid Hartman, decided to bring major league professional basketball to Minneapolis. After a year of research the group went ahead and acquired the financially-strapped Detroit Gems of the National Basketball League (NBL) for the whopping sum of $15,000, and moved them to Minnesota, where they would be renamed as the Minneapolis Lakers. They then hired John Kundla, who was coaching at St. Thomas, to be their coach, and former fight manager and restauranteur Max Winter to serve as their general manager.

The Lakers opened the first four games of their inaugural 1947-48 season with Jim Pollard at center. Pollard was an All-American at Stanford, but was a forward playing in the pivot. The club knew it needed a true center and had a plan on just how to get one. You see, the Lakers, by virtue of having the worst league record from the season before as the Gems, were now entitled to the first pick of a league-wide dispersal draft. (The Gems had posted a horrible 4-40 record that season — the worst in modern history! But Hartman and Co. knew that the league was about to go belly-up all along, and that is why they bought the team.) So, it came as no surprise to anyone when they selected the star of the NBL champion Chicago Gears, Center George Mikan — the game's greatest player at that time.

Although the Lakers held Mikan's draft rights, they still had to sign him to a contract. So, Winter flew the young center to Minneapolis with the hopes of wining and dining him. George came to the Twin Cities but wasn't sure if he wanted to be a Laker. The two sides were unable to come to terms on a deal, so George decided to go home to Chicago. That's when Sid Hartman, who handled the teams wheelings and dealings, saved the day by mysteriously getting lost while driving big George to the airport. As a result, Mikan missed his flight and was forced to stay one more night. That next day, George sat down with Winter again, this time inking a deal. It would be the beginning of a beautiful relationship.

In addition to Mikan and Pollard, Tony Jaros and Don "Swede" Carlson, both of whom had previously starred at the U of M as well as at Minneapolis Edison High School, were also added to the roster.

With that, the Lakers came out and dominated behind their new big man. Mikan was awesome. At six-foot-ten he was a giant that teams simply couldn't stop. The Lakers then went on to win the Western Division title that year by 13 games over runner-up Tri-Cities.

It was now off to the playoffs for the upstart Lakers. There, they breezed through the quarterfinals against Oshkosh, three games to one, and then swept Tri-Cities in the semifinals to advance to the NBL Finals against the Eastern Conference champion Rochester Royals. Before the Finals though, the Lakers accepted an invitation to play in the annual World Professional Tournament in Chicago. (Believe it or not, at that time winning the WPT was considered a bigger deal than an NBL title.) There, the Lakers rolled over the Wilkes-Barre Barons, 98-48, in the opening round, and then knocked off the Anderson Packers by three points in the semifinals. They then took on the defending champion New York Rens, an all-black barnstorming team, in the title game, and led by Mikan, who set a tournament record with 40 points, the Lakers beat the Rens, 75-71, to win the title.

Minneapolis now had just one day of rest before taking on Rochester in their best-of-five series at the Minneapolis Armory. (Their usual arena, the Minneapolis Auditorium, was full of campers and fishing boats for the annual Sportsman's Show, so they incredibly had to find another venue!) The Royals, led by a pair of guards from Seton Hall, Bob Davies and Bobby Wanzer, were a finesse squad. The Lakers meanwhile, had garnered a reputation as a bunch of bruisers. The big news for Rochester though, was the fact that their six-foot-nine All-Star Center, Arnie Risen, had suffered a broken jaw and would miss the entire championship series — a real break for Minneapolis.

The series opened to a jam-packed Armory with the Lakers taking Games One and Two. It then shifted to New York for the remaining games, as the Royals came back to take Game Three, 74-60, despite Mikan's 32-point performance. Then, in Game Four, the Lakers came out and dominated. They led from the opening buzzer and thanks to 27 points from Mikan and another 19 from Pollard, the Lakers cruised to an impressive 75-65 win — taking the NBL Crown in just their first year in the league.

For the season Mikan finished with a record 1,195 points, (nearly doubling the league's old mark), while averaging 21.3 points per game and leading the NBL in virtually every offensive category. For his efforts he was named as the league's MVP. In addition, he and Pollard were both named to the NBL's All-Star team. The upstart Minneapolis Lakers were now kings of the court, and quietly, a new sports dynasty was born.

"We were being judged on whether or not we could make it in the world of professional basketball," said Mikan, "and the excitement of winning that first Laker championship was just fantastic. It put us on the map, because at the time, big cities looked at Minneapolis as a tiny hick town. Well, we 'hicked' them all-right — we became league champions."

From the Windy City to the City of Lakes

George Lawrence Mikan Jr. was born in 1924, in Joliet, Illinois. He went on to enroll at DePaul University, where he learned the game under legendary Coach Ray Meyer. Meyer worked his prized pupil mercilessly, putting him on a regimen which greatly improved his agility, quickness and coordination, with drills that included skipping rope, throwing the medicine ball, shadowboxing and even ballet dancing. He would even tell George to try and dance with the shortest and smallest girls he could find at school dances, forcing him to either improve his footwork, or never get a date! Then, at the end of each practice, he would make him take 250 right-handed hook shots followed by another 250 with the left — a grueling repetition which would later become known simply as the "Mikan Drill" in basketball "how-to" manuals everywhere. Mikan went on to become the nation's biggest college star, leading the Blue Demons to the 1945 NIT title along the way.

Following his playing days at DePaul, George entered the then uncertain world of professional basketball, first with his hometown Chicago American Gears of the National Basketball League, and then with the Minneapolis Lakers, where he would lead his team to six world championships. Mikan revolutionized the game. Whereas in the past, guards and occasionally forwards had been the games' stars, Mikan redefined the center position. While most teams used them only to rebound and set picks, because most big men were considered too awkward to actually shoot the ball, George quickly changed all the rules. With his wide shoulders and firm elbows, he began to dominate the game like no other before him.

In a very "Jordanesque" way, George was the big draw for the new league. Fans came from all over the Upper Midwest to see the gentle giant. One time, in 1951, the Lakers were playing New York at Madison Square Garden, and the marquee in front of the Garden advertising that night's game read: "GEO. MIKAN vs. KNICKS." As game time neared, Mikan found himself to be the only player dressed for the game in the locker room. So, finally he said to his teammates, "Come on, gentlemen, we have a ballgame to play." His teammates then jokingly replied back: "No, George. You have a ballgame to play, and we can't wait to see how You do against the Knicks!"

Opposing teams soon found out that the best way to beat the Lakers was to simply try to keep the ball away from Mikan. In 1950, the Fort Wayne Pistons refused to shoot the ball and dared not give up their possession, ultimately just sitting there and stalling out an unbelievable 19-18 victory. (That was the lowest scoring game in NBA history and ultimately resulted in the creation of the 24-second clock.)

And that wasn't the only rule change in basketball that was a direct result of Mikan. You see, George did most of his damage down in the lane, which, at the time, was only six feet wide. This allowed him to set up in the low post right next to the basket, making him virtually impossible to stop. Because he was so much taller and stronger than everybody else, he simply dominated in those days. So, in 1951, the league doubled the width of the foul lane to 12 feet. This move was aimed at big men in general, but Mikan in particular. (The league, in an attempt to level the playing field, even tried raising the basket to 12 feet. Luckily though, that experiment lasted for just one game before cooler heads prevailed.)

On September 24, 1954, Mikan, who by now had received his law degree from the U of M, announced his plans to open his own law practice and retire as an active NBA player. Financially, he was set, and as the game's first bigger-than-life star, he had a bunch of endorsement deals lined up for everything from sneakers to beer to chewing gum. Regularly featured on magazine covers and on television, George was famous and wanted to settle down to raise his family. So Winter, wanting to focus his attention on landing an NFL franchise for Minnesota (ultimately the Vikings), then sold his stock to Mikan, announcing that the big fella would succeed him as the team's general manager. George attempted a comeback in 1956, but struggled, eventually becoming the Laker's coach in 1957-58. But with a 9-30 record, Coach Mikan once again left the game he loved.

A Laker from 1948-54, and again in 1955-56, his statistics were incredible. Mikan became the first player in history to score 10,000 points, ultimately finishing with 11,764. (At the time of his retirement the next closest player, Joe Fulks, was more than 3,700 points behind him.) A perennial seven-time All-Star, four times he led the league in scoring. And, amazingly, George missed only two games in his career with Minneapolis. He was the Lakers leading scorer 348 out of the possible 458 regular-season games that he played in, finishing with career averages of 22.9 points and 13.4 rebounds per game.

He returned to pro basketball again in 1967, this time as the first ever commissioner of the upstart American Basketball Association. With their trademark red, white, and blue ball, the new rebel league distinguished itself from the mighty, yet conservative, NBA. There, Mikan was influential in creating many of the innovations that are commonplace in the game today, such as the three-point shot, as well as non-basketball halftime and on-court entertainment for fans. When the ABA moved its headquarters from Minneapolis to New York City in 1969, Mikan resigned.

And, although Wilt Chamberlain, Bill Russell, Kareem Abdul-Jabbar and Shaquille O'Neal would follow, Mikan was the NBA's first truly dominant center and the first big man capable of car-

rying his entire team. In 1950, Mikan was named as the "Greatest Basketball Player for the First Half of the 20th Century" by the Associated Press, and 46 years later, as part of the NBA's 50th Anniversary Celebration, George was named as one of the "50 Best Players" in league history. In 1959, he was inducted as a charter member of the Pro Basketball Hall of Fame.

After basketball, Mikan, who ran a very successful law firm in the Twin Cities, also got into real-estate as well as the travel business. He later resurfaced onto the hardwood once again in the mid-1980s as the head of a task force which ultimately brought professional basketball back to Minneapolis — in the form of the expansion Minnesota Timberwolves. A tremendous family man, George and his wife Pat raised six children and settled down in Scottsdale, Ariz. (One of George's sons, Larry, a former Gopher, also played pro ball with Cleveland in the early 1970s.) Sadly, George passed away in Scottsdale on June 1, 2005, of complications from diabetes and other ailments.

Among his many accolades, his greatest tribute might have come at the Minneapolis Target Center on April 8th, 2001, when he was honored in a "Celebration at Center Court" during the halftime of a game between the Los Angeles Lakers and Timberwolves. There, in front of dozens of his former teammates, George was presented with a life-size bronze sculpture — which now stands proudly in the arena's lobby. Fittingly, it depicted the 6-foot-10 legend with his back-to-the-basket and his arm extended into the pose of a hook-shot — George's signature move as he was about to score a game-winning basket. It was a larger-than-life tribute to a larger-than-life man who has certainly made us all very proud. A true gentleman, George Mikan's contributions to the sport and his impact on the NBA still loom as large as his enormous frame. The cornerstone of the league's first dynasty, George was simply the best.

"He was the greatest competitor and team player I ever had," recalled former Lakers Coach John Kundla of his star player. "He made the Minneapolis Lakers, and made this town a major-league city. I remember Wilt Chamberlain and Bill Russell telling George that he was their idol growing up, and the two said that he was partially responsible for much of their success in the NBA. He brought big league basketball to Minneapolis and did so much for Minnesota. He is 'Mr. Basketball,' and I owe all my success to him. He is the greatest."

Laker Tombstone: "Well, I guess I would want to be remembered as 'Mr. Basketball,' I earned that honor."

1948 RUNNER-UP: ROY CAMPANELLA

The Saint Paul Saints, the minor league farm-team of the Brooklyn Dodgers, win the 1948 American Association "Junior" World Series. The Saints were led by future Hall of Fame manager Walt Alston, and featured several star players, including: Duke Snider, Spider Jorgenson, Eric Tipton and Pat McGlothin. Late in the season, catcher *ROY CAMPANELLA* became the first African American to play in the league when the Dodgers optioned him to St. Paul. The future Hall of Famer was called up about a month later after hitting .325 with 13 homers and 39 RBIs in 35 games.

HONORABLE MENTION: VERN GAGNE

Gopher wrestler *VERN GAGNE* wins his first of two straight NCAA championships — first as a 191-pounder and then as a heavyweight. Gagne, who grew up on a farm near Hamell and graduated from Wayzata High School, is arguably Minnesota's greatest all-time grappler. Gagne also played football for the Gophers and later played briefly for the NFL's Green Bay Packers. He retired from football, however, to become a professional rassler, where he would garner fame and fortune over the next half century. As the heavyweight champ of his American Wrestling Association (AWA), he entertained legions of loyal fans around the world as one of the industry's top grapplers and promoters.

JIM POLLARD
The Lakers Win Back-to-Back Titles

The Lakers made a major decision during the 1948-49 off-season when they, along with the Rochester Royals, Fort Wayne Pistons and Indianapolis Jets, opted to jump ship and defect from the struggling NBL and join Maurice Podoloff's upstart rival Basketball Association of America — which had just completed its second year of operation. The BAA was already an eight-team circuit that featured franchises in several major markets including: New York, Philadelphia, Boston, Baltimore, St. Louis and Chicago. Now, the four new NBL teams, which took up residence in the BAA's Western Division, along with Chicago and St. Louis, would make up a perfectly balanced 12-team league. The addition of the four clubs really bolstered the BAA's reputation as well. It already had the marquis arenas in the major markets, but this gave it the big-name players it needed. The biggest of those names, of course, was George Mikan — who was very excited to now get the chance to showcase his talents in big venus such as New York's Madison Square Garden.

Minneapolis opened the 1948-49 season in Baltimore against the defending BAA-champion Bullets with Laker Forward Herm Schaefer's 23 points leading the way to a 84-72 victory. There were several new faces on the roster that season, including Johnny Jorgensen, a former teammate of Mikan's at DePaul, Mike Bloom, a former All-American forward at Temple and Guard Earl Gardner from Depaw. (During the season the Lakers would also add University of Utah Forward Arnie Ferrin, as well as NYU's Don Forman and DePaul's Whitey Kachan.)

On November 24, the Lakers set a single-game BAA scoring record when they dumped the Providence Steamrollers, 117-89. Mikan then made history a few weeks later when he unloaded for 48 points to set another new league mark. Mikan topped the 40-point plateau on seven different occasions that season while twice surpassing 50, ultimately fending off Philadelphia's Joe Fulks to win the league scoring crown with 28.3 points per game.

Minneapolis also played the Harlem Globetrotters that season as well, splitting the home-and-home battle with the legendary club. Both Jim Pollard and Swede Carlson sat out the away game in Chicago, but returned to lead the Lakers past the Trotters, 68-53, in front of a record 10,122 fans at the Auditorium. In the game, Laker Guard Don Forman decided to perform some crowd-pleasing antics of his own, including a dazzling dribbling exhibition that brought the crowd to its feet.

The Lakers wound up finishing the regular season with a 44-16 record, good for second in the Western Division, one game behind their old nemesis, the Rochester Royals. The playoffs opened that March with the Lakers sweeping the Chicago Stags on Mikan's two-game, 75-point effort.

From there, Minneapolis took on Rochester in another best-of-three series in the Western Division Finals. And, while Royals Center Arnie Risen had been absent in the '48 Finals, he was rarin' to go this time around. The series opened in New York with the Lakers watching a 17-point lead wither away behind an amazing rally which gave the Royals a two-point advantage with just under a minute to go in the game. That's when Tony Jaros nailed what proved to be the game-winning basket with just 18 ticks on the clock as the Lakers hung on for a dramatic 80-79 win. Back at the St. Paul Auditorium for Game Two, the Lakers went on to outscore the Royals 18-3

in the fourth quarter as they cruised to a 67-55 victory and a berth in the BAA Finals.

Next up for Minneapolis were the Eastern Division champs from Washington. The Capitols, who were guided by legendary Coach Red Auerbach, were led by six-foot-nine Center Bones McKinney, Forwards Bob Feerick and Kleggie Hermsen, and Guards Freddie Scolari and Sonny Hertzburg. The best-of-seven series opened at the Minneapolis Auditorium and behind Mikan's 42-point performance, as well as a pair of last-second free-throws by Carlson, the Lakers hung on to take Game One, 88-84. Auerbach's strategy of isolating his defense to blanket Mikan in Game Two worked out as they held the bigman to just 10 points. But the rest of the Lakers lit it up with Carlson and Schaeffer each tallying 16 and 13 points, respectively — as Minneapolis took a 2-0 lead with a 76-62 win. The series then shifted to Washington's tiny Uline Arena for Game Three, where Mikan poured in 35 points to lead the Lakers to a 94-74 win and a 3-0 lead.

The Caps came out strong in Game Four though, beating Minneapolis by the final of 83-71. Bones McKinney played Mikan tough throughout the game, but George hung in there to score 27 points — despite chipping a bone in his wrist early in the game on a flagrant foul by Kleggie Hermsen that knocked him into the first row of seats.

Mikan recalled the play in Roland Lazenby's 1996 book, "The NBA Finals: A 50 Year Celebration," "Red told them to drag me off the court and get the game going. Hermsen made sure he fouled out quick after that. There's such a thing as retribution in sport. You didn't necessarily have to get back at someone because your teammates would." (Hermsen, a former Gopher and native Minnesotan, feared that if the series shifted back to Minneapolis, the hometown crowd might want to lynch him for his tackle of Big George!)

So tough was Mikan that he scored 22 points in Game Five with a huge cast on his right wrist. He played on though, despite being hacked at by the Caps throughout the game.

"I can remember playing with my broken arm held up in the air during that game," said Mikan, "and on one play in particular, the Washington players were going for my arm and not the ball — which was on my other hand!"

The Caps were simply too much in the end and won the game, 74-66, to bring the series to three games to two. And, despite the obvious attempts by the Caps to hack at his injured wrist, Big George kind of liked having the cast as part of his artillery. His opponents were already fearful of his powerful drop-step and this just added to the fun.

"That cast was hard as a brick; it fit right in with his elbows," Bones McKinney would later recall. "It would kill you. And it didn't bother his shooting a bit."

The Lakers got serious in Game Six (now back at the St. Paul Auditorium because of the annual sportsman's show), however, as Mikan scored 29 points to lead the team to a 77-56 victory. The more than 10,000 screaming fans loved every minute of it as the defending NBL champs were now the champs of the BAA as well.

While Mikan averaged a league-best 28.3 points per game, Pollard, who was often left wide open thanks to George's double and triple-teaming, also averaged 15 points. In addition, Guard Herm Schaefer averaged 10.4 points and Swede Carlson chipped in with 9.5 tool. By now the team was selling tickets like crazy and was operating in the black. A big part of that success came from the team's booster club, the "Laker Clubhouse" (one of the first organized booster organization's in pro sports), which was a group of civic leaders who helped to promote and sell season tickets. Things were looking very good for the organization as they headed into the decade of the '50s.

The Kangaroo Kid
Jim Pollard will always be remembered for the spring in his legs and his amazing jumping ability, hence the nickname: the "Kangaroo Kid." In fact, he had such leaping ability that he became the first bona fide "dunker" in pro basketball, although his acrobatic dunks were done mostly in practice — because dunking during a game in those days was

thought to be ungentlemanly! They didn't measure the players' vertical leaping ability back then, but if they would have, Pollard's would've certainly been astonishing, even by today's standards. He was truly the Michael Jordan of his day.

Born on July 9th, 1922, Jim Pollard's roots were formed in Oakland Calif., where he starred on the Oakland Technical High School basketball team. Full of promise and potential, Pollard took his talents to Stanford University, where as an All-American he led his squad to the 1942 NCAA championship. From there, he joined the U.S. Coast Guard and played on several service teams over the next couple of years, followed by a few semi-pro AAU clubs as well. It was there where he really started to make a name for himself..

The story of how Pollard became a Laker is as interesting as the man himself. Just before the Lakers first season in 1947-48, GM Sid Hartman was assembling the pieces to put together yet another winning roster. Specifically, they were trying hard to land a young six-foot-five jumping jack out of the California Industrial League named Jim Pollard, who was playing for the local AAU Oakland Bittners. (On the East Coast, pro basketball was all the rage, but on the West Coast, there were only the AAU leagues, and they were every bit as good as the eastern pros. In fact, a lot of pro teams had previously tried and failed to sign Pollard, who had been training for a spot on the coveted 1948 Olympic team.)

But somehow, someway, Sid was able to persuade the young star to forego his Olympic dreams and move to the tundra. The news spread quickly that somebody had finally talked him into signing. Oakland Mayor Joe Smith even called Pollard and pleaded with him not to go. But Jim liked the tenacious Hartman and agreed to sign a Laker contract. There was one catch though. In addition to his $12,000 annual salary, plus his $3,000 signing bonus, Pollard made Sid agree to bring along three of his Bittner teammates. He reluctantly agreed, and with that Pollard went on to become one of the game's all-time great ones. The rest, they say, is basketball history.

"We used to know when Pollard had been in the building," recalled Washington Capitols star, Horace "Bones" McKinney, in Roland Lazenby's 1993 book, "The Lakers: A Basketball Journey," "because the tops of the backboards would be clean where he raked them. Pollard was fast, too. You couldn't press him either. He was too good moving with the ball. He'd get by you in a cat lick."

In 1955, Jim Pollard announced his retirement from the Lakers to accept the head coaching position at LaSalle College in Philadelphia, where he would ultimately post a modest 48-28 record. Then on January 2, 1960, after a three-year stint in Philly, Pollard rejoined his beloved Lakers, this time as their coach, taking over the reigns in mid-season from John Castellani. He would have his work cut out for him though. The Lakers were 11-25 at that point, and things were not looking good. Minneapolis would finish the season at 25-50, and, while they did upset Detroit in the first round of the playoffs, they ultimately lost to the St. Louis Hawks in the Division Finals. That season would be Pollard's last, as well as the last for the Lakers in Minneapolis. (He would later go on to coach the Chicago Packers, an NBA expansion team run by Sid Hartman in 1961-62, the ABA's Minnesota Muskies in 1967-68, as well as the Miami Floridians from 1968-70 — when the

Muskies franchise was relocated from the Twin Cities to Florida.)

Pollard, the team's first captain, was the last of the original Lakers. A fabulous rebounder and all-around team player, he would finish his illustrious eight-year career with 6,522 points — good for a 13.1 points per game scoring average. He also grabbed 2,487 rebounds from 1950-55 as well, good for 5.0 per game. (Rebounds were not tracked until the 1950 season, so there were undoubtedly plenty more that went unrecorded.)

Along with George Mikan, Pollard was the only Laker to be a member of all six championship teams. And, while Big George had been named the "Best Basketball Player of the First Half Century" by the Associated Press, two years later, all of the players who had been in the league since its inception were given another poll as to who they thought was the greatest player ever. This time they chose Jim Pollard. The four-time NBA All-Star, who was the high scorer of the 1954 All-Star Game in Madison Square Garden with 23 points, was inducted into the Basketball Hall of Fame in 1977. Sadly, he died in 1993 at the age of 71.

TRIBUTES

"We were very close friends and roommates for several years," said Vern Mikkelsen. "He was probably the best athlete that I have ever played with or against. He was a very moody player, but on the floor, he played way above his head. He was just a marvelous athlete and a great friend. I miss him."

"Jim Pollard was probably the most graceful ballplayer that I ever had," said John Kundla. "He could do everything: run, pass, shoot, jump or whatever. He was the creator of the jump-shot. He was so graceful and smooth with everything. He could be playing today. When they put the press on, Jim would bring the ball down the court and nobody could guard him. We didn't keep track of assists back then, but he had a ton of them — most of them going to George! He was just an excellent all-around ballplayer with and without the ball."

"The Kangaroo Kid, he was one fabulous ballplayer," said George Mikan. "He was just an extraordinarily fine basketball player who could do it all. He could run like a deer, and had a great ability to pass the ball. His pin-point passes were just amazing. What can I say, he was just a tremendous leaper, a great player and a fine person."

"He was one of those guys who could do everything," added Bud Grant. "Just like Julius Erving, he could take off at the top of the circle and glide into the basket and lay it in. He could hang in the air and shoot with different hands. He was special."

1949 RUNNER-UP: JOE HUTTON

The Hamline Pipers, under legendary coach **JOE HUTTON**, beat Regis College of Colorado to win the 1949 National Association of Intercollegiate Athletics (NAIA) championship. (Incidentally, Hamline was the first school in the entire nation to play a formal intercollegiate basketball game. According to Basketball Hall of Fame records, the momentous game happened on February 9, 1895, when Hamline played the Minnesota Agriculture School. From there, the Pipers would go on to become Minnesota's first national powerhouse, thanks to Hutton. Hutton, who took over at Hamline in 1930, guided the Pipers to three NAIA championships in 1942, 1949 and 1951. Over the next 35 years Hutton racked up an incredible record of 588-186 (.760), en route to winning 19 MIAC titles and qualifying for 12 NAIA post-season tournaments. At the time of his retirement, Hutton ranked sixth all-time among the nation's top basketball coaches in total wins.)

HONORABLE MENTION: LEO NOMELLINI

Gopher defensive tackle **LEO NOMELLINI** is named to his second straight All-American football team. From there, "The Lion" went on to become a 10-time Pro-Bowler in the NFL with the San Francisco 49ers. He was later inducted into the Pro Football Hall of Fame in 1969.

JOHN KUNDLA
The Lakers Make it Three in a Row

By the 1949-50 season the BAA had severely crippled the NBL financially, and a truce of sorts was called when the two rival leagues decided to merge. The result was the newly created National Basketball Association, or NBA. The league's 17 charter members included the BAA's: Minneapolis Lakers, Baltimore Bullets, Boston Celtics, Fort Wayne Pistons, Washington Capitols, Rochester Royals, Philadelphia Warriors, Chicago Stags, New York Knickerbockers and St. Louis Bombers. The NBL provided the: Anderson Packers, Syracuse Nationals, Indianapolis Olympians, Tri-Cities Blackhawks, Denver Nuggets, Waterloo Hawks and Sheboygan Redskins.

It was a wild time for pro basketball at this juncture with many of the clubs joining the upstart circuit literally teetering on the verge of bankruptcy. Trying to arrange the travel logistics and coordinate the scheduling all of those games was a huge headache as teams were suddenly scrambling just to find local gyms and arenas to play their games in. The Lakers, now playing in their third league in as many seasons, were placed in the Central Division along with Chicago St. Louis, Rochester and Fort Wayne. The others were then divided into both the Eastern and Western Divisions.

The Lakers played well and went on to finish the regular season on top of the Central Division with a 51-17 record. They then won six straight playoff games, sweeping Chicago, Fort Wayne, and Anderson, to gain yet another shot at their third straight league title. Now, in the NBA Finals, the Lakers would face-off against the Syracuse Nationals, who were led by their fiery Player/Coach, Al Cervi, and star, Forward Dolph Schayes. Syracuse, winners of the Eastern Division championship, came into the series with a regular season record of 51-13. Both teams, however, had lost only one game apiece at home during the course of the regular season.

The best-of-seven series kicked off at Syracuse's State Fair Coliseum. In Game One, behind George Mikan's 37 points, the Lakers pushed the Nationals into overtime. Behind 66-64 with about a minute to go, Coach John Kundla called for a double pick with Jim Pollard taking the final shot. The ball swung around as designed, but when Pollard got the ball, instead of shooting, he threw it to Bud Grant.

Said Grant: "I was the most surprised guy in the place, but I took a long shot and it went in to tie the game." Then in overtime, Laker swingman Bobby Harrison drained a 40-footer at the buzzer to win the thriller, 68-66.

The Nats then went on to win Game Two, evening the series at one game apiece. The Finals now headed back to the Twin Cities, but with the annual Sportmen's Show occupying the Minneapolis Auditorium, the Lakers suddenly found themselves homeless. They tried to book the Minneapolis Armory, but that, too, was booked, so they looked to the University of Minnesota and the Gophers' home, Williams Arena. Nervous about the basketball competition though, U of M Athletics Director Frank McCormick had already pushed through a Big Ten rule that prohibited pro teams from playing in conference facilities. Ultimately, the Lakers wound up at the St. Paul Auditorium. The unfamiliar surroundings didn't seem to bother them though, as they took Games Three and Four.

It was now back to New York for Game Five. There, Syracuse rebounded to defeat Minneapolis, narrowing their series lead to three games to two. Back in Minnesota they had finally cleared out the fish-

ing boats and campers from the Minneapolis Auditorium just in time for Game Six. Feeling right at home, the Lakers battled the Nats in a wild one that would ultimately go down as one of the most memorable in franchise history.

Epitomizing the style of play which was commonplace of the era, the Lakers took it right to the Nats. Fights broke out all over the place as Pollard squared off with Paul Seymour, while Slater Martin and Swede Carlson both went at it with Billy Gabor before the police rushed in to break it up. To make it even more exciting, the volatile Cervi got tossed in the third quarter and four Lakers fouled out in the fourth. When it was all said and done, Mikan had poured in 40 and Pollard added 16 of his own in a 110-75 blow-out. The team celebrated at half-court and the crowd went nuts. The Lakers were now officially a dynasty.

"We had won a championship in all three different leagues at that point," said Kundla. "That was really a wild series. I remember Harrison sinking that 40-footer to win the first game at the fairgrounds. Then in the final game, I remember Seymour was guarding Mikan, and he was pinching George every time he got the ball. Finally George got so upset that when he went up for a shot, he gave him an elbow right to his forehead, giving Seymour a giant knot right on the noggin. George blew his top and I had to take him out of the game, but he did make the shot and the ref even called a foul on Seymour. Cervi, the player-coach, was really a mean competitor, and his teams would fight anybody. That series was a real brawl and at the time it was even more meaningful because our teams didn't like each other very much. It was a great series, and it is always special winning a championship, particularly that one, because it was our first NBA title."

The Original "Coach K"

John Kundla was born on July 3, 1916, in Star Junction, Pa., and grew up in Minneapolis, where he attended Central High School. After a great prep career, he went on to play basketball under coach Dave MacMillan at the University of Minnesota. Kundla also played baseball at Minnesota, but his main sport was hoops. In basketball, he earned three varsity letters and led the Gophers to the Big Ten co-championship in 1937. He captained the Gophers in 1939 and also earned All-Big Ten Conference honors that year as well.

Following graduation, he played one season of professional baseball with Paducah in the Class C Kitty League. Kundla also stayed active as a player during this time, even leading his semi-pro Rock Spring Sparklers, of Shakopee, to the 1943 World Pro Tournament in Chicago.

Kundla then returned to Minnesota and served as a basketball assistant to MacMillan at the U of M before accepting the head coaching job at DeLaSalle High School in downtown Minneapolis. There, he coached the Islanders to a pair of Minnesota State Catholic Championships in the mid-1940s. Following a two-year stint in the Navy in World War II, Kundla then decided to get back into coaching, this time in the college ranks at St. Thomas, where he coached the Tommies to a modest 11-11 record in 1947.

By this time, the Minneapolis Lakers had come to town. Originally, they had offered the head coaching position to coaching legend Joe Hutton, who had been Hamline's skipper since 1931 and had built the Pipers into a national small college power. But, when Hutton politely declined, the Lakers decided to hire the 31-year-old Kundla as their first ever coach. He then left the security of St. Thomas and signed a three-year deal with Minnesota's upstart professional basketball franchise for a whopping $3,000 annual salary.

He would go on to serve as the head coach of the Lakers for 11 years, compiling an impressive career record of 466-319. At the time of his retirement, only the great Red Auerbach of the Boston Celtics had more professional coaching wins. Kundla also won 70 playoff games while losing just 35, a record that translated into an amazing six world championships for the state of Minnesota. In addition to coaching four NBA All-Star Games (1951-54), he also became one of only three coaches in NBA history to have guided teams to three consecutive world titles.

"I've seen a lot of great teams, at least on paper, that won nothing," said the legendary Auerbach. "Sure, Kundla had great teams, but he did great things with them."

In 1958, tired of the stress and travel demands, Kundla stepped down as coach of the Lakers and became the teams' general manager. (By now the team was under new ownership.) In his first move as G.M., he hired George Mikan to be his coaching predecessor. It was a short-lived move though, as Kundla found himself back on the bench shortly thereafter. He would stick it out for one more year before finally calling it quits at the end of the 1960 season. In fact, the day after the Lakers lost to the Celtics in the NBA Finals that year, he announced his resignation. The Lakers were gone too, to Los Angeles.

Coach K then returned to his alma matter to take over as the head coach of the basketball Gophers. He would guide the Maroon and Gold for nine seasons, from 1959 to 1968, earning 110 career wins against 105 losses along the way. He also guided the U.S National Team into competition in 1964-65, and also served on the NCAA Rules Committee. In 1968, University of North Dakota Coach Bill Fitch took over for the Gophers, and Kundla went over to the U's St. Paul campus, where he became the school's Physical Education Director.

In 1995 Coach Kundla was inducted into the Pro Basketball Hall of Fame alongside his star pupil, Vern Mikkelsen, making it the first time a coach and player were enshrined with one another.

"I can still remember Ray Meyer walking me down the aisle in Springfield, at the Hall of Fame, it was such a thrill," Kundla recalled. "My family was all there, and I don't think I will ever experience anything any better than that."

Kundla, a humble and quiet man, always kept an even demeanor on the court. Even as a young coach, he displayed sound judgement and always stuck to his beliefs that defense and discipline were the keys to success. A tremendous tactician, his greatest asset as a coach might have been in recognizing the strengths of his players, and then utilizing them. He somehow managed to keep three superstars: Mikan, Mikkelsen and Pollard, all happy and content — a feat nearly impossible by today's standards. He was a "players coach" and for that his men loved him. He will forever be remembered as one of the game's greatest.

What did it mean for you to be a Laker?

"I was very lucky to be a Laker, and there is no greater thrill than winning a world championship," said Kundla. "The national recognition we got for the state of Minnesota was such a thrill for me to see."

"Sid Hartman actually talked me into becoming the Laker coach," added Kundla. "They paid me twice as much as I was making at St. Thomas. How lucky could I get? I mean the first player we got was Pollard, then we got Mikan, and then Mikkelsen two years later! I didn't even have to coach them. They were so good that they did it all themselves. Those guys were just great players with great talent and so much character."

What did it mean for you to be a Gopher?

"It meant a lot to me. It was such a thrill just to play for the University of Minnesota. I can still remember winning the Big Ten co-championship in 1937. Playing with guys like Gordy Addington, Gordy Spears, Paul Maki, Martin Rolick and Butch Nash was just great. Then, to be able to come back and coach my alma mater was something very special to me. It was a great honor to be a Gopher player and later their coach."

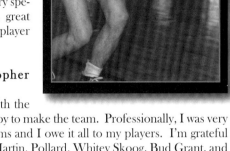

Laker and Gopher Tombstones:

"As an active player with the Gophers, I was just happy to make the team. Professionally, I was very proud of our Laker teams and I owe it all to my players. I'm grateful to Mikan, Mikkelsen, Martin, Pollard, Whitey Skoog, Bud Grant, and all the others. We had players with such character, team spirit, and a will to win. I was very lucky to be their head coach."

John and his wife Marie later settled down in Minneapolis, where they had six kids and many grandkids. He remains active in the Twin Cities to this day and still follows the game. In 2002 Kundla, along with several other former Minneapolis Laker greats, were honored by the Los Angeles Lakers for their achievements. It was a fitting tribute for the Hall of Famers that was long overdue.

TRIBUTES

"John Kundla is one of the greatest coaches of all time," said Vern Mikkelsen. "He's never been given the proper credit simply because everyone said that anyone could've coached our championship teams. I sort of look at John similarly today as I did with the Chicago Bulls head coach, Phil Jackson. Like Jackson, John was wonderful at coaching each of us at our own individual levels, and that really motivated us to play for him and win. I am just very grateful for the fact that he gave me the opportunity to play with the Lakers."

"John is just an excellent guy," said George Mikan. "He had a great way about him, and he could keep the players focused on the game. He also had the ability to help you when things weren't going your way. He could critique your game and correct any problems that you had so you could get back out there. He was also great at analyzing team defenses and was a master at setting up plays that would help us excel. He is a wonderful person and a great coach."

"John Kundla just got better and better, until he was one of the greatest coaches in basketball," said Bud Grant.

1950 RUNNER-UP: BERNIE BIERMAN

Legendary Gopher football coach **BERNIE BIERMAN** retires. In 1932, after serving as the head coach at both Mississippi A&M and Tulane, Bierman took over as the head coach at the University of Minnesota, where he became a living legend. During Bierman's first 10 years in Gold Country (1932-41), better known as the "Golden Era," the Gophers not only won seven Big Ten titles, they won five national championships as well (1934, 1935, 1936, 1940 and 1941). During one amazing span, Minnesota went three straight seasons and half way through a fourth without a defeat. The Litchfield native would ultimately retire in 1950 with a 146-62-13 career record and was later inducted into the College Football Hall of Fame.

HONORABLE MENTION: RAY DANDRIDGE

Led by third baseman **RAY DANDRIDGE**, a future Hall of Famer who earned league MVP honors that season, the Minneapolis Millers won the 1950 American Association pennant. Among the highlights that year were a pair of no-hitters by pitchers Dixie Howell and Kirby Higbe, as well as 15 wins by future Hall of Fame knuckleballer, Hoyt Wilhelm. Bert Haasalso also finished No. 2 in the MVP voting.

In 1951 the boys from Eveleth came down to the State High School Hockey Tournament at the St. Paul Auditorium with the title of "three-time defending undefeated champions" in front of their names. These Iron Rangers were somewhat of an enigma with the Twin Citians, who by now had heard of them much like they had heard about Paul Bunyan and Superman — with a sort of mythical God-like connotation. The team was guided by one of Minnesota's greatest all-time coaches, the legendary Cliff Thompson, who coached the Golden Bears from 1920 to 1958, finishing with an astounding 534-26-9 record.

Led by All-Staters John Mayasich, Ron Castellano and Dan Voce, the Bears came in to the state tourney riding an amazing 66-game winning streak. And, they were fresh off of yet another undefeated 16-0 season in which they scored 179 goals, while yielding only 30.

The Bears began their title defense by taking on Williams in the quarterfinals. There, in a replay of the 1951 title game, the Bears came out smoking. John Mayasich scored just 57 seconds into the game and didn't stop until he had scored three more in that first period alone. This one got ugly early as Eveleth went on to hammer the Wolves, 12-0, and advance onto the semifinals.

In the semis Mayasich showed why he was the greatest ever, scoring an unbelievable tournament record seven goals against Minneapolis Southwest. After a quick goal by Eveleth winger Dan Voce, Mayasich tallied three quick ones in the first period to get warmed up. Southwest then rallied back to make it interesting behind three goals from the Meredith brothers. That was just the wake up call Mayasich would need though, as he scored again in the second, and added another hat trick in the third. The Castellano's each added one as well for the Bears, as they cruised to an 11-5 victory.

That put the Golden Bears into the title match against St. Paul Johnson, who had beaten Thief River Falls in the other semifinal contest by the score of 6-2, thanks to a pair of goals each from Bob Youngquist and Ray Youngberg.

So, on Saturday, February 24th, 1951, in front of 7,163 Auditorium fans, Eveleth hit the ice to try and make it four-straight crowns. Johnson's own legendary coach, Rube Gustafson, knew that he would have to get a near perfect performance from his boys if they were going to have a chance. There was speculation before the game as to what kind of defense the Governors were going to throw at the Bears. Some teams had achieved a marginal level of success against them that season by running a "1-5" defense, in which one skater stayed at the blue line and the other four hung around the goalie. Or, perhaps he would just have the other four hang around Mayasich? Deciding to play it straight and take their chances, Johnson came out strong and held the Bears scoreless through the first on tough goaltending by Johnson keeper Warren Strelow. But, just a minute into the second, who else but John

Mayasich beat Strelow to put Eveleth up 1-0. Ten minutes later he scored again, and decided to add two more in the third just for good measure. His fourth and final goal of the game was a beauty, beating Strelow on a 20-foot blast from the point. Johnson's Bob Schmidt added a goal late in the third, but by then it was too late, as Eveleth and Mayasich prevailed, 4-1.

For Mayasich, who finished with 15 goals and three assists for 18 points, which is still a tournament record, it was as sweet as it gets. He would finish his storied prep career with four consecutive state tourney titles and an un-

believable all-time prep record of 69-0.

"I remember that St. Paul Johnson game was a tough one," recalled Mayasich, "and there was a lot of pressure on us to keep the winning streak going through that fourth year. As far as the streak went, every year we were expected to play better than the one before, so I looked at it that way and played that way myself. When it was all over we couldn't believe what we had done, it was very special."

"When we were growing up, we didn't think about college hockey or the Olympics or the pros," he added. "We thought about making the high school team and getting to the state tournament. Eveleth had won the first state tournament in 1945, when I was in sixth grade, and that gave us something to strive for. In Eveleth you were expected to win and it was just assumed you would. As a result, we didn't take any time for sightseeing when we came down to St. Paul. All we did was watch and play hockey."

Minnesota's Best Ever

John Mayasich has long been regarded as one of the finest amateur hockey players ever produced in the United States, and is without question the greatest to ever lace em' up in Minnesota.

Mayasich grew up playing hockey in Eveleth. "We got our start learning hockey on the ponds and outdoor rinks in the city," he recalled. "The older kids would pick sides and the younger kids would learn from them. It went on from generation to generation. When the ice melted, we played street hockey and broomball. We had a lot of fun and we learned a lot playing those sports as well."

Eveleth has often been referred to as the birthplace of American hockey because of its wonderful puck traditions and roots that can be traced back to the sport's American beginnings. That's why the U.S. Hockey Hall of Fame is situated in this relatively small town on the Missabe Iron Range, an hour's drive north of Duluth. Many hockey greats came from this hockey Mecca, names that ooze with tradition: Mariucci, Brimsek, Karakas, LoPresti, Matchefts, Ikola, Finnegan, Dahlstrom, and Palazzari, among others.

After high school Mayasich headed to the University of Minnesota, where he would join up with another Eveleth hockey legend, Gopher Coach John Mariucci, who had taken college hockey by storm after playing in the NHL with the Chicago Blackhawks.

In 1953, Mayasich's sophomore year at the U of M, the Gophers won the Midwest Conference championship and went all the way to the NCAA Finals in Colorado Springs. In the semifinal game they knocked off R.P.I., 3-2, only to get upset in the championship game by rival Michigan, 7-3. That next season, they made it to the NCAA Finals once again, this time crushing Boston College, 14-1, in the semis, only to lose this time to their old nemesis, R.P.I., in a 5-4 overtime nail-biter for the title.

"It's a loss that sticks with me still today," said Mayasich on the loss to R.P.I.. "To lose in overtime was bitter. It's not the ones you won that you remember, it's the ones you lost. To me, that was probably my biggest individual disappointment in all my years of hockey."

Before his career was over, the perennial All-American had tallied Gopher records of 298 career points and 144 goals. His totals worked out to an incredible 1.4 goals per game average for nearly three points per game. (To put it into perspective, Pat Micheletti, the next Gopher player on the career goal-scoring list, had 24 fewer goals despite playing in 51 more games. In other words, in his 162 games, Micheletti would have had to amass 435 points just to match Mayasich's per-game average. That's an additional 166 more than his career total!) Mayasich also holds the records for most goals and most points in a single game. In his senior year, he had an incredible six-goal game against Winnipeg and also tallied eight points against Michigan that same season as well.

At the end of his playing career with the Gophers, Mayasich fulfilled his military obligations and then went on to play with eight U.S. Olympic and National Teams. He was also a member of the 1956 silver medal-winning U.S. Olympic hockey team in Cortina, Italy. The

MAYASICH'S STATE TOURNEY RECORDS

Most All Time Total Points:	46	(1948-1951)
Most All Time Total Goals:	36	(1948-1951)
Most Consec. Games Scoring:	12	(1948-1951)
Most All Time Hat-Tricks:	7	(1948-1951)
Most Points One Tournament:	18	(1951)
Most Goals One Tournament:	15	(1951)
Most Points One Game:	8	(1951)
Most Goals One Game:	7	(1951)
Most Points One Period:	5	(1951)
Most Goals One Period:	4	(1951)

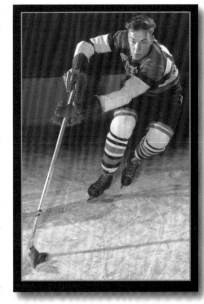

highlight of that tournament came against perennial power Canada, which had won seven of the eight Olympic gold medals since the Games had begun. There, John played an incredible game, scoring a hat trick, en route to leading his squad past the mighty Canucks. The Americans played tough in the tournament, but wound up losing the gold to the Soviets.

The most celebrated of his Olympic events, however, was the first "Miracle on Ice," the 1960 U.S. Olympic team, which won the gold in Squaw Valley, California. The U.S. team beat the mighty Russians for the first time that year, and, in the process, put hockey on the map across the United States.

"At the time we were thinking it would be a great accomplishment if we could win a bronze, we had no idea we would win a gold," he said. "Beating the Russians was amazing and very similar to the 1980 team victory as well. I think for both teams, playing at home, in America, was a big factor, because it's nice having the fans there to support you. This was probably one of the biggest thrills of my life."

John Mayasich was a "velvety-smooth skater," with a keen, sixth sense into the psyche of opposing goaltenders' every move. He is credited as being the first college hockey player to develop the slap shot, a new weapon that instilled fear into an already perplexed group of goalies who had been trying to stop him. John was an artist with his stick and his stick-handling skills were legendary. On opponent's power-plays, he could kill penalties by toying with opposing defenses. He used to take the puck and simply weave around the rink without ever passing to a teammate until the penalty had been killed. With amazing ability like that, it's hard to believe that he was often criticized for passing too much.

"The camaraderie was the best, those friendships go back 40 years now," recalled Mayasich on his playing days at the U of M. "Playing with the players who I had played against throughout my high school career was really exciting. We had great Gopher players like Dick Meredith, Dick Dougherty, Gene Campbell, Ken Yackel, Wendy Anderson and Stan Hubbard. I got to see the world through hockey, and the purity of the game is the bond that keeps those friendships together today. It was quite a time to be involved with the Gopher program as it was just taking off back then. It made me proud of the fact that I was there when all of this was happening. Now, to see what the program has

grown into today, and to think that maybe, in a small way that I had something to do with it, is incredible. My time at the U of M was great."

Declining professional hockey opportunities in the then six-team NHL, Mayasich devoted his remaining pro hockey career to the minor league Green Bay Bobcats. After his hockey career, John went into business with his old Gopher teammate Stan Hubbard, where he worked as an executive for KSTP Radio for the next several decades.

Mayasich received numerous honors during his hockey days, including being the first Minnesotan to be voted into the National High School Athletic Hall of Fame. In 1976 he had a homecoming of sorts, being inducted into the U.S. Hockey Hall of Fame in his native Eveleth, and in 1998 John received the coveted Lester Patrick Award, for his outstanding contributions to American hockey. In addition, in 1998 John became the only Gopher ever to have his number retired when his No. 8 was hung into the Mariucci Arena rafters forever.

Things have changed in the world of hockey since Eveleth's incredible run. While the attendance for the entire 1951 high school tournament was 18,582, the attendance in the new millennium exceeds 120,000. However, in all those years, no one has come close to topping Mayasich's records, nor his legend. He remains the best hockey player ever to hail from the Gopher State, and is a real living legend. But as great an athlete as he was, so is his humility. Often in the limelight, he is always quick to share the credit and the glory with his teammates and coaches. That is what makes the man so beloved by those who know and respect him.

Gopher Tombstone:

"I was blessed with the opportunity of playing with and against some great players. I was at the right place at the right time with the right people, and made contributions through a lot of hard work and effort."

TRIBUTES

"John Mayasich brought college hockey to a new plateau," said John Mariucci. "He was the Wayne Gretzky of his time, and if he were playing pro hockey today, he would simply be a bigger, stronger, backchecking Gretzky. The words to describe him haven't been invented. When I say he's the best, that's totally inadequate."

"John was a quiet fox," added former Gopher Coach Doug Woog. "He was the best player I ever saw play in Minnesota. Hockey made his life. What can I say, he is just such a wonderful guy."

1951 RUNNER-UP: WILLIE MAYS

The "Say-Hey Kid," *WILLIE MAYS*, plays 35 games for the Minneapolis Millers and hits .477 with 8 home runs and 30 RBI, before getting called up to the big leagues with the New York Giants. Mays would go on to superstardom in the Majors, garnering a career batting average of .302 from 1951-73. He would hit 660 home runs, third all-time in MLB history, and drive in more than 100 RBI on eight different occasions. In addition, he won 12 Gold Glove Awards and was voted Most Valuable Player in the National League in both 1954 and 1965. He was inducted into the Hall of Fame in 1979 and is widely considered to be the greatest all-around player ever in Major League Baseball history.

HONORABLE MENTION: SLATER MARTIN

The Minneapolis Lakers win the Western Division title with a 44-24 record, but lose to the Rochester Royals, three games to one, in the divisional finals. George Mikan played valiantly with a broken ankle, but just couldn't get his team over the hump. One of the stars of the team was point guard *SLATER MARTIN*, a seven-time NBA All-Star who was inducted into the Pro Basketball Hall of Fame in 1982.

The 1952 Lakers added some depth when they signed Rochester's six-foot-two, two-handed set-shot sniper, Pep Saul. In addition, the Lakers also added a couple of local homers in former Gopher star Whitey Skoog, and a pair of Hamline stars: Joe Hutton Jr. and Howie Schultz.

The Lakers got off to a good start that season, eventually finishing in second place in the West with a record of 40-26, one game back from rival Rochester. There were some highlights along the way too, including Mikan's 61-point performance in a double-overtime win over those very Royals. He also set an NBA record by hauling in 36 rebounds in one game, beating Syracuse's Dolph Schayes' old mark of 35. The Laker's big three of Mikan, Pollard and Mikkelsen each topped the 1,000 point mark that year, giving the team its most balanced scoring attack ever. So dominant were the trio that famed Basketball commentator John Devaney noted that "standing shoulder to shoulder, Mikan, Mikkelsen and Pollard looked like a ragged row of alpine mountains...".

By the end of the season Skoog was sidelined with a bum knee, something the team would have to work around. In the playoffs, however, Minneapolis breezed past Indianapolis in the opening round, then headed to Rochester for the start of a best-of-five semifinal series against the defending champion Royals.

There, the Lakers lost Game One by 10, despite Mikan's 47-point effort, but came back to take Game Two. Minneapolis then took Game Three back home, and thanks to Pollard's last-second game-winning stuff-in, was able to also take the deciding Game Four, 82-80, to win the series. The Lakers then prepared to do battle with the New York Knicks, who, under Coach Joe Lapchick, were making their second consecutive trip to the NBA Finals. Led by such stars as Max Zaslofsky, Sweetwater Clifton, Al & "Tricky Dick" McGuire, Connie Simmons, Ernie Vandeweghe, Harry Gallatin and Vince Boryla, the Knicks would be a formidable opponent.

The Finals opened at the St. Paul Auditorium, where Jim Pollard led the way with 34 points in a 83-79 win. The game wasn't without controversy though, as Al McGuire had a basket go in that wasn't counted. Amazingly, the refs, who gave him two foul shots on the play, didn't see the ball go in, and despite protests, refused to count it. The 10,000 fans there that night saw it go in, but didn't complain too hard when the overtime game ended with their Lakers victorious. The Knicks rebounded to take game two, 80-72, only to see Minneapolis come back to take Game Three, 82-73. The game was played in New York's 69th Regiment Armory because Madison Square Garden was being occupied by the circus. Game Four was another overtime thriller with the Knicks, who held Mikan to just 11 points, etching out a 90-89 win. Pollard, who had injured his back in the game, was replaced by Bob Harrison. Game Five, which saw Mikan and Pollard each tally 32, was all Minneapolis, 102-89. Game Six, however, went to the Knicks, 76-68, setting up a decisive Game Seven back in the Minneapolis Armory — a place the Knicks had never won a game in. There, thanks to Mikan's 22 points and Pollard's 10 down the stretch, the Lakers blew out New York, 82-65, to capture their fourth championship in five years. And, for their efforts, the players received a whopping $7,500 bonus.

The Askov Iron Man

At six-foot-seven and 230 pounds, Vern Mikkelsen cleaned the boards and scored down low in the paint with such reckless abandon that he was considered by many to be pro basketball's first real power forward. A rock-solid defender, "Big Mik" was also beloved by his teammates for his relentless work ethic. The ultimate team-player, he became a fixture on one of the game's greatest all-time front-lines alongside the likes of fellow Laker Hall of Famer's George Mikan and Jim Pollard. A gentleman in every sense of the word, Vern Mikkelsen is truly a Minnesota basketball legend.

The original "Great Dane," Arild Verner Agerskov Mikkelsen was raised in the tiny town of Askov, a small Danish community of just 300 souls, nestled halfway between Minneapolis and Duluth in northeastern Minnesota. The son of a Lutheran minister, Mikkelsen went on to lead his Askov High School team to the District Finals during his senior year of 1945, only to lose to rival Pine City.

Vern, who also participated in baseball and track, went on to graduate that Spring. "I was ranked No. 4 in my graduating class, but still finished out of the upper third," he said jokingly of his eight other classmates. By now though, the three-time All-Conference Center had grown to six-foot-five and had inklings of playing college basketball. He thought about giving the University of Minnesota a shot, but reconsidered when he found out that All-State Center Jim McIntyre, who just led Minneapolis Henry to two straight state high school titles, had also signed up to play for Coach Dave MacMillan's Gophers.

Then something happened that forever changed Vern's life. That summer, Al Holst, a Hamline professor who used to travel the rural Minnesota countryside to check out basketball recruits for Coach Joe Hutton, was on his way up to the Iron Range to check out a hot prospect. As luck would have it, on his way up north he got a flat tire in Askov. So he pulled into the local Chevy dealership where Elmer Morgansen, who just happened to be a Mikkelsen family friend, got to visiting with him while he was fixing his flat. When Al explained to him that he was a basketball recruiter, Elmer said that as long as he was there he might as well check out Askov's star player. Al obliged and with that, set out to find Vern, who was working that afternoon in his neighbor Chris Hendricksen's rutabaga field.

"I can still remember seeing him pull up in his 1936 Buick,"recalled Vern. "We all knew that he had to be someone important because nobody in our town had a car like that."

Sure enough Al found his way there and before he knew it, wound up coming back to the Mikkelsen's home for dinner. There, he was able to sign up the Piper's next prized recruit.

"Back in those days my parents didn't have a lot of money," said Vern. "So, my Lutheran father, himself an accomplished gymnast back in his native Denmark, quickly overlooked the fact that Hamline was a Methodist school. It was an opportunity of a lifetime and something that seemed too good to be true. It was as if I had hit the lottery!"

With that, at just 16, Vern enrolled at Hamline University, where he was about to play basketball under legendary coach Joe Hutton. Now, although Hamline was considered a small college (back then there were no Division I, II or III classifications), the school played a big-time national schedule against many colleges and universities which would be considered D-I powers by today's standards.

Also a Piper track and field standout, Vern would go on to become one of college basketball's finest players, leading his Pipers to three straight MIAC conference titles as well as the 1949 NAIA National Championship. By his senior year Vern, who was averaging better than 17 points per game, had grown to be six-foot-seven and weighed in at 235 pounds. He quickly became one of the most coveted NBA recruits in the nation.

With his Physical Education degree nearly in hand, Vern, who would graduate with honors, was now ready to take that next step into the world of pro hoops. And as luck would have it, his hometown Minneapolis Lakers wanted him badly. By this time the Lakers, who had already won the 1948 NBL and 1949 BAA crowns, were a basketball dynasty. They were on a roll, and saw Vern as the perfect compliment to their star center, George Mikan. With that, the Lakers then used their "territorial draft choice" (which allowed teams to select a

local player from within its own 50-mile area in the first round by substituting their regular draft position) to select Vern.

Mikkelsen started out his pro career by seeing very little playing time, instead serving as an understudy to big George. Then something happened that truly changed the game of basketball. In a game against Fort Wayne, Laker coach John Kundla decided to play both of his big men at the same time. Calling his creation the "double pivot offense," Coach Kundla stationed both Mikan and Mikkelsen as a pair of centers — with Mik playing high and George down in the low post. The new "twin tower" lineup was good, but ultimately clogged up the narrow six-foot lane. So Kundla went back to the drawing board, this time putting Mikkelsen out on the perimeter and facing him towards the basket. In so doing, the coach had inadvertently created the NBA's first true power forward. Mikkelsen's new role was not to score, but primarily to rebound, set picks, and pick up Mikan and Pollard's missed shots. Although he would develop a great two-handed overhead set-shot, Vern's new position was not an easy transition for him. The center spot had been the only position he had ever known, and now, as a professional, he was being asked to change everything.

Teams were so intimidated by Mikan and Mikkelsen's brute strength, size and technique that they would use stalling tactics to simply keep the ball away from them for minutes at a time. As a last resort, the league finally evened the playing field by widening the lane from six to 12 feet and later instituted the 24-second shot clock, thus giving the other teams a fighting chance. (Both rules were credited as "Mikan Rules" as a result of just how much Big George truly changed the game.)

Known as the Lakers' "Iron Man," Mikkelsen went on to play in 699 games out of a possible 704 — a stretch which included an amazing run of 642 consecutive games played. For 10 glorious seasons, which included four NBA championships and a pair of runner-up spots, the "Great Dane" was a Laker fixture. He played on six NBA All-Star teams, was named All-Pro four times and served as the team's captain for five years, ultimately finishing with 10,063 career points (14.4 ppg) and 5,940 rebounds (8.5 rpg). (Vern was only the sixth player in NBA history to reach the prestigious 10,000 point club.) He also added 1,141 points (13.4 ppg) in 85 playoff games as well.

His amazing achievements still rank him among the all-time leaders in nearly a dozen Lakers statistical categories, right alongside fellow Hall of Famers Wilt Chamberlain, Jerry West, Kareem Abdul-Jabbar, Magic Johnson and Shaquille O'Neal. (Just how tough was Big Mik? He even still holds the NBA record for most game disqualifications, with 127!)

Vern ultimately decided to hang up the sneakers after the 1959 season, one year before the team was sold to a group in Los Angeles. He clearly had the ability to keep playing (just two months before he retired he hit for a career high 43 points against Cincinnati), but wanted to leave the game on his own terms.

Laker Owner Bob Short tried to convince him to stay on as a player/coach, even offering him a whopping $25,000 salary and a 25% ownership in the franchise. Vern passed on the offer though because he wanted to devote more time to his family and his aspiring insurance business. Five years later Mikkelsen can still remember coming down

to breakfast and having his wife Jean show him the newspaper headline revealing the news that Short had sold the Lakers to Los Angeles businessman Jack Kent Cooke for a whopping $5 million. Said Vern jokingly, "She knew exactly what 25% of five million dollars was!"

Following his NBA retirement, Mikkelsen, who later got his masters degree in Educational Psychology from both the Universities of Minnesota and Oslo, in Norway, built a very successful insurance business. But, in 1967, he got that basketball itch one more time and accepted the offer to become the GM of the upstart Minnesota Muskies of the American Basketball Association. The team got into some financial problems later that season though and wound up moving to Florida. That following summer, George Mikan, who was the commissioner of the league, called Vern to tell him that the defending ABA champion Pittsburgh Pipers, and their star Connie Hawkins, were in financial trouble and were moving to Minnesota. They needed a GM, and once again Vern reluctantly agreed. But, like the Muskies, the team lasted just one season and wound up moving back to Pittsburgh.

From there, other than a brief stint as Breck High School's basketball coach, Vern's affiliation with the game would evolve into a purely fun one. He still continues to do fundraising work for his beloved Hamline University, and also does some public speaking. The ultimate honor for Vern finally came on May 15, 1995, when he became the first native Minnesota player ever to be enshrined into the Naismith Memorial Basketball Hall of Fame. Escorted down the red carpet by fellow Hall of Famer and friend, Bob Pettit, of the St. Louis Hawks, Mik would later say of his former rival: "That was the longest time I ever spent with Bob without having him score a point against me!"

One of Vern's most recent achievements was to help coordinate the 2001 George Mikan Gala at the Target Center, which included the presentation of a life-sized bronze statue and tribute honoring his long-time friend and teammate. A proud grandparent, Vern and his late wife Jean have two sons, Tom and John, and he currently resides in Wayzata.

TRIBUTE

"He was the first power forward," said George Mikan. "He was a fantastic guy and a fierce competitor on the court. He was a great rebounder and he learned to shoot from the outside. He was a good friend and a very important part of our team."

1952 RUNNER-UP: "BIGGIE" MUNN

CLARENCE "BIGGIE" MUNN wins the first of what would prove to be undefeated back-to-back NCAA National Championships as the head coach of Michigan State University. Munn was a tough guard who earned Big Ten MVP and All-American honors for the football Gophers in 1931. Munn, who also played fullback and punted, was a sprinter on the U of M track team as well. After graduation, the Minneapolis native got into coaching, where, over a period of 22 years, he coached at Albright, Syracuse and Michigan State. As head coach at MSU from 1947-53, Munn led the Spartans to an impressive 54-9-2 record. After retiring, Munn went on to become the school's athletic director.

HONORABLE MENTION: KEN YACKEL

The 1952 U.S. Olympic team wins a silver medal in Oslo, Norway, with of a handful of Minnesotans, including a St. Paul Humboldt grad by the name of **KEN YACKEL**. "Yack" was a three-sport star (football, baseball and hockey) at the University of Minnesota, where he earned All-American honors in hockey before going on to play professionally for more than a decade in the AHL and NHL. He later coached in the college and pro ranks with the Millers and Gophers in the '60s and '70s, while also guiding the 1965 U.S. National Team.

PAUL GIEL
The Winona Phantom's Heisman Run

Paul Giel is one of Minnesota's greatest ever athletes and could seemingly do it all. On the football field he lined up all over the place and forced opposing coaches to account for his every move. While Giel's storied gridiron career consisted of three fabulous seasons, 1953 stands alone. The football gods blessed Paul during his senior campaign. And why not, it was the greatest individual season any Gopher has ever had in Gold Country.

Optimism was running high in the Land of 10,000 Lakes in 1953, as the Gophers looked poised to finally make a run for the roses. Minnesota, under Head Coach Wes Fesler got off to a very slow start that year, and after losses to USC, Michigan State and Northwestern, was just 1-3 heading into its big showdown against Michigan. The game was significant because it was the Silver Anniversary of the Little Brown Jug, the team's vaunted traveling trophy. Many of the stars from 1903, including Sig Harris and Ed Rogers, were even on hand for the festivities and the atmosphere was electric. Fesler knew it was a big game, and came down hard on his players that week. He knew that if they were to win though, it would all come down to the play of one player — Paul Giel.

Giel, who had the authority to call his own plays and audible at the line whenever he felt necessary, was ready to make history and turn the season's misfortunes around that afternoon. And boy did he ever. In what many have called the greatest-ever single performance in Gopher history, Giel single-handedly crushed the Wolverines.

The game got exciting early when Gordy Holz recovered a Michigan fumble on the Gopher 29-yard line. Just four plays later Giel called his own number, and after deking out several Wolverines, found himself standing in the end-zone with his squad up 7-0. He would repeat that feat yet again in the first quarter, leading a 62-yard drive which was capped by another run around the end to make it 14-0.

Giel provided more heroics in the third when he returned a punt 41 yards, down to the Michigan 34-yard line. From there, after nice runs by Bob McNamara and Melvin Holme, Giel connected with Bob Rutford on a perfect pass in the end-zone to make it 20-0. The Gophers added a late safety to make the final score 22-0, and regain the precious Jug that had eluded them for a decade. Giel set a Big Ten record that day by handling the ball on 53 of 63 offensive plays, of which he ran for 112 yards. He also completed 13 of 18 passes for another 169 yards, returned one kickoff for 24-yards, and had four punts for 59-yards too. Oh yeah, on defense the cornerback also intercepted a pair of Michigan passes to end a couple of key drives. Not bad! It was an unbelievable performance from an unbelievable player.

"They had kicked us around pretty good in those previous years and I really wanted to beat them badly," Giel later said. "From a personal standpoint, I would have to say that it was my best all-around game ever."

The Gophers then went on to beat Pittsburgh, 35-14, behind Giel's three touchdowns, and Indiana, 28-20, before getting shut out by Iowa, 21-0. They ended the season by tying Wisconsin, 21-21, this time fumbling on the Badger two-yard line with just a minute to go, to finish with a 4-4-1 record — far short of preseason expectations.

Giel averaged more than 100 yards per game that year though, and for his efforts was again named as a unanimous All-American. In addition to being awarded the prestigious Big Ten Medal of Honor, he also became the first-ever two-time Big Ten MVP. In addition, he was given the Walter Camp Award for "Back of the Year," and was chosen as UPI's "Player of the Year" as well. The highlight, however, was his runner-up finish to Notre Dame Halfback Johnny Lattner in the Heisman Trophy race. It was so tight that it remains the closest balloting ever recorded. Many felt he would've won the nation's top honor had the Gophers won more games. It didn't matter. Minnesotans knew that he was the best all-around player in college football that season, regardless of the final voting.

The Winona Phantom

As a young boy, Paul Giel grew up playing football and baseball on the sandlots of Winona during the Great Depression. There, he would often try to emulate the smooth moves of his childhood hero, Heisman winning Gopher Halfback Bruce Smith. Paul's imagination was refueled every Saturday morning, when he religiously listened to his beloved Gophers on the radio. Soon he grew into an incredible prep athlete in his own right, starring in football, baseball and basketball at Winona High School. By 1950, not only was he one of the most celebrated prep football prospects in Minnesota history, he also had an opportunity to sign on with several major league baseball teams right out of high school as well. The kid was a natural, and luckily for us, he had decided long ago that he too was going to wear the Maroon and Gold.

"Coming out of high school in Winona, I was really steeped in the tradition of the Gophers, and because of guys like Bruce Smith, I wanted to be a Gopher," said Giel. "Also, because I could play both football and baseball there, it was even better. It meant everything for me to be a Gopher."

Giel came in and literally took the Gopher sports world by storm. By the time he had finished his illustrious career in Minnesota, he had shattered most of Bruce Smith's records, while single-handedly rewriting the record books. All in all, he rushed for 2,188 yards, caught 281 passes for 279 yards, and posted 417 return yards on both punts and kicks, for a total of 3,165 career all-purpose yards. He also had 22 touchdowns — a number that still ranked in the top-10 all-time more than 50 years later.

He was a throwback. Not only was he an unbelievable halfback, he was also an tremendous quarterback, defensive back, punter, punt returner, kick returner and kicker. It is a wonder how he ever had time to come off the field to catch his breath!

Giel's offensive regime is often credited for developing what was then called the "spread formation," which by today's NFL standards is called the "shotgun." It was that set-up that defenses feared most. In it, Giel lined up five yards back from center. This is where he could do the most damage. Having the advantage of not having to take a seven-step drop to get set to throw, he could see the defense from the pocket, giving him valuable time to raise holy hell in the backfield. Often he would pass, lighting up the secondary. Other times he would follow his fullback up the middle or his halfback around the end. He could hand-off the ball to Gopher All-American Bob McNamara or split wide in the single wing formation to run the option. Sometimes he would line up at the running back position behind either quarterback Geno Cappelletti or Don Swanson in the power-T formation and blast full speed ahead. Occasionally he would fool the defense and pull a quick kick or even punt the ball. Whenever he got into trouble, he would scramble — and boy could he scramble. On the other side of the ball Giel played cornerback, constantly making spectacular tackles. And with a quarterback's instincts, he could anticipate pass patterns to force timely interceptions. He was simply unstoppable.

In addition to all of that, he also starred on the baseball diamond, where, as a pitcher on Coach Dick Siebert's Gopher Baseball teams, he dominated. In fact, Siebert said "Pitching Paulie" Giel was the hardest-throwing pitcher he had ever coached. From 1952-54 he was named to the All-American and All-Big Ten teams. On the mound, he earned 21 wins, and had the same number of complete games. His record for the most career strikeouts, 243, stood for more than 50 years and he remains fifth all-time for the most single season strikeouts, with 92. He finished his brilliant career with a 2.16 ERA.

So, with a resume like that, what was Paul to do after graduation? "I knew in my heart that I wanted to play baseball over football, and I was trying to be realistic about myself," said Giel. "I wondered where in the heck I would play in pro football. I mean I wasn't fast enough to be a halfback in the pros, and I couldn't have made it as a pure drop-back quarterback. So, I thought I still had a shot to make it in baseball."

His tenure as "Mr. Everything" at the U of M would ultimately prove to be a springboard for bigger and better things to come in the world of sports. With that, despite being drafted by the NFL's Chicago Bears, Giel opted to instead try his hand at professional baseball with the New York Giants. He would make his big league debut for legendary Manager Leo Durocher on June 29, 1954, striking out the side in the 9th inning of a 10-7 loss at home to the Pirates. It would be the beginning of a steady six-year Major League career, interrupted only by a two-year stint to serve his country in the military. From New York he went to San Francisco, and then to Pittsburgh for two seasons before finishing up his pitching career with his hometown Twins in 1961. He would hang up the spikes for good that same year, finishing his career with an overall record of 11-9, and a modest ERA of 5.39.

From there, Giel simply did it all, working first for the Vikings doing public relations and game management; followed by an eight year career as Sports Director of WCCO Radio — broadcasting prep, college and pro sports throughout Minnesota. In 1972 he was asked to return to his alma mater and serve as the University's Athletic Director, a position he would gladly accept and perform masterfully for more than 17 years. When that was up he even became a Vice President with the North Stars. Having seemingly covered every sport possible in the Land of 10,000 Lakes, in 1990 Giel settled down and took over as the Vice President of the Minneapolis Heart Institute Foundation, where he raised millions for heart health research and education. It was only fitting that a man with a heart as big as Paul's round out his illustrious career at such an appropriate place.

Tragically, Paul died in the Summer of 2002, leaving behind a legacy that will never be equaled in Minnesota sports history. A true legend at the University of Minnesota, Giel was one of those players who comes around once in a millennium. He played the game like no one will again, and did it with an unpretentious demeanor, earning the respect of his teammates and his opponents alike. It has been more than a half century now since he first lived out his dream of playing football and baseball for his beloved Golden Gophers. The old brick stadium is gone and so is that old baseball diamond, but memories of Paul Giel will live on forever.

On Prep Football in the New Millennium:
"I'm glad to see that many of our kids today are getting the opportunity to play and learn at major Division I schools, because that's what it's really all about. Sure, it's not the same as the old glory days back in the 1930s and '40s, when the University's rosters were lined with all Minnesota kids, but as a state, we are contributing more and more onto the national scene. Our coaches are doing a great job of recruiting, land-

ing and developing more and more of the local and national blue-chippers, which is imperative to our program's success."

"In addition, I really like the fact that we have so many Division II and III schools here for kids to play at as well. We have a lot of pretty dog-gone good football players in this state and it's great to see so many kids who maybe don't have a shot at playing D-I, striving to go on and play at the next level after high school. The MIAC is a wonderful conference, and our D-II schools: Mankato, Duluth and St. Cloud, have great programs too. I remember going to a St. John's vs. St. Thomas game up in Collegeville, and I have to tell you, that is some darn good football! In addition to being entertaining, it was great to see those kids playing for the love of the game, knowing that none of them are receiving any scholarships. All in all though, with the exception of the youth game, football today is big business. And frankly, I don't miss the pressure of it all."

Perhaps Big Ten Commissioner Ken Wilson said it best when he described Giel as being a great ambassador for collegiate athletics: "He was not only an inspiration to his teammates, he was an inspiration to anyone who was privileged to watch him play. A modest unassuming individual off the field, on the gridiron, Giel seemed to be inspired."

What Did it Mean for you to Be a Gopher?
"Being a Gopher meant so very much to me that it is really hard to put it into words. It had been a dream of mine since I was a kid and it was without question the wisest decision I ever made in my entire life. The opportunities that it afforded me both academically and athletically were immeasurable. It truly made me who I am today. To play for my home-state school, in front of so many wonderful fans who supported me so much through all those years was an honor I can't even begin to describe. Sometimes I have to pinch myself because it seems like a dream come true."

Gopher Tombstone:
"I owe everything I have to the University of Minnesota. It gave me a chance academically, athletically, and because of my visibility as a Gopher, it got me a chance to work with the Vikings and later WCCO, where my name meant something. I might have been angry with a few individuals at the time I left the position of Athletics Director, but not with the University itself, and certainly not the Athletics Department. It was a great experience for me."

1953 RUNNER-UP: "WHITEY" SKOOG

The 1953 Lakers win their fifth world title with an overall record of 48-22. One of the stars of the team was Brainerd native, **MEYER "WHITEY" SKOOG**, who joined the squad after earning All-American honors for the Gophers in 1951. It was at the U of M where Skoog also made history for inventing what we now know as the jump shot — a technique that revolutionized the game of basketball. Skoog played for six seasons with the Lakers, averaging 8.2 points per game and playing a pivotal role in leading the franchise to three straight NBA titles from 1952-54. In 1957, after suffering a career-ending back injury, Skoog headed to St. Peter, where he served as the head basketball and golf coach at Gustavus for nearly a quarter century.

HONORABLE MENTION: DICK DOUGHERTY

John Mariucci's hockey Gophers, after beating RPI, 3-2, in the semifinals, lose to Michigan in the 1953 NCAA Finals, 7-3. One of the stars of the team was International Falls native **DICK DOUGHERTY**. A two-time All-WCHA first-teamer, Dougherty later went on to win a silver medal as a winger on the 1956 U.S. Olympic team. From there, he would go on to play for seven seasons with the semi-pro Green Bay Bobcats of the USHL. He was later enshrined into the U.S. Hockey Hall of Fame in 2003.

JOHN MARIUCCI
The Gophers Make a Run for the NCAA Title

John Mariucci is the godfather of American amateur hockey and the patriarch of the puck sport in our state. In fact, what John did for the sport was immeasurable. With his passion for competing, teaching, and spreading the gospel about the sport he loved, Mariucci went on to become the country's most important figure in the development of amateur hockey. After a storied career as an NHL enforcer, Mariucci came home to his alma mater to coach the Gophers. Although he never won an NCAA championship during his 14-year tenure at the U of M, he came pretty darn close in 1954 with the best line ever to play college hockey.

When the 1953-54 collegiate hockey season started, the U of M was on a mission to avenge their NCAA Finals loss to Michigan the season before. After losing the first two games of the new season, the Gophers got back on track and lost only one of their next dozen games. After splitting with Michigan, Minnesota then swept Michigan State twice, Michigan Tech, North Dakota, and Denver, only to get beat twice by Michigan at season's end. The Gophers finished the year with a 24-6-1 record, the best in the nation, and won their second straight WIHL Conference crown.

Hockey fans were anticipating a rematch in the NCAA Finals in Colorado Springs between Minnesota and Michigan. But the Maroon and Gold had to first get by Boston College in the semifinals. There, Minnesota pummeled an outmanned BC club, 14-1, behind an amazing effort from the best line in college hockey: John Mayasich scored three goals and added four assists, Dick Dougherty scored four goals and added two assists, while Gene Campbell added three goals and two assists. Then, to the Gophers' disappointment, they found out that the Michigan Wolverines had been knocked off by unheralded Rennselaer Polytechnic Institute (RPI) in the semifinals.

Minnesota was clearly favored to win it all, (by five goals) in most spreads. Colorado Springs' Broadmoor Arena was packed with puck fanatics as the title game got underway with the Fighting Engineers striking first at 17:07 of the first, on an Abbey Moore back-hander that beat Gopher Goalie Jim Mattson. Then RPI scored a shorty on a Gopher power-play to make it two-zip. At 2:45 of the second, the Engineers threatened to run away with it when they scored again to make it 3-0. The Gophers were stunned, but, 24 seconds later, Minnesota got on the board with a Kenny Yackel blast, followed by a Dougherty one-timer from Campbell that made it 3-2. Then, after peppering the Engineer goalie, Mayasich put in a back-hander to even it up at three-apiece in the third. Four minutes later Mayasich set up Dougherty on a pretty "five-hole" goal to finally take the lead. But, at 16:10 the men from Troy, N.Y., evened things up one more time, as Moore scored again to send the game into overtime.

Then, at 1:54 of the extra session, after a mix-up out in front

of the net, RPI's Gordie Peterson, grabbed a loose puck on the doorstep and promptly slammed it home to win the game by the final of 5-4. It was a devastating defeat and a big blow to Mariucci, who wanted so badly to win the big one for Minnesota. After the game, the players huddled around their coach to shield him from the press and their cameras. It was the first and only time Minnesota hockey players would ever see this giant of a man shed a tear. Despite the loss, Yackel, Mattson, Dougherty and Mayasich were all named to the All-American team.

Growing up in "The Hockey Capital of the World"
John Mariucci was born the son of Italian immigrants on May 8, 1916, on the great Missabe Iron Range in Eveleth — the birthplace of hockey in the United States. He grew up on Hay Street, also referred to by locals as "Incubator Street" because it was said that there were so many nationalities living there, and every house had eight or nine kids inside. Many of the kids of the immigrants would play hockey to stay out of trouble. Some kids didn't even have skates, so they wore overshoes, while others used tree branches for sticks. John found his first pair of skates in a garbage can and, because he didn't have money to buy equipment, wrapped old magazines around his legs for shin pads.

Even though it was a mid-sized Minnesota Iron Range town, Eveleth was as sophisticated as New York City when it came to hockey. Eveleth even had a team in those days, the "Reds," which played big-time pro hockey against cities such as Toronto, Philadelphia and Chicago. Eveleth kids would try to emulate the many Canadians who were imported to the city to play hockey as one of the forms of entertainment provided for the iron-ore miners. John learned the game from legendary hall of fame coach Cliff Thompson, whose tenure as the Eveleth High School hockey coach lasted nearly 40 years.

In 1936, Mariucci left the Range and headed south to the University of Minnesota. There, he starred as a defenseman for Larry Armstrong's Gopher hockey team and also played offensive and defensive end alongside Butch Nash under legendary football coach Bernie Bierman. In 1940, led by Goalie Bud Wilkinson, the future football coaching legend at the University of Oklahoma, Mariucci captained the National AAU Championship team. (At the time that was the only championship available in college hockey.) After the season, Mariucci, who was named as an All-American, was offered the head coaching position at the U of M, but turned it down to play in the pros.

After a brief stint with Providence in the American Hockey League, Mariucci joined the Chicago Blackhawks to finish out the 1940 season. At that time the NHL employed few Americans and not many college-bred players. (To put this into perspective, by 1968, only six Americans and five collegians had ever played in the NHL!) Mariucci played there until 1942, when he was summoned to join the U.S. Coast Guard in New York. There, he played for the Coast Guard team in the Eastern Amateur League during WWII. After turning down another offer to coach at the U of M, he returned to the Hawks for the 1945 season. In 1947 Mariucci even became the first American-developed player ever to captain an NHL team.

The rugged "Maroosh," as he was known, was one of the biggest celebrities in Chicago during his playing days there. He became famous amongst Windy City hockey fans for his legendary brawls. One in particular, with Detroit's Black Jack Stewart, remains the NHL's longest ever — lasting more than 20 minutes. In 1948, Mariucci left the Hawks having scored 11 goals and 34 assists for 45 points over 223 games. He also played in two Stanley Cup playoffs. More importantly though, he led the team in penalty minutes, racking up more than 300 over his career. A goal-scorer he wasn't. Mariucci was a role-playing hatchet-man who protected and defended his teammates. That's why they loved and appreciated him so much.

Mariucci then went on to play for St. Louis of the American League, St. Paul and Minneapolis of the U.S. League, and again with a Coast Guard team before hanging up his skates for good as an active player in 1951. From there, he got into coaching, opting to become the skipper of Minneapolis Millers of the A.A.L.

After a year with the Millers, Mariucci finally decided to come home to coach the Gophers, replacing former Blackhawk and Gopher, Doc Romnes. It was only a part-time job for him though, as he continued to work as a salesman for the Martin Falk Paper Company as well. In his first season in Gold Country he was awarded Coach of the Year honors. It would be his first of many such honors.

He got Minnesota residents excited about college hockey, and they responded by coming out in droves to see his Gophers. The U even had to add an upper tier of seats to the Williams Arena rink to accommodate them all. Always a kidder, Mariucci was always trying new things to keep the fans interested and was constantly looking for new recruits. One time while watching the giant Bill Simonovich, from Gilbert, Minn., play with the varsity basketball team, Mariucci, ever the character, said: "Man, what a goalie he'd make! Give him a couple of mattresses and a pair of skis and nobody would ever score on him."

In a sport dominated by Canadians, Mariucci championed the Americans and in particular, Minnesotans. After watching an NCAA Final one time, he said: "It's asinine that the only two Americans on the ice for the college championship game were the referees." Mariucci was a visionary and saw the potential growth of the sport.

"College could be a developmental program for our own country, for the Olympics and for the pros," he said. "College hockey is a state institution and should be represented by Minnesota boys. If they're not quite as good as some Canadians, we'll just have to work a little harder, that's all."

It became political for him as he battled to stop the importation of the older Canadians and give the American kids an equal playing field. In the late 1950s, the U's Athletic Director, Marsh Ryman, refused to play Denver's Canadian-filled teams. This ultimately led to the end of the WIHL and the creation of the WCHA in 1959.

"What I was against was the junior player who played in Canada until he was 21, then, if the pros didn't sign him, he would come to this country to play college hockey as a 22-year-old freshman against our 18-year-olds," said Mariucci. "It wasn't fair to our kids, who were finishing college at the same age Canadians were freshmen."

The "Noble Roman" left the University in 1966 with a record of 207-142-15, including conference championships in 1953 and 1954, as well as three NCAA playoff appearances (including another Final Four appearance in 1961). Included in his tenure was an Italian homecoming of sorts, when he led the Americans to a silver medal in the 1956 Olympics in Cortina, Italy. There were 11 Minnesota natives on the team that stunned heavily favored Canada before falling to the Soviet Union. Mariucci's successor at the U of M would be Glen Sonmor, a former teammate with the Minneapolis Millers and close friend.

In 1966, another chapter of Mariucci's storied life unfolded as he became chief scout and special assistant to Wren Blair, GM of the NHL's expansion Minnesota North Stars, where he was able to apply his vast knowledge of recruiting, coaching, and scouting. In 1977 Mariucci coached the U.S. National team and a year later he rejoined the North Stars, this time as the Assistant GM under his former player with the Gophers, Lou Nanne.

"One word of advice to all you coaches," quipped Mariucci. "Be good to your players, you never know which one might someday be your boss...".

John's accomplishments and honors are far too great to list here. Some of his more notable ones, however, include: Being inducted as a charter member of the U.S. Hockey Hall of Fame in his hometown of Eveleth; being inducted into the NHL Hockey Hall of Fame in Toronto; and receiving the NHL's coveted Lester Patrick Award for his contributions to U.S. hockey. He also made a difference by back giving to others. In fact, he devoted much of his life to Brainerd's Camp Confidence, for the mentally-retarded, a cause he

dearly loved.

On March 2, 1985, in an emotional ceremony to give thanks and immortalize the man forever, the U of M renamed the hockey half of Williams Arena as Mariucci Arena, in his honor. It was also declared as "John Mariucci Day" in Minnesota by then-Governor Rudy Perpich. During the ceremony, longtime friend Robert Ridder said: "During the 1980 Olympics, a U.S. Destroyer passed a Russian ship and signaled to it: 'U.S.A. 4, Russia 3.' Probably nobody on that boat ever heard of John Mariucci, but it wouldn't have been possible without John Mariucci." In 1987 Maroosh died at the age of 70 after a long bout with cancer. He had seven children and several grandchildren.

This gentleman brawler was a legend, on and off the ice. Although he was tough as nails, his wit, intelligence, and personality were one-of-a-kind. John was one of the toughest Italians who ever lived. His face has often been referred to as a "blocked punt," because it was so beat up. But what separated him from the goons was that he wouldn't just knock his opponents down, he'd pick them up and then make them laugh.

Perhaps Herb Brooks said it best: "In all social causes to better an institution, there's always got to be a rallying force, a catalyst, a glue, and a magnet, and that's what John was for American hockey. The rest of us just filled in after him."

Full of wit, he was described as a newspaperman's dream-come-true. From his famous brawls, which included once breaking thumb-wrestling champion Murray Warmath's thumb, Mariucci was tough as nails, yet soft as a pillow. Local reporters found themselves having a lot of dinners that turned into breakfasts while listening to his endless stories. The sports community was in awe of him, and he made journalists who hated the sport of hockey want to start covering it.

He was also the pioneer in the development of hockey in Minnesota. Because of that, his legacy will live on forever. Every kid that laces up his or her skates needs to give thanks to the man that started it all. Mariucci started grassroots youth programs, put on coaching clinics, attended new arena openings in countless cities across the state, helped former players find coaching positions, and even encouraged hockey moms to write to city councils to encourage building new rinks and to develop recreation programs. Because of him, hockey in Minnesota carries the same pedigree as basketball in Indiana or football in Texas. Described best by his friends and players as "father-like, magical, and even super-human," he was simply the greatest. He *WAS* the godfather.

1954 RUNNER-UP: CLYDE LOVELLETTE

The Lakers win their sixth world championship with an overall record of 46-26. One of its stars was big-man *CLYDE LOVELLETTE*, who was the team's first round draft pick out of Kansas University in 1952. The first player in history to play on an NCAA, Olympic and NBA championship team, Lovellette pioneered being able to move outside to utilize the one-handed set-shot. This ultimately extended his shooting range and enabled him to play either the small forward, power forward or center positions — forcing the opposition's center to oftentimes play out of position. Lovellette would go on to play in more than 700 NBA games with Minneapolis, Cincinnati, St. Louis and Boston, averaging 17.0 ppg and 9.3 rpg. The three-time All-Star was inducted into the Basketball Hall of Fame in 1988.

HONORABLE MENTION: MURRAY WARMATH

MURRAY WARMATH is hired as the head coach of the football Gophers, replacing Wes Fesler. The Tennessee native would make history in Gold Country, leading the Gophers to a pair of Rose Bowls and an NCAA National Championship in 1960. He would step down in 1971 with an overall career record of 86-78-7. From there, the "Autumn Warrior" went on to serve as an assistant coach and scout with the NFL's Minnesota Vikings. In all, Warmath would spend 65 years in the game of football, playing, coaching and scouting.

Chuck Mencel could flat-out shoot, and that's why he was one of the greatest guards ever to play for the University of Minnesota basketball Gophers. Mencel had poise, court-savvy, tremendous ball-handling skills, and was extremely accurate from the field as well as from the line. He worked hard at the fundamentals and optimized the cliché, "lead by example." In 1955, Mencel was honored as the first Minnesota player ever to be named as the Big Ten MVP. But, he would have surely traded it all to knock off the powerful Iowa Hawkeyes that year for the conference title.

Minnesota was coming off a respectable third place finish in the Big Ten in 1953-54, with a 10-4 conference mark. The outlook was cautiously optimistic for the 1954-55 season. Although the Gophers were young, they had returning All-Big Ten players Chuck Mencel and Hibbing's Dick Garmaker, both of whom were named as the upcoming season's co-captains. The other three Gopher starters were Forward David Tucker, Center Bill Simonovich and Guard Gerald "Buck" Lindsley.

The season opened in the Windy City, where Ray Meyers' DePaul Blue Demons knocked off the Gophers, 94-93, in an overtime thriller. Minnesota rebounded a week later when the Blue Demons came to Minneapolis as part of a home-and-home series to kick off the season, and this time the Gophers prevailed, 94-84. From there, the Gophers were beaten by Oklahoma A&M, but rallied to win their next four games — the first two of which took place at Williams Arena against SMU and Notre Dame. The Maroon and Gold then flew south to play in the Dixie Classic in Raleigh, N.C. There, they defeated Wake Forest and Duke, but lost to North Carolina State for the championship.

It was back to Chicago for Minnesota, as they took on Northwestern to open the Big Ten Conference schedule. In a heart-breaker, the Wildcats beat the Gophers, 72-74. Next stop, Iowa, where the Gophers beat the arch-rival Hawkeyes, 81-80. That would prove to be a pivotal game for the squad as they sent a clear message to the Big Ten that they meant business. The U of M went on to win its next two over Indiana and Purdue before losing to Michigan State, 75-87. From there the team rattled off seven straight wins, including triumphs over Northwestern, Purdue, Ohio State, Illinois, Indiana, Michigan and Wisconsin.

In the game against the Badgers, Mencel poured in 23, while Garmaker had 28 to lead the way. Wisconsin, led by Dick Miller, who scored 31 in the game, rallied to go up by seven at the half. In the second, Garmaker took over, scoring 12 points in first five minutes to get the score to 49-48. The Badgers held the lead until Garmaker's tip-in made it 63-63. It then went back and forth with less then two minutes to go as Mencel stripped the ball from Miller. He quickly passed it up to Garmaker, who then put it in to make it 69-apiece. Now, with only 15 seconds to go, Mencel took the ball upcourt and got fouled. With only six ticks left on the clock, Mencel nailed both free throws to ice the game, 71-69.

The stage was now set for the Big Ten title game as hated Iowa came to town for a much-anticipated rematch. A record crowd, of 20,176 fans, showed up at Williams Arena in anticipation of the dynamic duo of Mencel and Garmaker bringing down the vaunted Hawkeyes. Williams Arena had never held so many spectators for a basketball game, and it will never again as fire codes now prevent such an occurrence. The contest went

back and forth early on as Minnesota shot 43 percent in the first half to take a 35-33 halftime lead.

The Hawks were led by their big man, Bill Logan, who had 15 of his 25 points in the first half. In the second half, the battle continued as both teams sparred like heavyweight champions. With just over four minutes to play, Mencel scored six straight of his team-high 27 points to give the Gophers a 70-67 lead. But at 2:23, Iowa's guard play brought the Hawks back on top, 71-70. With two minutes to go, Mencel missed a key shot, which was then followed by Buck Lindsley's missed free throw at the end of the game which would have gotten the Gophers back into it. Iowa hung on, shooting an incredible 67 percent in the second half to beat the Gophers, 72-70.

It was an incredibly crushing loss for Minnesota and somewhat ironic in that Iowa, the league's worst from the charity stripe, won the game on the line, beating Minnesota — the league's best free throw shooting team.

The last game of the year then featured a rematch with the Badgers. The Gophers not only needed to win the game, but also had to have some help from Lady Luck to have any chance to win the conference title. This would ultimately be the great Mencel's farewell to Williams Arena. And, appropriately enough, his last game was against his home-state Badgers. Minnesota, its backs to the wall, hung it all out on the line that night. Coach Ozzie Cowles' boys held the lead at the half, 32-31, and looked confident.

The Badgers then went ahead, but the Gophers rallied with 12 minutes to go, narrowing the gap to 50-48 off a pair from Lindsley, who scored 17 points in the game. At the four-minute mark the Gophers were still in it at 72-67, but that would be as close as they would come in the season finale. Cowles removed Mencel and Garmaker with a minute left and the crowd responded with a thunderous roar of appreciation for all their hard work over the years. Minnesota lost by the final of 78-72, and as a result, Iowa was now off to the NCAA Tournament.

How good was Iowa that year? Led by Logan, Carl Cain, and Sharm Scheuerman, the Hawkeyes waltzed past Penn State and Marquette before losing to All-American sensation Tom Gola and LaSalle in the NCAA Final Four by the tally of 76-73.

"It was a letdown for me at the time, but it also became the springboard to a much more expanded view of opportunity, both in an athletic and business sense," Mencel would later recall. "I'm not going to say we should have won the Iowa game, but we could have easily won it. I've got a video tape of the game, and I still bring it out and watch it every now and then. It was a great, great game — a disappointment — but definitely my most memorable as a Gopher. The thing that stands out for me most, was that it was probably my best game as a Gopher, but we still lost. And then losing to Wisconsin in the next game was a tough way for me to bow out."

The Gophers led the conference in defense that season and finished the year with a 10-4 record in the Big Ten, 15-7 overall. But because of the Wisconsin disappointment on the last day of the season, they wound up as the conference bridesmaids. Mencel was named as the team's MVP that year and was also named to the All-Big Ten and All-American squads. For his efforts he was also awarded the Silver Basketball Award, signifying the Big Ten's most valuable player.

The Golden Touch

Chuck Mencel was born in Phillips, Wis., the oldest of three children. He grew up spending much of his time shooting hoops at the YMCA.

"When my parents got divorced while I was in the seventh grade, the basketball gymnasium became my safe haven," said Mencel.

He went on to play basketball at Eau Claire High School, becoming the only non-senior to make the squad. His team made it all the way to the Wisconsin State High School Tournament Finals, but lost in the championship game to St. Croix Falls. During that season, he broke his school's single-game and season scoring records. Then, after his senior year, he was selected to the national high school All-

American team. After a stellar prep career, Mencel accepted a scholarship to attend Bradley University in Peoria, Ill. But when allegations of a basketball betting scandal broke out that summer, Mencel elected to transfer to Minnesota instead.

"The scandal was a big red flag for me, so I immediately decided to attend the U of M," said Mencel.

Because of the Korean War, freshmen were now allowed to participate in intercollegiate sports, and Mencel took every advantage of his playing time. Interestingly, while at the U of M, he wound up living in possibly the most athletic dorm room of all time. That's because his roommate was Gopher Hockey All-American John Mayasich.

Averaging 16 points per game, Mencel held five Gopher scoring records during his tenure at the U, and he still ranks among the best in career scoring, with 1,391 points. He would hold the school's scoring record for nearly a quarter of a century, until Mychal Thompson came along and broke it in the late 1970s. He also set the record for the most field goals attempted, with 1,635. In addition, during his sophomore, junior, and senior seasons in the Big Ten, he scored 766 points, then a school record. An outstanding student, he graduated that same year with a bachelor's degree in Business Administration. What's even more impressive is that he did it all while taking care of his family. You see, Chuck married his high school sweetheart when he was a sophomore at the U, and before he graduated, he had two children.

Mencel's partner in crime during the mid-50s was fellow All-American Dick Garmaker, a transfer student from Hibbing Junior College. Garmaker was a tremendous rebounder, defender and free-throw shooter who could also do a lot of damage with his jump shot. Over his career at Minnesota, Garmaker would set eight scoring records. Later, he and Mencel even played together for a couple of years with the Minneapolis Lakers. Garmaker ultimately went on to finish his NBA career with the New York Knicks.

"Dick Garmaker and I were the two seniors on an otherwise underclass team," said Mencel. "We had a great time playing together for the Gophers and, later, the Lakers. He was certainly my closest friend on the team and he was a great player. We're still close today."

Mencel had the golden shooting touch and was acknowledged as one of Minnesota's greatest team players. He was widely regarded as the premier pure shooter of his day and, because of his quickness and shooting ability, revolutionized many aspects of the game. There's no telling just how good Mencel would have been if he had played in the NBA after the dawn of the three-point line. Although he didn't bring home the hardware for Minnesota in 1955, he made Minnesota proud of the U's basketball program and got people all over the state excited about college hoops again.

After his illustrious career at Minnesota, Mencel was drafted by the Minneapolis Lakers. But, that summer before his first season, he was invited to play on the traveling team that played the Harlem Globetrotters. It was a 24-city tour and he was paid $100 per game. By the way, this was a real team Mencel played for, and not the stooge teams like the Washington Nationals that we see today. They played it straight in those days and Mencel had to work for everything he got.

After that Chuck went on to start as the point guard for the Lakers. He averaged seven points per game and led the team in assists

with three per game. His career was cut short after only two years in the NBA though, due to the fact that he was required to fulfill his military obligation, which he had deferred out of college. With that, he joined the Army as a second lieutenant in the Transportation Corps and was stationed in Fort Eustis, Va. After that, Mencel decided to abandon the NBA altogether and enter the world of business, where he applied that same zealous attitude of hard work and success that he had on the court. Following his playing days he went on to become the President and CEO of Caterpillar Paving Products, in Brooklyn Park.

What did it mean for you to be a Gopher?

"In hindsight, it really set the table for a lifestyle that was unparalleled in my expectations as a young person. To have played and been successful at a major institution like the U of M, and in a conference such as the Big Ten, was just incredible. As an athlete, it was wonderful stepping stone to the business world that gave me the ability to raise my family and live a standard of life that I never dreamed would be possible. If I had not come to Minnesota — who knows? I can't imagine that it would have been any better for me anywhere else. It was a wonderful experience."

Gopher Tombstone:

"I see myself as a very fierce competitor, never giving up hope of a victory. I hope that I demonstrated that during my playing time. I felt like I always expected victory, but I was never discouraged by defeat."

TRIBUTES

"Chuck was such a good, sound ballplayer," said Laker Coach John Kundla. "He was solid with the fundamentals and, not only that, he had such a great shot. He had that jump shot of his down pat! He was a super guy and a great player. He had a great career at the University and he was a great addition to our Laker teams."

"He had a nice career here with both the Gophers and the Lakers and was just a real good player," said George Mikan.

"I met Chuck as a freshman in Pioneer Hall, and we became roommates and best friends," added John Mayasich. "I really admired him as an individual. He had such a wonderful personality. We were like brothers. We helped each other socially, athletically and academically. He was a great athlete, student and friend. He exhibits the same traits today, and we're still the best of friends."

1955 RUNNER-UP: AL WORTHINGTON

The Minneapolis Millers beat the Rochester Red Wings to win the 1955 Junior World Series — the team's first title in 23 seasons. The Millers closed out the series with a 9-4 victory, highlighted by future Hall of Famer Monte Irvin's home run. It would be the final game ever played at Nicollet Park, as the team would move into the newly constructed Metropolitan Stadium in Bloomington that next Fall. One of the stars of the club was pitcher *AL WORTHINGTON*. The Birmingham, Al., native would go on to pitch for 14 seasons in the Major Leagues with the Giants, Red Sox, White Sox, Reds and Twins (1965-69). Considered the first great closer in Twins history, "Red" compiled a 75-82 career record with 110 saves and a 3.39 ERA.

HONORABLE MENTION: CAL MARVIN

CAL MARVIN'S Warroad Lakers beat the Grand Falls Americans (Montana) to win the 1955 U.S. Senior National Intermediate Championship. Marvin, the venerable godfather of Warroad hockey, coached the Lakers for more than 50 years, leading them to two Canadian Intermediate titles in 1964 and 1974, along with three straight Allen Cup titles from 1994-96 — the pinnacle of amateur hockey in North America. A true pioneer who gave everything he had to grow the game, Marvin also coached the 1958 U.S National team as well.

DICK SIEBERT
The Baseball Gophers Win the NCAA Title

There were plenty of reasons for optimism as the University of Minnesota baseball team headed into the 1956 season under Coach Dick Siebert. The Gophers were coming off a respectable 19-9 campaign that previous Spring and had all the necessary confidence to make a legitimate run for the Big Ten title.

The Maroon and Gold finished the regular season that year with an outstanding 33-9 overall record, as well an 11-2 conference mark. They captured the Big Ten title, but didn't stop there. They went on and become the first Gopher baseball team to win the NCAA championship at the College World Series in Omaha.

It was a storybook year that saw the club breeze through its competition and coast into the Mideast Region Semifinals, which were held in Minneapolis. There, the Gophers edged Notre Dame, 4-3, in Game One. They could only manage a 5-5 tie in Game Two, but they rebounded in Game Three, crushing the Irish, 10-1, to take the series. Minnesota then kept it going that next week in the Mideast Regional Finals in Athens, Ohio, where they swept Ohio, 5-0 and 6-2, to advance to the College World Series.

Gopher Pitchers Jerry Thomas, Rod Oistad and Ron Craven all made big contributions in leading Minnesota to its first national championship. Thomas, an All-American, would appear in three games during the World Series, going 1-1 with two complete games, while Oistad and Craven would each earn a complete-game victory as well. On June 9th, the Gophers opened up the big dance by downing the University of Wyoming, 4-0. In Game Two the Gophers, behind Pitcher Jerry Thomas' three-hit gem, topped Arizona, 3-1. Then, in Game Three, they beat up on Mississippi, 13-5. On the fourth day of tournament play Minnesota just kept on rolling, beating Bradley, 8-3. But then, in the first game of the Finals, the Gophers finally got beat, losing to Arizona, 10-4, in the double-elimination tournament. They rebounded in that next game though, thoroughly pounding those same Wildcats, 12-1, to claim their first ever NCAA championship.

The Gophers jumped out to a quick 1-0 lead in that championship game when Bill Horning led off the first inning with a single, stole second, and then scored on a Doug Lindblom double. Minnesota never relinquished the lead after that. Doug Gillen followed with another double and, before you knew it, coach Siebert's boys were up 3-0. It became 4-0 in the fourth after two walks, plus another Horning single, and 10-0 after a six-run fifth inning which saw the Gopher bats really come to life. With the score 10-1 in the seventh, Horning belted his second homer of the game to put the final nail in the Wildcat coffin. Along with Horning's four hits, other Gophers who played big in the game included Gillen, McNeeley and David Lindblom, who each had a pair of hits, while Jack McCartan, Jerry Kindall, R. Anderson and Gene Martin, each added one apiece.

Gopher Pitcher Jerry Thomas pitched masterfully, giving up only five hits en route to mowing down four Wildcats while walking only one batter. Amazingly, Thomas retired the side 1-2-3 in six of the nine innings and at the plate, even added two hits for the cause. It was only after an error and a questionable wild pitch that Arizona even got on the board. For his efforts, Thomas, who earlier had also beaten Arizona, 3-1, was selected as the MVP of the Series. After the final out, Siebert rushed out to the mound to give his star pitcher a hero's ride on his a shoulders back to the dug-out.

With the convincing final score of 12-1, the Gophers had won their first ever NCAA baseball championship.

In 1956, Minnesota featured a superb blend of intimidating hitting, dominating pitching and smooth fielding. Led on the mound by All-American Jerry Thomas, who won 12 games that season while going 5-0 in conference games, the Gophers made history. Leading the way offensively was slugger Jack McCartan, who was not only an All-American third baseman on the baseball team, but was also an All-American goalie on the John Mariucci's Gopher Hockey team. Another key member of that squad was Shorty Cochran, who stole 22 bases that year as well.

The Gophers hit .320 as a team that year while posting an amazing .976 fielding percentage. The conference title ended an 18-year drought for the program, which was typically at an arctic disadvantage geographically against the southern and western schools, which had the luxury of having longer and more temperate weather to practice in.

"You're always prejudiced about your own kids, but I think this was the greatest team that ever played in the College World Series. This was my greatest thrill, barring none," said Coach Siebert on winning his first NCAA crown.

Two weeks later All-American Gopher Shortstop Jerry Kindall, who hit a record 18 home runs that year in Gold Country — a single-season record that would stand for 40 years, turned pro by signing with the Chicago Cubs. (It is interesting to note that Kindall, who would later play with the Twins, would make history some 20 years later when, as head coach of those same Arizona Wildcats, he led his teams to three NCAA national titles. In the process, he became the only person ever to win a College World Series championship as both a player and coach.)

The Chief

A native of Fall River, Mass., Dick Siebert began his baseball days at St. Paul Concordia High School and went on to attend Concordia Junior College. From there, he moved to the Concordia Seminary in St. Louis with full intentions of becoming a Lutheran minister. But the lure of baseball was too much for the calling of the pulpit, so Dick started his pro baseball career in 1932. Originally a pitcher, Siebert switched over to first base when he developed some arm problems.

He went on to play in the minor leagues with teams in Ohio, Pennsylvania and New York, eventually paying his dues as a member of the Brooklyn Dodgers, Chicago Cubs and St. Louis Cardinals farm systems. Finally, in 1938, he made it to the big leagues when he became a regular first baseman for the Philadelphia Athletics under the legendary Connie Mack.

Siebert played for the A's through 1945 and even appeared in the 1942 All Star game. He was chosen as an all-star again in 1945 only to see the game canceled due to wartime restrictions. Siebert later recalled his greatest day in the big leagues was when he broke up a no-hitter by Cleveland great Bob Feller. Siebert played in 1,035 games over his big league career and finished with a very respectable .282 lifetime batting average.

Siebert's pro career came to an abrupt end in 1946 due to some unfortunate contract problems with management. So, he simply traded in his first-baseman's mitt for a microphone and decided to become a sportscaster with WTCN radio in Minneapolis. But, only one year later, Siebert would get the baseball itch one more time. This time it was to take over as head coach of the Golden Gophers. (Later he would do radio and television work with WCCO as well.)

Siebert took the reigns as the University of Minnesota head coach in 1947 from then-head coach David MacMillan. The "Chief," as he was affectionately known, would go on to become one of the greatest coaches in college baseball history.

Siebert helped develop baseball at all levels in Minnesota. A true pioneer of the game, he was also credited with introducing the aluminum bat and designated hitter to college baseball as well. As a coach, he emulated many of the mannerisms of his long-time mentor, Connie Mack. He was tough but fair, and his players respected him for his honesty and integrity. He also got involved, serving as the president of the American College Baseball Coaches Association.

When it was all said and done, Siebert had compiled one of the most incredible records in college baseball history. At the time of his retirement in 1978, Siebert was the winningest coach in Gopher history with a 754-361 record, and a .676 winning percentage. The record would stand until 2002, when his former player and current Gopher coach John Anderson finally broke it. He is also one of just a handful of coaches from a major university to have guided a team to more than 700 wins. In all, he sent five different teams to the College World Series and, of course, he brought home three NCAA National Championships in 1956, 1960 and 1964 — following a three year presidential cycle. His teams also captured 11 Big Ten titles as well. Amazingly, he endured only three losing seasons over his illustrious career in Gold Country.

Among his many honors and accolades, Siebert was twice named as college baseball's Coach of the Year. He is also a member of the College Baseball Hall of Fame and was a recipient of college baseball's highest award, the Lefty Gomez Trophy, which recognizes the individual who has given the most outstanding contribution and service to the development of college baseball.

Siebert coached 31 seasons in Minnesota, with his last season being that of 1978. Sadly, on December 9, of that same year, the Chief died, succumbing to numerous respiratory and cardiac illnesses. Dick was survived by his wife Marie and their children: Marilyn, Beverly, Richard, and Paul — who went on to play ball in the Major Leagues with the Mets and Cardinals.

In his last year of life, Siebert was quoted as saying: "I actually expected my coaching job at the U to last a few years and then I would go into business. No one in the world could have convinced me then I would still be here 31 years later. But I loved it, working with great young men and staying active in the best form of baseball I knew, the college game."

The entire baseball world mourned his passing, and tributes to the coach poured in from every corner of the baseball world. Fittingly, on April 21, 1979, the University of Minnesota Baseball Stadium was officially renamed "Siebert Field," in honor of their great coach and friend.

For more than three decades, the Chief brought honor and respect to the University of Minnesota baseball program. Siebert was a true ballplayer and a real throwback to another era. A tireless worker, his life was consumed with Gopher baseball. The cold weather was no match for the Chief because he worked at his craft all-year long. Whether it was from his old Cooke Hall office, or from the fieldhouse, he was always trying to improve and help his teams find a way to get better.

He was a man who learned virtually every aspect of the game of baseball throughout his life and chose to teach others what he had learned. He was a teacher, a coach, a mentor and a friend. We appreciate coach Siebert for all these things, but also, and maybe especially, for the fact that he did so much of it with local home-grown talent.

He will be forever thought of as the standard to which all other coaches will be measured against, and will go undoubtedly go down in history as one of the best of the very best.

TRIBUTES

"He was a tremendous teacher," said Paul Molitor. "I think baseball at the University of Minnesota was successful under him because of the fact that he knew how to teach college players to be fundamentally sound. He taught us how to execute and gave us a chance to be competitive with any college team in the nation. When you played for the Chief, you were playing for a man with a national reputation. He felt he never had to go out of the state to get his players, and he competed on a national scale. The Chief put a lot of pride in that Minnesota uniform for us."

"Dick Siebert was a great coach, and I really enjoyed my playing days at the University of Minnesota working with him," said Dave Winfield. "I felt that I was as good a hitter as I was a pitcher in college, but they wouldn't let me hit, insisting instead that I become specialized. My friends would come to the games and yell at him, 'Put in Winfield and let him hit, because he's the best hitter you've got!' But it didn't matter how good or bad you were, you had to get out there and work when you played for the Chief. You could be a star on his team, but he played no favorites and treated everyone alike. I learned a lot playing for him."

"Dick Siebert was just a heck of an all-around guy," said Paul Giel. "He was a very fine coach, and I had so much respect for him as a man. He knew the fundamentals of the game so well, but he had a sense of humor and made it fun for you. I learned the game from Dick, and even while I was in the Majors, I still felt like he was better than most of the managers that I had. Every person on the team respected him and he got a lot out of his kids."

"When you think about Dick, you don't just think about his record at Minnesota, which is distinction enough in itself," said Jerry Kindall. "But I don't think people realize what he did for college baseball in general. Dick was one of the leaders in restoring good relations with Major League Baseball. There was a time when there was an antagonistic, very tense, relationship between the colleges and the pros. He overcame that. And he was the biggest expert of all college baseball coaches on the rules of the game too. He served on virtually every committee that college baseball has instituted. I think it's safe to say — and I don't think I'm stretching it at all — that Dick was the most highly respected and honored coach in collegiate baseball."

1956 RUNNER-UP: WENDELL ANDERSON

The U.S. wins a silver medal at the 1956 Winter Games in Cortina, Italy, under the leadership of Gopher coach John Mariucci. Among the seven Minnesotans on the team is a kid from the east side of St. Paul by the name of **WENDELL ANDERSON**. Anderson, a St. Paul Johnson grad who played for the Gophers from 1952-54, would go on to pursue a life in politics — later serving as the Governor of Minnesota from 1971-76, and U.S. Senator from 1976-78.

HONORABLE MENTION: FORTUNE GORDIEN

Gopher track and field star **FORTUNE GORDIEN** wins a silver medal in the discuss at the 1956 Winter Games in Cortina, Italy. The Minneapolis native attended the University of Minnesota from 1942-48, taking a two-year layoff for World War II. In 1948, he led the Gophers to their first-ever NCAA track and field championship, after the team had finished third the year before. That year the shot put and discus thrower won his third consecutive NCAA discuss title. Gordien was a three-time Big Ten champion, six-time AAU national champion, and a three-time Olympian (1948, 1952 and 1956). A one time world record holder, Gordien won a bronze medal at the 1948 Summer Games in London as well.

PATTY BERG
An Incredible Year for Golf's Grand Dame

Arguably, the greatest golfer ever to hail from Minnesota, Patty Berg was truly a links legend. Born in Minneapolis in 1918, Berg's storied career as a golfer began in 1933, when, at the age of 15, she entered her first tournament. It wasn't exactly an auspicious beginning, but from there she would go on to accomplish more than any other woman in the history of the game. She is without question the matriarch of women's golf, as witness to the fact that she was a founder of the LPGA (Ladies Professional Golf Association) in 1949, while also serving as its first president.

Berg's career resume is a Who's Who and What's What of women's golf; her list of tournament victories, lifetime achievement awards, honors, and tributes rendered her by organizations within and without of the sports world, borders on the incredible.

In 1940, having won 28 amateur titles, and having decided she wanted to make a career in golf, Berg turned professional. Amazingly, from 1941 through 1962 she won 57 professional tournaments, 15 of which were deemed as "majors." (Incredibly, that is a record that still stands!) In all, throughout her career as both an amateur and a professional, she won a mind-boggling 85 tournaments.

One of her best years without a doubt was 1957. That year she was named Woman Athlete of the Year by the Associated Press after she won five tournaments, two of them majors — the Titleholders Championship and the Western Open. Her other victories included the World Championship, the All-America Open and the Havana Open. With earnings of $16,272, she was that years leading LPGA money-winner. (Incidentally, another Minnesotan, Bev Vanstrum, won a couple of professional tournaments on the LPGA Tour that year as well.)

Even as a youngster, Berg showed signs of being a natural athlete. She played baseball, took part in track and field events, and as a member of the Minneapolis Powderhorn Club won several national medals as a speed skater. She even played quarterback on her neighborhood football team, called the "50th Street Tigers." Patty was the quarterback because, as she puts it "I was the only one who could remember the plays!" Another famous Minnesota athlete, Bud Wilkinson, was a tackle on that team. Wilkinson, of course, went on to the University of Minnesota where he became an All-American football and hockey player for the Gophers.

According to Patty, it was only after Wilkinson suggested she "was too short and too slow, and that there was no future in football for me that I gave it up." Furthermore, her parents wanted her to specialize in a less violent sport, one that didn't tear her clothes. So the freckled-faced tomboy swapped her sneakers for golf shoes.

Patty's father came home one day in 1931 only to find his daughter digging up the back yard with one of his golf clubs. So, Herman Berg, a successful grain merchant, took his 13-year-old daughter to play at the prestigious Interlachen Country Club. It wasn't too long before she was outplaying her father. The kid was just a natural.

Ready to test her newfound skills, patty entered her first ever tournament — the 1933 Minneapolis City Ladies Championship. "I qualified for the last flight with a 122," she recalled. "Then the woman I played in the first round beat me like a drum!"

A self-proclaimed perfectionist, Berg vowed to learn from that experience by going home and practicing for an entire year. "I said I'm going to work, and I'm going to work, and I'm going to see if I can't do better," she said. "And I worked. I concentrated and took my lessons, and finally, a year later, I came back and I won that same Minneapolis City Ladies Championship!"

It was this relentless determination and pride that made her the premier player she was to become.

Patty won the Minnesota state title in 1935, then finished as runner-up to one of her golfing idols, Glenna Collett Vare (the woman for whom the LPGA's low annual scoring average honor is named) in the U.S. Women's Amateur, which was played at Interlachen. Three years later, and in between stints at the University of Minnesota, Patty won the U.S. Women's Amateur title and was also named as the Associated Press' Woman Athlete of the Year.

Patty's father had a big influence on her as she grew up. In many ways her persona as a gallery favorite was shaped by him as he encouraged her both as a player as well as an entertainer.

"I had played nine years of amateur golf, and during that time, when I wasn't in a tournament, my father had me play in a clinic and exhibition every weekend around the state of Minnesota to promote golf," said Patty. "I'd take a popular football player or amateur golfer with me. The local club pro would put it (a clinic) on and we'd hit shots. Dad said that I had to do something for the game, and he felt this was a great idea." On train rides between exhibitions, Patty recalled reciting her favorite poems, particularly "Casey at the Bat," to keep herself busy.

In 1940, after winning 28 amateur titles, including three Titleholders Championships, which were then considered majors, Patty signed a contract with the Wilson Sporting Goods Company. Wilson took advantage of her outstanding communication skills as a motivator and educator by having her give clinics and exhibitions at colleges and universities throughout the country. An already famous woman and only in her early 20s, her name now appeared on several different lines of Wilson golf clubs for women.

In 1941, after winning the Western Open, the Asheville Open, and the Lake Champlain Invitational, Patty was involved in an automobile accident that seriously injured her knee. As a result, she was sidelined for a year and a half. Then in 1943, with the nation at war, Patty enlisted in the Marine Corps, serving as a first lieutenant and doing what she did best — recruiting, public relations, and promotions.

Over the next six years Patty won 15 tournaments including the first-ever Women's National Open Golf Championship, two Westerns, and one Titleholders Championships — all considered major wins. As the first half-century ended, women's golf was gaining momentum, and there were new LPGA tour stops being created across the nation with the prize money increasing annually.

Golf's Grande Dame

Throughout the ensuing years Patty was a vital, driving force behind the growing and struggling women's professional golf tour. From 1950 to 1962 she won 41 tournaments, seven of them majors, including four Western and three Titleholder Championships. She also received her third AP Woman Athlete of the Year award in 1955. In 1959 at the U.S. Women's Open at Churchill Valley Country Club in Pittsburgh, she made a hole-in-one, becoming the first woman ever to do so in the event. As of the new millennium, her 57 tour victories rank third all-time for women, only behind Kathy Whitworth's 88 and Mickey Wright's 82. A true legend, her amazing stats will surely stand the test of time.

It must be remembered that Patty Berg once literally dominated women's golf. Accordingly, she has received nearly every major golf award known to the sport. Other accomplishments included setting a world record for a par 72 golf course by shooting a 64 (which stood for 12 years); becoming the LPGA top money winner in 1954, 1955, and 1957; and winning the Vare Trophy three times. As an amateur, she also was a two-time member of the U.S. Curtis Cup Team which competed internationally.

Along with being inducted into the LPGA, American, Minnesota, Florida, and PGA Halls of Fame, Patty was formally inducted into the World Golf Hall of Fame at Pinehurst, N.C., in 1974. Her fellow inductees included such legends as Jack Nicklaus, Ben Hogan, Arnold Palmer, Sam Snead, Gary Player, Byron Nelson and Gene Sarazen.

The LPGA even later named one of its top awards after Patty in recognition of attributes that include sportsmanship, diplomacy, goodwill, and overall contributions to the game. Then, in 1995, Patty became the first woman ever to receive the PGA's coveted Distinguished Service Award. It placed her in some fast company alongside such dignitaries as Gerald Ford, Gene Sarazen, Byron Nelson, Arnold Palmer and Bob Hope.

Patty has won nearly every major award for sports achievement and humanitarianism. What she did for, and gave to, golf is immeasurable. In great demand throughout the U.S. as a speaker, she once was described as having the delivery of "Winston Churchill and FDR rolled into one." And she was sure to give everybody goosebumps at the end of her talks when she said, "God be with you and God Bless America!"

One of Patty's former golf students, fellow LPGA Hall of Famer Kathy Whitworth, recalled, "We all accused Patty of being a frustrated actress. Her clinic was really a staged production. It ran like clockwork. Even though we all knew each line, we'd still laugh and get tickled every time we heard her."

In a business relationship that stretched nearly six decades, the Wilson company eventually rewarded Patty with a lifetime contract. What started as a speaking job for the company evolved into a clinic and exhibition routine she called her "golf show." It has been estimated that she alone has entertained several million golfers worldwide at her humorous yet informative instructional clinics and exhibitions. "She has done more to promote golf than any person in the history of the game," said LPGA great Betsy Rawls.

Known for her shot-making ability as well as her showmanship, she will be remembered as one of the game's all-time best. Much of her marvelous iron play and pin-point accuracy can be traced back to the teachings of former University of Minnesota golf coach, Les Bolstad, who advised her for more than 40 years.

"I learned so much from Les over the years," said Patty. "He always told me that I had to learn the golf swing so that I could always teach myself how to conquer my flaws. He also taught me that all the clubs were equal, and one was no more important than another."

"Patty was a colorful performer and drew big crowds," said Bolstad. "She had it right from the start. Champions are a breed apart. They have a little extra stamina, talent, and coordination, plus a will to win. They can do things ordinary mortals can't do. They just stand out. Patty Berg was one of them, and she was a scrapper. She made clutch putt after clutch putt from above the hole to win tournaments."

A Goodwill Ambassador

Patty's name is synonymous with golf in that she has transcended gender and age to become one of the game's great goodwill ambassadors. Undoubtedly she's the best female promoter golf has ever had. And

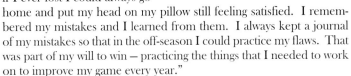

she truly made a difference in the world. One of its most admired and highly respected women, she is a sports role model kids can truly look up to. She was a pioneer, a good friend to all who knew her, and she devoted her entire life to the game she loved. And there's a generous and humanitarian side to her as well, as she continually gave of herself — evidenced by her name on the cancer wing of the Southwest Medical Center in Fort Myers, Florida.

Golf Tombstone:

"I always tried to do the very best that I could, and that way if I ever lost I could always go home and put my head on my pillow still feeling satisfied. I remembered my mistakes and I learned from them. I always kept a journal of my mistakes so that in the off-season I could practice my flaws. That was part of my will to win — practicing the things that I needed to work on to improve my game every year."

On giving back to the game:

"Golf has been so wonderful to me. In return, I enjoy doing something for it. If I can help somebody play a little better it makes me happy. If I feel that through showing them different shots, and making them laugh a little bit, and putting a few smiles on peoples' faces, well, that makes me happy, too."

What would you change?

"I wouldn't change anything, I couldn't be this lucky twice."

Gone But Never Forgotten...

Sadly, Patty passed away on September 10, 2006 in Fort Myers at the age of 88. She remained active in her later years, even working on keeping her game sharp by regularly hitting balls at the practice range. As enthusiastic as ever, she continued to be involved wherever there was a need. She made speeches, met with groups of her devoted fans, received awards and honors annually, and continued to give her time to junior programs and youngsters who sought her guidance and wisdom. She also lent her name and support to two annual charity tournaments — one for women, the other for men — that raised funds for the American Cancer Society. In addition, Patty was active in the staging of an annual youth tournament known as the Nolan Henke/Patty Berg Junior Masters that was played on her home course, the Cypress Lake Country Club in Fort Myers. Dearly missed, Patty's legacy will always be tied to her passion and love of the great game of golf — a sport she tirelessly promoted and gave to until the day she died.

1957 RUNNER-UP: DICK GARMAKER

With a modest 42-38 record, the Minneapolis Lakers finish in a three-way tie for the Western Division title, along with St. Louis and Fort Wayne. The team then went on to beat Fort Wayne in the semifinals, only to get swept by the Bob Petit-led St. Louis Hawks in the Divisional Finals. One of the stars of the Lakers that season was Hibbing native **DICK GARMAKER**. Garmaker, who played his first two years of basketball at Hibbing Junior College, went on to set eight scoring records with the Gophers, averaging 24 points per game from 1954-55. The six-foot-three sharp-shooter was signed by the Lakers in 1955 as a "territorial draft pick."

HONORABLE MENTION: WALLY JOHNSON

The Gopher wrestling team wins the Big Ten title under coach **WALLY JOHNSON**. Johnson grew up in Detroit Lakes and went on to become a three-sport star at Minnesota as a wrestler, boxer and football player. Johnson guided the Gopher wrestling team from 1952-86 and posted a career record of 392-209-11. In addition to capturing a pair of Big 10 Championships in 1957 and 1959, he also coached 35 individual Big 10 titlists, four NCAA champs and more than 40 All Americans. Among his many honors, in 1976, he was named NCAA Coach of the Year and in 1977 he was inducted into the Minnesota Wrestling Hall of Fame.

GENE MAUCH
The Minneapolis Millers Win it All

The remarkable baseball history of the minor league Minneapolis Millers goes way back to the good old days at Athletic Park in the late 1880s, then over to Nicollet Park in the early half of the century, and finally ends at Metropolitan Stadium in the 1960. The late '50s were the golden years for the Millers, highlighted by two Junior World Series titles in 1955 and 1958, as well as a legendary runner-up finish against Fidel Castro and the Havana Sugar Kings in the series of 1959.

No good story would be complete without a rival, and the Millers' cross-town counterparts were the St. Paul Saints. The Millers were the triple-A farm club of the New York Giants and later the Boston Red Sox, while the Saints were the triple-A affiliates of the Brooklyn Dodgers. The Millers-Saints rivalry was a legendary one that often featured weekend double-headers at each stadium. Fans would take the trolley between the games from Nicollet Park in Minneapolis to Lexington Park in St. Paul, cheering all the way. A lot of Hall of Fame players played for the Millers over the years on their way to the big leagues, including the likes of Willie Mays, Carl Yastrzemski, and the great "Teddy Ballgame," Ted Williams.

In 1955, the Millers celebrated their ninth American Association pennant en route to winning their first ever Junior World Series title against the International League champion, Rochester Red Wings. They were led by the Association's MVP, Shortstop Rance Pless, and wins leader, Pitcher Al Worthington. The 1955 Junior World Series saw the last game ever played at old Nicollet Park near Lake Street and Nicollet Avenue, however, as the Millers moved outside the city to the newly constructed Metropolitan Stadium in Bloomington that next season.

Two years later, when the Giants moved from New York to San Francisco, the Millers were moved to Phoenix, Arizona, where they became the "Phoenix Giants." To fill the vacancy, the San Francisco Seals (a Boston Red Sox farm team) were moved to Minneapolis to fill the void. The "new" Millers then hit the field with a feisty player/manager by the name of Gene Mauch and a first base coach by the name of Jimmie Foxx – a future Hall of Famer. In addition, the Millers were blessed with a 19-year-old rookie by the name of Orlando Cepeda that year, who would also go on to become a Hall of Famer as well.

Mauch, who was the team's manager and second baseman in 1958, led his ballclub to a third place finish in the American Association that year with a record of 82-71. Things looked promising for the young club as they steamrollered into the playoffs, knocking off Wichita right out of the gates. From there, they proceeded to upset Denver in the next round, and with that they found themselves right back in the Junior World Series. Their opponent this time would be the mighty Montreal Royals, who were led by a young pitcher named Tommy Lasorda. The Millers took Games One and Two, 6-2 and 7-2, followed by Game Three, 3-2. Then, in Game Four, the Millers completed the sweep by downing the Royals in their own backyard, 7-1, to claim their second Junior Series Championship in just three years. It was a truly amazing season for the new ballclub.

"I remember sweeping Montreal four in a row and winning it all in 1958," said Mauch years later. "I was still playing and managing at that point, and it was a pretty special championship for me. That year was great, and I even still have the pennant from when we won that series."

Now, while the Millers were kings of the world in

1958, the 1959 squad might even be a better story. That year the Millers finished second in their division with an impressive 95-57 record. They then opened the playoffs against Omaha, where the series went back and forth until both teams had split two games apiece. Then, back home at the Met for the fifth game of the series, the Millers newest recruit, who had just been activated before the game, scored the game-winning run in the bottom of the tenth inning. His name was Carl Yastrzemski. (Like Ted Williams had done 22-years earlier, "Yaz" spent a season in Minneapolis playing triple-A ball before heading to Boston, where, ironically, the Hall of Famer would succeed the great Ted Williams in the outfield.)

The game was officially protested by Omaha, who challenged Yaz's series eligibility. The Omaha officials were proved to be right, and with that, the league president ordered the game replayed. So, even without the services of Yaz, the Millers went out and still won the next game, to take the series. Led by Mauch, their feisty manager, they then went on to beat the Fort Worth Cats for the league title, thus earning a trip to the Junior World Series against the Havana (Cuba) Sugar Kings. (Incidentally, Fort Worth was led by a couple of Minnesotans in former Gopher Jerry Kindall and former Mankato State star Bob Will.)

This Junior World Series would prove to be one of the most amazing spectacles in sports history. The first two games were played at Metropolitan Stadium, where it proceeded to rain and even snow. During the first two games of the series, the Sugar Kings, not quite used to Minnesota's balmy climate, could be seen in their dugout guzzling hot coffee and huddling around a fire they had lit in a trash can to stay warm. An early highlight was a two-run-homer hit by Mauch's brother-in-law, Roy Smalley, Sr., in a 6-5 Game Two victory. (Incidentally, Smalley's son, Roy Jr., would subsequently go on to play a key role in Twins' history as a very popular middle infielder.)

Following Game Two, it was decided that the rest of the series would be played in Havana, where it was much warmer than Minnesota. Now, Cuba in 1959 was anything but a tropical paradise. The Cuban Missile Crisis and Bay of Pigs were just around the corner, and it was basically a military state under President Fidel Castro. They loved their baseball though and the five games that were played in Havana drew more than 100,000 fans, not counting the thousands of gun-toting soldiers, who were stationed throughout the stadium. Down three games to one, the Millers rallied in the series to win Games Five and Six.

With the series tied at three games apiece, the stage was now set for the much anticipated Game Seven. (Stew Thornley captured the scene best in his book "On to Nicollet.") As Fidel, a former pitcher himself, made his entrance to the game, he walked by the Millers' bullpen with his hand on his revolver and said to the Minneapolis pitchers, "Tonight we win...". It was looking great for the Millers as they built a two-run lead going into the eighth, but Havana came back. They evened it up in the eighth, and then in the bottom of the ninth, Havana's Don Morejon ripped a liner into center field. Raul Sanchez, who was on second, then rounded third and slid home ahead of Umphlett's throw to score what proved to be the winning run. The crowd erupted as the Sugar Kings had won the Junior World Series crown. The Millers came home dejected, but happy to be alive!

"I imagine it was about as gripping a time as I had ever experienced," said Mauch, who first met Castro when the two played together in the Cuban winter league in 1951 and got to know him personally. "It was standing room only every night," he added. "Fifteen minutes before game time, Castro would come walking in through center field with his entourage. Every fan rose and waved a white handkerchief and yelled 'Fidel,' 'Fidel!' Then he would come sit down behind home-plate. No baseball player in history was ever greeted the way he was greeted down there. About half of my players were afraid to win the title game because there were Cuban soldiers on the bench with loaded rifles and bayonets. In fact you couldn't get from the batters box to the dugout without wading through 50 to 100 soldiers. A lot of my players were fearful and wanted to get the hell out of there, I know that. The whole thing was quite an experience."

On October 27, 1960, it was announced that Calvin Griffith was moving his Washington Senators to Minnesota. As a result, Major League Baseball would mean the end of the Millers and Saints. One golden era of baseball was over, but the Twins would start another.

A Managerial Icon

Gene Mauch was born in Salina Kan., on November 18, 1925. At the age of 13, his family moved to Los Angeles. Gene grew up playing sports and in high school played football, baseball and basketball. He had the opportunity to attend USC or Stanford on football and baseball scholarships, but instead went into the service where he became an air cadet. After the service, he went back to his true love, baseball.

Mauch would go on to play a total 16 seasons in the Major Leagues. He first started out playing in the minors in Durham, NC, in 1943, and from there the list of cities is long: Montreal, Brooklyn, St. Paul, Pittsburgh, Indianapolis, Chicago (AL & NL), Boston (AL & NL), St. Louis, Milwaukee, Atlanta, Los Angeles, and finally the Minneapolis Millers, where he retired as an active player. He would leave the game with a respectable career .239 batting average.

From there, Mauch got into managing at the age of 27, first with the Atlanta Crackers in the Southern Association. He continued to manage with the Millers in the late '50s and got his big break in 1960 when he took over for the Philadelphia Phillies. He remained in Philly until 1968, when he left to guide the expansion Montreal Expos.

Mauch then managed the Twins from 1976-80, posting a career record of 378-394. Next he went on to guide the Angels for three seasons, until finally hanging it up for good in 1987. He is among a select fraternity of big-league skippers on the all-time seniority list, having managed for more than three decades. He also holds the dubious distinction of managing the most years (26) without winning a pennant.

Sadly, Gene passed away on August 8, 2005 in Rancho Mirage, Calif., from cancer. Mauch was an intense competitor, and a great ambassador of baseball. He played when it was still a game and was a true throw-back to another era. He will be forever remembered as an integral thread in the fabric of Minnesota's baseball history.

On the Twins:

"It was a wonderful experience. I worked with some great, great people: Calvin Griffith, Rod Carew, Tony Oliva, Larry Hisle, Lyman Bostock, Butch Wynegar, and my nephew, Roy Smalley. I mean being able to have the opportunity to manage guys like Rod Carew and Tony Oliva, I felt like my time in Minnesota wasn't a job, it was a privilege."

Any Regrets?

"Originally, when I came to Minneapolis, I thought that I would eventually go on to become the manager of the Red Sox, because we were their triple-A farm club. One of the biggest disappointments of my life came in 1959, when Boston didn't name me to be their manager. Bucky Harris, the Red Sox G.M., said I was too young and didn't think that I would be able to handle guys like Ted Williams, who, at the time, was older than I was. Not being able to manage some of those kids

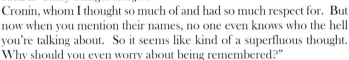

like Carl Yastrzemski, who played for me in Minneapolis, with the Millers, was a real disappointment."

On the Fans:

"I loved the people up there, they were just outstanding, super people, and were just wonderful to me. Hell, they even gave me a new car! I was just so intrigued by Minnesota and was really thinking of moving there. I had many close relationships with a lot of people from that area."

Millers and Twins Tombstones:

"There were guys in baseball, such as Casey Stengel and Joe Cronin, whom I thought so much of and had so much respect for. But now when you mention their names, no one even knows who the hell you're talking about. So it seems like kind of a superfluous thought. Why should you even worry about being remembered?"

TRIBUTES

"We went through some tough times together in 1977 and 1978, when the fans were on us about nepotism," said his nephew, Roy Smalley, Jr. "It was a difficult situation, but it was also a great situation to be in, at the same time, because we were able to be together. I learned that being successful takes care of everything, and once I realized that, everything took care of itself. We have a lot of love and respect for each other. He was one of my heroes growing up. I've played for 15 managers throughout my career, and there was nobody that could hold a candle to him. He was just the best. I learned more baseball in my time with him than with all the rest combined. He was the best prepared, best tactical, and best teaching manager I've ever been around. I can't imagine a better manager in the game, ever."

"Gene was one of the best managers that I ever played for," said Rod Carew. "He could really get the best out of his players and teach them the correct way to play the game. We both had tremendous respect for each other. I knew that if I ever had any problems on or off the field, I could always go in and talk with him, and he would always help me through it. He was a great person."

"He managed a long, long time, and he was a great manager," said Tony Oliva. "He was very serious about his job, and he wanted to win no matter what. He knew a lot about the game and was just a great person to be around."

"I liked Gene very much," added Harmon Killebrew. "I thought he was a very good manager and certainly an intense guy. When he was managing the Twins, he asked me to come back to the club to help out as a hitting instructor, and I was grateful for that."

1958 RUNNER-UP: TED WILLIAMS

The minor league Minneapolis Millers beat their parent club, the Boston Red Sox, on June 16, 14-10, in an exhibition game at the newly constructed Metropolitan Stadium in Bloomington. *TED WILLIAMS*, who played for the Millers in 1938 as a 19 year old, and hit .366 with 43 homers and 142 RBI before being called up by the Red Sox the next season, hit a home run in the loss. "Teddy Ball Game" would go on to become, arguably, the greatest hitter ever and was later inducted into the Baseball Hall of Fame in 1966.

HONORABLE MENTION: JACK McCARTAN

What an amazing year it was for Gopher great *JACK McCARTAN*, who earned All-American honors in both baseball (as a third baseman) and in hockey (as a goalie) in 1958. The St. Paul native also led Minnesota to an NCAA baseball title in 1956 — the program's first ever national championship. After his senior year, McCartan received the Big Ten Medal of Honor for his athletic and academic achievements. Upon graduating, McCartan made history when he led Team USA to a gold medal at the 1960 Winter Olympics in Squaw Valley, CA. From there, he embarked on a 15-year career in pro hockey — starting with a two year stint with the NHL's New York Rangers and ending with a two year stint with the WHA's St. Paul Fighting Saints.

ELGIN BAYLOR
The Lakers Make One Last Run

1959

The only good thing that came from the fact that the Lakers finished in the cellar in 1957, was that they would now get the first pick in the upcoming draft. The team was going to need a miracle, and, incredibly, that's just what they were going to get. Their savior, was none other than Elgin Baylor, a flashy young six-foot-five rookie small forward out of the University of Seattle, who, as the nation's leading rebounder, had just taken his Seattle Chieftains to the NCAA Finals. Blessed with the ability to somehow hang in mid-air, Baylor would become known as the league's first sky-walker, long before the likes of Dr. J., Air Jordan and Kobe Bryant.

Laker execs knew going in that it was not going to be easy to sign the kid to a contract though. Baylor had publicly stated his intention to complete his senior year at Seattle and not enter the NBA draft. But with draft day nearing, and the Minneapolis franchise's future in doubt, team owner Bob Short opted to gamble and drafted Baylor with his first pick. Needless to say, they eventually signed him after a month of negotiating. Short was later quoted as saying that if Baylor had turned him down, the club would have "gone out of business and declared bankruptcy." The NBA had put the Lakers on financial probation and specified that if the club didn't average at least $6,600 in gate receipts for home games that season, the league would have the power to take over the team. All of that changed, however, when the fans started pouring into the Minneapolis Auditorium to see their new phenom.

Baylor, who started opposite Forward Vern Mikkelsen, was joined by Center Larry Foust and Guards Dick Garmaker and "Hot Rod" Hundley — giving Johnny Kundla's Lakers a solid starting five. Baylor was also joined by new teammates Alex "Boo" Ellis, and the six-foot-eight Steve Hamilton, who would later go on pitch for the New York Yankees. The Lakers came together late in the season to post a marginal 33-39 record, good enough for second place in the West and a trip to the post-season.

Baylor wasted little time in making his presence known in the NBA by becoming the first rookie ever to garner MVP honors at the All-Star Game. Another highlight from the regular season came near the tail end, when the Lakers played Boston in a real barn-burner. By the time the dust had settled in this one, the Celtics had beaten Minneapolis by the final score of 173-139 — which was good for a new NBA record for total points.

From there, they beat Detroit, two games to one, in the first round of the playoffs. Now, the 1959 NBA Finals were supposed to feature the two best teams in the NBA that year, Boston and St. Louis, in what would've been their third-straight meeting for the championship. However, in the West, the Baylor-led Lakers knocked off the defending world champs from St. Louis in the conference finals. The Hawks had won two of three to start the series against the Lakers, but

Minneapolis won the final three by the scores of 108-98, 98-97 (in overtime at St. Louis), and 106-104, back in Minneapolis, to set the stage for the mighty Celtics. It wouldn't be easy though, as the team had lost 18 straight against the Beantowners, and, to make matters worse, Baylor was nursing a badly bruised knee.

The rejuvenated Lakers quickly realized that Red Auerbach's squad, which featured Bill Russell, Bob Cousy, Tommy Heinsohn, Bill Sharman and Frank Ramsey, was going to be a handful. Owner Bob Short even tried to motivate his players by offering

them presents such as new sets of tires and sport coats if they won the championship. While that might have spared Kundla from any Knute Rockne-like motivational speeches that he had to deliver to get his players ready to play the mighty Celtics, it certainly didn't help much.

With that, the Celtics came out and sent a message to Minneapolis right out of the gates, spanking them in Games One and Two, 118-115 and 128-108, respectively. By the time the series had returned back to Minneapolis, it was all but over. The Celtics were dominant and took no prisoners. After a Celtics' victory in Game Three back in Minnie, 123-110, the Lakers decided to make Game Four interesting. Baylor and Bob Leonard would combine to give the Lakers a brief 95-93 lead early in the fourth quarter, but Boston clinched the series with a 118-113 victory thanks to Bill Sharman's phenomenal outside shooting. Baylor had 30 points, while Leonard finished with 21, but it was too little too late. Even though they kept the margins of victory to within less than five points for three of the games, the Celtics were able to sweep the Championship Series four games to none. It was the first time ever that an NBA Finals would end in a sweep, and for the Celtics, it was their first of what would amount to eight straight world titles — making them a true dynasty.

For the season Mikkelsen averaged 13.8 points and 7.9 rebounds while Foust contributed 13.7 points and 8.7 rebounds. It was Baylor who was the real star though, leading the team in nearly every offensive category en route to averaging 25 points, 15 rebounds and four assists per game. For his efforts he was named as the NBA's Rookie of the Year and was also named as a first team All-Pro. He finished third, behind Bill Russell and Bob Pettit, in the Player of the Year voting as well.

"My rookie year with the Lakers was a great one for me," said Baylor. "Being the number one player chosen in the draft, playing on the NBA All-Star team, and just to be playing in the NBA was wonderful. The reception by my teammates in Minneapolis was great, and I was accepted and treated like one of them right away. The year before the team had finished in last place, so it was a thrill because no one thought we would get close to the Finals. We beat the defending world champion St. Louis Hawks to win the West, and we were all very proud of our accomplishments that season. Minneapolis had a good year, we made a great run, and a lot of wonderful things happened that season, but the Celtics had a better team and they beat us."

The Original Sky-Walker

Born and raised in Washington D.C., Elgin Baylor went on to star at Washington's Springarn High School. From there, he opted to first attend the College of Idaho in 1954 on a football scholarship. Then, after being noticed by the school's basketball coach, he joined the basketball team, leading his squad to a 23-4 record while averaging 31 points and 20 rebounds per game. The following season Elgin transferred to Seattle University and, after sitting out the year because of the NCAA transfer rule, he led Seattle to a 22-3 record. Baylor, who pulled down 508 rebounds and averaged 30 points per game that season, went on to average 32.5 points and 559 rebounds per game that next year.

Although the top-rated senior in college basketball in 1958 was Indiana's Archie Dees, Baylor was the player every team wanted. He led the nation in rebounding that year and guided his Chieftains to the NCAA Finals before eventually losing to Kentucky.

The All-American had publicly stated his intention to complete his senior year at Seattle and not enter the NBA draft. But the Lakers rolled the dice and drafted him anyways. He would prove to be the savior of the franchise. His popularity was unlike anything they had ever seen and he immediately wound up becoming one of the team's biggest fan-favorites.

So good was Baylor that the next season, when he got called to fulfill his military commitment in the Army Reserve Medical Corps training program in San Antonio, the team moved its entire training camp to Texas just so that he wouldn't miss a beat. The team even hired John Castellani, who had been Baylor's coach at Seattle University, that next year to replace the retired Johnny Kundla.

Ironically, while Baylor may have saved the Laker franchise from going out of business in 1959 by leading the club back to the NBA Finals, in the process he also helped the team become good enough to become sellable on the open market. With the team's stock on the rise, Lakers Owner Bob Short up and moved the franchise to Los Angeles the following season. Minnesota wouldn't see NBA action again for another 29 years, when the expansion Timberwolves came to life. Baylor, of course, would go on to even bigger stardom in L.A.

Baylor was more than the first of the great skywalkers, he was an explosive scorer whose career scoring average is exceeded only by Wilt Chamberlain and Michael Jordan. Baylor used his body control and unbelievable creativity like no other before him. His Laker career stats from 1958-1972 included averaging: 27.4 PPG, 13.5 RPG, 4.3 APG. The 10-time All-NBA first teamer appeared in 11 All-Star games as well. Among his many honors and accolades, Baylor was enshrined in the Basketball Hall of Fame in 1976 and later named to the NBA's 35th Anniversary All-Time Team in 1980.

He is also considered among the greatest rebounders the NBA has ever known, posting-up any big man, regardless of his size or stature. He could pass and dribble with the best guards in the league, and his speed made him a stellar defender. Baylor, who teamed with Jerry West to form one of the most feared scoring duos in NBA history, retired early in the 1971-72 season due to nagging knee injuries. Ironically, the Lakers won the NBA championship that year, an achievement that somehow eluded him over his amazing career. He was undoubtedly the greatest NBA player never to win a title. His Los Angeles teams lost in the Finals seven times in 11 years, with three of them being decided in seventh games with the Celtics — which the Lakers lost by a combined total of seven points.

"It was really exciting for me to be a Minneapolis Laker," said Baylor. "In college I never thought about playing professionally. The only thing I thought about was being able to go to college. Growing up, I knew my family could not afford to send me to college, so I really hoped that I could just get a scholarship either in football or basketball. So, to be able to play for Minneapolis was very special to me. The honor, the pride, and the glory of just being a pro in the sport of basketball was great. Playing with and against the best players in the world was tremendous. All the traveling, meeting people, and making friends was all very special to me. I loved Minneapolis. It still is a great city and the people there were great to me."

Baylor may be best remembered for his unbelievable driving, twisting, lay-ups which featured spectacular mid-air antics. The terms "hang time" and "body control" became synonymous with him. He was also known for following his own shot, and it has been said that if that statistic would have been kept, he may very well hold the NBA record for scoring the most points off of his own put-backs. Often, during the course of a tight game, when the Lakers really needed him, he would switch from the forward to guard or even center, whatever the situation warranted. And, when the opposition was engaged in a full-court press, Baylor was the only one trusted to bring the ball upcourt.

He has even been referred to as the "father of the modern aerodynamic game." Boston Celtic great Bob Cousy remembers:

"Elgin was the first one who would go up for the jump shot, hang up there for 15 seconds, have some lunch and a cup of coffee, and [then] decide to shoot the thing. Elgin was that spectacular. He was the first guy who literally couldn't be stopped."

After basketball Baylor went on to become the Head Coach of the Utah Jazz, before settling down as the long-time General Manager of the Los Angeles Clippers. Elgin and his wife Elaine have two daughters and a son and reside in the Los Angeles area.

Laker Tombstone:
"I would want to be remembered as a person who cared about other people and cared about his profession. I felt like I gave it all that I had and I played as hard as I could."

TRIBUTES

"I can't say enough about Elgin," said John Kundla. "He could play an entire game without getting tired because he had more stamina than any player I ever saw. He was a tremendous all-around ballplayer. He could just hang up in the air and he could do it all — passing, shooting, dribbling, jumping and defending. He was just great. His first year with us was so terrific and right away I knew he was one of the best all-around athletes I ever saw play the game of basketball. One time, he scored 50 points in a game off of only two field goals he shot from the outside. His other points came off of rebounds and put-backs. He was a truly special player."

"My last year with the Minneapolis Lakers was Elgin's first, and we were kind of a rag-tag bunch when he came in as a rookie," said Vern Mikkelsen. "Coach Kundla wanted me, as team captain, to teach Elgin about how to play the pro game. He didn't need any teaching. Elgin had a pocket full of press clippings, and he was the best there was to came out of college at that time. I could tell he was in a class by himself. He had all the ability in the world and became such a fabulous player. But, at first, he was also kind of a loner, and we couldn't really get him into being a part of our bunch. Later he joined the poker-playing group of players called the 'dead-enders,' which consisted of Dick Garmaker, Hot Rod Hundley, Slick Leonard and I. Garmaker used to say that he would pick Elgin up at his house and bring him to the airport for the road games because he didn't want any chance of him missing the plane. Dick said that he made more money off Elgin in poker games than he made in salary! Elgin had a wonderful career with the Lakers, both in Minneapolis and LA, and he is a great person."

1959 RUNNER-UP: JEAN ARTH

St. Paul's *JEAN ARTH*, arguably Minnesota's greatest women's tennis player of all-time, teams up with Darlene Hard to win the 1959 Wimbledon and U.S. Open Doubles championships. The duo also won the U.S. Open in 1958 as well. Arth graduated from St. Paul Central High School in 1952 and went on to attend the College of St. Catherine's. Among her many honors, Arth has been inducted into the Minnesota Sports, Minnesota Tennis and Wilson International Tennis Halls of Fame.

HONORABLE MENTION: CARL YASTRZEMSKI

The Minneapolis Millers win the American Association crown, only to lose to the Havana (Cuba) Sugar Kings in a thrilling seven-game series for the Little World Series title. Leading the way for the Millers that post-season was future Red Sox star outfielder, *CARL YASTRZEMSKI*, who arrived in the Twin Cities after leading his Double-A Raleigh Capitals with a .377 average. "Yaz" played for the Millers in 1960 as well, before being called up to the Sox, where he would spend the next 23 seasons. There, the 18-time All-Star won seven Gold Gloves, became a member of the 3,000 hit club, and was inducted into the Baseball Hall of Fame in 1989.

The football Gophers made history in 1960, and it started in the opener, when they beat the No. 2 ranked Nebraska Cornhuskers, 26-14, in Lincoln. Quarterback Sandy Stephens led the charge in this one, running three yards for one touchdown while passing for another. That following week Minnesota spanked Indiana, 42-0, which was followed by a 7-0 win over Northwestern that next Saturday. Tom Brown led the defensive surge to shut-out the Wildcats, while Stephens' lone four-yard touchdown run was enough to give Minnesota the victory. Next up were the Illini, a team Minnesota would hang on to beat, 21-10, on a fourth quarter rally. Stephens was once again the hero, capping a 66-yard game-winning scoring drive with a nine-yard touchdown — his third on the day.

At 4-0, Minnesota was starting to gain some respect in gridiron circles. They would make some more believers that next week, when they blanked a very good Michigan team, 10-0, at Ann Arbor, to re-claim the Little Brown Jug. The Gophers forced five fumbles that day and held the Wolverines to just 76 yards rushing and 68 yards passing. Jim Rogers capped a 44-yard scoring drive when he ran in what would prove to be the game-winner from the two yard line.

Kansas State then fell to the Gophers, 48-7, setting up an epic showdown between the suddenly No. 2 ranked Gophers and the No. 1 ranked Iowa Hawkeyes. Forest Evashevski's Hawks had owned the Gophers over the last five years, surrendering just 21 points over that time period. More than 65,000 Gopher fans somehow jammed into the 53,000-seat Memorial Stadium on that November 5th to see the Gophers beat the Hawks, 27-10. The hero of the game was Tom Brown, who won the Outland Trophy that year as the nation's top line-man. "Brownie" stuffed the Hawkeye linemen all day and dominated both sides of the line. On one particular third-down play, with the ball on the Gopher five-yard line, Brown fired through the line just as the ball was snapped and knocked the center into the quarterback, who then flew back into the fullback — pancaking all three of them on their butts for a five-yard loss. After that game Brown proudly hoisted the Floyd of Rosedale trophy over his head for all to see.

With the big win, Minnesota found itself as the No. 1 team in the land. That's when last-place Purdue came to town and wrecked everything, upsetting the Gophers, 28-14. Down, but not out, the Go-phers traveled to Wisconsin for the final game of the regular season with a Big Ten title and possible Rose Bowl berth laying in the balance. Minnesota "rose" to occasion that afternoon though, scoring a pair early and a pair late, as their top-rated defense shut down the Badgers to se-cure a 26-7 victory.

By now the Gophers found themselves at the top of both the AP and UPI final polls, declaring them as consensus national champi-ons for the first time in two decades. And, although they had a better record, the Gophers had to share the Big Ten title with Iowa. This was due to the fact that their early rout of Indiana, which was on probation for re-cruiting violations, did not count in the final standings. Fittingly, Murray Warmath was named as the college foot-ball Coach of the Year.

With their Big Ten title, the first in two decades, the Gophers would now have to sit back and wait to find out if, and where, they would be spending New Year's Day. You see, at the time, the Big Ten-Pacific Coast Rose Bowl pact was not in effect, which therefore allowed the PAC-10 champion, Washington, to choose its opponent. Luckily, they chose Minnesota, and with that the Gophers were off to Pasadena to face the Huskies in their first-ever Rose Bowl.

Once there, the Gophers were showered by well-wishers who simply couldn't get enough of their Cinderella story. When the game got going though, it became a different tale. Washington, unlike the star-struck Gophers, had been there before, crushing Wisconsin just the year before by the final of 44-8.

Nearly 100,000 fans were on hand to watch what would later be viewed upon as a tale of two halves. The game got underway with the Huskies scoring early on a 34-yard field goal by George Fleming. From there, they went on to score a pair of touchdowns in the second quarter, thanks in large part to the efforts of Husky Quarterback Bob Schloredt, who threw for one and ran in the other from 31-yards out to give his squad a 17-0 half-time lead.

The Gophers, meanwhile, could muster just two first downs the entire half, while Stephens' interception didn't help matters either. It was a different story in the second though, as the Gophers came out and rallied behind a Bob Deegan fumble recovery which set up an 18-yard touchdown pitch from Stephens to Bill Munsey. Minnesota threatened to get back in the game by driving to the Washington six-yard line midway through the fourth, but were held when Stephens was blitzed for a 13-yard loss. The Gophers then tried a little razzle-dazzle by going for a fake field-goal on fourth-down, but came up short when Stephens, the holder, pulled up and threw an interception on a pass intended for Tom Hall at the Husky one yard line. The Gophers got the ball back late, but were unable to get past the 35-yard line. Wash-ington added a field goal to ice it, and the Gophers, who ended the game with 60 more total yards than did the Huskies, came up on the short side of a 17-7 game.

"We didn't play as well as we could of, and on that day we played one of the best football teams I've seen in 18 years at Min-nesota," Coach Warmath would later say. "But as the game wore on, we started coming on fast and they were fading. Another 15 minutes and we maybe would have won."

Despite losing the Rose Bowl, the Gophers still remained as National Champs, due to the fact that the voting was done prior to the post-season. That wasn't the only award the team would win either as Bobby Bell and Tom Brown each earned All-American honors. Brown also went on to be named as the Big Ten MVP, and even fin-ished as the runner-up in the Heisman Trophy voting — a first for a lineman.

"We made some stupid mistakes, but we knew we had a good team," said Stephens. "After the game, I recall that I had never felt so bad after losing. However, it was a fantastic experience for me. The Rose Bowl was everything I thought it would be and more. The whole first half we were sort of awe struck, but the second half we were ready to play. I think they only got one first down in the entire second half, and that was off a long quarterback sneak. We just couldn't get any of-fensive momentum going at that point. I don't want to take anything away from the Huskies, they were a fine team. But they were just a bet-ter football team on that day. We lost the game, but were still national champions, and they can't take that away from us."

A True Trailblazer

Sandy Stephens grew up in Uniontown, Pa., in a household where his parents strongly encouraged his academic and athletic endeavors. Upon graduating from high school, more than 50 colleges and univer-sities, eight from the Big Ten alone, recruited him. Sandy felt pretty strong about his football roots: "We always felt that those of us who lived in Western Pennsylvania had the best high school football in the country, bar none — including Ohio and Texas too."

Stephens was a tremendously gifted all-around athlete, earn-ing nine letters in football, basketball and track. He garnered high school All-American honors in football, was an All-State basketball player, and, although he never played high school baseball, was a good enough pitcher and centerfielder to be romanced by several major league baseball teams — including his home state Philadelphia Phillies, who drafted him out of high school.

With assurances that he would be given a shot at quarterback, as well as the opportunity to play baseball, Stephens enrolled at the University of Minnesota in the fall of 1958. So did an old friend and high school rival from Clairton, Pa., who would be his roommate for the next four years, running back Judge Dickson. In so doing, the two became pioneers for all young African American men who wanted to play college athletics in the predominantly white northern schools.

Still considered by many to be one of the top five all-time greatest players ever to wear the Maroon and Gold, Stephens is a football legend in Gold Country. From 1959-61, he threw for nearly 1,500 yards, rushed for a record 20 touchdowns, and twice he led the team in punting. In 1961, he led the Gophers to their second consecutive Rose Bowl and defeated UCLA by the score of 21-3. He also led the team in rushing that year with 534 yards while throwing for nine touchdown passes as well. For his efforts in leading the conference with 1,151 yards of total offense that year, he was named as the Big Ten MVP. In addition, he was also named as an All-American, becoming the first-ever African American player ever to be so honored. He also won College Back of the Year and finished fourth in the balloting for the Heisman Trophy as well.

After college, Sandy was drafted in the first round by the New York Titans of the American Football League. "At the time," Sandy said, "the Titans didn't want a black man playing quarterback. Cleveland had my NFL rights, but the NFL still wasn't ready for a black quarterback. So, I was forced to play in Canada." With the promise that he would be given a chance to play quarterback, Sandy then went north of the border to the Montreal Alouettes. Montreal had finished last in the Canadian Football League the year before, but with Stephens at the helm, he led the Als to the CFL Finals.

After three years in Canada, Sandy's life was abruptly changed when he was involved in a nearly fatal car accident. The doctors said that he would never walk again, but Sandy was determined. In 1964, Sandy's old teammate and friend, Bobby Bell, asked his Kansas City Chiefs coach, Hank Stram, to give his old buddy a shot at a comeback. Sandy overcame the odds and went on to play with the Chiefs for two seasons, both as a defensive halfback as well as a quarterback. He retired from the NFL in 1970.

Among his many honors, in 1997 Stephens was inducted into the Rose Bowl Hall of Fame. "Getting this honor now, after all these years, is thrilling and definitely a high point in my life," he said. In addition, Sandy's No. 15 jersey was retired at half-time of the 2000 Minnesota vs. Iowa game which celebrated the 40th anniversary of the 1960 national championship.

Before his tragic death in June of 2000, Sandy had been recognized as a major influence in the breakthrough of African American athletes in collegiate athletics. He was a real pioneer both on and off the field and a was a true trailblazer in life. Long considered the greatest quarterback to ever wear the Maroon and Gold, he blessed the University of Minnesota football program with his talents and leadership like no other, before or since.

Gopher Tombstone:
"I hope that they'll remember the championship teams that we had. That's my biggest thing. I have always been a team player. The only reason that you achieve accolades is because of the teammates that you have, and I had great teammates all the way through. We were all champions."

TRIBUTES
"Sandy was a great quarterback," said Bobby Bell. "If they would've given Sandy the opportunity to have played in the NFL, he would have been the first black quarterback in league; that's how good he was. He was a player that just

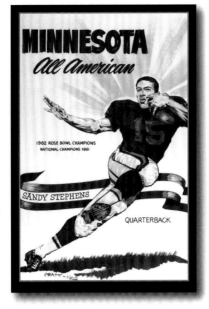

wanted to win. He had the quickness, the speed, the arm and the agility. Defenses couldn't pin him down and contain him because he was so fast and so smart. He could beat you in a lot of ways, but especially one-on-one. He was so versatile; he would punt, pass, run, and do just about anything for the team. He hated to lose. I don't care if you were playing ping-pong, he wanted to beat you. He drove us to win and to be national champions. He was an all-around fun guy to play with and a tremendous competitor."

"He was a great leader and commanded a lot of respect from everybody," said Tom Brown. "His teammates really liked him and always played hard for him."

"He was the field general in the truest sense of the word," said Carl Eller. "He was in command out on the field, and there was no question about it. We had total confidence in him and we knew that he could get it done. He would tell us in the huddle that we were going to either run over my side or over Bobby Bell's side, and we would do it. He had a lot of confidence in us. He was just a fabulous player."

"I grew up only a block away from Sandy, and we grew up together playing sports," said Bill Munsey. "After my senior year, I had received 58 full scholarship offers, but I chose to go to Minnesota because my best friend Sandy was there. I saw those big Swedes and Norwegians on the line and thought about the possibility of playing with Sandy in the backfield. He was stubborn, and there is probably no cockier person in the world than Sandy, but to play quarterback you have to have those ingredients. He had so much ability and was just a great natural athlete."

"He was a hell of a great football player, but he was never given the publicity and acclaim he deserved," said Murray Warmath. "He was one of the greatest football players I ever saw. He was a great running back, a good passer and an excellent defensive player. He could do everything and do it well."

1960 RUNNER-UP: TOM MOE
The Gopher baseball teams wins its second NCAA national championship in four seasons in dramatic fashion, edging USC, 2-1, in a 10-inning thriller. With the bases loaded in the bottom of the 10th, Gopher third baseman Cal Rollof got walked, allowing Dave Pflepsen to score the winning run. Second baseman John Erickson was named as the tournament MVP. One of the stars for the Gophers that season was *TOM MOE*, who hit .333 and finished third on the team with 26 RBI. Moe also starred on the gridiron for the Gophers, earning team MVP honors in 1959. The Edina native went on to become a successful lawyer and later served as the Gopher's Director of Men's Athletics from 1999-2002.

HONORABLE MENTION: BILLY & ROGER CHRISTIAN
With eight Minnesotans on its roster, the U.S. Olympic hockey team wins gold at the 1960 Winter Olympics in Squaw Valley, CA. After upsetting the Canadians and Soviets, the underdog Americans topped the Czechs, 9-4, in the gold medal game. Two of the stars of the team were Warroad natives *BILLY & ROGER CHRISTIAN*, who would later become household names for their popular "Christian Brothers," hockey sticks. Incidentally, Billy's son David also won a gold medal as a member of the 1980 "Miracle on Ice" team.

The defending national champs from Minnesota weren't going to sneak up on anyone in 1961 like they had done the year before. The Gophers, who lost a few key players to graduation, including Tom Brown and Joe Salem, still had a nucleus of stars in Bobby Bell, Sandy Stephens, Bill Munsey, Judge Dickson, and a new sophomore Tackle by the name of Carl Eller, who stood six-foot-five and weighed in at 240 pounds. Eller and Bell, a pair of outstanding tandem bookend Tackles from North Carolina, would anchor the Gopher defense and ultimately lead the squad back to Pasadena.

The team's season opener against Missouri attracted a lot of national interest because the Tigers were the team that Minnesota had climbed over to earn the No. 1 ranking in the polls after the last week of the 1960 season. The playing conditions that day were less than desirable, to say the least. "It was the worst game in terms of weather conditions that I ever played in," said Stephens. "It was just awful, and it was so cold that I couldn't feel the ball when it was centered." Amidst constant rain and wind, the Tigers hung tough and upset the Gophers by the score of 6-0.

Minnesota went on to win six in a row after that though, starting with Oregon, who they rallied to beat, 14-7. Stephens scored both Minnesota touchdowns in this one, with the speedster from Fairmont, Jimmy Cairns, adding a two-pointer for good measure. Then, against Northwestern, Stephens tallied on a one-yarder, while Judge Dickson added a 31-yard field goal of his own to give the Gophers a 10-3 victory. Against Illinois, Stephens beat the Fighting Illini all by himself, passing for four touchdowns and scoring a fifth on a short run.

In the 23-20 win over Michigan, Stephens (who was married just two days prior), played one of his best games ever, racking up over 300 all-purpose yards in yet another come-from-behind victory. Then there was the 13-0 shut-out over the top-ranked Michigan State Spartans at Memorial Stadium, where Munsey, who had recovered from an injury that sidelined him from the Wolverine game the week before, scored both touchdowns for the Gophers.

Next up was Iowa. After giving up an early safety, Tom Loechler's field goal early in the second gave Minnesota a 3-2 lead. Then, in the third, Stephens tallied on a 39-yarder, followed by a touchdown on a blocked punt by Dick Enga, which was recovered in the end zone by John Campbell to give the Gophers a thrilling 16-9 victory.

Purdue was next, as an all-time record crowd of 67,081 crammed into Memorial Stadium to watch the Gophers beat the Boilers, 10-7. Minnesota went ahead 10-0 on Tom Loechler's 25-yard field goal, followed by Stephens' four-yard score. Purdue rallied back to score, but the Gopher defense, which yielded just 27 yards of rushing that day, stood firm in what turned out to be one of the most bruising battles in team history.

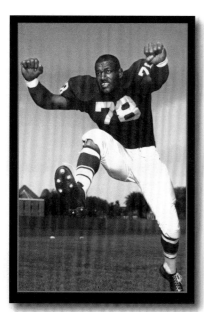

By now, only the rival Wisconsin Badgers stood in the way of the Gophers' first perfect Big Ten record since 1941. But Wisconsin Coach Milt Bruhn, an ex-Gopher, had a different idea, as his quarterback, Ron Miller, connected with Pat Richter for two touchdowns in leading his Badgers past Minnesota, 28-21. In the loss, Sandy Stephens and tight end Tom Hall combined for an 80-yard touchdown bomb, followed by Jerry Jones' 22-yard score. Stephens then connected with Al Fischer with just under two minutes to go in the game, but sadly it was just too little too late.

Normally a 6-1 Big Ten record would make a solid case for winning the title, but, in 1961, the undefeated Ohio State Buckeyes would receive that honor. However, in a bizarre twist of fate, Woody Hayes' Buckeyes, who were invited to play the UCLA Bruins in the Rose Bowl, declined the invitation. If an official Big Ten-West Coast agreement had been in effect at that time, Minnesota would have been ineligible to play in the big game two years in a row — but there was no such contract that year. As a result, the Rose Bowl committee selected the Gophers, and for the second time in as many years, they were off to Pasadena for a run at the roses.

"This time," Warmath would later say, "we stayed at a monastery where we were isolated and could get a lot of rest. We were better prepared mentally because it was a team of veterans. We had a more professional attitude, and we wanted to redeem ourselves for what happened the year before. UCLA was not as good a team as Washington was the year before, but we played an excellent game."

(Incidentally, the pressure was on to perform well for the cameras during this game. That's because it was the first college football game to be televised nationally in color.)

Reminiscent of the '61 Rose Bowl, when Washington scored a field goal on the opening drive, UCLA would also strike first. After being held deep in Gopher territory, the Bruins settled for a 28-yard field goal by Bob Smith just seven minutes into the game. The 98,214 fans that had poured into Pasadena's Rose Bowl to see the game could sense early on that Minnesota wasn't just happy to be there. In fact, that would be all the scoring the Bruins would do that day against the stingy Minnesota defense. The Gophers, haunted by the previous year's finale, rallied back late in the first on a one-yard touchdown plunge by Stephens, which was made possible by Dickson's fumble recovery a few plays prior. Coach Warmath had decided early on that he wasn't going to play as conservatively this go-round, and his Gophers went for it on several pivotal fourth down plays, picking up a first down on one, and scoring on another. Just before the half, Stephens marched the Gophers 75 yards for a second touchdown, with Munsey scoring this time on a reverse.

Dominating the game with their amazing defense, the Gophers looked poised in the second half. Stephens led the Gophers on an incredible 84-yard scoring drive late in the final period, tallying his second touchdown of the game from two yards out. The 19-play drive ate up 11 minutes off the clock, leaving little time for UCLA to do anything but wonder what could have been. The Gophers controlled every aspect of the game, compiling 21 first downs while holding UCLA to eight. Led by the outstanding defensive play of Bell and Eller, Minnesota held the Bruins to a paltry 107 yards of total offense and a mere field goal. Minnesota would not be denied in their second run for the roses, winning the game, 21-3, for the team's first and only Rose Bowl victory. As Coach Warmath was carried off the field, it was said that his smile could be seen all the way back in Minnesota.

"We went out the year before and lost to Washington, so this year we were going to win the Rose Bowl, no matter what," said Bobby Bell. "We beat UCLA pretty bad, and I'd have to say it was amazing. It was one of the greatest things that ever happened to me in college. I was playing with cracked ribs during the game, but at the time I didn't care because I wanted to win so badly. I can remember our defensive coach was saying to us, 'Hey, if you let these guys run three or four yards up the middle, then we are not players at all, we might as well pack up, put our dresses back on, and go home.' Their running back, All-American, Charlie Smith, was a great player, but every time he got close to that line, we were all over him. We shut him down completely. It was great, and when it was over, we were sitting on top of the world."

"It wouldn't have mattered who we would have played this go around," said Big Ten MVP, Sandy Stephens. "I would have died before I lost that game, even if I had to win it all by myself. We just completely dominated UCLA from the moment after they made that opening field goal. The game started out similar to the Rose Bowl of the year before, and that shocked us and woke us up pretty quick. That was the first and last time UCLA would score on us that day."

"I don't know if this is something that is very well known," said Carl Eller, "but I think that a lot of the senior players weren't sure if they even wanted to go back to the Rose Bowl in 1961. We actually had a team meeting on whether or not we should even go. Many of the players didn't want to go if Coach Warmath, who was a task-master, was going to lock them up in a retreat again when they were right down the street from Hollywood. Now, I was only a sophomore at the time, so I didn't have a voice on the team like the juniors and seniors did, but I felt like there was a mutiny going on. So, I stepped up and said, 'Hey guys, I don't want you to rob me of my chance to go to the Rose Bowl.' I didn't care what hotel we stayed at, I just wanted to go to the Rose Bowl! I think in retrospect, he (Warmath) probably did relax a little bit on us out there, and we had a great time that year. We had a very strong team in 1961, and we just overpowered UCLA, physically dominating them. It was a tremendous experience."

One of the Greatest Ever

Growing up in Shelby, N.C., Bobby Bell played quarterback for his high school six-man football team, until his senior year when he finally piloted an 11-man team. Bobby originally came to Minnesota with every intention of playing quarterback for the Golden Gophers. As a sophomore, he could run as fast and throw farther than all the quarterbacks in practice. But Coach Warmath had already begun to mold the great Sandy Stephens as his quarterback, and since the talented Bell was too good to keep on the bench, as Stephens' replacement, the coach put him in the line-up as an offensive and defensive tackle. Bell, who just wanted the chance to play, accepted the role and eventually became one of the greatest tackles not only in Gopher history, but in Big Ten history.

The 6-4, 220-pounder's transition from signal-caller to tackle was hailed by sportswriters of the day as one of the modern wonders of college football. He led Minnesota to a 22-6-1 record during his tenure, including a national championship and Rose Bowl victory. There aren't many All-American tackles today that could boast to have the same sized 28 inch waist as Bell did back in 1961.

Bell is one of only eight Minnesota football players to earn All-America honors in two different seasons, 1961 and 1962. He was awarded the prestigious Outland Trophy his senior year by a landslide vote, recognizing him as the nation's top interior lineman. During his career at the University, Bell won the conference MVP in 1962 and was All-Big Ten in both 1961 and 1962 as well. He was later elected to the College Football Hall of Fame in 1991.

Bell was such a fantastic athlete that he was actually recruited by several other U of M athletics programs in addition to the football team, including the gymnastics and baseball squads. Wanting to do more, he even became the first African-American to play a varsity game for the Gopher basketball team. Gopher Hockey Coach John Mariucci even tried to talk him into playing goalie. "He told me that I had the quickest reflexes that he'd ever seen and that I was going to be the first black hockey player in the country," said Bell. "Now, coming from North Carolina I had never even seen hockey before. So, when we got out on the ice and someone nearly took my head off with a puck, I told

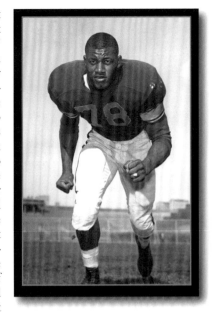

him that the only way I'd get out there is if he turned the net around in the other direction!"

As a professional in the NFL, Bell made another transition, this time to linebacker, where he guided the Kansas City Chiefs to two Super Bowls. In fact, Bell was one of the stars of the team that stopped the Vikings, who were led by his old teammate and friend Carl Eller, in Super Bowl IV in 1970. He would go on to play 13 years in the NFL, was an all-pro for eight consecutive seasons, and became the Chiefs' first inductee into the Pro Football Hall of Fame in 1983. Bobby Bell was undoubtedly the greatest lineman and one of the greatest athletes ever to wear the Maroon and Gold.

"I thought I had died and gone to heaven when I arrived at the University of Minnesota," said Bell. "Coming from North Carolina, I remember the first time I ever saw snow, it was so exciting. Being on campus as a Gopher was one of the most exciting things in my life. Playing in those Saturday football games was just so great. The fans and everybody were just really involved in the game. The night before our games we would stay at a hotel in St. Paul. Then, on Saturday, we would drive down University Avenue with a police escort, and it was just wall-to-wall people everywhere yelling and screaming for us. My heart started to pound like crazy. I was so excited, and my stomach was churning. I couldn't wait to get my uniform on. Getting off that bus and seeing all the people hanging out of the frat house windows was incredible. Seeing all that excitement in one place was fantastic. Everybody was so into it! Tickets to our games were nowhere to be found. I had so much fun there, and to this day I have a real love for the University of Minnesota."

Gopher Tombstone: "He gave it his all."

TRIBUTES

"He had great ability and range on the football field," said Tom Brown. "He had so much tenacity, and he was just an incredible ball player."

"Bobby was probably the most versatile player that I ever had the pleasure of playing with," added Sandy Stephens. "I don't know of anyone else who could have gone from quarterback to tackle. When he came in, the only place we had open was at left tackle, and coach Warmath realized that since he was such a good athlete, he had to play him somewhere. Bobby said that he just came here to play and didn't care where it was that he lined up. He was one of the only guys that could throw a football further than me, and I could throw it 80 yards."

1961 RUNNER-UP: THE VIKINGS & TWINS

The ***MINNESOTA VIKINGS*** and ***MINNESOTA TWINS*** arrive in Minnesota, truly putting the state on the national sports radar — while also easing the pain for the loss of the Lakers, who moved to L.A. in 1960. Both teams would play at Metropolitan Stadium in Bloomington. The Twins were relocated from Washington DC, where they had been playing as the Senators. The team would win its first ever game on April 11, 1961, beating the Yankees in the Big Apple, 6-0, ultimately finishing their inaugural Major League Baseball season with a modest 45-49 record. The Vikings, meanwhile, an NFL expansion team, played their first game against Chicago on September 17, 1961. There, led by rookie quarterback Fran Tarkenton, the purple stunned the Bears, 37-13. The team came back to earth after that, however, finishing in last place with a 3-11 record.

HONORABLE MENTION: ROGER MARIS

Hibbing native ***ROGER MARIS*** hits a record 61 home runs with the New York Yankees. The right fielder made history that season when he topped Babe Ruth's single-season home run record (60 in 1927), a mark that would stand for 37 years. In 12 Major League seasons, Maris played in four All-Star games and participated in seven World Series.

CARL ELLER
The Gophers Play a Wild One in Madison

In 1962, Carl Eller and Bobby Bell stood like two giant oak trees in a forest of outstanding college football players. The two anchored perhaps the greatest defensive unit in Gold Country history. In seven games, Minnesota's Big Ten opponents averaged less than 60 yards rushing per game. Minnesota's defense was so tough that they allowed a mere 61 total points in nine games (34 alone came in a freak loss upset by Northwestern), while five of those nine opponents were held scoreless. In an era of high scoring, wide-open play, this was truly an amazing feat.

With Sandy Stephens gone, Duane Blaska took over the quarterbacking duties in 1962. He was joined by a solid backfield that year as well, with Bill Munsey, Jerry Jones, Jim Cairns, Bill McMillan, Bill Crockett and Jerry Pelletier. It would be the defense, however, that would be the trademark of this team, which was poised to make even more history after winning a national championship and Rose Bowl victory the two seasons prior.

After opening the season with a tough 0-0 standoff with Missouri, Minnesota went on to blank Navy, 21-0, even holding the Midshipmen to negative 31 yards rushing. From there though, the squad was upset by a pesky Northwestern team. They rebounded to post a pair of 17-0 shut-outs over Illinois and Michigan (Michigan was held to negative 46 yards rushing as well), followed by wins over Michigan State, 28-7, Iowa, 10-0, and Purdue, 7-6. With a 5-1 Big Ten record, the Gophers needed a win at Wisconsin to secure the conference title and a repeat trip to Pasadena. The Badgers, also at 5-1, were ready and waiting when the Gophers came to mix it up at Camp Randall Stadium in Madison.

Unfortunately, what followed was considered by many to be one of the most bizarre and disturbing games ever played in college football history. When the dust finally settled, it became clear that the officials, not the players, played a pivotal role in a game that will long be remembered for all of the wrong reasons in Gold Country.

The Gophers opened the scoring in the second quarter with Duane Blaska connecting with Jimmy Cairns on a 15 yard scoring strike. The extra point, however, was no good. Wisconsin Quarterback Ron VanderKelen then rallied his Badgers back with a 65-yard scoring drive to take at 7-6 lead.

In the second half, the game started to turn into a penalty-filled freak-show, capped by the Gophers being penalized 15 yards for illegally aiding the advance of a runner — in this case, Bill Munsey. Minnesota settled for a Collin Versich 32-yard field goal, and the scoreboard read: Minnesota 9, Wisconsin 7. OK, so far so good.

The Gophers later punted, and the coverage team, seeing the ball hit a Badger player, jumped on the loose ball rolling in the end zone, claiming a touchdown. The officials didn't see it that way, however, and returned the ball to Wisconsin out on the 20-yard line. The Gophers, dejected, assumed that the refs probably just didn't see it, and figured they would get it right the next time. Wrong! That's when "IT" happened — an event that will live in infamy. On the Gopher 43 yard-line, VanderKelen dropped back to pass and was sacked hard by Bell. The ball then flew into the awaiting arms of Gopher John Perkovich, only to have the referee nullify the interception. Incredibly, he even called Bell for roughing the passer. At this point, Coach Warmath could no longer contain himself. The 15-yard roughing call suddenly turned into 30 when the ref slapped the Gopher bench with an additional 15-yard unsportsmanlike conduct penalty. So, instead of Minnesota having the ball at mid-field, the Badgers now had a first down on the Minnesota 13-yard line with less than two minutes to go. Three plays later Wisconsin scored to make it 14-9.

Then, amazingly, the officials, who were feeling the heat, decided to even things up and let the Gophers back into the contest by first calling the Badgers for a personal foul penalty on the ensuing kick-off, followed shortly thereafter by a pair of pass interference calls. Suddenly, with a minute to go in the game, the Gophers found themselves with a first down on the Wisconsin 14 yard line. Then it got downright weird. Mysteriously, all communications from the press box to the Gopher bench disappeared, and the assistant coaches who had the bird's eye views of the on-field action, were silenced with jammed head-sets. So, on first down, Blaska, not knowing otherwise, went for it all. But, his pass was picked-off in the end zone to kill the rally. Wisconsin had won the Big Ten title. The irate Gopher fans had just witnessed their third straight Rose Bowl appearance vanish before their very eyes.

"I was called for roughing the Badger quarterback," said Bell, who would go on to receive All-American honors for the second straight year, "but you could see on the film that he still had the ball in his hands, so it couldn't have been roughing. It was a blown call. It was a mess, and they ended up getting about 45 yards out of the whole thing, which ultimately led to them winning the game. It was the craziest game I ever played in. I bet that I've received hundreds of letters and newspaper clippings from around the country about that one play, and people still want to talk to me about it. The referee's name was Robert Jones. I will never forget that guy."

The run was over. For three glorious seasons in the early 1960s, Minnesota had produced a very respectable 22-6-1 record, entitling them to a National Championship, a Big Ten title and a Rose Bowl victory. Carl "Moose" Eller would stick around for one more year in Gold Country before going on become one of the greatest defensive ends in NFL history as a member of the Vikings legendary "Purple People Eaters" defense of the 1970s.

The Moose
A native of Winston Salem, N.C., Carl Eller stared as a two-time All-American Tackle for the Golden Gophers from 1961-63. The six-foot-six 260 pound terror was then selected by the Vikings with the sixth overall pick of the first round of the NFL draft. He went on to play 225 regular-season games over 15 years for the Vikings before spending one final season with the Seattle Seahawks in 1979. He was named All-Pro six times, was the NFL's Most Valuable Defensive Lineman twice, and played in six Pro Bowls. He was also voted as the NFL's Defensive Player of the Year in 1971. Eller would retire as the Vikings all-time sack leader, with 130, and a whopping 44 from 1975-77 alone. He also recovered 23 fumbles, a number that still ranks in the top five in NFL history. Eller's leadership and abilities were a big reason for the Vikings 11 division titles, three NFC crowns and four Super Bowl appearances. He retired after 16 professional football seasons in 1979 but probably could've kept right on playing if he really wanted to. He was just that good. Known for his outstanding speed, power and agility, Eller was elected to the Pro Football Hall of Fame in 2004.

Eller has very much become synonymous with football in Minnesota and will always be remembered not only for his big smile, but as a fierce competitor as well. In his first season at the U of M, he even played with a broken hand, tossing aside his cast that he wore in practices come game day. And football wasn't all Carl could do. He once played MacBeth at the Guthrie Theater and was even voted one of Esquire Magazine's "Best Dressed Jocks" in 1972. He later starred in a B-Movie about bikers called "The Black Six," with Mean Joe Greene and Mercury Morris. Eller has also been a huge inspiration and role-model to kids everywhere by speaking to them about the dangers of drugs. Carl went on to make a career working for the State of Minnesota and later operated his own satellite communications company. He has three children and lives in the Minneapolis area.

What Did it Mean for You to Be a Gopher?

"Being a Golden Gopher was great," said Eller. "Going to the U was one of the better choices that I made in my life. Being on a metropolitan campus and being a part of the Saturday football scene at Memorial Stadium were wonderful experiences for me. Sure, it was a culture shock because I had come from a segregated town in North Carolina. Everything at the U was a new and incredible experience for me, and it was my first exposure to big-time football. Yes, it means a lot for me to be a Gopher."

What Did it Mean for You to Be a Viking?

"It still means a lot. But, truthfully, I felt I was totally misunderstood by the media. You see, when I played, I felt like I was an artist. I could have easily been the equivalent of a violinist, or a painter or whatever. Football is a mental game and I was a craftsman who had great skill and technique. The culmination of all those things made me a great player. Professional football was a real test of all my skills and I looked at playing as a performance. In other words, when I would do things like putting on a pass rush, or stopping a double-team, or making a tackle behind the play, I had to push and test myself to the limit to do those kinds of things that were just barely humanly possible. I had to be quick off the ball, and I had to beat my opponent to the ball. Sometimes I had to beat two guys, and sometimes I would have to hold one guy off with one arm and try to grab the quarterback with the other, all while trying to maintain my leverage, and all while watching out for the back who was coming to cut me at my knees. You had to do all that in a split second, and I took great pride in being able to do it well."

Does Never Winning a Super Bowl Still Hurt?

"Well, we had four shots at winning the big one. People can look at it whatever way they want to, but the four losses never came off as a negative to me. I can say that we were champions of the National Football Conference three times and NFL once. We went to four Super Bowls, defeated some great teams, and lost to some of the best football teams ever in Miami, Oakland, Pittsburgh and Kansas City. It wasn't like we took a dive in our Super Bowls, or anything like that. I have nothing to be ashamed of. I have nothing to regret. We lost four games fair and square. But we didn't lose because we didn't put our best effort out there. We didn't lose because we weren't the best team to make it there. Regardless of what anybody says, those were my greatest moments. Those games were great Vikings moments and an unforgettable part of the great Vikings' history. We never quit. It takes a lot of strength and character to come back time and time again. I think that says a lot more about the Vikings than perhaps some of the teams that actually won the Super Bowl."

TRIBUTES

"Carl was a very talented football player," said Alan Page. "He was strong, quick and agile, and he was a very intense player."

"Moose was a great talent," said Bud Grant. "He got a lot of sacks and knocked down a lot of balls back then, he was just a domi-

nant player. He played his best against the best players, and would dominate each team's top players that they put up against him."

"He was one of the biggest, strongest, toughest guys to come down the pike," said Jim Marshall. "When he wanted to destroy an opponent, I don't think there was anyone who could stop him. He was a great, great football player and I have so much respect for him. We played throughout our entire careers together. He was my roommate and one of my closest friends."

"These guys, the Purple People Eaters were household names when I grew up," said Ahmad Rashad. "It was so great to play on the same team with them, because if we scored seven points — it was a blow-out. We would win because the other team wasn't going to score on them. I used to love watching Carl battle. I couldn't wait for the offense to get off the field so I could watch him go up against those huge 300-pound lineman. It was a massive battle of the titans watching them go at it out there, and Carl would usually win."

"He was the enforcer," said Chuck Foreman. "Carl wasn't just a great football player, he was a great athlete. He was also a very bright guy. He was probably the greatest defensive end that ever played the game."

"As great a player as Carl was, I always admired the confidence that he added to our team each time we went onto the football field," said Joe Kapp. "He was like a chieftain out there. He was as big, as fast and as tough as anybody in the league, and yet he had such a will and spirit to win. Confidence is what separates losing teams from winning teams and Carl passed that quality onto our team."

"We named him the moose, because he was a so big and strong," said Sandy Stephens. "Being from North Carolina, he hated the cold, so we had to indoctrinate him to the balmy Minnesota weather! He had so much enthusiasm and was just a great player."

"He was an all-around athlete," said Bobby Bell. "I got recruited with Carl from Winston Salem. He was so tough and strong, that's why we named him the 'Moose'. He was a happy-go-lucky, fun guy, and he was a guy you could coach. I remember playing that great Michigan State team where they had the No. 1 offense in the country and we had the No. 1 defense in the country. I think they were averaging something like 550 yards of offense per game, and at half-time they had like 26 yards — we shut them down. Carl was just unstoppable. We unbalanced the line that game so he could come down to my side and double-down. Carl would drive their guy into the ground every play and our offense took over. He was the greatest."

1962 RUNNER-UP: JACK KRALICK

Pitcher *JACK KRALICK* throws the first no-hitter in Twins history, a 1-0 win over the Kansas City A's at the Met on August 26, 1962. Kralick was just two outs away from throwing what would have been the first perfect game in the Majors in nearly 40 years, but wound up walking pinch-hitter George Alusik late in the ninth inning. He hung in there though and tossed a 97-pitch complete-game gem that would go down in history. Ironically, he would be traded just nine months later to Cleveland in exchange for pitcher Jim Perry.

HONORABLE MENTION: CONNIE PLEBAN

The University of Minnesota-Duluth Bulldogs, under coach *CONNIE PLEBAN*, make the leap to play Division I hockey after dominating the Minnesota Intercollegiate Athletic Conference (MIAC) for nearly a decade. Finally, after winning a record 56 straight conference games, the school decided to join the Gophers in the ranks of big-time college hockey. They would play a D-I independent schedule in 1961-62, and later go on to become members of the Western College Hockey Association (WCHA) in 1965 — joining Minnesota, North Dakota, Colorado College, Denver, Michigan Tech, Michigan State and Michigan.

1963
JOHN GAGLIARDI
The Football Johnnies Win Their First National Title

In 1963, a dynasty of sorts officially began. This was the year that football coach John Gagliardi, of St. John's University, in Collegeville, Minn., won his first national championship, beating Prairie View A&M (Texas) in a thriller.

The 1963 Minnesota Intercollegiate Athletic Conference (MIAC) season was very successful for the Johnnies. Gagliardi's team was led by Halfback Bob Spinner, who won his second straight MIAC scoring championship in the season finale during a 32-6 drubbing of rival St. Thomas.

Next, it was off to the small-college playoffs for St. John's, where they met the College of Emporia (Kansas). This one wasn't even close as the Johnnies cruised, 54-0, en route to waltzing through the playoffs and advancing to the title game. There, the Johnnies would face Prairie View A&M in Sacramento, Calif., in the Camellia Bowl.

Prairie View A&M was the dominant black college team in America at the time. They played a big-time schedule against teams like Grambling State and Florida A&M and dominated them all. Prairie View also had some great players on their team who would go on to become stars in the NFL, such as Hall of Famer Otis Taylor, and Jim Carnie, who would later become an All-Pro defensive back for the Kansas City Chiefs.

The Johnnies were decisive underdogs going into the contest. Prairie View had 40 "free-ride" football scholarships for their players while St. John's had none. The only thing the Johnnies did have in their favor was the a-typical California weather on that day, which was a chilly 39 degrees — downright freezing to a Texan.

Prairie View scored first on a 29 yard roll-out by Quarterback Jimmy Hall. The Johnnies answered though, on Bob Spinner's 41-yard punt return in the second, making it 7-6. But the Panthers came right back on Jimmy Kearney's 61-yard pass to Otis Taylor to make it 14-6.

St. John's defensive back John McCormick then returned an interception 44 yards, and Johnnie Quarterback Craig Muyres later hooked up with Halfback Bernie Beckman to make it 14-13 at the half.

In the third, the Johnnies took the lead for good on Muyres' 23-yard pass to Hardy Reyerson. Muyres then hit Ken Roering for the extra point and St. John's led 20-14. Late in the same period Beckman, off a double reverse, connected with Roering on an 18-yard touchdown strike.

The Panthers rallied back in the fourth as Kearney threw a 14 yard TD pass to halfback Doug Broadus, cutting the margin to 26-21. But the Johnnies answered, this time on a 19-yard Muyres to Reyerson aerial, followed by a Spinner extra point catch. Prairie View scored on an Ezell Seals one yard plunge, with only 2:15 to go on the game clock. But it was too little too late, as Roering recovered the Prairie View on-side kick to seal the deal. The Johnnies had done it, upsetting the mighty Panthers, 33-27, as the 12,220 fans, many of whom had make the trek from Minnesota, went wild.

Beckman, the smallest man on the field, ran for 52 yards, caught three passes for 43 yards, including a conversion, and played brilliant defense. For his efforts he was named as the game's MVP.

"It was a tremendous win for us," said Gagliardi. "Prairie View is the best team we played all year. Believe me, we knew we weren't going to be playing St. Catherine's! I mean it, it was like coming back after two nine-count knock-downs. And the second knockdown really had us hanging on the ropes. I give credit to the team. They managed to come through with the big play when it was needed all season, especially Craig Muyres, who I believe is the best clutch quarterback in the United States."

A Living Legend

John Gagliardi was born in 1927, the son of an Italian-born body shop owner in Trinidad, Colo. To fully understand this man's life-long calling of coaching, however, you have to go way back to Trinidad Catholic High School. You see, Gagliardi's storied coaching career ironically began when his high school coach was drafted into World War II. Without a coach, the school was just going to drop the football program until he talked the administration into letting him do the coaching. Gagliardi, the teams' captain, took over the reins at the age of just 16. Even at that young age people could see that he had a gift for teaching, working with young people, and instilling in them a winning attitude. Upon graduating, he put himself through school at Colorado College, where he coached the high school team for two more seasons. He then took over as C.C.'s head coach for his junior and senior seasons as well. His teams would win four conference titles in six years.

After graduating from Colorado College in 1949, the 22-year-old accepted his first college coaching position at Carroll College, a small Catholic liberal arts school in Helena, Mont. There, he coached not only the school's football program, but also the basketball and baseball programs as well. Inheriting a Carroll College athletics program in utter disarray, he turned things around in a hurry, leading the football and basketball teams to three straight championships.

His success drew the attention of another small college — St. John's University of Collegeville, Minn. St. John's needed a coach to succeed the mythical Johnny "Blood" McNally, a former Green Bay Packer and Duluth Eskimo great who was a charter member of the Pro Football Hall of Fame. SJU had not won a conference title in 15 years, and Blood, their departing head coach, offered these inspiring words to the new coach: "Nobody can ever win at St. John's."

In 1953, all John Gagliardi was given was a mandate to turn the program around and nothing else that was tangible. Amazingly, he immediately quieted the skeptics by winning the MIAC title that Fall with the help of his first great halfback, Jim Lehman (the father of Minnesota golfing great Tom Lehman), who led the country in scoring. Gagliardi also went on to turn around the Johnnies' track and hockey teams too, proving his unique coaching methods and motivational skills could make any team a winner.

There have been more than 25,000 head coaches in college football history. Just 10 of them have won more than 300 games. The top five are (ranked by most wins): John Gagliardi (St. John's), Eddie Robinson (Grambling), Bobby Bowden (Florida State), Joe Paterno (Penn State) and Bear Bryant (Alabama). Of them, only Gagliardi, Bowden and Paterno are still coaching. Bowden and Paterno, both in their 42nd seasons of coaching, have 373 wins as of 2008. Gagliardi, meanwhile, now in his 58th year behind the bench, has a whopping 453. Translation: nobody is ever going to catch him.

One of his biggest moments in coaching and perhaps in life happened in 1993, when his Johnnies pulverized Bethel, 77-12, for his 300th career win. After that historic event the eyes of the world of sports were suddenly upon him. The national media invaded Collegeville for words of wisdom from the man who had became known nationwide as a coaching genius. It was quite the scene.

Without question, Gagliardi has built one of the nation's top NCAA Division III programs at St. John's. The attitude and winning tradition he instills in his players is unprecedented. Among this seven-time national coach of the year's many achievements are his four small college championship teams. First, in 1963, then two years later, when they crushed Linfield College of Oregon, 35-0 (Amazingly the Johnnies' defense allowed just 27 points to be scored against them that entire season!), in 1976, when they beat Towson State of Maryland, 31-28, and most recently in 2003, when they beat Mount Union, Ohio, 24-6.

As a collegiate coach Gagliardi's teams have won 28 conference titles and have appeared in 56 post-season games. In the past 41 years, St. John's has been nationally ranked 40 times, and it owns a 39-17 post-season record as well. In 1993, the team averaged 61.5 points per game, setting a record that may never be broken.

Among his numerous awards and achievements, Gagliardi has been inducted into the Minnesota and Montana Halls of Fame and is a member of the College Football Hall of Fame as well. He has been the subject of a Sports Illustrated cover story and was awarded the Football Writers of America Citation of Honor. Perhaps his greatest honor came when the NCAA honored him by naming the Division III equivalent of the Heisman Trophy after him — the Gagliardi Trophy. There have even been a couple of books written about him.

The winningest coach in college football history, Gagliardi entered the 2008 season with a 453-122-11 (.782) career record. And Gagliardi's teams are still setting the standard for MIAC competitors. In 1993, SJU became the first NCAA team since the 1904 Gophers to score more than 700 points in a season. Then, in 2000 St. John's made the national title game, followed by a national semifinal appearance in 2001. In 2003 the won it all yet again, this time going undefeated. Gagliardi's 60 years of collegiate coaching is the most in college football

history, surpassing the old record of 57 years held by former University of Chicago coach Amos Alonzo Stagg (1890-1946). He has also coached more games than any coach in history as well, at nearly 600.

Gagliardi's success is attributable to more than mere football strategy and tactics. He is an astute judge of talent. He creates an environment of fun along with high expectations, and he concentrates on methods and practices that truly focus on winning football games. Gagliardi has built a legacy that is unrivaled in college football, and what's frightening for all the other MIAC schools is that he may just be getting his second wind.

Today John and his wife Peggy live in Collegeville and have four children. It's business as usual for the coach though as he enters his 60th season behind the bench. With no more records or honors to shoot for, he is content in having fun and making a difference to the student athletes he teaches and coaches on a daily basis.

St. John's Tombstone:
"I dared to do a lot of things that no one else dared to do — like the way we practice. We've never gone 'full-go' in practice I am proud of the fact that I saved a lot of guys from permanent injuries because of that. I've been a lucky guy and I've always had great athletes to make me look good along the way."

1963 RUNNER-UP: BUD WILKINSON

With an astounding 145-29-4 career record at the University of Oklahoma, *BUD WILKINSON* retires as the winningest coach in college football. Wilkinson, who attended the Shattuck School in Faribault and then went on to earn All-American honors in both football and hockey for the Gophers in both 1934 and 1935, led the Sooners to 14 conference crowns and three national championships. Additionally, from 1953 to 1957, his teams won 47 consecutive games over five straight undefeated seasons — an all-time national record.

HONORABLE MENTION: PAUL JOHNSON

The Minneapolis Millers, with a 36-32-2 record, come up just short in the International Hockey League (IHL) Finals. The Mill City boys beat Omaha in the first round of the playoffs, but then lost to Fort Wayne in the championship series. (Incidentally, both the Millers and St. Paul Saints would fold that off-season, but were replaced by two new franchises in the Central Professional Hockey League: the Minneapolis Bruins and St. Paul Rangers — both minor league teams of the Boston Bruins and New York Rangers.) Leading the way for the Millers that year was a kid from West St. Paul by the name of *PAUL JOHNSON*, who scored 28 goals and 18 assists. Johnson played on two U.S. Olympic teams; winning gold in 1960 at Squaw Valley, CA; and then again in 1964 in Innsbruck, Austria. He would play professionally for 13 seasons, in the CHL, IHL & USHL.

HARMON KILLEBREW
The Killer Wins the Home Run Crown

While a young right fielder by the name of Tony Oliva was named as the Rookie of the Year in 1964, the big story of the season was that of Harmon Killebrew, who led the American League with 49 home runs — his fourth straight season of 45 or more dingers. Major League Baseball's sultan of swat won the home run crown for the third straight year that season, putting him in a very select class. Only seven players had ever led their leagues in home runs for three or more consecutive years up to that point. The Pittsburgh Pirates' Ralph Kiner holds the all-time record of seven straight years, and Babe Ruth had two streaks — four in a row from 1918-21 and six in a row from 1926-31.

Killebrew finished the 1964 season with some other very impressive stats. He hit a modest .270, scored 95 runs and drove in 111 RBIs to boot. With the addition of teammate Bob Allison's 32 homers, the two combined for 81, the most prolific homer-twosome ever for the Twins. At a sports banquet in Baltimore, Killebrew was presented with a crown of jewels, symbolic of the major league home run championship. He would join a select fraternity of prior winners, which included Mickey Mantle, Ted Williams, Ernie Banks, Eddie Mathews, Hank Aaron, Willie Mays and Roger Maris.

"Over my career I led the league six times in home runs," said Killebrew, "but that year was special because it was the first time I hit 49. That was probably one of my best years ever as an individual, but unfortunately we didn't win anything as a team."

Despite the efforts of those two players, however, the team finished with a disappointing sixth-place finish at 79-83. Pitching and defense were again where most of the finger-pointing turned to, as the team finished tied for worst in the league in overall defensive performance. So desperate were the Twins at second base that after trying five different second basemen, they went out and traded Lenny Green and Vic Power for former Gopher star Jerry Kindall. He was decent, but did not solve the answer to their riddle. They did acquire a few new pitchers that year though in Jim "Mudcat" Grant, Al Worthington, and Johnny Klippstein — all of whom would make contributions. Kaat was the ace with 17 wins, while Pascual and Grant added 15 and 11, respectively.

Despite the team's struggles on the field that year, there was some good news. The season was just a warm-up to the fabulous World Series run in 1965 — and Harmon Killebrew would be leading the charge.

Mr. Baseball

Harmon Killebrew grew up playing baseball on the vacant lots of Payette, Idaho. Their, the neighbor kids would emulate the late Hall of Famer Walter Johnson, who had played semi-pro ball just 15 miles away. What set Killebrew apart from other kids though was his intense dedication to the game and his desire to improve himself. While many boys were content simply to play the game, Harmon would practice for hours in the backyard of his home, swinging his bat at imaginary pitches. From there, he would become an Idaho high school football, basketball and baseball sensation. After earning 12 high school letters, he decided to accept a scholarship from the University of Oregon to play both football and baseball.

But, after being heavily recruited by both colleges as well as major league baseball scouts, Harmon suddenly was presented with another inter-esting option. At the time, Idaho Senator Herman Welker was a close friend of Washington Senators owner Clark Griffith, and one of Welker's favorite subjects was talking about a certain local star playing baseball back in his home-state of Idaho. Welker persuaded the Old Fox to check out the kid, Killebrew, so Griffith immediately dispatched scout Ossie Bluege to Idaho. As the story goes, the first time Bluege saw him play, the 17-year-old Killebrew hit a 435-foot shot out of the park and into a sweet potato field, prompting Bluege to call Griffith and say, "Sign him up!"

Harmon truly wanted to go to college that fall, but when Griffith flashed a $30,000 signing bonus in front of him, he just couldn't refuse. With that, Killebrew had become the Senators first bonus baby. (The bonus-baby rule meant that players were forced to spend at least two seasons in the big leagues before being sent down to the minors. The rule was notorious for damaging young ballplayers by depriving them of necessary minor-league teaching and experience.)

Harmon spent the required two seasons riding the pines in Washington, D.C., before spending several more years in the Senators' farm system. He received a "last look" in 1959 when he was finally placed on the team's Major League roster. Three major league managers had expressed doubt that he would ever make it as a big league ballplayer. They saw his potential as a power hitter, but needed to be sold on Harmon the fielder, runner and thrower.

That's when Calvin Griffith, who had succeeded his uncle as president of the Senators, decided to see what the family money had bought and insisted that Harmon be given an extended shot with the Senators. The new Washington third baseman surprised everybody in 1959 by becoming one of the most feared sluggers in the American League. Harmon led the usually dormant Senators, finishing the season with a whopping 42 homers and driving in 105 runs. Killebrew even tied Cleveland's Rocky Colavito for the home run title as well.

When the Senators moved to the Twin Cities in 1961, Killebrew continued his torrid home run hitting pace, winning three successive home run titles from 1962-64. He rose to Hall of Fame stardom in the early 60s in Minnesota, becoming the primary attraction at Metropolitan Stadium. On the field, Harmon assumed the position of the Twins team leader. His hustle and tenacity made him the complete player that had eluded him earlier on in his career. He became known as a fierce competitor, a solid fielder and a true gentleman — both on and off the field.

"I was really apprehensive about moving to Minnesota to tell you the truth," recalled Harmon. "I liked playing in Washington. I thought it was a great place to play and I really enjoyed the excitement of seeing and meeting all the presidents, congressmen, senators, and other famous people who would attend our games. Although I didn't like playing in the cold Minnesota weather, the warm hearts of the people made it warm up in a hurry. They were great. I really enjoyed the years I spent playing in the Twin Cities. The fans were just wonderful to me. The 1960s were an exciting time for sports in Minnesota with the Vikings' success as well."

Killer went on to win the American League MVP in 1969 when he hit 49 dingers with 140 RBIs and 145 walks, all team records. In 1974, sensing that the end was near for his aging veteran, Griffith encouraged Harmon to retire and become a manager in the Twins farm system — grooming him to be an eventual Twins skipper. Killebrew wasn't quite ready to go out to pasture, however, and wanted to play one more season. So, he declined Calvin's suggestion and signed on as a designated hitter with the Kansas City Royals. Killebrew's playing career in Minnesota was over.

On May 4, 1975, Harmon returned to Met Stadium, this time as a member of the opposition. His No. 3 was officially retired in a pre-game ceremony, and to top it all off, he smacked a homer to left field in his first at-bat. Minnesota fans went crazy as he rounded the bases in what some have said was the loudest ovation Twins fans have ever given an opposing player.

"I think that being a Twin meant that I had an opportunity to play on a lot of great ballclubs, and play with some great players over the years," said Killer. "Just putting on that uniform and walking on that Met Stadium field to represent the Twins was about as big a thrill as anything for me."

Harmon Clayton Killebrew, Jr., will be remembered as one of the greatest home run hitters in history with 573 career round-trippers. He was second only to Babe Ruth in the history of the American League to hit more than 40 home runs, (eight times), 30-or-more home runs, (10 times), all while driving in 100-plus RBIs (nine times). Over his career he tallied 1,584 RBIs, while garnering 2,435 hits and playing in 10 All-Star games.

Killebrew was also the consummate team player, always more interested in the team's achievements rather than his own, "You know, it's fine to hit homers, but it's RBIs that mean the most," he said.

Because of his tremendous contributions to the game of baseball, on January 10, 1984, Killebrew became the first Twin ever to be inducted into the Baseball Hall of Fame. At the induction ceremony, he went on to tell the gathering that he attributed much of his success to his father, who had once explained to someone who had commented on the families' sports-worn front lawn, by saying that he was "raising children, not grass."

Harmon was more than just a slugger. He overcame his early fielding problems and emerged as a solid all-around baseball player. Twins manager Sam Mele recognized him as a genuine team leader whose presence in the line-up inspired the other players to do their best. Quiet and unassuming, Harmon was always more interested in his team rather than personal accolades, and he is the first to deny his greatness. He is also quick to give thanks and appreciation to the game of baseball for everything it has done for him and his family.

Just outside the town of Payette, there is a sign that says, "Home of Harmon Killebrew." There also is a street named for him, and his No. 12 football jersey still hangs prominently in the halls of his high school for all the kids to see. His hometown didn't forget him — nor will baseball. Killebrew ranks as one of the greatest right-handed sluggers of all time. "One of the quietest team leaders of all time," remarked a sportswriter, "but a leader nevertheless."

"When they originally told us that we were moving from the nation's capital to Minnesota, I was, frankly, a bit apprehensive about it," said Harmon. "But when it finally happened it was just great. The people of Minnesota immediately embraced me and I grew to love it up there. The fans in Minnesota are as good, if not better, than any fans in baseball. They showed me so much love and respect, and I will never forget that."

"When I came to Minnesota I was already aware of the great baseball tradition that they had here. In fact, I had actually played against the Minneapolis Millers and St. Paul Saints in my earlier days. Old Nicollet and Lexington Parks had a lot of great ballplayers come through their gates through the years and that just added to Minnesota's great baseball history."

"The one thing that I always took away from my time in Minnesota is that the people up there really cherish their free-time and know how to have fun — especially in the summertime, when they are not cooped up in the house. And, whether they are out in the yard or

up at the lake, it always seemed like the fans made time to tune into the ballgame and support us. I never forgot that. Overall, I can't thank the fans of Minnesota enough for their amazing generosity and hospitality towards me over the years. It is a state with a wonderful baseball heritage and I was truly proud and honored to be a part of it."

TRIBUTES

"He was a steadying influence on our teams," said Rod Carew. "The greatest thing that I learned from Harmon was here was a man who would hit two or three home runs in a ballgame one day, and then maybe strike out four times the next night. But, I never once saw him get upset or gesture to the fans even when they booed him. His whole career was one of dignity. I watched him day in and day out and saw that here was a future Hall of Famer who could handle harassment from the people in the stands and not let if affect him as a player. I knew that if he could do that, then I could, as well. Harmon was a great hitter and a great ballplayer." "Harmon was just what you would expect," said Jim Kaat. "He was the perfect poster-boy for the Minnesota Twins. He was this big, hulking power hitter, very soft-spoken gentleman in every sense of the word, and he was the perfect person to be identified and associated with the Twins. I respect what he did on and off the field, and it was a great pleasure playing with him. Just the way he carried himself during good times and bad times was a great influence on all of us."

"You couldn't have played with a better person than Harmon," said Tony Oliva. "I think he was almost too nice to be a Major League ballplayer. He is just a wonderful person, and I considered it to be an honor to be able to say that I played baseball with him."

"I had the dream of being a Major Leaguer as a kid and, of course, being from St. Paul and following the Twins, I regarded Harmon Killebrew as the one player who I tried to emulate when I was playing out in my backyard," recalled Paul Molitor. "I was always fascinated by his home-run power and by just what he had meant to the Twins. Harmon is a tremendous gentleman. You know, sometimes you get deflated if and when you are finally lucky enough to get to meet your childhood hero. This was by no means the case when I met him though. If anything, my respect for Harmon has only grown by getting to know him."

"Harmon is just so loved here in Minnesota," added Kent Hrbek. "He was an idol of mine when I was growing up in Bloomington. He was just a fantastic player and is probably the best right-handed home run hitter of all time."

1964 RUNNER-UP: RON WOJCIAK

The Gopher baseball team wins its third NCAA national championship in nine years, beating the top ranked Missouri Tigers, 5-1, in the College World Series finale. What made the event even more exciting was the fact that Missouri had just beaten Minnesota two nights earlier, 4-1, allowing just one hit. Gopher pitcher Joe Pollack answered back in the tourney's final game though, allowing just four hits of his own. Pollack was dominant, garnering three of the team's four victories in the World Series. Leading the way for the Maroon and Gold that season was catcher **RON WOJCIAK**, who earned All-Big 10 and All-American honors that season. The Columbia Heights native would go on to sign with the Minnesota Twins the following season.

HONORABLE MENTION: JEAN HAVLISH

Bowler **JEAN HAVLISH** has the season to remember in 1964, winning the top division of the Women's International Bowling Congress Singles Title, as well as the All Events Championship. The St. Paul native first made her mark in the sports world back in the mid-1950s as a star shortstop for the Fort Wayne (Ind.) Daisies of the All-American Girls Professional Baseball League. From there, Havlish went on to become Minnesota's most famous all-time bowler. She is a member of the International Bowling Hall of Fame, and was even listed as one of the "50 Greatest Minnesota Sports Figures" by Sports Illustrated for its 50th Anniversary edition.

1965

ZOILO VERSALLES
The Twins' Amazing World Series Run

The 1965 Twins were historic. They came out of nowhere and shocked the baseball world while taking the fans of Minnesota on a ride they would never forget. They opened up the season on April 12th with a 5-4 win over the Yankees — perhaps an omen of good things to come for this promising bunch of kids. The season got off to a great start and by mid-season the team was poised to make a run for its first-ever trip to the post-season.

Meanwhile, on July 13th, the baseball Gods shined down on Minnesota by letting Metropolitan Stadium host the state's first-ever All-Star game. And, while the National League won the 36th mid-summer classic, 6-5, local slugger Harmon Killebrew thrilled the 47,000 fans in attendance by smacking a tater for the American League. The AL had rallied back from a 5-0 deficit to tie it up before Ron Santo's RBI single in the seventh proved to be the eventual game-winner.

From there the Twins got on a roll, building a five game lead in the Division by playing smart baseball. By season's end the team was hitting on all cylinders. Leading the charge was shortstop Zoilo Versalles, who led the league in at-bats, runs scored, doubles and triples. Outfielder Tony Oliva batted .321 and won his second straight batting title. Mudcat Grant won 21 games to lead the league and Jim Kaat won 18. To top it off, the Twins had four 20-plus home run hitters in Jimmie Hall, Bob Allison, Don Mincher and Harmon Killebrew. (Mincher came off the bench to hit 22 home runs and 65 RBIs during the pennant drive while filling in for Killebrew, who was hurt following a collision with Baltimore's Russ Snyder.) There was also the bullpen of Al Worthington, Johnny Klippstein, Jim Perry, and Bill Pleis, who were at times, untouchable. The Twins won with smart pitching, a solid defense, and clutch hitting.

On September 26, after battling Chicago and Baltimore for the right to represent the American League in the World Series, the Twins, behind Jim Kaat, clinched the pennant when they beat the Washington Senators on their home field, 2-1. Champagne corks popped following the win as the team knew it was now playing the role of Cinderella. (That Sunday, back at Metropolitan Stadium, the Twins' score was displayed on the scoreboard during the Vikings game against the Lions. When the fans saw it, they rose en masse to cheer them on.) Minnesota finished in first place during that magical year, seven games ahead of the pack with a club-record 102 wins. They would then go on to face the mighty Dodgers of Los Angeles in that fabled October get-together, the World Series. L.A., which had to win 14 of their final 15 games to edge out the San Francisco Giants, were playing red-hot baseball. It would prove to be a study in contrasts as the power of the Twins would challenge the speed, defense and pitching of the Dodgers.

The Twins now were presented with the monumental challenge of facing the heavily-favored Los Angeles Dodgers and their ace pitchers, Sandy Koufax and Don Drysdale, who had won 26 and 23 games, respectively. "The Twins are game, but they are not in the same class as the Dodgers, they'll be lucky if the Series goes to five games," one sportswriter noted.

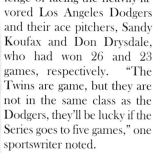

Finally, on October 6, Game One got underway at the Met with Vice President Hubert Humphrey tossing out the first ball. From there, Mudcat Grant opened the festivities by taking to the mound. He would be driven by the familiar chatter of his shortstop, Zoilo Versalles, as he barked

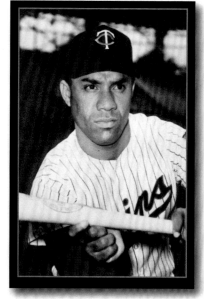

out his routine chatter of encouragement for his burly pitcher: "Hubba-Hubba-Hubba—Cat!" In a shocker, Dodger ace Sandy Koufax had decided to sit out the opener to attend Yom Kippur — the holiest of Jewish holidays. His place was taken by the almost equally feared Donny Drysdale, a six-foot-six right-hander. The Dodgers struck first with a Ron Fairly home run in the second, but Minnesota answered with a homer of their own, this one from Mincher. Minnesota scored six unanswered runs in the third, highlighted by a Versalles three-run homer. The 47,797 fans watched their Twins take Game One, 8-2.

Game Two featured a pitcher's duel between two of the greatest baseball has ever seen, Koufax and Kaat. Scoreless through five, Left Fielder Bob Allison then made an historic diving, sliding circus catch off of Jim Lefebvre's sinking liner to end a fourth-inning scoring threat. The game was still scoreless until the sixth, when Oliva doubled to score Versalles, with Killebrew coming in on the next play. In the bottom of the seventh Versalles tripled and scampered home on a Perranoski wild pitch. Then, to add some salt to the wound, Kaat knocked in Allison and Mincher with an eighth-inning liner. Minnesota was shocking the baseball world, winning, 5-1, and threatening to sweep Los Angeles.

Back at Chavez Ravine in L.A. for Game Three, reality bit as Dodger lefty Claude Osteen faced off against Camilo Pascual. The stars were out in force for this one as well, with Frank Sinatra, Gregory Peck, Doris Day and Milton Berle among the spectators in attendance. The Twins threatened early with Killebrew and Versalles on the corners, but that would be as close as the Twins would get that day, as they were both thrown out in run-downs. The Dodgers' John Roseboro then singled in the fourth, knocking in Fairly and Lefebvre. L.A. added two more runs late, as the Minnesota bats remained quiet. The Dodgers went on to take Game Three by the final count of 4-0.

Then, in a replay of Game One, Grant and Drysdale were re-matched for Game Four. Errors and miscues were the story of the day for the Twins though, as the Dodgers got two easy runs early. Killebrew and Oliva smacked solo homers to make it 3-2, but errors by Hall, Oliva, and Frank Quilici in the sixth, accompanied by a Lou Johnson solo homer in the eighth, opened the flood gates. Los Angeles went on to win the game, 7-2, tying the series at two games apiece.

Game Five featured a rematch of the titans, Kaat and Koufax. Koufax tossed a gem in this one, thrilling the nearly 56,000 Dodger fans in attendance. When it was all said and one, he had won the game by the final score of 7-0, while striking out 10 Twins hitters in the process to earn the huge shut-out victory. Maury Wills led the Dodgers with a four-hit performance that equaled the entire Twins' hitting attack. With the win, the Dodgers went ahead three games to two. The series now shifted back to Minnesota for Games Six and Seven.

The Twins were now 0-for-Osteen in their last seven tries. But the Mudcat, despite not feeling very well, had the performance of his life in the sixth game of this epic battle. With catcher Earl Battey aboard, Allison started off the festivities in the fourth by slamming an Osteen offering over the Met's left field wall. In the fifth, Grant masterfully pitched his way out of a bases-loaded, no-outs jam. Then, Mudcat amazed the Metropolitan Stadium crowd by going deep for a home run with Allison and Quilici on board to make it 5-1 in the sixth. Fairly homered for the Dodgers in the seventh, but it was way too little, way too late for Los Angeles. The Mudcat had pitched a six-hit, complete-game gem of his own to tie the series at three games apiece. It would now all come down to the pivotal Game Seven out at the Met.

In what turned out to be their third World Series go-around, it was Koufax vs. Kaat one last time. No one could believe that both pitchers were going to take the hill on only two days rest, but they did. In the third, Versalles singled off Koufax and then stole second, only to have the home plate umpire wave him back to first. Dodger announcer Vin Scully, explained the controversial call to the millions of radio and TV listeners across the nation: "Umpire Ed Hurley has just ruled that batter Joe Nossek interfered with Catcher Roseboro's throw. Versalles is going back to first, and Manager Sam Mele is coming out of the dugout." Mele protested, but the call stood. The next batter, Oliva, struck out, ending the potential rally.

In the top of the fourth, Kaat served up a dinger to Johnson to give LA a 1-0 lead. Ron Fairly followed with a double and scored on a Wes Parker single. That would be all for Kaat as Relief Pitcher Al Worthington was sent in with the Twins down by the score of 2-0. In the fifth, Twins Second Baseman Frank Quilici doubled off the left field wall. Then Rich Rollins, batting for Worthington, walked, setting the table for Versalles. Zoilo ripped the Koufax offering down the line, only to have L.A.'s Jim Gilliam make the catch of his life, robbing Versalles in dramatic fashion. Koufax then retired 12 Twin batters in a row before Killebrew could manage a single off him in the ninth. With the tying runner at the plate, Koufax stuck out Battey on three straight. Allison would be the team's last hope. But, with the count 2-2, the Twins left fielder whiffed to end the ballgame. With that, the Dodgers stormed the field to celebrate. They were officially World Series champions for the second time in three years. Koufax, meanwhile, ended up tossing a three hit shut-out, striking out ten in one of the greatest World Series Game Seven pitching performances ever.

After the season Versalles was named as the American League's MVP. There had been some question as to whether or not he would win it, after all, his competition was a regular who's who of baseball: Yankees Pitcher Mel Stottlemyre; Tigers Shortstop Dick McAuliffe; Oriole Third Baseman Brooks Robinson; and Red Sox Right Fielder Carl Yastrzemski. At the annual team dinner, Twins Owner Calvin Griffith gave Zoilo the good news: My next announcement should wipe away any last doubts as to why the Twins won the pennant this year," he said. "I've just received word from the commissioner's office of the choice for the MVP in the American League for 1965. The choice is Zoilo Versalles of the Minnesota Twins!"

Upon receiving the honor, Zoilo was asked to say a few words. He stood silent for a moment, as a hush fell over the audience. Perhaps he was thinking just then of growing up on the dusty streets of Marianao, Cuba, and all he had gone through in his life to get to where he was at that moment. As he stood next to the trophy, he said: "I am just lucky. Lucky to get a base hit, lucky to get a home run, lucky to steal a base, and lucky to be here." Yet, Zoilo would insist that the honor be given to his best friend, Tony Oliva. "Tony's hitting brought us the pennant," he said. "He was the most valuable to our team."

Zoilo the Great!

Brought into this world on December 15, 1940, in a one-room straw hut in Marianao, Cuba, Zoilo Versalles was born to baseball and poverty. Although he was still small, at the age of 12 he was fast enough to play sandlot baseball with the big boys. Not being able to afford a glove of his own, he shared with opposing players when the teams switched sides. At 14, he had all the tools that made up a great shortstop: the arm, the hands, the eyes and the speed. As he grew older, he taught himself to read by slowly sounding out the player's names on the rosters and in the sports pages of the local paper. Baseball had become his life, and would eventually be his ticket out of poverty.

Zoilo was discovered by "Papa Joe" Cambria, a Washington Senators scout who found him in Cuba. He then helped him come to

America where he would become a hero to his native Cubans. Cambria's advice to the young Zoilo: "Eat, sleep, and think baseball." Cookie Lavagetto, manager of the Washington Senators, had a simple formula for his team's success: "Tight pitching and a healthy Zoilo at short."

Zoilo Versalles was one of the greatest players ever to play for the Twins. From 1961-67 his Twins career batting average was .252. In addition, he had 1,046 hits, scored 564 runs, belted 86 homers, knocked in 401 RBI's and stole 84 bases in a total of 1,065 games. His greatest season, of course, was that of 1965, when he led the Twins to the World Series and was named as the American League's MVP.

On November 28, 1967, Zoilo was traded to the Dodgers for pitcher Ron Perranoski and catcher John Roseboro. He would bounce around for a few more seasons before finally retiring from the game in 1971. Sadly, Zoilo, who made his home in the Twin Cites area, passed away in 1995 at the age of just 55.

TRIBUTES

"Zoilo was the best Twins shortstop ever," said Tony Oliva. "And, there was nobody better in the league than Zoilo in 1965. He could hit and could catch everything. He covered a lot of ground at shortstop, so nothing got by him. He was a great friend and was like my brother. It was comforting for me to have someone to talk Spanish to, because I too spoke very little English."

"Zoilo had a real fine year in 1965," said Harmon Killebrew. "He played a great shortstop and he hit real well too. He was kind of erratic at times as a young player, but he certainly learned to play the game. He was a big reason we won the pennant that year."

"We had played together in the minors as well, and he was a great talent," said Jim Kaat. "He had as good a year as any ballplayer could have in 1965. I don't know how he did it all, because mentally there was so much additional pressure on him because he was taking care of his family responsibilities on top of everything else. Coming out of Cuba from a situation that we all would consider poverty, and then all of a sudden becoming a star in the Major Leagues was very difficult for him to handle and his career fizzled out a lot quicker than it should have."

"He was a hero of mine as a kid, so I really looked up to him," said Dave Winfield. "He had a unique style and flare and was just a great ballplayer. I once got a chance to meet him, and it was a genuine thrill for me."

1965 RUNNER-UP: EARL BATTEY

The Major League Baseball All Star Game is held at the Met. Six Twins were named to the team, with catcher *EARL BATTEY* being the only player to get the nod as an American League starter. The other Twins who were selected to play in the game as reserves included: Zoilo Versalles (SS), Tony Oliva (OF), Mudcat Grant (P), Harmon Killebrew (1B) and Jimmie Hall (OF). Battey would play in the Major Leagues for 13 seasons, batting .270 with 104 home runs and 449 RBI.

HONORABLE MENTION: RUMMY MACIAS

The Mankato State Mavericks win the NCAA Division III wrestling national championship. Leading the charge for the Mavs was legendary head coach *RUMMY MACIAS*. The Davenport, Iowa, native guided the Mavs from 1950-88, leading the program to a pair of NAIA national titles in 1958 and 1959, to go along with nine conference crowns. In addition, Macias had 93 of his wrestlers attain All-America status, with 19 of them earning individual national champion honors and 62 earning individual conference champion honors. A member of seven halls of fames, Macias also served as the MSU golf coach for many years as well.

JIM KAAT
Kitty Wins 25 Ballgames for the Twins

The Minnesota Twins, coming back to earth after their phenomenal World Series run of 1965, encountered some tough luck and caught a few bad breaks in 1966. Led by their ace pitcher, Jim Kaat, who had the season of his career with a 25-13 record, the Twins finished in a respectable second place behind Baltimore in the American League with a record of 89-73.

Injuries hindered Bob Allison and Camilo Pascual, who both sat out for much of the season. In addition, Manager Sam Mele was none too pleased when his overweight catcher, Earl Battey, who after an apparent single in a game that season against Boston, was thrown out at first base from right field. Battey's performance prompted the wry sportscaster Halsey Hall to recall some years later that watching him round second base "looked like he was pushing a safe."

That season, Mele juggled the line-up to shake things up. Harmon Killebrew was moved to third, Don Mincher went to first and Bernie Allen was posted at second. Ted Uhlaender filled in for the injured Allison, while Jimmie Hall and Tony Oliva rounded out the outfield. Killebrew wound up with 39 home runs and 110 RBIs, while Tony Oliva hit .307 with 25 homers and 87 RBIs.

Shortstop Zoilo Versalles, coming off his incredible MVP season, seemed to be only a shadow of his 1965 self, leading the American League not in hits, but in errors. One of the bright spots for Minnesota that season though was the effort of Mr. Versatility, Cesar "Pepe" Tovar, who hit in the lead-off spot, while playing short, second and in the outfield.

The pitching staff was OK, but struggled to find itself all year long. Along with Kaat's 25 wins, Jim Merritt and Mudcat Grant each added 13, Dave Boswell came up with 12, and Jim Perry, who would win the Cy Young four years later, won 11. Camilo Pascual sat out most of the season with a sore arm, but managed to win eight games as well. In addition, Al Worthington was steady in the bullpen, adding six wins and 16 saves.

With a phenomenal league-leading 25-13 record, Kaat was the real deal. He posted an impressive 2.74 ERA that season while striking out 205 hitters. And, in 41 outings he pitched 304 innings, completing 19 games. He finished fifth in the MVP voting and was named the American League Pitcher of the Year by The Sporting News. He was the savior of the pitching staff and truly led by example. The even-keeled hurler never got too emotional out on the mound, but earned a great deal of respect from his opponents.

"For a pitcher, and all pitchers realize this, sometimes it's not always how you pitch, but when you pitch," said Kaat. "Sometimes you have those years when you pitch mediocre, your team scores a lot of runs, and then when you pitch well, you win 2-1. That's the kind of year I had in 1966. I won a lot of games by blow-outs, but I also won the close ones. I think maybe my best year personally, was probably 1971, when my record was 13-14. But in 1966, it all just came together for me and I just happened to pitch on the right day a lot that year."

"Kitty-Kaat"

Born in Zeeland, Mich., Jim Kaat was the model of baseball consistency. From 1959 to 1983, the red-headed southpaw become the first pitcher in Major League history to ply his trade for 25 years. Winning 20 games several times throughout his career, he was more than just a good pitcher; he ranks up there with the likes of Bob Gibson and Bob Lemon as among the best at all aspects of the game. Though he only had a lifetime .185 batting average, Kaat was nevertheless highly respected as a hitter, considering he belted out 16 home runs over his career. What might be most amazing, however, was the fact that he was awarded 16 consecutive Gold Glove awards for his spectacular fielding abilities, a record unlikely to ever be matched by another pitcher.

After a remarkable 25 seasons in the Majors, Kaat had appeared in 898 games, placing him fifth in history in the category, and he won 283 of them. With a lifetime ERA of 3.45, Kaat fanned 2,461 batters, had 31 career shut-outs, 180 complete games and 18 career saves.

As a member of the Minnesota Twins from 1961-73, Kaat won 189 games, posted a 3.30 ERA, struck out 1,824 batters, and played in a pair of All-Star games in both 1962 and 1966. Known as an "inning-eater," Kaat was known for his durability. He could always be counted upon for more than 200 innings per season, yet in 1966 he threw in a whopping 304. During his stint with the Twins, he also pitched 23 shut-outs, yet another testament to not only his durability, but his dogged determination to finish whatever he started. The opening-day pitcher in both 1965 and 1967, Kaat also received the Twins Pitcher of the Year Award in 1966 and 1972 as well.

A huge fan-favorite, it was a shocker when it was announced on August 15, 1973, that Kaat was unceremoniously being sent packing for the Windy City to join his new team, the White Sox.

"I would have liked to have played my entire career in Minnesota," he said. "I was heartbroken when I heard Calvin Griffith had put me on waivers. Yet, in the back of my mind, I knew what was going on because the Twins had gradually phased me out of being a regular starter and made me into a long reliever. In 1973, I was coming back from a wrist injury that had happened the year before while I was sliding into second base. It took me a while that year to get my stuff back together, and I knew that I was getting stronger and healthier, but could sense the end was near."

"I remember getting a phone call from Calvin while I was golfing at the Minnetonka Country Club, and he told me that the White Sox had picked me up on waivers. That night I went in to clean out my locker and to personally thank Calvin for the years I had in Minnesota. Calvin said 'You know, I really would have liked to have kept you, but my manager told me that he didn't think you could pitch in the big leagues anymore.'

"Then, when I went down to the locker room to pack my bags, I saw Frank Quilici, the manager, and said to him, 'Thanks a lot, good luck, and I appreciated the opportunity.' Frank's words were, 'You know, I would have liked to have kept you, but Calvin didn't think you could pitch in the big leagues anymore.'

"I remember driving to Chicago that day, and it was a very difficult trip for me, reminiscing on my days in the Twin Cities. I really enjoyed it in Minnesota and would have loved to have finished my career there. Looking back, in retrospect, it was a great break for me. Going to Chicago was a stepping stone for me to play another 10 years in the Majors, and I even got to experience a World Series win with St. Louis in 1982."

After his days as an active player ended, Kaat returned to the Twin Cities as a broadcaster, teaming with Ted Robinson to do Twins TV broadcasts from 1988-93. In 1993 he moved to the Big Apple to broadcast Yankees games for the next 15 seasons. There, in the media capital of the world, he became known as one of the best color-men in the business.

One of the game's all-time greats, Jim Kaat will be undoubtedly be remembered as not only one of the best pitchers ever to throw for the Twins, but also for being one of the organization's classiest and most respected gentlemen.

Most Memorable Game as a Twin
"Winning Game Two of the 1965 World Series. That was really special."

On playing in the 1965 World Series

"We had such a good team that year. When you're in your mid-twenties, it is so exciting just being there, and I don't think you ever realized how difficult it was just to get there. My feeling at the time was that we were good and going to the Series was going to happen to us more than once. So, maybe I didn't think there was enough sense of urgency. We were enjoying all the festivities, and that may have taken a little of the focus off our winning as well.

"From an individual standpoint, I can remember sitting on the bench next to our pitching coach, Johnny Sain, in Game Two. I had never seen Sandy Koufax in person, and I had heard a lot about him. After seeing him pitch for a few innings, I remember telling Johnny that if we gave up just one run, this game would be over.

"What stands out in my mind is just thinking that there was no way we could win against him, because he looked completely unbeatable. I remember what a dominant pitcher Sandy was. I mean we had a really good hitting ball club that year, and we couldn't touch him at all."

Did you Always Want to Play Baseball?

"Growing up as a kid in Michigan, my first exposure to baseball was the 1945 World Series between the Cubs and the Tigers. From that point on, I just always knew that I wanted to play baseball. It was my dream."

When Were Your Happiest Days?

"I was happiest very early on in my career. I can remember a former Twins minor league manager of mine, Del Wilbur, who said to me 'Kid, when you get to the big leagues don't be content to just live there, accomplish something while you're there.' I enjoyed getting there but was driven to make my mark. After you win 20 games, make an All-Star team, and play in a World Series, your career kind of settles in from there."

What Was It Like to Win a World Series?

"Winning the World Series with the Cardinals in 1982 was unbelievable. I was 44 years old, and it had been 17 years since I had been in a World Series. I had been given up on a couple of times up to that point, and here I was contributing to a team that won the World Series. I think that was probably as satisfying a year as I ever had."

Were Twins Pitchers Forgotten Heroes?

"The Minnesota Twins have always been known as the lumberjacks, with all those great home-run hitters through the years, but you have to have pitching to win too. I don't think the pitchers who have gone through that organization have gotten the same high recognition that the Twins hitters have. I'm speaking of pitchers like Frank Viola, Bert Blyleven, Mudcat Grant, Camilo Pasqual, Jim Perry and myself. That's not sour grapes on my part; it's a matter of fact."

Which Player of the Modern Era Reminds You of You?

"I would say probably Yankees Pitcher Andy Pettitte. I enjoy watching him, and when I see him both personally and the way he conducts himself on the mound with his competitive nature, I think I see a lot of him in me, and me in him. There are some similarities; we're both tall lefties. Although, back then I wish I could have had the poise that he shows nowadays, as well as his unbelievable pick-off move."

Twins Tombstone:

"I think after 25 seasons in baseball, I can look back and honestly say that I never gave less than a maximum effort. Throughout my career, I never had to turn the ball down and was ready to play every day. I take pride in the fact that I never missed a start because of a sore arm, and I felt that I gave the Twins their best days work for their money. I'll never go down as one of the all-time greats, but in my mind I feel good about the fact that I got the most out of my abilities. It meant a lot to me that my teammates had confidence in me, and that I was the guy that they wanted on the mound when we had a big game to win."

TRIBUTES

"Jim was a great pitcher and was always a great competitor," said Harmon Killebrew. "He was one of the finest fielding pitchers that I have ever seen. I mean, he won 16 gold gloves as a pitcher — that's just incredible. He should be in the Hall of Fame."

"Jim was great to be around," said Rod Carew. "He was one of the best hitting pitchers in baseball and one of the top left-handers in the game. Being around Jim and watching him perform day in and day out was an inspiration to me as a young player coming up. He is a very classy person."

"He is a very nice guy and was a good teammate," said Tony Oliva. "He was a pitcher that was great to play behind because if you ever made an error, he would never say anything bad to you about it. He would just say 'come on, let's go!' He was a pleasure to play with, and I really like him."

"I really like Kitty," said Jack Morris. "He was a great pitcher. He does a super job broadcasting and is just a super guy."

"He is a great guy and a great announcer," added Kent Hrbek. "I saw Kitty play at the old Met many times. He had a very unorthodox pitching style, and he would just come right at you with whatever he had. He would tell you to your face that his pitches probably couldn't even break a pane of glass, but, nonetheless, he knew how to pitch and was just a great pitcher."

1966 RUNNER-UP: LOU HUDSON

The basketball Gophers go 14-10, good for fifth in the Big 10. Leading the charge for the Maroon and Gold is senior All-American guard **LOU HUDSON**, who averaged nearly 20 points and 8 rebounds per game in 1966 — despite the fact that he had a cast on his right (shooting) hand and had to shoot lefty for much of the season. From there, the Greensboro, NC, native was selected No. 4 overall in the NBA draft by the St. Louis Hawks. "Sweet Lou" would go on to play in the NBA for 13 seasons, garnering six All-Star appearances. In all, he would average 20.2 points per game en route to finishing 12th on the league's all-time scoring list.

HONORABLE MENTION: LARRY ROSS

The International Falls High School hockey dynasty, complete with a 58-game undefeated streak, finally comes to an end after three straight state championships (1964-66) — not to mention a fourth in 1962. (Incredibly, they would have won five straight titles had it not been for a 4-3 overtime loss in the 1963 semifinals to Roseau.) Leading the way for the Broncos is legendary coach **LARRY ROSS**. The Duluth native was a two-time All-American goalie for the Gophers in 1951 and 1952 before getting into coaching. A true hockey icon, Ross posted a 566-169-21 career record in the Falls, including 13 state tourney appearances and six championships.

1967

LOU NANNE
The North Stars Hit the Ice

On March 11, 1965, National Hockey League President Clarence Campbell announced that his six-team league would expand, creating six new teams for the NHL's Western Division. A group of nine Twin City businessmen led by Gordon Ritz, Bob McNulty, and Walter Bush, Jr., then joined in a partnership to control the new franchise. Plans were swiftly put into motion and the ground in Bloomington was broken for the new $7 million Metropolitan Sports Center. The structure was erected in less than a year (on the site just north of the Mall of America), just in time for the North Stars' maiden season.

On June 6, 1967, the draft was held. Wren Blair, a hockey veteran of junior and minor league coaching, scouting, and player personnel, was named as the team's first GM and later its first coach. It would be his job to set about the difficult task of selecting the team's first 20 players from a dispersal draft pool of players from the original six teams. So, with the first pick, Blair opted to draft a young goaltender from the New York Rangers by the name of Cesare Maniago, who was already known by the locals from his minor league playing stint with the Minneapolis Bruins of the CPHL. Among the other skaters he chose that day included two diamonds in the rough from Boston: Wayne Connelly and Bill Goldsworthy. Goldsworthy, of course, would emerge as the team's first superstar, carrying the franchise on his back for its first decade of existence.

The Stars were anxious to make an immediate impact in the league, and as a result, gambled away a lot of their future draft picks in order to obtain some immediate talent. Because the established clubs had been stockpiling talent in the minor leagues, they were able to pawn off their youngsters, who were green, as well as their veterans, who were too old, onto the expansion teams. Add to that the fact that the established clubs could bargain with the expansion teams with the lure of cash and future considerations to entice their counterparts to "pass over" their most coveted unprotected players, and it was a mess. Finally, when it was all said and done, Blair was a bit skeptical to say the least about his new roster of has-been's and cast-off's.

"Good Lord," said Blair to his scouting staff after the draft on the 20 players he had just obtained, "just look at this mess. This is supposed to be a major league hockey team. There are only four guys on this list that are major league players. Your job and mine is to unload the other 16 just as fast as we can, any way we can. I'll trade 10-for-one if I have to."

Blair even wanted to stop taking players at one point in the draft, but Clarence Campbell told him that he had to take all 20. With that, the stage was now set. The anticipation for big-time hockey in Minnesota was immense, and season ticket sales soared even well before the team could hit the ice. The team was forced to play its first four games on the road, however, because the arena's new seats weren't quite finished being installed.

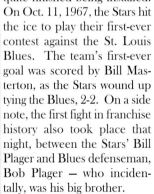

On Oct. 11, 1967, the Stars hit the ice to play their first-ever contest against the St. Louis Blues. The team's first-ever goal was scored by Bill Masterton, as the Stars wound up tying the Blues, 2-2. On a side note, the first fight in franchise history also took place that night, between the Stars' Bill Plager and Blues defenseman, Bob Plager — who incidentally, was his big brother.

Finally, on October 21st the Stars faced off against the Oakland Seals for their inaugural home opener. The packed Met Center crowd, who had seemingly waited a lifetime for the NHL to finally

come to Minnesota, was delighted to see a young blonde-haired kid from Kitchener, Ontario, tally the team's first-ever goal in the new arena. His name was Bill Goldsworthy, but they would soon come to know him simply as "Goldy." The two teams excited the crowd that night with a brand of hockey that Minnesotans had never known before, ultimately skating to a 3-3 tie.

Midway through the season, the Stars would encounter a tragedy that was to influence hockey players of all ages for years to come. On what seemed to be just another normal play in a game that season, winger Bill Masterton was fatally injured after falling and striking his head on the ice. Masterton, a very popular player, was a long-time minor leaguer who was enjoying his first NHL season with the Stars when the accident occurred. (Today all NHL players are required to wear a helmet because of that incident more than 40 years years ago.)

With the memory of Masterton's tragic death on their minds, the Stars played inspired hockey the rest of the way through their inaugural campaign. They finished the regular season with a modest record of 27 wins, 32 losses and 15 ties — good for fourth in the Western Division, just four points out of first. Wayne Connelly led the team in scoring that year with 35 goals and 21 assists for 56 points, while Ray Cullen and Andre Boudrias each chipped in with 53 points as well.

It was off to the playoffs for the rookie North Stars, who were matched against the Los Angeles Kings. L.A.. which was led by goalie Terry Sawchuk, took the first two games of the best of seven series, only to see Minnesota rally back to even the series. The Kings then went up 3-2, only to see the Stars come back one more time to tie it up. Stars forward Milan Marcetta won the sixth game with an overtime goal, and with the momentum on their side, the Stars went on to rout the Kings in Los Angeles, 9-4, to take the series. Minnesota, who scored a club record nine goals to win the quarterfinal contest, would now face St. Louis to determine who would play in the Stanley Cup Finals.

Now, even though the Stars were a hot commodity, they weren't commanding a lot of respect around town, as evidenced by the fact that the powers-that-be who ran the Met Center went ahead and booked the Ice Capades during the second-round of the playoffs. Figuring the team would be swept in the first round, they basically wrote them off — forcing the team to play five of the seven games of the series on the road in St. Louis.

Undeterred, the Stars marched ahead by winning two of the first three games of the series. Game Four was a grinder though. Through the third period the Stars were up 3-0, only to see the Blues tally twice within a two minute span. Then with only 11 seconds to go in the game, Blues Forward Jim Roberts scored his second goal of the game to send it to overtime. Then, only two minutes into the extra session, Gary Sabourin scored on a wrister to win it for the Blues.

Excited to finally play in the Met Center, Minnesota got back on track in Game Five, only to lose another overtime heartbreaker. With their backs against the wall, they came back in front of a packed house and crushed St. Louis in Game Six, 5-1.

The Seventh and final game, which shifted back to the Gateway-Arch City, would go down as a classic. It would come down to which goaltender wanted it more, Cesare Maniago or St. Louis' Glenn Hall. The game was scoreless through the first two periods until Stars Winger Walt McKechnie blasted a goal past Hall with only four minutes to go in the game. But, only seconds later, the Blues would tie it up at 1-1 and force an overtime. Midway through the extra session, Stars winger Wayne Connelly broke loose on a breakaway, only to get mugged by a Blues defender. As Connelly went down, the fans back home thought for sure that there would be a penalty shot issued, but it never came. Deadlocked at 1-1, the teams then headed into double overtime. There, just three minutes into the second OT, the Blues' Ron Shock blasted a slapshot past Maniago for the game-winner. After nearly 83 minutes of fantastic "old-time" hockey, the Cinderella Stars' fairytail season had come to an end. Incidentally, the Blues, who were absolutely spent by the end of this emotional and physical series, went on to get swept by Montreal in the Stanley Cup Finals.

"It was just a phenomenal experience," said Lou Nanne, a Gopher All-American who joined the team shortly after playing in the Olympics that year. "To be able to have NHL hockey right in your own back yard and see it every week was something that I was really excited about. Playing with the North Stars was just a thrill for me and that first season we had a pretty good year, making a great playoff run. The Stars got some credibility after that playoff series with the Blues."

"Sweet Lou From The Soo"

Lou Nanne has become synonymous with the game of hockey in Minnesota. A native of Sault Ste. Marie, Ontario, Louie grew up playing Junior hockey with hall of famers Phil and Tony Esposito. Originally wanting to go to college to be a dentist, Nanne came to Minnesota and played for John Mariucci's Gopher hockey teams from 1961-63. Nanne refers to Mariucci as his "second father," and is forever grateful to him for giving him the opportunity to play hockey at Minnesota.

Earning Gopher captain and All-American honors in his senior year, Nanne tallied a career-high 74 points, becoming the first defenseman to win a WCHA scoring title. For his efforts the newly naturalized American citizen was named as the league's MVP.

"I loved playing hockey at the University of Minnesota," said Nanne, "it was a real privilege. I had tremendous fun all the way through, and it was just a great experience. I really enjoyed the atmosphere, and it was something I will always cherish."

Upon graduating from the University, Nanne was drafted by the NHL's Blackhawks. Nanne got into a contract dispute with the organization, however, and ultimately refused to play for them, which led to a five year lay-off from pro hockey. While he sat out, he worked for Minneapolis businessman Harvey Mackay's envelope company and also coached the Gopher freshman hockey team for four years as well. During that time, he played on and off with the USHL's Rochester Mustangs, and also served as the captain the 1968 Olympic hockey team in Grenoble, France. Then, when the NHL expanded, Nanne became a free agent and decided to play for Minnesota's new expansion team, where he quickly emerged as one of the squad's first stars.

Nanne quickly earned a reputation as being a great all-around player for the Stars. Polished at killing penalties, he also developed into a fine checking forward who was often matched against the other teams' top line. Nanne would go on to play defense and winger for the North Stars through 1978, becoming the only player to play with the Stars in all of the first 11 years of the team's existence. He also represented USA during the 1975 and 1977 World Championships, where he served as team captain. In addition, he played for the U.S. in the 1977 Canada Cup series, and later served as GM of Team USA for the Canada Cup in 1981, 1984 and 1987. For his career with the North Stars, including the playoffs, he tallied 72 goals and 167 assists for 239 points.

In 1978 the All-Star defenseman went from player to coach, and later served as the team's longtime general manager, eventually serving as the team president from 1988-90.

"It was a lot of fun as a general manager, making very important day-to-day decisions, but there is not a better job in the world than actually playing the game on the ice," said Nanne. "Whenever you can

play something that you loved as a kid and get paid for it, well it doesn't get any better than that."

As a GM, Nanne quickly became known as a shrewd wheeler and dealer of talent. He had clout with the other GM's around the league and parlayed that into his favor. For instance, in 1979 he claimed Dave Semenko from Glen Sather's Edmonton Oilers in the expansion draft for the sole purpose of dealing him right back to Sather in a "gentleman's agreement" that would leave Neal Broten available for them in that year's upcoming amateur draft. Neal, of course, went on to become a legend with the Stars. And, of the players on the 1981 Stanley Cup team, only five were left from the roster that Nanne took over in 1978. Bobby Smith was his first pick and Mike Modano would be his last.

Although Canadian by birth, Nanne became a well-known advocate of the Americanization of the NHL. He was one of the first to scout U.S. colleges for American talent and to take an active role in the support of player-development programs, which also included Olympic and international competition. He also wasn't just involved with the North Stars. For his many contributions to USA hockey, Nanne was honored as a recipient of the 1989 Lester Patrick award. And, in 1998 he was inducted into the U.S. Hockey Hall of Fame.

Possibly the most recognized hockey figure in the "State of Hockey," Nanne is extremely well liked and respected by his peers. He had been a fixture with the North Stars from start to finish and is the authority on hockey in Minnesota today. His quick wit, colorful sense of humor and knowledge of the game also landed him several TV commentating jobs, including Stanley Cup playoffs and Finals for "Hockey Night in Canada," CBS and NBC. But his favorite colorman gig is still covering the annual State High School Hockey Tournament, something he has done now since 1964. Nanne has also gone on to become a very successful businessman, serving as an executive vice president with the Minneapolis-based Voyageur Asset Management Co. Louie is a winner. Period. In addition to beating prostate cancer, he also wrote a fantastic coffee-table book about the history of his beloved North Stars in 2007.

On the North Stars Moving to Dallas:
"It was like losing a relative, a really disheartening experience for me."

Gopher & North Stars Tombstones: "He always played with the philosophy of never letting anybody beat you because they outworked you."

1967 RUNNER-UP: BOB STEIN

The football Gophers finish with an overall record of 8-2, good for a three-way tie for first place in the Big Ten alongside Purdue and Indiana. Despite the fact that the Gophers had already beaten Indiana that season, 33-7, the Hoosiers were chosen to represent the Big Ten in the Rose Bowl because, according to the rules, Minnesota had played in the big game most recently, in 1961. One of the stars of the team that season was two-time All-American defensive end **BOB STEIN**. Also a two-time academic All-American, Stein would go on to play for eight season in the NFL with Kansas City, Los Angeles, San Diego and Minnesota. He retired in 1975 and went on to become a very successful lawyer and businessman, even serving as the first general manager and president of the NBA's Minnesota Timberwolves when they arrived on the local sports scene in the late '80s.

HONORABLE MENTION: DEAN CHANCE

Pitcher **DEAN CHANCE** throws a pair of no-hitters and wins 20 games for the Twins. Chance, who was acquired in a trade with the Angels just prior to the season, tossed his first no-no on August 6th in a 2-0 win over Boston, and got his second of the season just three weeks later in a 2-1 decision over Cleveland. Chance only pitched for the Twins from 1967-69, but still holds the team record for career ERA at 2.67.

1968

JIM MARSHALL
The Vikings Win Their First Central Division Title

With a year of Coach Bud Grant's conservative play-calling under their belts, and a bunch of new faces on the field, including the addition of new offensive coordinator Jerry Burns, the Vikings came out and posted a much improved 8-6 record in 1968, giving them their first divisional title. Top draft pick Ron Yary, the highly touted Offensive Tackle out of USC, would join the team that year as part of the deal which sent quarterback Fran Tarkenton to New York. Also included in the package were Safety Charlie West, fullback Oscar Reed and quarterback Bob Lee. Safety Paul Krause also came to Minnesota in a trade with the Redskins, while wide receiver John Henderson and linebacker Wally Hilgenberg were claimed on waivers. Krause and West would join an already solid secondary which was led by corners Ed Sharockman, Earsell Mackbee, Dale Hackbart and Karl Kassulke.

After jumping out to a 3-1 start, Minnesota lost three straight, won its next three, dropped two more, and then needed to win its final two games to have a shot at making it into the playoffs. After beating San Francisco, 30-20, the title hung in the balance as the Vikings went off to Philadelphia to meet Grant's former team, the Eagles.

"We had to win our last game against the Eagles to clinch it, and I remember it was snowing and icy," recalled Grant. "We ended up scoring a couple big play touchdowns on a bad field. Usually teams play conservatively on bad conditions, but I had played enough games on bad fields to know that you can make big plays on bad fields easier than on good fields. So we got a couple big plays and won the game. Then we sat in the locker room and listened to the outcome of the Packers vs. Bears game. The Pack won, 28-17, and we had our first divisional title. (Reporter) Sid Hartman was relaying the information over the phone to us. It was a great feeling."

The Vikes then headed east to face the mighty Baltimore Colts in the Western Conference Playoffs. There, led by Coach Don Shula, the Colts went on to defeat Minnesota in a rainy and muddy Memorial Stadium by the final of 24-14. Earl Morrall, who had taken over for Johnny Unitas, was the top ranked quarterback in the league that year and made his presence felt that day by throwing a pair of TD passes. Meanwhile, six-foot-seven, 300-pound defensive end Bubba Smith tattooed Vikings quarterback Joe Kapp to force a fumble which was then returned 60 yards by Mike Curtis, to get the Colts up 21-0 in the third quarter. Kapp rallied the troops late in the game, completing a record 26 of 44 passes for 287 yards, and throwing for a pair of TD passes to tight end Billy Martin and running back Bill "Boom Boom" Brown.

"It was a rough game," said Kapp, who took a bloody beating but played like a hero. "The Colts blitzed us with everything they had, sometimes with as many as a nine men at once, and it caused a lot of problems for us."

After the loss, the Vikings went on to play the loser of the Miami vs. Dallas game, where they lost to the Cowboys, 17-13, in the NFL's "Runner-up Bowl." In that game, rookie cornerback Bobby Bryant returned a punt 81 yards for a touchdown, and Fred Cox kicked two field goals to help Minnesota build a 13-0 lead. But Cowboy quarterbacks Don Meredith and Craig Morton each tossed touchdown passes to rally Dallas to victory.

The Vikings were a team on the rise and one of their emotional leaders, Jim Marshall, played an important role in leading the team to the NFL championship the following season.

"Winning the divisional title in 1968 was very special," said Marshall. "We worked very hard to get there, and we knew that we had a great core of guys that could go even further."

"As for the following season, unfortunately, in our first Super Bowl, we were in a cloud," he added. "I think we felt that there was no way we could lose. We were very confident that we could go out, perform, give our best, and win it all. I was deeply saddened at the loss to Kansas City, but it was a wonderful experience just getting there."

The Iron Man
Jim Marshall was born in 1937, in Danville, Ky., and attended East High School, in Columbus, Ohio. He went on to become an All-American defensive end at Ohio State, and was one of the stars of the 1959 Rose Bowl title team that beat Oregon, 10-7. After playing in the CFL and then with the Cleveland Browns for one season, in 1960, he was acquired by the Vikings, where he anchored one side of the infamous "Purple People Eater" defensive line from 1961-79. The two-time Pro-Bowler also served as the team's captain, an honor extremely fitting of the type of amazing player that he was.

When it as all said and done the numbers were simply astounding. For 19 seasons Marshall somehow played in an NFL record 270 consecutive games, and 302 consecutive regular season and post season games combined. Like dog-years, in football-years that's got to be close to 100 years. One of the reasons he was able to survive that long down in the trenches was because of Bud Grant's willingness and understanding of what made each guy tick. He knew that Marshall hated to practice and would do anything he could go get out of it. So, every now and then, Bud would accommodate one of his many "mystery" illnesses that would pop up from time to time in order to let him take a sauna and get some much deserved rest.

Marshall's legend and lore includes several incredible stories that exemplify the many obstacles he hurdled over the course of his career. For example, a few months before joining the Browns, while stationed at an Army training camp, Marshall was stricken with encephalitis. Although he lost over 40 pounds, he still reported to camp and insisted on playing. Marshall was a warrior in the best sense of the word. He loved adventure and on more than one occasion it nearly killed him, literally. In 1964, while cleaning his gun, Marshall accidentally shot himself in the side. Once during training camp, he was hospitalized when a grape, of all things, became lodged in his windpipe. Another time, while visiting the U.S. troops during the Vietnam War, he underwent a tonsillectomy that resulted in severe hemorrhaging.

In 1971, Marshall almost died in a snowmobile accident on a trip throughout the Grand Teton Mountains in Wyoming. After his snowmobile went over a cliff and nearly crushed him in the midst of a blizzard, his group was forced to burn $20 bills to keep warm on their three-day ordeal. Marshall later said, "It was the toughest thing I've ever encountered in my life, I thought we were all going to die." As a matter of fact, one member of his 16 person group did. Then, in 1980, he survived a near-fatal motorized hang-glider accident. He was an enigma, and that's one of the reasons why everybody loved him so much. It was as if they wanted to live their own lives vicariously through him.

How he played through all of those injuries that would keep 90% of today's players out of the line-up is unconscionable. He played for the love of the game and lived for Sundays. Perhaps former teammate Ahmad Rashad summed it up best when he described Marshall as "A Viking among men and a giant among Vikings."

On his unbelievable durability and ability to play through pain, Marshall would modestly reply, "I played because I loved the game."

One of the initiation rituals for many Vikings rookies was to make the road-trip to training camp in Mankato, with Marshall behind the wheel. For most humans that trip took ninety minutes, but Jim usually made it in about 45 minutes, with the rookies screaming the entire

52

way. He just loved adventure, wherever it presented itself.

But there is also another side of Marshall — the one who studied Oriental philosophy, wrote poetry and even modeled men's clothing. He once took a brokerage test and was given a genius rating. He described life like this: "Life is wonderful, with so many things to be enjoyed. I think too many times we restrict ourselves to a small box with a limited wish list on each wall. I like to raise my head above the walls and look out into the horizon and think about all the possibilities that are out there to better enjoy my life. That outlook makes life interesting. It gives you the opportunity to grow as a person. I want to enjoy everything as much as I can while I still occupy this physical body. Because one day, when I no longer have this earthly vehicle, I want to feel as though I truly had an opportunity to enjoy everything that was available to me."

Known simply by his teammates as "the captain," Marshall will always be remembered as a Vikings legend. Fittingly, on Nov. 28, 1999, in a game against the San Diego Chargers, the Vikings celebrated "Jim Marshall Day," officially retiring his No. 70 jersey in front of a thrilled and appreciative sell-out Metrodome crowd.

Another way Jim will always be remembered, for better or for worse, is the now infamous "Wrong-Way-Play." In 1964, while playing in San Francisco against the 49ers, Marshall was involved in a play that will forever be a part of NFL film anthologies. During the game, he picked up a San Francisco fumble and ran for the end zone — only it was the wrong end zone! He motored 66 yards right into his own end zone, in the process handing the 49ers two points for a safety. Luckily though, to Marshall's considerable relief, the Vikings still beat the Niners, 27-22.

When asked about the play Jim said, "It was very simple in my mind. It was one of those things where I just got all turned around. I picked up the ball and thought I was going the right way. Of course I wouldn't have run at all if I didn't think I was going the right way. So I crossed the goal-line and threw the ball out of bounds to celebrate, and then, Bruce Bosely, a 49er, ran up to me and said, 'Thanks Jim!' He was giving me the razz, and then it hit me. Uh oh, I had really done something bad. But, what nobody remembers is that during that game, I went back and caused the fumble that Carl Eller picked up to score the game-winning touchdown. They don't talk about that now do they?"

Today Jim is a cancer survivor who enjoys giving back to his community. He participates in a wide variety of civic and volunteer activities and is involved in fund raising for many worthwhile organizations that support kids in need. He also co-founded Life's Missing Link Inc., a non-profit organization dedicated to helping inner-city youth realize their potential and find a better way of life than doing drugs or participating in gang warfare.

Most Memorable Game?

"We were playing the Rams in the playoffs, and they were on the one-foot line ready to score the game-winning touchdown. But we dug in, held them, and eventually blocked a kick to win the game. It was an amazing experience."

When Were You Happiest in Your Career?

"The early 1970s and particularly 1970, when we lost to the Niners in the playoffs, 17-14. We had our best team that year, maybe of all time. It was unfortunate that one bad call by the referee changed everything. Overall, it was my happiest season and also the saddest season at the same time. I really felt like we were headed back to the Super Bowl."

Vikings Tombstone:

"I would like to be thought of as a guy who gave everything he had to give on the football field and did whatever was necessary for his team to help win the game. I had fun doing it, and I tried to give the best that I could give to win."

TRIBUTES

"Jim Marshall was one of the finest athletes I have ever coached," said Bud Grant. "He had durability, and that was the greatest ability you could have. He was one of the finest competitors the Vikings have ever had, period."

"He was the best," said Carl Eller. "He epitomized the term 'Viking.' I am still very good friends with Jim, and I cherish our friendship very dearly. Together we went through a lot out there and he was just a fabulous football player. He was so quick off the ball and was just fearless. I have a lot of respect for him as a player and as a person."

"Jim was a phenomenal football player and a really good friend," said Alan Page. "He is somebody who was dedicated and committed to the game of football and to his franchise. I guess the best way to describe him would be when you look up the definition of professional football in the dictionary, you should find Jim Marshall's name."

"Jim Marshall was our leader," said Chuck Foreman. "A guy that anybody would follow. He is a unique man in that he had the greatest mind control of anybody I've ever seen. He was the heart and soul of the Minnesota Vikings."

"Captain Marshall! Man, he was fearless," said Ahmad Rashad. "He was the epitome of a football captain. He should definitely be in the Pro Football Hall of Fame. No, they should have a separate wing in the Hall of Fame just for him."

"To me, aside from being a magnificent player, Jim was the spirit of the Vikings," said Joe Kapp. "He represented the essence of spirit and leadership. There would be no player who would stand up more for basic, fundamental, consistent values in team sports than Jim Marshall. He was always there for his teammates on and off the field, and he is a wonderful person."

1968 RUNNER-UP: CONNIE HAWKINS

The Minnesota Muskies, under coach Jim Pollard, complete their first season as members of upstart American Basketball Association (ABA). The team finishes the season with the second best record in the league, at 50-28, and advances on to the Conference Finals. There, after beating Kentucky in the semis, the team loses to the Pittsburgh Pipers, and future NBA Hall of Famer **CONNIE HAWKINS**. The Muskies then move to Miami, that off-season, and are replaced with the Pittsburgh franchise that had just gone on to beat New Orleans for the ABA title. The "new" Minnesota Pipers, led by Hawkins, which played games at both the Met Center as well as the DECC in Duluth, finished the season in fourth place with a 36-42 record. They then lost in the first round of the playoffs to the former Muskies, the Miami Floridians, in seven games. With that, the Pipers packed up and promptly moved back to Pittsburgh — thus ending the ABA's wild ride in Minnesota.

HONORABLE MENTION: DUANE BAGLIEN

The Edina Hornets boys basketball team's (national record) winning streak of 69 straight games is finally broken by Richfield, thus ending the "Edinasty." Led by center Bob Zender and coach **DUANE BAGLIEN**, the team won three straight state titles from 1966-68. Baglien also led the baseball team to a title that year too.

The Vikings finally turned the corner as one of the NFL's premier teams in 1969, going 12-2 and earning a trip to their first ever Super Bowl. Being seen on Sunday afternoons at the Met was the "in" thing to do by this time, as tail-gating outside of the old stadium had taken on a life of its own by now. The fans were crazy for the purple and the team was front-page news on a daily basis. Led by their emotional leader, quarterback Joe Kapp, the Vikings embraced a new campaign slogan for that season called "40 for 60," which meant that 40 men playing together for 60 minutes, couldn't lose.

The season started out on a downer, however, as the Vikes lost their opener, 24-23, to Fran Tarkenton's New York Giants in Yankee Stadium. Minnesota rebounded to pound Baltimore that next week, 52-14, thanks to Kapp's amazing seven-touchdown performance. He connected with everybody on that "spiritual" day including: Dave Osborn, Bobby Grim, Kent Kramer, John Beasley, Jim Lindsey, and a pair to Gene Washington. That next week against Green Bay, the Vikings made history by playing at the U of M's Memorial Stadium. (The Twins were playing Baltimore in the American League playoffs that day at the Met, so they got kicked out.) No problem though, as the Vikes went on to beat the Pack, 19-7.

From there, Minnesota didn't look back, as the team's unstoppable defense led them to a record 12 consecutive victories. In Week Three the "Purple People Eaters" sacked Bart Starr eight times, only to sandwich Chicago's Bobby Douglass nine times just four weeks later. In Week Eight the Vikings scored on their first nine possessions en route to a 51-3 win. In Week 10 Safety Paul Krause picked-off Pittsburgh quarterback Dick Shiner and took off 77 yards for a touchdown. The score put the Vikes into the lead, and they went on to crush the Steelers, 52-14. In Week 12 they beat the Rams out in L.A., 20-13, ending the "lamb's" 11-game winning streak. After beating the 49ers the next week, Minnesota found itself with a 12-game winning streak — the NFL's longest in 35 years. Only a 10-3 loss in a torrential rainfall down in Atlanta, against former Vikings coach Norm Van Brocklin's Falcons, in the season finale (with Grant resting many of his starters for the playoffs), prevented the team from winning 13 in a row.

The Vikings were by far the NFL's best team that year, scoring the most points in all of pro football and yielding the least by an unthinkable 379-133 margin. (Their average of 9.5 points allowed per game was the lowest since World War II.) So, with their Western Conference championship in hand, they prepared to battle the Rams in the playoffs.

On Dec. 27, in front of some 48,000 frozen fans at the Met, the Vikes played the Rams in a game that ranks as one of the most exciting in team history. The Rams, guided by their fiery coach, George Allen, were led by defensive stars Merlin Olsen and Deacon Jones, as well as quarterback, and NFL MVP, Roman Gabriel. L.A. went up early in this one, scoring early off the recovery of Bill Brown's fumble. Minnesota then rallied back behind a thunderous crowd that the players had never seen the likes of before. With the fans stomping and absolutely going nuts, the Vikes drove 75 yards to tie the score on Dave Osborn's tough one-yard dive up the middle. The Rams answered though, only to take a 17-7 lead on a field goal, followed by a two-yard touchdown pass from Roman Gabriel to Tight End Billy Truax just before half-time. The Vikings roared back in

the third quarter behind a 41-yard pass from Kapp to Gene Washington which set up another Osborn one-yarder to make it 17-14. Kapp then took over late in the fourth quarter, capping a 65-yard drive by plunging into the end-zone for a two-yard touchdown. Then, with just a few moments left to go in the game, Carl Eller crashed into the end-zone to sack Gabriel for a safety that secured a dramatic 23-20 victory.

From there, Minnesota went on to face the Cleveland Browns in the NFL Championship Game. The stage was now set. The field was slick, the sidelines out at the Met were piled with snow, and the frigid eight degree temperature made the illusion of Minnesota's cold weather invincibility even more intimidating. Joe Kapp started it off by hitting Gene Washington for a 33-yard gain when he beat cornerback Walt Sumner, who had slipped on the icy field. Kapp then ran over a couple of Brown defenders to score on a seven-yarder. Shortly thereafter, Kapp connected with Washington on a 75-yard bomb to give the Purple a 14-0 first quarter lead. After Fred Cox nailed a 30-yard field goal, Dave Osborn then chewed off 20 of his game-high 108 yards rushing by finding the back of the end-zone late in the second quarter. Cox then added another 32-yarder late to seal the team's first-ever NFL Championship, 27-7. With that, Minnesota had become the first modern expansion franchise to advance to the Super Bowl.

After the game the players, bloodied, cold and battered, all celebrated with a champagne party in the lockerroom. For that moment, it was all about a bunch of kids, Black, White and Latino, who had all come a long, long way. They would now go on to face the AFL champion Kansas City Chiefs in Super Bowl IV in New Orleans.

More than 80,000 fans crowded into Louisiana's Tulane Stadium on January 11, 1970, to watch the Vikings do battle with the Chiefs in what would prove to be the AFL's last-ever game. That's because the 10-year-old AFL would merge that following season with the NFL, despite the notion by most gridiron fans that the AFL was inferior to the NFL with regards to quality of play and calibre of players. And, because the Jets dispelled that very notion just the year before by shocking the mighty Colts in Super Bowl III, many were expecting Minnesota to restore the balance of power back to the established NFL. The oddsmakers also agreed with that sentiment, declaring the Chiefs, who lost to Baltimore in Super Bowl I, as two-touchdown underdogs.

Kapp, bothered at suggestions made by the media that he lacked a classic throwing style, was quoted as saying: "Classics are for Greeks. Who is a classic quarterback? I think I can play some ball."

Before the game, a hot-air balloon with the Vikings logo on it crashed into the stands, nearly decapitating a group of nearby Sugar Bowl Princesses. It was, sadly, a dreadful omen of things to come. The Chiefs, led by quarterback Len Dawson's short, precision passing, picked apart the now world-famous "Purple People Eater" defense. On the other side of the ball, the Chiefs huge defensive linemen simply out-muscled the smaller Vikings on the line of scrimmage, stuffing Minnesota's highly touted running game. In addition, the Chiefs used an elaborate trapping scheme to neutralize the Vikings great pass rushers, Alan Page and Carl Eller, who were blitzing from the ends. To make matters worse, leading the way for the Chiefs defensively were a bunch of ex-Gophers: Bobby Bell, Aaron Brown and Bob Stein. Very methodically, and without flash, Kansas City dominated the game — capitalizing on five very costly Minnesota turn-overs.

The game started out rough for the Vikings when Charlie West bobbled the opening kick-off and lost the wind-blown offering, giving the Chiefs the ball deep in purple territory. Jan Stenerud then kicked the first of his three field goals in the first half, ultimately giving the Chiefs a 9-0 lead midway through the second. West then fumbled the ball again on the kick-off following Stenerud's third field goal at the Vikings' 19-yard line. A few plays later Kansas City's Mike Garrett scored on a five-yard run, as the Chiefs went into the locker room at the half up 16-0. Needless to say, coach Bud Grant was not pleased.

The Vikings came out primed in the second half and appeared to be mounting a rally when they forced the Chiefs to punt. They then capped off a 69-yard, 10 play drive with a Dave Osborn four-yard touchdown run. Kapp had driven the team down masterfully, hitting wideout John Henderson for a key first down to keep the drive alive and set up the touchdown. (Incredibly, Minnesota didn't even get a first down until the second half!) The Chiefs didn't flinch though, as Dawson drove down after the ensuing kick-off and hit Otis Taylor for a 40 yard touchdown. It would be the final nail in the coffin.

Minnesota had three possessions in the fourth quarter but couldn't capitalize, as each drive ended in an interception. The final blow to the Purple came midway through the fourth, when Kapp, battered and injured, had to be helped off the Tulane Stadium field after badly injuring his shoulder while being sacked. Back-up signal caller Gary Cuozzo then came in and completed two passes: one to the Vikings and one to the Chiefs. Adding insult to injury was the Chiefs' bombastic coach, Hank Stram, who, while wired with a microphone during the game for NFL Films, said of the Vikings: "They can't figure us out. They don't know what they're doing. It's like a Chinese fire drill out there!" Although the 23-7 loss to the Chiefs stunned the Minnesota faithful and most of the NFL, it did not diminish the accomplishments of an otherwise fantastic season.

As Tough as Nails

Joe Kapp grew up as a sports fanatic in southern California and later attended the University of California at Berkeley, where he played football and basketball for the Golden Bears. At Cal he quarterbacked a Rose Bowl football team and even played on a couple of championship basketball teams as well. After graduating, he decided to head north of the border to try his luck in the Canadian Football League. There, he would ultimately play for eight years with Calgary and then British Columbia, where he won a Grey Cup as a member of the Lions.

In 1967 Kapp was lured to Minnesota by an old CFL colleague by the name of Bud Grant, who was now coaching the Vikes. Minnesota had just dealt Fran Tarkenton to New York and needed a veteran signal-caller. Kapp obliged and became an instant fan-favorite in Minnesota. He was a throwback and played simply for the love of the game. He had the mentality of a linebacker and actually loved to punish his would-be tacklers by putting his head down and letting them have it. He occasionally threw spirals, but seemed to be able to will his team to victory on pure heart and emotion alone.

Following the season Kapp was named as the team's MVP, but he turned down the award, citing the fact that there was no most valuable player on a team of 40 men working together. (Incidentally, Joe bought a Mustang convertible with his Super Bowl bonus money, and still drives it today!)

After three seasons in Minnesota, Kapp got into an ugly contract squabble and wound up being shipped off to the Boston Patriots, where he would begrudgingly play one more year before hanging up the cleats for good.

Kapp led the Vikings in passing all three years he played for the purple with 4,807 yards on 351 of 699 attempts. He also tossed 37 touchdowns while surrendering 47 interceptions. He left the game, not necessarily on his own terms, but will always be remembered as one of the guttiest players in NFL history. Among his many honors and accolades, Joe is a member of the Canadian Football Hall of Fame, the

College Football Hall of Fame and the University of California Hall of Fame.

The man Sports Illustrated once called the "Toughest Chicano of all-time," Kapp later became head football coach at his alma-mater, Cal. In fact, Kapp was the coach during "The Play," the famous 1982 five-lateral kick-off return by the Cal team to score the winning touchdown on the final play against rival Stanford. Kapp also served as the GM of the British Columbia Lions as well. Kapp later got the acting bug and went on to appear in a number of movies. Today he resides in Los Gatos, Calif., where he owns a restaurant and has four children.

Viking Tombstone:

"When I played, the effort showed, and I think that's why people appreciated me as a player. You accept the responsibility of playing quarterback for a team and building excellence takes value points such as toughness, determination, persistence and fortitude. All of the those are things that a player brings with him, in addition to skill, and those are the things that make winners."

TRIBUTES

"Joe was a football player who probably did not have a sense of what was good for Joe Kapp as an individual," said Carl Eller. "In other words, what Joe was about was what was good for the team. It didn't matter whether it was good for Joe or not, he was a true team player."

"Joe is a guy that you would want to be in an alley fight with," said Jim Marshall. "He would do anything that was necessary to get that ball down the field and to make something happen. He didn't throw the prettiest passes in the world, but, he threw winning passes. It didn't make any difference what his passes looked like; they always got to his target. He made some great efforts in the short time he was with the Minnesota Vikings. He is one of my most dear friends, and I am so respectful of his ability and his qualifications. Most of all I'm respectful of the attitude and toughness that he brought to the team. No quarterback that I know of ever had that kind of toughness, period. I've seen him fight linebackers, and come out winning. I've seen him put guys like Jim Houston, one of the toughest all-pro defensive ends in the league, out of a game. He didn't care who you were, he was going to hit you as hard as you were going to hit him. As soon as that ball left his hand he was looking to deliver a blow to someone who was coming at him. You don't find that anymore. He was a genuine throwback to the earliest days of professional football."

1969 RUNNER-UP: BILLY MARTIN

The Twins, led by first year manager **BILLY MARTIN**, win the newly created American League Western Division with a record of 97-65, but lose to the Baltimore Orioles in the American League Championship Series. Game One saw Baltimore's Mark Belanger score on a Paul Blair squeeze play in the 12th to give the O's a dramatic 4-3 win. Game Two was another pitchers duel, with Minnesota's Dave Boswell scattering seven Baltimore hits over 10 scoreless innings before giving the reins to Ron Perranoski in the 11th. O's Pitcher Dave McNally gave up only three hits in this one, and it all came to an end when pinch hitter Curt Motton lined a single off of Perranoski to score Boog Powell in the 11th. In Game Three, back at the Met, Baltimore pounded Minnesota's pitchers for 18 hits, while Jim Palmer cruised to the easy 11-2 series-clinching win. The infamous Martin, meanwhile, was fired that off-season following a brawl in Detroit with one of his pitchers, Dave Boswell.

HONORABLE MENTION: DANNY GRANT

The North Stars finish in just sixth place in 1968-69, with an 18-43-15 record. One bright spot, however, was the play of winger **DANNY GRANT**, who earned NHL Rookie of the Year honors that season after leading the team in scoring with 65 points. Grant would play in the NHL for 14 seasons, scoring 535 career points.

1970

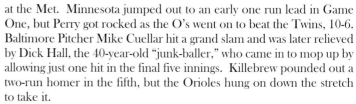

TONY OLIVA
The Twins Win the West

Led by All-Star right fielder Tony Oliva, the Minnesota Twins won the American League Western Division for the second year in a row in 1970. This was indeed a wild year for Minnesota baseball, and it all started out with a pre-season managerial change. The popular Billy Martin, who had led the Twins to an impressive 97-65 record and the American League West title only the year before, was fired by owner Calvin Griffith and replaced with former Minneapolis Miller player-manager Bill "Captain Hook" Rigney. (Rigney earned his nickname "Captain Hook" because he used to pull his pitchers early and often when they got into hot water out on the mound.)

There was endless speculation as to why the fiery Martin was fired. Maybe it was because he punched the Twins traveling secretary; or maybe it was his fight he got into outside a Detroit bar; or possibly it was because he publicly aired his grievances about the Twins front office management to the press. Regardless of the reason, the fact remained that Calvin canned him. The whole mess didn't bode well with the fans. *"Bring Billy Back"* bumper stickers were everywhere, and there was even a country-western song that uttered, *"Are you leavin' Billy Martin? It's a shame, it's a shame."*

But Rigney, the Twins new skipper, ignored the distractions and went on to guide his team to an impressive 98-64 record and their second straight Western Division title. The season started off well for the Twins. But, midway through the season, Pitcher Luis Tiant broke his shoulder, so the Twins brought up a 19-year-old rookie to replace him by the name of Bert Blyleven. Blyleven went on to have a pretty good year, winning 10 games for the Twins. One of the highlights that season came on May 20th in a 10-5 win over the Kansas City Royals, when Rod Carew became the first Twin ever to hit for the cycle. (Carew had his knee torn up by a runner at second base early that year though, and sat out for much of the season as Frank Quilici and rookie Danny Thompson filled in for him.)

The pitching staff was led by Jim Perry (the brother of future Hall of Famer Gaylord), who, with 24 wins, a modest 3.03 ERA, and 168 strike-outs, became the first Twin ever to win the Cy Young Award. And, whenever Perry needed help, Closer Ron Perranoski came in to mop up. Perranoski's American League leading 34 saves, combined with Stan Williams' 15, made up the best bullpen in the league. Throw in Jim Kaat and Tom Hall, and statistically the Twins had the second best pitching staff in the AL.

The Twins bats were also hot in 1970, as Harmon Killebrew hit 41 dingers with 113 RBI's, while Rod Carew, Cesar Tovar and Oliva all hit .300 or better. As a team, the Twins would lead the American League in batting. Individually, Tony-O had another fabulous season, cranking out the most hits in the American League for the fifth consecutive year, with 204, and once again leading his club to the post-season. He led the team in batting with a .325 average, while driving in 107 RBI's, scoring 96 runs and hitting 23 homers. He also hit a league-leading 36 doubles as well.

The Twins, champions of the American League West, entered the 1970 playoffs in a rematch of the year before with Baltimore. Being swept by the Orioles the season prior, observers might have presumed that some sort of revenge factor would've been motivating the Twins. Needless to say, they were wrong in their presumption.

On October 3rd, the Twins opened the American League Championship Series at the Met. Minnesota jumped out to an early one run lead in Game One, but Perry got rocked as the O's went on to beat the Twins, 10-6. Baltimore Pitcher Mike Cuellar hit a grand slam and was later relieved by Dick Hall, the 40-year-old "junk-baller," who came in to mop up by allowing just one hit in the final five innings. Killebrew pounded out a two-run homer in the fifth, but the Orioles hung on down the stretch to take it.

In Game Two it got a lot worse. Baltimore topped their first game power surge by crushing the Twins, 11-3, despite homers by Oliva and Killebrew. Baltimore held a close 4-3 lead after eight and then exploded in the 9th, peppering Perranoski and Luis Tiant for seven runs, including a Davey Johnson three-run homer.

Back in Baltimore for Game Three, Rigney pitted Kaat against Jim Palmer. It wasn't even close, and Earl Weaver's Orioles went on to complete the sweep. Palmer struck out 12 and allowed just six Minnesota hits in this one as Kaat was replaced in the third by Blyleven. Baltimore scored five runs in the first three innings and another in the eighth to ice it. In the first two years of the ALCS the Twins were 0-6 with all six losses coming at the hands of mighty Baltimore. The O's would go on to win the World Series, shutting down Cincinnati's "Big Red Machine" in just five games.

"Losing two years in a row to the Orioles was tough," said Tony Oliva, who batted .500 in the ALCS. "After the first game, I thought that we had a chance to beat them, but we lost a very tough playoff series to a really good team. That year was a lot of fun and winning the West for the second time was a real thrill. We had a great ball club back then and it was too bad that we just couldn't make it past that next round to get to the World Series like we did in 1965. There were a lot of great players on that 1970 team, and we were really like a family."

Regrettably, for the Twins, this would be the end of the line for a while as the team would struggle over the next several years. For the previous six seasons the team had played outstanding fundamental baseball, but would go downhill quickly from there. After the season Bob Allison retired. Killebrew, although one of the game's best ever, never again hit more than 28 home runs, and Tony-O would go on to suffer a series of knee injuries which would hobble him for years to come. Perry, Kaat and Blyleven were a solid 1-2-3 starting rotation, but the team just couldn't get anything going after that. They had holes in their infield and could not find an effective stopper either. As Minnesota was aging, the Oakland A's were coming of age — and it was soon to be their turn to shine in the American League West.

Oh, Tony-O

Pedro "Tony" Oliva grew up in the western province of Cuba, on his family farm in Pinar del Rio, about 100 miles from Havana. There, he went to school through the 8th grade in a two-room wooden schoolhouse. He grew up as one of 10 kids — five boys and five girls. (He told his father he was a lucky man because he had hit .500!) Baseball consumed his life as a young boy, and it would ultimately be his ticket to prosperity.

"When I was a boy, we would help my father with the work on the farm after school, and then play baseball," said Oliva. "We grew tobacco, oranges, mangos, potatoes, corn, and raised cows, pigs, chickens and horses. My father loved the game and always found time for my brothers and me to play it. He helped all the kids play and enjoy the game by going to Havana to buy gloves, bats and balls for us. Once, he came back to the farm with nine gloves. We kept them in our house and when the kids came to our farm to play, they used them."

Oliva got his big break when he was spotted by Cuban scout "Papa" Joe Cambria, who brought him to the United States for a tryout. His teammates on his Cuban team even chipped in to buy him some clothes for the big trip.

"Since I didn't have a passport, I had to use my brother, Antoine's. So, everyone started calling me Tony," said Oliva. "I found that I liked the name even better than Pedro, so I didn't ever tell anyone my real name."

The newly christened Tony was invited to training camp with the Twins, and in 1961, he led the rookie league with a .410 average. After one-year stints in Class A and AAA, he got called up to the Majors in 1964. Oliva wasted little time in making a name for himself, hitting .323, and becoming the only rookie ever to win the league batting title. He was even named Rookie of the Year, earning every penny of his lavish $7,500 salary.

That same year, Tony got a new teammate from his native Cuba, Zoilo Versalles. The two became instant pals. "Best roommate I ever had," said Versalles of Oliva. "He doesn't smoke, doesn't drink, and doesn't snore. All he does is eat, sleep, and breathe baseball."

Oliva would go on to become one of the greatest players in Twins history. One of the highlights of his career was when he led the Twins to the World Series in 1965, his sophomore year, winning another batting crown en route to being named A.L. Player of the Year.

"It was a great series and something I will never forget," said Oliva. "I look at it this way, there were two champs — one from the American League and one from the National League. But, only one team can win when you play seven games. Anything could've happened that last game, and we got beat by the Dodgers."

Tony won a Gold Glove in 1966 and captured a third batting crown in 1971. In 15 seasons, six of which were affected by a knee injury, Oliva finished with 1,917 hits, 220 home runs, 947 RBI's and had a career batting average of .304. His prowess as a hitter was demonstrated by the fact that he led the league in hits five times. An eight-time All-Star, Tony's No. 6 was officially retired on July 14, 1991.

From 1962-76 Oliva was simply awesome. He could hit for power and average, as well as run, field and throw. His versatility made him one of the most feared hitters of his day. If not for agonizing knee problems which cut short his career, Oliva would have been a certain choice for the Hall of Fame. Tony finally retired from the game in 1976 and began coaching for the Twins. Incredibly, he has been there ever since, working as a hitting instructor in the Twins minor league system, while also serving as a scout for the club as well.

Tony-O will forever be remembered as one of the Twins all-time greats. From his infectious smile to that Cuban accent that is as strong today as it was 40 years ago, he is a real living legend and a true treasure for Minnesota baseball.

A Twins Legend
"I would like to be remembered as a ballplayer that gave 100 percent and also as a person that was able to get along with everybody," he said. "I think the fans here in Minnesota are great, and it was a pleasure to play here for them. I have lived here for over half of my life, so my family and I am grateful to the good people of Minnesota."

As far as the Hall of Fame goes, Tony knows that had he not suffered through countless knee injuries in the latter stages of his career that he would be a shoe-in. Let's just hope that the Veterans Committee comes to their senses in the coming years so that this outstanding ballplayer and person can be enshrined into his appropriate place in history. Tony, however, has his own views on baseball immortality and remains cautiously optimistic.

"Everybody thinks I should be in the Hall of Fame except for the people that vote. I feel a little bit disappointed. I think I should be in the Hall because I achieved so much. It was too bad that I got hurt, but there were people that did less in the same amount of time than I did that got in. A lot of pitchers now in the Hall of Fame, who pitched against me, have told me over the years that when they were asked by baseball writers who they felt should be in the Hall that isn't, they said me. I had a lot of great accomplishments in my career, and I hope I can still make it in through the back door."

TRIBUTES
"He was like a brother to me," said Rod Carew. "He was the one who took me under his wing when I was a rookie. He even taught me how to tie my first necktie. He allowed me to be his roommate for nine years, and he taught me how to handle myself and how to handle people. He always had that great smile about him too. He was never upset at people for anything, and that was one of the reasons that even today the people have a great love affair with this guy. He is a tremendous person aside from being a tremendous baseball player. We knew where we came from. We came from nothing — countries where we wouldn't have been able to make the type of living that we were to make by playing professional baseball."

"Here's a guy that deserves to be in the Hall of Fame," said Harmon Killebrew. "He was a Rod Carew type hitter with power. He was one of the finest hitters that I have ever seen. He could hit the ball all over the park and he was the best off-speed hitter that I ever saw. You could throw him 99 fast-balls and one change-up, and he'd hit it out. He was such a great hitter."

"Tony is special to me," said Jim Kaat. "Tony has been short-changed with regards to the Hall of Fame. He was one of the greatest hitters and all-around players in all of baseball. If you were to ask catchers from the 1960s who they feared the most with the winning run on base: Killebrew, Carew, or Oliva, and they would say Tony was the guy pitchers feared most. Jim Palmer and I have talked about that at length and that's how he felt too. Tony was a combination of average, power, speed, and he could drive the ball to produce runs. He was as good a pure hitter as there was."

"I think if you cut his head open, a bunch of baseballs would fall out," said Kent Hrbek. "That's all he knows is baseball. Tony-O was one of my heroes growing up, and I even wore his No. 6 on my first T-ball jersey."

1970 RUNNER-UP: PAUL KRAUSE

The Vikings win the NFC Central Division title with a record of 12-2, but wind up losing to the 49ers in the first round of the playoffs, 17-14. One of the highlights of the season came in Week One, when the purple beat the Kansas City Chiefs in the "Super Bowl Revenge Game," 27-10. Starring on the defensive side of the ball that season was All-Pro safety *PAUL KRAUSE*, who came up with six interceptions. Krause's total of 81 career interceptions over his illustrious 16-year pro career (53 of which came while wearing the purple), is an all-time NFL record that will probably never be broken. Krause was named to eight Pro Bowls, was voted All-NFL four times, and started at safety in four Super Bowls. For his amazing efforts and contributions to the game, the Flint, Mich., native was inducted into Pro Football Hall of Fame in 1998.

HONORABLE MENTION: HAZELTINE INTERNATIONAL

The U.S. Open, pro golf's biggest annual event, is held at *HAZELTINE INTERNATIONAL* in Chaska. Britain's Tony Jacklin, fresh off of his British Open title, endured 40 mph winds on the opening day to outduel the likes of Arnold Palmer, Gary Player and Jack Nicklaus. Jacklin led the tourney from start to finish and was the only player to come in under par — a full seven strokes ahead of his nearest competitor, Dave Hill.

1971

ALAN PAGE
An MVP Season From One of the Best Ever

In 1971 the Vikings reloaded with some new talent. Among the new faces in camp were defensive tackle Doug Sutherland, defensive end Bob Lurtsema, guard Ed White, tight end Stu Voigt, defensive backs Nate Wright and Jeff Wright, and quarterback Norm Snead. Snead would prove not to be the solution the team was so desperately looking for that year though. He was brought in to compete with Gary Cuozzo and Bob Lee for the starting job, but thanks to coach Bud Grant's decision to play musical chairs, they all got to see some action that year.

In the first game of the season Cuozzo got the nod, and responded by sparking the Vikings to a 16-13 victory over the Lions. Then, after a 20-17 home loss to the Bears, Snead came off the bench to take over. While Snead led the Vikings to back-to-back shut-outs over Buffalo and Philadelphia, Grant decided to shuffle the deck once more, this time putting Cuozzo back in for the next five games. Lee's number then got called for four of the final five games of the season, assuring Grant of one thing — he needed a new quarterback.

Over that stretch Minnesota went on to win 11 out of 14, even going nine consecutive quarters at one point without surrendering a point. In addition, their defense, which was led by tackle Alan Page, forced 33 fumbles and 27 interceptions, including seven by Charlie West and six each by Paul Krause and Ed Sharockman, en route to giving up just 139 points — an average of nine points a game. That awesome defense also tallied 49 quarterback sacks for 360 lost yards.

While the team did win their fourth straight NFC Central Division title, the quarterback problem was making more headlines than the team's unbelievable defense, just fueling the debate as to who was going to score the most points each game — the offense or the defense. Clint Jones did rush for 675 yards and receiver Bob Grim was able to catch 45 passes for a modest 691 yards, but the offense was flat. It was the team's achilles heel, and was about to become exposed.

The purple entered the playoffs that year with high hopes of returning to the Super Bowl. It was Christmas day at the Met, and nearly 50,000 Minnesotans were on hand to watch the Vikes do battle with the hated Cowboys. Dallas jumped out to an early lead in this one, going up 6-3 after an early fumble recovery and an interception, which led to two Mike Clark field goals. After kicker Fred Cox answered on a 27-yarder, Dallas exploded in the third quarter for a pair of touchdowns. The first of the two scores came on Cliff Harris' interception which was returned 30 yards to the Minnesota 13. Then, on the next play, running back Duane Thomas took a hand-off up the middle for a 13-yard touchdown. The Viking offense sputtered and was forced to punt again, which led to a Roger Staubach nine-yard touchdown pass to Bob Hayes. Minnesota rallied in the fourth behind an Alan Page safety, followed by a six-yard touchdown pass from Cuozzo

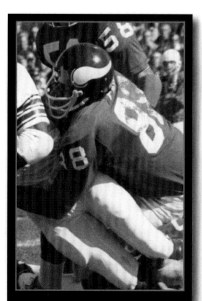

to Stu Voigt, but it was too little too late. Dallas hung on to beat the Vikes, 20-12. Once again, it was the team's inability to hold onto the ball that did them in. Five turnovers, including a pair interceptions each from Bob Lee and Gary Quozzo, negated the fact that the purple actually out-gained the Cowboys in total yardage, 311-183.

The undisputed bright spot of the season, however, was the inhuman play of Alan Page, who simply took his game to another level. His passion for the game was unparalleled and he simply hated to lose. In the Detroit game, Page had a coming out party

of sorts. You see, Page was lightening quick, almost to the point that he made everyone else on the field look like they were in slow motion. It would just so happen that in this particular game the referees weren't that familiar with his ability to get across the line of scrimmage and wreak havoc on the opposing team's offense. As a result, Page was called on two consecutive encroachment penalties for what they perceived as him jumping over the line before the ball was snapped. Page went nuts, threw his arms in the air and demanded justice. He would get none, so he took out his rage on the defenseless Lions, who just had no way of stopping him.

Page released an onslaught of blitzes and bull-rushes that completely destroyed Detroit's game plan. His cat-like quickness proved to be no match for double and even triple teams that were thrown at him. That day he blew threw the line time after time and smothered the Lion's quarterback and halfback from sideline to sideline. He caused a couple of fumbles, had a few sacks and simply took all of the rhythm out of their passing attack. They were all so afraid of him that seemingly everyone on the line had one eye on him, which of course let Eller and Marshall have a feast of their own. When the Lions punted the ball away on that day, it wasn't for strategy, it was to get Page off the field and provide a little mercy for the team's offense. Coaches who later saw the game on film said Page's superhuman performance was a never-before seen case of one lineman somehow being able to dictate the flow of the game all by himself. Said one Lion after the game: "They could call this guy murder. We couldn't block him. He played like we weren't even there. He was unreal."

That season Page posted 10 sacks, 109 tackles, 35 assists, 42 hurries and three safeties. It might possibly have been the single-greatest season ever recorded by a defensive lineman. For his efforts, Page made history by becoming the first defensive player in NFL history of to win the league's MVP, something he later downplayed.

"The MVP award was by somebody else's measure," he said. "Certainly 1971 was a good year for me, but there were other good ones in there too. For me, it was trying to be the best that I could be. That was something that was constant for me, and it wasn't something that took place one year and not in others. When I look back, I look on a whole career, not any one season. I had a lot of success in a lot of successful seasons."

The Honorable Alan Page

After starring on the 1966 Notre Dame NCAA National Championship team as an All-American defensive tackle, Page was selected by the Vikings in the first round of the 1967 draft. The first rookie ever to start for Bud Grant, he would go on to become one of the greatest players the NFL would ever know. Page was selected as a unanimous All-Pro on six different occasions while receiving nine Pro Bowl invitations. From 1967-78 the anchor of the "Purple People Eaters" defense posted 108 career sacks, although, unofficial records show that he recorded 173 sacks. (Sacks weren't counted back in the day like they are now.) In addition, he also recovered 23 opponents' fumbles and blocked 28 kicks and punts. Page was even the inspiration for the now common pass-rushing statistic known as the "hurry," which is issued when a defender forces a quarterback throw the ball before he wants to.

Page was a nonconformist, often bucking heads with Coach Grant. Later in his career he began to attend Law School at the U of M, and even began running marathons. As a result, Page thinned down to about 230 pounds, which was very small for an NFL defensive tackle. Finally, when he went against the wishes of the coaching staff to keep his weight up, he was released on waivers for $100. Undeterred, Page went on to play another three seasons with the Bears before retiring in 1981. When it was all said and done, his numbers were staggering. He had played in 236 straight games, was a four-time Defensive Player of the Year, earned All-NFL honors nine times, played in nine Pro-Bowls, recovered 23 fumbles, blocked 28 kicks and punts, and recorded 173 sacks.

"There really isn't much to think about on a football field," said Page of his retirement. "Playing the game requires physical ability and a tremendous emotional commitment. Intellectually, it doesn't require much. There are a finite number of things that can take place on a football field. After 10 years, you probably have done most of them. Football to me became repetitious and boring."

When Page's career was over he had a homecoming of sorts. You see, he grew up in Canton, Ohio, the home to the Pro Football Hall of Fame, and actually worked on the construction crew that built the museum one summer during the late 1960s. In 1988 he was inducted into that very shrine. However, he did it in typical Alan Page style, declining the opportunity to swap gridiron gossip, as most of the football brethren do at their induction's, and instead shocked the pro football establishment by choosing Willarene Beasley (the principal at Minneapolis North High School) as his presenter. Never in the Hall of Fame's history had a person not in the football fraternity made an induction speech. Page selected her because of the fact that she was an educator and, as a black woman, represented minorities. Alan's speech was about the values of education, not football; about learning to tackle issues, not quarterbacks; and about ABCs, not Xs and Os.

"I wanted to take advantage of that recognition and use the day as a mechanism for something meaningful," said Page, who, following her introduction speech, launched the Page Education Foundation from the steps of the Hall of Fame.

On why Page decided to use that forum to speak of education rather than football, Page recalled a pre-season afternoon practice some years ago, when, during a defensive meeting, one of the coaches asked some of the players to read aloud from the playbook. It was at that moment that Page realized that several of his teammates couldn't read, while several others were struggling to just get by.

"In that moment, listening to my teammates unable to read a simple playbook, everything crystallized for me," Page said. "I don't know why it took me so long to realize it, but at that moment it became clear that this wasn't a dumb-jock problem, or an athletic problem. These men were supposed to learn to read in first, second, or third grade, long before they were football players. You think about something, and you think about it again, but you can't point your finger at it. Well, that day, I realized the problem I wanted to try to address was education. Pure and simple."

Page has a great outlook on life. "I saw a quote once that read that success is not a place where you arrive at, it's a manner of travel. The success and the joy is in working to get there, not getting there. Once you're there, what's interesting about that? I learned that lesson very early on as a football player. When I was selected as the league's MVP early on in my career, I felt that was about as good as it gets in professional football. It was at that point that I figured out that the fun was in the journey, not arriving at the destination. The journey never ends."

Today Page sits on the Minnesota Supreme Court. He had always battled adversity, and his journey to the bench would be no exception. By 1979, Page had earned his law degree and moved from the gridiron to private practice. Soon he was working in the attorney general's office. After spending several years there, he decided to seek an even higher office. Typically, new judges are appointed temporarily

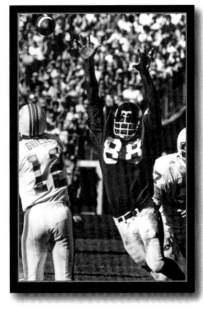

and then elected without competition. But, when his opportunity to run kept being denied, he sued then Governor Arne Carlson. A substitute Supreme Court then ruled in Page's favor, allowing him to run successfully, with opposition, in 1992. As a result, he became the first African-American to sit on the state's highest court — or on any Minnesota state appellate court, for that matter. Today, with his spectacles and trademark bow-tie, Associate Justice Page is a member of the Minnesota Supreme Court. He and his wife Diane live in the Twin Cities and have four children. An avid jogger, Page still remains active in his Page Education Foundation, which to date has helped thousands of minority students attend college.

Vikings Tombstone:
"If I could choose a way to be remembered, it wouldn't be my association with football. Football is in the past — a good past, but nonetheless it is the past. I'd want to be remembered with children — with my children and other children."

TRIBUTES
"As a football player, I feel very proud to have played with Alan Page," said Jim Marshall. "I think he was one of the guys that truly changed the game. They stopped calling holding (penalties) because Alan was so quick and elusive, and he was so disruptive to the other teams. They (referees) intentionally allowed holding on him, because that was the only way anybody could block him. They gave more freedom to offensive lineman in the way they used their hands, and a lot of that was because of his elusive play. Never in the history of the game, and I have looked at film since the beginning of organized football, have there been any rule changes like they made in the 10 years that Alan was out there. Everything changed with the advent of television, and people wanted to see a more potent offensive representation on the field. That handcuffed the defensive teams. Today football is more of a form of entertainment, rather than the sport that it was back in those days. I think a lot of that had to do with the play of Alan Page."

"Alan had a vision about his own personal life," said Carl Eller. "To a great extent, within his greatness, he saw his own limitations. He felt that he really had to do something significant outside of football. I think that Alan felt consumed by his own greatness on the field, and it was probably too much for him. He was a torch-bearer right from the very beginning."

BILL MUSSELMAN
The Gopher Basketball "Iron Five"

The University of Minnesota Golden Gopher basketball program has been through a lot of ups and downs over the course of its history, but one of its most colorful eras involves a coach by the name of Bill Musselman and his unbelievable 1972 Big Ten championship run.

The 1971-72 Gophers, under new Coach Bill Musselman, hit the court with one of the most talented line-ups in the country. In addition to returning upperclassmen center Jim Brewer, forward Corky Taylor, and guards Bob Murphy and Keith Young, Musselman added three junior college transfer players in six-foot-nine swingman Ron Behagen, who had been playing at Southern Idaho Junior College, six-foot-eight forward Clyde Turner, who came over from Robert Morris Junior College (Illinois), and six-foot-three guard Bob Nix, from Henderson County Junior College in Texas.

The JUCO transfers that Musselman brought in were not without controversy though. He knew he needed to surround Jim Brewer, one of the best centers in the country, with some talented new players. So, he went outside the system and got some players who could help him right away. While this is practice is commonplace today, back in the early 1970s it was extremely taboo. Back then, it was just understood that coaches recruited kids, red-shirted them, and developed them. What Musselman did, in the eyes of many coaches, was to take a shortcut, and "cheat" the system. But Musselman didn't care. He had finally arrived to the big-time after paying his dues for many years and simply didn't want to wait around to someday be a contender. He wanted his players to execute a physical, tough rebounding, in-your-face style of basketball, and he now had the tools to do some immediate damage in the Big Ten.

Musselman now had the players but knew he still needed to fill Williams Arena with plenty of fans and excitement. So, this consummate salesman and promoter took his players around the state for intra-squad games to sell tickets. In addition, he even instituted one of basketball's greatest pre-game warm-up shows, which was similar to that of the old Harlem Globetrotters. The pre-game warm-up saw the players enter into a darkened arena, run through a giant spotlight, and form a circle. There, in addition to basketball finger-spinning, they would pass balls back and forth by zipping them through their legs, behind their backs and off their heads. The opposing coaches and players hated it, but that didn't bother Musselman.

"It was the greatest exhibition of ball-handling that a lot of people had ever seen," said Musselman. "It was precision ball handling to music like 'Sweet Georgia Brown.' We used to fill up the arena an hour before game time so that people could watch our warm-up."

The Gophers went into their Big Ten Conference schedule with a modest non-conference record of 6-3. They even picked up a new walk-on player early in the season — a young man who would go on to become a pretty decent athlete in his day. Who was he? Well, in 1971, the U of M intramural basketball champs were a team called the "Soulful Strutters." The Strutters were led by a six-foot-six specimen from St. Paul Central High School by the name of Dave Winfield, who was also a star pitcher on the Gopher baseball team at the time. Now, because the Strutters were the best intramural team on campus, they often-times scrimmaged against the Gopher Junior Varsity squad — usually whipping them pretty good. When J.V. Coach Jimmy Williams saw Winfield play during one of those

games, he couldn't believe his eyes. So, he told Musselman that he better give the kid a look. He did, and immediately asked him to join the team.

The Gophers opened their Big Ten schedule against Indiana at the old Barn, where the second-largest crowd in school history (19,121) showed up to watch Musselman do battle with his old childhood pal from Ohio, Bobby Knight. Turner, Behagen, Nix, and Young all scored in double figures in this one as Minnesota went on to win the game, 52-51, thanks to a blocked shot by Brewer and a pair of last-second free throws by Nix.

Minnesota would add three more victories to go 4-0 in conference play. Their next opponent was Ohio State. It was a big game and everyone knew it. There were several sidebars going in as well — including how Buckeye Coach Fred Taylor didn't appreciate Musselman, a fellow Ohioan, recruiting JUCO kids. The media was all over it too. In fact, while the NHL All-Star Game was being played across town at the Met Center that same night, most of the media attention in the Twin Cities was focused on the basketball game. The Gophers had a chance to move into a first-place tie with a victory and the crowd was pumped. What the fans didn't know, however, was that this particular game would go down as one of the most significant in Minnesota history. This was the game that will forever be remembered as "The Fight" and the beginning of the "Iron Five."

With the Buckeyes leading 50-44 and 36 seconds left in the game, OSU's, star Center Luke Witte broke toward the basket. As Minnesota pressed, Witte outran the field and caught the inbound pass. In the process, he was fouled hard by both Turner and Taylor. Turner was then called for a flagrant foul and was immediately ejected. Then, amazingly and nearly simultaneously, Taylor reached out to help Witte, who was down on the court, up to his feet. But instead of helping him up, he proceeded to kick him in the groin. The crowd was stunned, and subsequent mayhem broke out. OSU's, Dave Merchant rushed over to help Witte, quickly pushing Taylor out of his way. Brewer and Taylor then ran down the court after Merchant, while Behagen, having already fouled out, came off the bench and attacked Witte.

For the next moments, complete pandemonium took over at Williams Arena. The nearly 18,000 fans in attendance were shocked, and many even jumped onto the court to partake in the mayhem. Big Dave Winfield even got into the act and it got ugly in a hurry. Several Buckeye players were taken to the hospital, and a near riot ensued. Minnesota's Athletic Director, Paul Giel, then decided, after consulting with the game officials, to simply end the game and declare Ohio State as the winner. Outside, they started to throw rocks at the police cars as they took the players to the hospital. When it was all over, a huge black eye was left on the University of Minnesota basketball program.

The opposing players had much different stories as to what really happened. "Witte was gong up to take the shot, and Clyde Turner and myself fouled him," said Taylor. "It was really how hard I fouled him that precipitated my helping him up. Basically, it was a situation where he had an easy two points and we were trying to make sure he didn't score. When I went to help Luke up, he spit at me and I got pissed! It was a very tough game, and I kicked him. When I turned around, the entire floor had erupted. It was a scary situation."

To better understand the entire "situation," you have to go back to the end of the first half, where an incident took place that may have instigated it all. As the players ran off the court and into the locker rooms, Bobby Nix waved to the pumped-up crowd by raising his fists in the air towards the scoreboard.

"Witte crossed in front of me," said Nix. "There's no question in my mind or anybody's that saw it. It was a deliberate elbow to my face. He just threw it, and he damn near decked me. It was seen by a lot of people, except the officials."

That night, following the incident, replays of the fight were played on virtually every newscast in the country. Every paper ran a story about it, and the next week, Sports Illustrated even featured the brawl as their cover story. Incredibly, all fingers pointed to Musselman as the instigator. They tried to paint a picture that his "win at any cost" attitude had somehow driven his players into a fit of rage. National media had concentrated only on the game-ending fight, and they never mentioned the half-time incident that precluded the retaliation. Attempts were made to dramatize and polarize Musselman and the Buckeyes' Fred Taylor, the two coaches (both with roots to Ohio). Taylor was a Big Ten coaching legend who built programs traditionally. Musselman, on the other hand, was a rookie who they said took short-cuts to success by obtaining junior college players. Racism and even the Vietnam War were thrown into the stew. People were searching for a scapegoat, and the media had found one in Musselman.

"A lot of things were said in print that were wrong," said Musselman in Bill Heller's 1989 book: "Obsession: Timberwolves Stalk the NBA." "I was blamed for the fight, or for not stopping the fight, yet the fight was the last thing I wanted. My insides were torn up. My hopes and dreams were shattered that night. I couldn't believe life was like that. I believed if you were dedicated and outworked everyone, you'd be successful. That night it seemed like everything I believed in was wrong. I went home and got down on my knees and prayed. And I thought then, 'Well, you asked for this; you wanted to coach in the big time.' Since then, my beliefs have been reaffirmed. But it was my background that got me through that situation. If I hadn't been mentally tough, I wouldn't have survived that incident."

"Obviously the fight was wrong, but I always felt that it was racially motivated," added Musselman several years later. "It was during the early 1970s, and there were a lot of racial overtones. The game got out of hand, and the officials let too much loose play go on. I took a lot of heat for it. It was ridiculous that people would insinuate that I wanted to have a fight. They tried to blame it on my pre-game warm-up routine, saying that it hyped the fans into a frenzy. It was too bad that it happened, but it was an intense heat of the battle thing. The sad part about it was the fact that all the players were good people. Back then our kids never got into any trouble, and they got their degrees. They all made a contribution to society and were all great kids."

Following the game, Behagen and Taylor were suspended for the remainder of the season. (Ohio's governor even suggested publicly that the two ought to be thrown in jail.) The new squad stayed focused though, and even used the suspensions as a personal vendetta to salvage the season. As a result, Musselman went almost exclusively with a five-man lineup: Turner and Winfield at the forwards, Brewer at center, and Nix and Young as the guards — the "Iron Five."

The next game was at Iowa. There were plain-clothed police officers everywhere and the fans were on edge. The Gophers stayed calm, however, and won the game, 61-50. They just kept on rolling from there. Late in the season, with Ohio State reeling in a tail-spin, Minnesota put it all on the line at Purdue with a chance to win the Big Ten title. There, behind Jim Brewer and Clyde Turner's 12-point performances, the Gophers hung on to beat the Boilers, 49-48, thus becoming the first Gopher team in 53 years to win an undisputed Big Ten title. It was an amazing run that nobody could have predicted.

Unfortunately, in their first-ever NCAA Tournament appearance, the team was upset by Florida State, 70-56, in the NCAA Mideast Regional in Dayton, Ohio. They did manage to come back to beat Marquette, 77-72, in the consolation game though.

With the top defense in the nation, the 10th ranked Gophers allowed just 58 points per game that season, finishing with an impressive 18-7 record. Brewer was named as the Big Ten's MVP, and both he and Behagen were named to the All-American team as well. (Incidentally, that next year all five Gophers would be drafted into the ranks of professional basketball.) Musselman, who said going in to the season that he did not believe in "rebuilding years," kept his word and made his first campaign in Gold Country one of the program's most exciting, and dare we say "eventful" in history.

Coach Muss

A native of Wooster, Ohio, Bill Musselman will always be remembered in Minnesota for a lot of reasons. Most importantly though, he will be remembered as a great coach. Attendance nearly doubled at Williams Arena during his four-year career in Gold Country, and he was the impetus, compiling a 69-32 record, for a .683 winning percentage — the best in school history. He rescued the program and, for better or for worse, got people excited about basketball again. Musselman would leave the University in 1975 under the shadow of allegations and investigations by the NCAA.

Musselman's collegiate coaching career included posting a record of 233-84 as a college coach at Ashland, Minnesota and South Alabama. He was also a head coach in four pro leagues as well — the NBA (with the Cleveland Cavaliers and Minnesota Timberwolves — whom he coached for two seasons, 1988-89 and 1990-91), CBA, ABA and WBA, where his overall career record was 603-426. In addition, he was named as the CBA Coach of the Year in 1987 and 1988, winning four consecutive titles with both Rapid City and Albany along the way. He later served as an assistant with the NBA's Portland Trailblazers until his tragic death in 2000, from cancer, at the age of 59.

Gophers & Timberwolves Tombstones:

"I think my teams always played hard and played together," said Musselman. "I think that I have always had the ability as a coach to get the most out of my players, and my teams have always played as hard as they could. I always taught my players to get out of life what they put into it. I think it is important to teach an athlete to be able to face and handle adversity. Mental toughness is important to me, and I always wanted my players to be able to be prepared to handle the good times along with the bad."

1972 RUNNER-UP: BILL GOLDSWORTHY

The NHL All-Star Game is played at the Met Center in Bloomington with the East, led by game MVP Bobby Orr, beating the West, 3-2. Representing the North Stars were **BILL GOLDSWORTHY**, Gump Worsley, Ted Harris and Doug Mohns. Goldsworthy would emerge as the team's first big star, complete with his own signature move — the "Goldy Shuffle," which he would perform after scoring big goals on the Met Center ice. The five-time All-Star was with the team from its inception and played in Minnesota for 11 seasons, scoring 267 goals and 239 assists for 506 career points. His No. 8 was retired at the Met in 1992.

HONORABLE MENTION: HENRY BOUCHA

The U.S. Olympic hockey team wins a silver medal at the 1972 Winter Games in Sapporo, Japan. Among the dozen Minnesotans on the roster was Warroad prep legend **HENRY BOUCHA**, an 18-year-old sensation who many consider to be the state's greatest all-time player. Boucha gained notoriety as a high schooler, when he was injured in an emotionally-charged 5-4 overtime loss to Edina in the 1969 state tournament. Boucha would go on to play in the NHL for six seasons, ultimately having his career cut short due to a brutal eye injury suffered in a 1975 game versus Boston, which ultimately forced him to retire at the age of just 24.

Minnesota recorded one of the greatest turn-arounds in pro football history in 1973, posting a 12-2 record and advancing to their second Super Bowl in just four years. Leading the way was the all-purpose wonder, Chuck Foreman, who was named as the NFL's Rookie of the Year for his 1,163 yards both rushing and receiving. The offense clicked that year because the ground game had forced opposing defenses to respect them. Quarterback Fran Tarkenton took full advantage of the situation too, by throwing for nearly 3,000 yards while hooking up with wide receiver John Gilliam 42 times for eight touchdowns.

The purple jumped out of the gates poised to do some damage in 1973, winning all five of their exhibition games. From there, the squad ran off nine straight wins in the regular season before finally losing at Atlanta in Week 10. They rounded out the season by beating Chicago, 31-13, getting shut-out at Cincinnati, 27-0, and then rebounding to beat both the Packers and the Giants by the identical scores of 31-7, to finish out the regular season at 12-2.

On December 22, 1973, the Redskins came to town to face the Vikes in the first round of the playoffs. It would be a game remembered for two reasons. First, because of the team's great second half comeback, and secondly, because of Carl Eller's half-time motivational speaking speech that ultimately caused the Vikings to have the aforementioned great second half comeback.

Washington got on the board first in this one after Bob Brunet recovered Bobby Bryant's fumbled punt at the Minnesota 21-yard line which resulted in a three-yard touchdown run by Larry Brown. Fred Cox added a field goal in the second, but the lethargic Vikes blew a chance to take a lead at the end of the half when Tarkenton threw an interception.

At half-time, Eller, who played like a man possessed, went ballistic. He screamed, shouted, pounded his fist on metal doors, smashed a chalk board against the wall and challenged every man in that room to give it his all. He was tired of losing big games and wanted more guts from everyone — right then and right there. The rest of the team sat in shock, staring silently, knowing that they had better step it up big-time, or they were going to have to deal with Carl after the game. And that's just what they did. Minnesota came out and took the lead in the second-half, thanks to Bill Brown's two-yard TD plunge which came on the heels of Oscar Reed's 46-yard scamper into the red-zone. Following a pair of Redskin field goals, Tarkenton capped a 71-yard drive with a 28-yard touchdown pass to Gilliam. Nate Wright then intercepted Billy Kilmer on the team's next offensive play, which led to Tarkenton again hitting Gilliam on an eight-yard touchdown pass. Freddy the foot then came in to nail a 30-yarder late in the fourth to ice it for the Vikes as they hung on to win, 27-20.

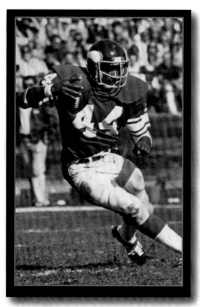

That next week the team headed to Irving, Texas, where they faced the hated Cowboys in the NFC Championship game. Minnesota came out and jumped all over the 'Boys in this one, thanks to an early Fred Cox field goal, followed by Chuck Foreman's five-yard TD run which capped a long, demoralizing 86-yard drive, mostly through the middle of the field. With two of their stars, running back Calvin Hill and defensive tackle Bob Lilly, out of the game with injuries, Dallas just couldn't get it going.

Golden Richards finally put Dallas on the board early in the third quarter when he

returned a punt 63 yards for a touchdown. Minnesota answered though, when Tark found John Gilliam open behind cornerback Mel Renfro for a 54-yard touchdown pass. Dallas added a field goal to make it 17-10, but Quarterback Roger Staubach threw two of his four interceptions in the fourth quarter — one of them right into the awaiting arms of Bobby Bryant, who promptly took it 63 yards for a score. Another interception set up a 34-yard field goal by Cox. Walt Garrison then ended a forgettable day for Dallas when he fumbled the ball away at the Minnesota two-yard line late in the fourth to kill their rally and end it at 27-10 in favor of the Vikes.

With that, the Vikings found themselves in their second Super Bowl, this time at Houston's Rice Stadium, where, on January 13, 1974, they took on Don Shula's Miami Dolphins. Yeah, the same Dolphins that had won 17 in a row just the year before to win Super Bowl VII. Their roster was a venerable who's-who of pro football: Bob Griese, Larry Csonka, Nick Buoniconti, Mercury Morris, Paul Warfield, Larry Little, Garo Yepremian and Jim Langer (a native of Little Falls).

Much of the pre-game excitement and controversy the week before the big game centered around the Vikings' miserable practice facilities at Delmar Field in Houston. You see, sparrows had moved in and built nests in the shower room, where most of the nozzles didn't work, nor did they spit out any hot water. In fact, the locker room didn't even have any lockers, just a bunch of rusty nails on the wall. Needless to say, Coach Bud Grant felt disrespected and was not pleased with the situation.

"This is shabby treatment," Grant told reporters at a press conference. "This is the Super Bowl, not some pick-up game. The NFL sets up the practice facilities and they had a year to do it right. Go look for yourselves, we don't have any lockers. Our seven coaches have to share one table for spreading out our clothes. These facilities definitely give the Dolphins the advantage."

Meanwhile, the prima-donna Dolphins, on the other hand, were working out at the Houston Oilers' plush practice facilities. Secretly, this was just what Grant wanted. He needed a juicy subplot to distract all of the hounding journalists and their endless questions, so he figured that this headline would be better than that involving of any of his players. Plus, it got his players fired up. They were already underdogs coming in, but now they were plenty pissed-off about being treated like second-hand citizens to the media darling Dolphins.

The reporters still hounded the players though, including Viking's tackle Gary Larsen, who found the whole Super Bowl hyperbole to be a bit much. "I hope you don't think I'm a wise guy when I add that we've sweated a long time for this opportunity, and a whole bunch of people will be watching on TV," he quipped. "But there are 800 million Chinamen who don't give a damn about what happens in Houston this Sunday afternoon!"

Maybe Gary was on to something, but all those people who did care about the game saw nothing more than a good old fashioned butt-kicking, as the Dolphins came out and thrashed the Vikes, thus becoming the second team in NFL history to win back-to-back Super Bowls. On paper, the game seemed to be a mismatch from the opening kick-off. You had the 23rd ranked Vikings run defense up against a relentless Miami ground attack, and Miami wasted little time in exploiting Minnesota's weaknesses. Before the Vikings could manage a first down, the Fish were up by the score of 14-0.

Following two time-consuming 62 and 56 yard drives, Miami Fullback Larry Csonka plowed in first on a five-yard run, followed by a Jim Kiick one-yarder. Garo Yepremian then added a 28-yard field goal to make it 17-0 at the half. The Vikings' only chance to get back in the game came late in the first half when they drove down to the Miami five-yard line, only to see Dolphins linebacker Nick Buoniconti crunch Oscar Reed on the next play to force a costly turnover.

Stu Voigt then got called for a clipping penalty during the kick-off to start the second half, negating John Gilliam's brilliant 65-yard return which would've given Minnesota the ball on the Miami 34-yard line. As a result, they were held on downs, and Csonka scored on a two-yard plunge the next series to make it 24-0. Tarkenton, who set a Super Bowl record by completing 18 passes, tried to mount a late comeback by capping a 40-yard drive on a four-yard TD run. He put together another drive with seconds to go, but it was foiled by Curtis Johnson's interception at the Miami goal line to end the game at 24-7.

Just how bad was it? Dolphins' quarterback Bob Griese had to throw only seven passes that entire afternoon, completing six. The 71,882 fans in attendance watched Csonka, named as the game's MVP, set a Super Bowl record by rushing for 145 yards and two touchdowns on 33 carries — doubling the rushing yardage of the entire Minnesota backfield.

"I've never tried to tackle anybody stronger," said linebacker Jeff Siemon of the "Zonk." "Once he got going, he just carried you on his back. He has to be the strongest running back I've ever faced."

"I don't have many good memories of that Super Bowl game against Miami," recalled Chuck Foreman. "There's not much to say except that they beat us on both ends of the ball. Of all the Super Bowls I've played in, that was the only one that I could justify losing in my mind. The Miami Dolphins had more talent and a better unit than we had. Personally, it was an incredibly exciting time for me being Rookie of the Year and playing in my first Super Bowl and all. Miami was the only team that I have ever played against that I could honestly say that they were better than us. It was just a tough loss after coming off the great season that we had."

Forty-Fourman

Chuck Foreman was raised just outside of Washington D.C. in Frederick, MD, where he grew up playing football, basketball and baseball. Originally recruited as a defensive tackle, he made the switch to running back at the University of Miami, where he quickly broke all of the Hurricane's freshman rushing records

In 1973 he was drafted by the Vikings as the 12th overall pick of the first round. The transition to the pro's was a smooth one for the powerful running back, who, after rushing for 801 yards, catching 37 passes, and scoring four touchdowns, was named as the NFL's Rookie of the Year. Not only was he a bruising runner, he also had amazing hands — which made him one of the game's greatest all-time offensive weapons. When he had the ball in the open field it was all over. His spectacular 360-degree spins became his trademark, as he oftentimes left his would-be tacklers dazed and confused in his vapor trail.

"I am sometimes surprised when I look at film of myself," said Foreman of his unorthodox running style in Klobuchar's book: "The First 15 Years." "I just do what's natural out there and live by instinct. It's like when you're riding your bicycle and all of a sudden, a mad dog starts chasing you. There's a little bit of fear in your heart, and you've got to get away. I look at running as an art."

In 1975, en route to leading the Vikings in rushing, receiving, and scoring, No. 44 also won the NFC scoring and receptions titles by hauling in 73 catches — the most ever by a running back. He followed that up the next year by rushing for 1,155 yards, including a 200-yard game against Philly, to be named as the NFC Player of the Year. Then, in 1978, Foreman, the hub of the Vikings offense for five seasons, suffered a knee injury which would ultimately lead to the premature end

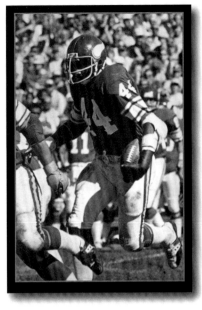

of his incredible career. He gained a career-low 749 yards in 1979 and saw his playing time slowly get gobbled up by back-up Ted Brown. That next season he was traded to New England, where he played one more year before retiring.

Without a doubt, Chuck "Forty-Fourman" was the greatest running back in Vikings history. No one could run the ball with the passion and desire like he did. Sure, Robert Smith was good, but Chuck was special and could do it all. Foreman led the Vikings in rushing for six consecutive seasons, set team records for yards rushing, with 5,879, and also combined yards (rushing and receiving), with 8,936. All in all, he scored 53 rushing touchdowns, while also catching 350 passes for 3,156 receiving yards and 23 receiving touchdowns. Had his knee not gone south on him, there is no telling just how many yards and touchdowns he would have racked up with the purple.

What Did it Mean For You to Be a Viking?

"I was always a big fan of the "Purple People Eaters" so I had to pinch myself when I was drafted by Minnesota. But, before I came up here to join the Vikings, I actually did a lot of research on the team and on its players. I wanted to know who played there and where they were from. I consider it to be a privilege to have been able to perform there."

TRIBUTES

"I think that Chuck was one of the finest running backs in the history of the NFL," said Jim Marshall. "At the peak of his career, he was one of the most highly skilled running backs that ever played the game of football. He was a great player."

"His talent is still unrecognized," said Carl Eller. "He was one the best running backs ever. Chuck was so good that the Vikings didn't realize how good he was. He was a great player, but as great as he was, I don't think they ever used his greatness to its fullest extent."

"It was too bad Chuck didn't play the game a little longer," said Bud Grant. "He was the best back in the league for five years. Running backs take a lot of wear and tear, and it was unfortunate that he got hurt."

"Chuck was the best all-around running back that I ever played with," said Ahmad Rashad. "He was an amazing athlete. He could block, tackle, run, catch and score. Chuck Foreman could just do everything."

"Chuck was just a great running back," said Alan Page. "He had the speed, talent, the moves, and he always came to play."

1973 RUNNER-UP: GLEN SONMOR

The upstart World Hockey Association (WHA), a rival to the NHL, sets up shop at the newly constructed St. Paul Civic Center. Steering the ship is head coach **GLEN SONMOR**, who left his post as the coach of the Gophers to take over as the Fighting Saints' first bench boss. The Saints finished the season with a respectable 38-37-3 record and managed to squeeze into the playoffs, ultimately losing in the first round to the Bobby Hull-led Winnipeg Jets, four games to one. Sonmor would also go on to coach in the North Stars from 1979-82.

HONORABLE MENTION: FRANK BRIMSEK

The United States Hockey Hall of Fame inducts its first ever class in the birthplace of American hockey, Eveleth, Minnesota. Among the initial enshrinees are a handful of Minnesotans, including a goaltending legend from right there in Eveleth by the name of **FRANK BRIMSEK**. Also known as "Mr. Zero," Brimsek didn't waste much time in making a name for himself in the NHL, earning Rookie of the Year honors in 1939 with Boston after posting shut-outs in five of his first six games. A two-time Vezina Award winner, emblematic of the league's top keeper, the two-time All-Star would play in the NHL for 10 seasons, posting a gaudy 2.74 lifetime GAA. In addition, Brimsek was also inducted into the Hockey Hall of Fame in Toronto in 1966.

1974

HERB BROOKS
The Hockey Gophers Win it All

Led by their fiery second-year coach Herb Brooks, the 1974 Gophers made history by winning their first ever NCAA hockey championship. After finishing sixth in the WCHA the season before, the Gophers came full circle that season, proving to the world that Minnesota was indeed the hockey capital of America.

After starting 0-4-1, the Gophers put together a nine-game winning streak that included series sweeps of North Dakota, Michigan State and St. Louis. Minnesota then went on win all but two of it's final 16 home games at Williams Arena, finishing with a 14-9-5 record, good enough for second place in the WCHA behind Michigan Tech.

From there, the Gophers went on to beat tough Michigan and Denver teams in the WCHA playoffs, and then found themselves on their way to Boston, where they would be pitted against the top-ranked, hometown Terriers of Boston University in the NCAA Frozen-Four. The Cinderella Gophers felt right at home in the Boston Garden though, as they proceeded to knock off BU in the semifinals, 5-4, thanks to Mike Polich's short-handed go-ahead goal at 19:47 of the third period. They would now face their old WCHA nemesis, Michigan Tech, for the right to be called national champion.

In the Finals, the Gophers went back and forth with the Huskies throughout the first period, until John Sheridan scored late to give the Maroon and Gold a one-goal lead. John Perpich then found the back of the net to make it two-zip in the second. The Huskies came back though, scoring at 3:24 of that same period, to make it 2-1. It remained that way until the third, when John Harris and Pat Phippen both scored 12 minutes apart to put the Gophers up for good. The Huskies added another one with less than a minute to go, but it was too little, too late. Goalie Brad Shelstad hung on down the stretch, making 22 saves in all. With an impressive 39 shots-on-goal, the Gophers held on to win the title, 4-2, giving the program its first ever NCAA hockey crown.

Brooks had led the Gophers to a 22-12-6 overall record that magical season. It was also the first team in 25 years to win the national championship with a team comprised exclusively of American players. And, he did it with only two years' worth of talent that he had recruited, exclusively from the state of Minnesota. For his efforts, Brooks was named as the WCHA Coach of the Year.

Team captain Brad Shelstad, a product of Minneapolis Southwest, was chosen as the tournament's MVP and was also selected as an All-WCHA selection. Les Auge and Hibbing's Mike Polich were named to the All-Tournament team as well. Polich and Harris led the team in scoring that season. Polich went on to a successful career in the NHL, while Harris emerged as a star in another sport, golf, where he would go on to win the 1993 U.S. Amateur Golf Championship and later play on the PGA's Champions Tour.

The 1974 team will perhaps be remembered most for their hustle, desire, and work ethic, all reflections of Brooks' hard-driving motivational style of coaching. Moving from last place in the WCHA to first could not have been accomplished without unique leaders.

"My first year, our two captains, Billy Butters and Jimmy Gambucci, were tremendous leaders who just did a great job of getting the program returned to a good, solid footing," said Brooks. "It was tremendously gratifying getting the school's first championship coming from where we did. The players weren't in awe of anything, and they were extremely strong mentally. Plus they could really compete. They played well on the road and they played against the odds to overcome a lot that season. That first title was very special to me."

Her-bee! Her-bee!

Herbert Paul Brooks was born in St. Paul on August 5, 1937 and grew up in a hockey-crazy family. His father was a well known amateur player in the 1920s, and his brother, David, played for the Gophers in the early 1960s and also on the 1964 U.S. Olympic team. As a boy growing up on St. Paul's tough East Side, Herb learned to skate on the frozen waters of Lake Phalen. He would go on to star at St. Paul Johnson High School from 1952-55. As a senior, the forward led Johnson to a 26-1-2 record en route to winning the state championship. In the title game, Brooks scored two goals in the 3-1 victory over their Mill City rivals, Minneapolis Southwest.

"Winning the state championship, that represented your neighborhood," said Brooks. "I would have to say that it was my biggest thrill ever. It was just the guys from neighborhood and that was special."

An outstanding athlete, Herb also earned three varsity letters as a first baseman on the baseball team as well. Before long, the colleges were calling.

"I had an interview with the Air Force Academy, because I really wanted to be a fighter pilot," he said. "Unfortunately, because I was slightly color blind, I washed out of the Academy. I also had a scholarship at Michigan, but my dad encouraged me to walk on at the U of M and try to play for John Mariucci, so that was the route I took."

At Minnesota, Brooks became known for his blinding speed. "He was one of the fastest, if not the fastest, player in college hockey in that era," said his coach, John Mariucci. Brooks would learn a lot from "Maroosh," saying that he had more to do with shaping his ideas in hockey than any other individual. Brooks wore a Golden Gopher sweater from 1957-59, scoring 45 points over his three-year career. He graduated from the U in 1961 with a B.A. in Psychology.

The next phase of Brooks' life involved his lifelong dream, the Olympics. After graduation, he began to build a successful career in the insurance business, but never fully got away from the game that continued to dominate his life. Herb tried out for the 1960 Olympic team and eluded every cut except the final one, when he was the last player ultimately to be released by Coach Jack Riley.

"My father said that they must have cut the right guy, because they won the gold medal," said Herb jokingly.

Brooks then spent the next decade playing on nearly every U.S. Olympic and U.S. National team, more than any player in the history of United States hockey – captaining the 1965, 1967, 1968 and 1970 teams to boot.

"The Olympics were always my goal," said Brooks. "Playing in 1964 and 1968 was really a big thrill, and all things considered, it was one of the biggest highlights of my career."

Brooks went into coaching after that, becoming an assistant under Coach Glen Sonmor at the U. At the same time, he pioneered Junior hockey in the state as the first coach of the Minnesota Junior Stars in the Minnesota/Ontario Junior-A League. Then, in 1971, Sonmor left to become the coach of the WHA's Fighting Saints and Ken Yackel, Sr. was brought in to finish the season as an interim coach. That next season Brooks was named as the new Gopher coach. The youngest college hockey coach in the country, Brooks would inherit a program that had just off finished in last place.

The chant "Herbee - Herbee" was an all too familiar sound throughout the tenure of the man who would become Minnesota's greatest hockey coach. Brooks instilled a new brand of pride and tradition that next season, starting with his newly designed jerseys which proudly featured the Minnesota "M" on the front. Brooks promised he would bring, "exciting, dynamic people into the program," and he kept his word. In only seven years, he would build a dynasty at Minnesota. More importantly, he did it all with Minnesota kids.

With his extensive knowledge and experience in European hockey, Herb became an advocate of the Russian style of play and in particular, the coaching style of Anatoli Tarasov. He would instill this philosophy in motivating his own players. From 1972-79, Brooks won the first three NCAA National Championships in University of Minnesota hockey history: 1973, 1976 and 1979.

While at Minnesota, Brooks won 175 games, lost only 100, and tied 20 for a .636 winning percentage. He guided five All-Americans: Les Auge, Mike Polich, Tim Harrer, Neal Broten and Steve Ulseth, while 23 of his protégés went on to play in the NHL as well.

"We went to the finals four of my seven years there, and we made a great run of it," said Brooks. "I think I put a lot of pressure on the players, and I had a lot of expectations of them. I didn't give them an 'out,' and I think I was always able to find the kids who were really competitive. The common denominator of all the guys who played throughout my seven years was that they were really competitive, very hungry, very focused, and mentally tough — to go along with whatever talent they had. I think that really carried us."

Do you believe in miracles? Yes! The next chapter of Brooks' life is the one that made him a household name, the "Miracle on Ice." After guiding the 1979 U.S. National team in the World Games in Moscow, he was asked to lead the 1980 U.S. Olympic team — fulfilling his destiny as a coach. Brooks guided the fabled squad to their incredible upset over the heavily-favored Soviet Union, setting the stage for the huge win against Finland for the gold medal. The accomplishment would go down as one of the most memorable moments in U.S. sports history. In fact, it would later be named as the "Sporting Event of the Century" at the time of the new millennium.

After a brief coaching stint in Davos, Switzerland, Brooks' coaching success continued with the NHL's New York Rangers, where he gained 100 victories quicker than any other coach before him and, as a result, was named NHL Coach of the Year in 1982. His Broadway stint with the Rangers, which included several Stanley Cup playoff runs, lasted until 1985.

Then, in an amazing move, Brooks came home and accepted the head coaching position at St. Cloud State University in 1986. He would be revered as the school's savior, leading the Huskies to a third place finish in the national small-college tournament, and more importantly, getting them moved to NCAA Division I status. He stayed for only a year, but with his clout, lobbied the legislature to the school a beautiful new arena and really put the Huskies' program on the map.

"I've never met Herb Brooks, but I feel like I owe him everything," said Bret Hedican, former Husky and current NHL All-Star. "He's done so much for St. Cloud Hockey, it's incredible."

The next stop in Brooks' hockey resume was Bloomington, to coach the Minnesota North Stars. This was another homecoming of sorts, as Herb took over the reigns from Lorne Henning and became the first Minnesota native to coach the NHL team. The season, however, didn't go well for Brooks. Unable to overcome an enormous number of injuries, the Stars finished in the Norris Division cellar. Citing philosophical differences with management, Brooks resigned and was replaced by Pierre Page that next season.

Brooks took some well deserved time away from coaching for

a few years after that to embark on a successful business career which included motivational speaking, TV analysis, NHL scouting and occasional coaching. Then, in 1991, he took over as the coach of the New Jersey Devils' minor league team in Utica, NY, and was later promoted to be the head coach of the NHL team in 1992. He got the coaching bug again a few years later, when he guided the French Olympic team in 1998. Following that he became a scout with the Pittsburgh Penguins, ultimately taking over as the teams' head coach in 1999. He then came full circle in 2002 when he guided the U.S. Olympic team to a dramatic silver medal at the Winter Games in Salt Lake City. Once again, Herbie had made America proud.

One of our nation's most charismatic and inventive coaches, Herb Brooks is a true American hero and a real Minnesota treasure. Among his many honors and accolades, Brooks is a member of both the Hockey Hall of Fame as well as the U.S. Hockey Hall of Fame. In addition, Brooks also received the coveted Lester Patrick Award for his contributions to American hockey. Brooks was also named as Sports Illustrated's Sportsman of the Year in 1980, along with his gold medal-winning U. S. Olympic team.

Sadly, Brooks was killed in a car accident on August 11, 2003, returning home from playing golf at the U.S. Hockey Hall of Fame annual fundraiser. That was Herbie, helping a cause he dearly loved right up until the day he died. He will surely be missed.

What Did it Mean For Your to Be a Gopher?
"It was very important to play for the University of Minnesota. It's not like it is today where there are a lot more hockey schools, and American kids have more opportunities. Playing for the Gophers then, when there were few opportunities, was real special."

On the Olympics:
"To me the Olympics are not about 'Dream Teams,' they're more about dreamers. They're not about medals, but the pursuit of medals. They're not about being No. 1, they're about sacrificing and trying to be No. 1. That's why the Olympics will always be special to me."

Minnesota Hockey Tombstone:
"The name on the front of the sweater is more important than the name on the back. They always forget about individuals, but they'll always remember the teams. That has always been the cornerstone of my coaching philosophy."

1974 RUNNER-UP: RON YARY

The Vikings win their sixth division title in seven years and their second straight NFC Championship Game, only to lose their third Super Bowl, this time to the Pittsburgh Steelers in New Orleans. (The game was actually played on Jan. 12, 1975.) Minnesota's lone score came off of a Matt Blair blocked punt which was recovered by Terry Brown. Freddy Cox's extra-point hit the up-right and that was as close as the purple would get that day as Pittsburgh, behind MVP running back Franco Harris, won the game 16-6. One of the Viking's unsung heroes that season was offensive tackle *RON YARY*. A seven-time Pro-Bowler, Yary played 14 seasons in Minnesota and only missed two games. He was inducted into the Pro Football Hall of Fame in 2001.

HONORABLE MENTION: CHARLES LINDBERGH

The nation mourns the loss of its greatest aviator, *CHARLES LINDBERGH*, who died at the age of 72. "Lucky Lindy," who grew up in Little Falls, MN, went on to make history on May 20, 1927, when he flew his plane, "The Spirit of St. Louis," from New York to Paris in a time of 33.5 hours — thus achieving the first solo non-stop transatlantic flight ever. Lindbergh was thrust into the spotlight shortly thereafter, becoming an instant international hero, and arguably one of the most famous men in the world.

The 1975 Vikings were arguably the best ever. The team came out of the gates just smoking, winning its first 10 games. It wasn't until Week 11, when they got upset, 31-30, at Washington, did they even come back down to earth. They then beat Green Bay the following week, lost at Detroit in Week 13, 17-10, and rebounded to finish the regular season with a 35-13 drubbing of Buffalo.

In addition to running back Chuck Foreman's brilliant season, quarterback Fran Tarkenton had a career year as well, passing for 25 touchdowns and earning the league's coveted MVP award. Things were looking great for a repeat trip to the Super Bowl. The offense was playing huge and was hitting on all cylinders. They had outscored their opponents, 377-180 and had won nine games by 10 or more points. They were primed to finally win it all that year. Everything had been going according to plan until, that is, the hated Dallas Cowboys came to town and pulled off one of the most infamous plays in the history of the NFL.

On December 28, 1975, the Vikes hosted the Cowboys for the NFC Divisional Playoff game. Minnesota, a veteran laden team which had battle scars from three Super Bowls, was expected to finally win the big one this year, while the 10-4 Cowboys on the other hand, were a young wild-card team with a cast of more than a dozen rookies. Sure, Dallas had lost Bob Lilly and Walt Garrison to retirement that year, but they still had their hard-hitting "Doomsday Defense," which was led by Ed "Too-Tall" Jones, Harvey Martin, Lee Roy Jordan and Cliff Harris. When this one was all said and done, it would go down as one of the NFL's greatest upsets and without question the Vikings' undisputed worst loss of all-time.

The game got underway and after a scoreless first quarter, something pivotal happened in the second quarter that would play an important role in the outcome of the game. Dallas felt that they were jobbed by the refs when Cowboy safety Cliff Harris, who was waiting to receive a Neil Clabo punt on his own four-yard-line, opted to let the ball sail into the end-zone for a touchback. The ball, however, took a crazy bounce and Vikings linebacker Fred McNeil jumped on it. Harris didn't know what was going on, but the officials claimed it touched his leg on the bounce, meaning that it was a live ball for anyone to claim. Dallas argued to no avail, and Chuck Foreman leaped over the goal line for a touchdown one minute later, making it 7-0.

After a missed 45-yard field goal attempt by Fred Cox, Dallas came back to tie it up on a Doug Dennison seven-yard TD run. Dallas then took the lead on Toni Fritsch's 24-yard field goal to make it 10-7. Then, with five minutes to go in the game, Minnesota regained the lead when Brent McClanahan capped an 11 play, 70-yard touchdown drive by taking it in from the one-yard line.

Dallas' offense sputtered on the next series and was forced to punt. But they held the Vikings in check, thanks to safety Charlie Waters, who blitzed and sacked Tarkenton for a three-yard loss on a key third down to force the Vikings to punt as well. The Cowboys then got the ball back on their own 15-yard line with just 1:51 to go. Quarterback Roger Staubach started out his drive by hitting Drew Pearson for seven yards. Then, on fourth-and-16 from his own 25, he found Pearson again at mid-field for another first down. The play, which had Staubach faking a post pattern and instead hitting Pearson angling for the side-line, was aided by cornerback

Nate Wright. Here's why. While the momentum of the pass probably would have carried Pearson out of bounds for an incompletion, the official ruled otherwise, declaring that Wright had forced him out. The Vikings, now frantically pointing their fingers and wildly criss-crossing their arms, claimed it would have been impossible for Pearson to have landed in-bounds. But the referee stood firm, and the drive continued.

Dallas now had a first down at the 50-yard line with 37 seconds left in the game. After throwing a pair of incompletions to receivers Golden Richards and Preston Pearson, Staubach then mishandled John Fitzgerald's poor snap and was dumped for a six-yard loss. Metropolitan Stadium was rocking. He got up though, and huddled his men at midfield. His bruised ribs from the week before were bothering him and Drew Pearson was exhausted. Pearson thought he could beat Wright, so Staubach told him to do just that. With that, he said a prayer and lined up against the vaunted "Purple People Eaters."

Now, with 24 seconds left on the clock, and after a bobbled snap, Staubach dropped back, pump-faked to keep safety Paul Krause from coming over to offer double-coverage, and let go a desperation heave into the semi-darkness of the late afternoon Minnesota haze. The wobbly pass hung up there and was slightly under-thrown to his sprinting receiver, Drew Pearson. But Pearson, who was shoulder to shoulder with cornerback Nate Wright in a foot-race down the side-lines, somehow came back, adjusted to ball and miraculously caught the 50-yard ball at the five-yard line, simply falling into the end-zone as time ran off the clock. With the ball pinned awkwardly in between his elbow and hip, the surprised receiver cautiously looked at the official for a penalty flag. But the offensive pass interference call never came. Pearson, who clearly pushed off of Wright, even knocking him down to gain better position on the play, had gotten away with murder. He then turned around, took a running start and fired the ball up at the cowboy hat wearing Marlboro Man cigarette billboard ad up on the scoreboard, as a sort of salute to all of Texas.

The more than 47,000 fans in the old Met sat in silence, shock and disbelief. Everyone thought that there would be a penalty called, and there was, only it was on Wright for interference. The Vikings players went berserk. The fans started booing and screaming: "Pearson pushed off!" Then, in what some crazy zealots later called "justifiable homicide," some drunk lunatic heaved a half-full "Corby's" Whiskey bottle from the 21st row of the Met's right field bleachers and decked the Official, Armen Terzian, square in the noggin. Foreman quickly ran to the aid of the now bleeding ref and pleaded with the fans to remain calm. The game ended a few seconds later, but for Tarkenton, things got much, much worse. Shortly thereafter, he learned that his father, a Georgia Minister whose name was, ironically, Dallas, had died of a heart attack while watching the game on television.

(After the game the whiskey bottle was seized as evidence, and a search for the psychotic fan began. A $5,000 reward was offered; the Bloomington Police Department released a sketch of the perpetrator; game tapes were scrutinized and more than a dozen suspects were interrogated. Six months later, a 21-year-old kid from Golden Valley was picked out of a line-up by a couple of witnesses and charged with simple-assault and disorderly conduct. He pleaded guilty and was fined a whopping $100 bucks.)

"It was just a 'Hail Mary' pass," said Staubach very impromptu-like after the game, "a very, very lucky play." "I just threw it and prayed. I'll admit that we were very lucky on that play. But on the other hand, that touchdown we gave the Vikings in the second quarter had to be some kind of a fluke. If you take away that touchdown by the Vikings and our so-called lucky catch, we still would have won by a field goal and I think we deserved to."

"The touchdown pass was a prayer that was answered," said Bud Grant. "From our side of the field, there was no question that Pearson shoved Nate Wright. It was as clear as day and night. He (Pearson) had nothing to lose. If they called a penalty on him, what had he lost? They would just line up and try another long pass. It was one chance in a hundred that he would get away with it, but it was the only chance he had."

In the era of modern football there are several historic and celebrated plays that will forever link certain teams with an era: Green Bay's "Ice Bowl" victory; Pittsburgh's "Immaculate Reception" by Franco Harris; "The Catch" by Dwight Clark from Joe Montana; the Raiders' "Holy Roller" play; and even the Tennessee Titans' "Music City Miracle" to beat the Bills in 1999. They were all amazing events to be sure, but none was bigger and stung more than has the infamous "Hail Mary."

Fran the Man

Francis Asbury Tarkenton was born on February 3, 1940, in Richmond, Va., and went on to attend high school in Athens, Ga., where he excelled in both football and basketball. From there, he became an All-American (and Academic All-American) quarterback at the University of Georgia, where he graduated with a business degree in 1961.

Tarkenton was then selected in the third round of the NFL draft by the expansion Minnesota Vikings that same year. He made quite a statement in his first game, torching the mighty Chicago Bears for four touchdowns and running in another en route to leading Minnesota to a dramatic 37-13 win — one of the biggest upsets in NFL history. Fran would play five solid seasons in Minnesota, even having the phrase "scramble" coined after his unorthodox way of running around to evade would-be sackers. He called his own plays and added a new dimension to the quarterback position by refusing to ever give up.

"Perhaps the best way I can sum up my scrambling activity," he said, "and also press home my deepest philosophies about fighting to win is this way: I was talking to a writer one time, and he wondered why I scrambled. He said, 'I guess there's no sense standing back there and getting clobbered.' You know, I had never thought about that aspect of it, and I quickly corrected him by saying that there was only one reason to scramble — to win a ball game. The only thing I think about on a football field is winning."

Then, in 1966, after five stormy seasons under Dutch Van Brocklin's conservative and temperamental coaching style, Francis was traded to the New York Giants. The final straw came near the end of the 1966 season when Van Brocklin benched Tarkenton before the Atlanta game, apparently out of spite — knowing that his friends and family would be watching back home. Fran demanded to be traded and Vikings General Manager Jim Finks pulled the trigger on a deal that sent him to the New York Giants for two first-round picks. The Giants desperately needed a marquis player much like their cross-town rival Jets had in Joe Namath, and they achieved that with Fran Tarkenton.

Five years later, in 1972, Coach Bud Grant engineered a deal that brought Fran back to Minnesota. By then Fran was a full-fledged celebrity though, and his interests weren't confined to the playing field. Fran was a smart guy and had already started to prepare for his life after football, where he was quite confident that he would become an even bigger star. He owned real estate, had several major commercial endorsement deals, and he read the Wall Street Journal as avidly as he read his own team's play book. He was handsome, rich and articulate.

The Republicans even begged him to run for public office. Yes, Fran had a plan, and football was just a part of it.

He was also pretty damn tough. Despite being just six-feet tall and weighing in at a measly buck-eighty, he could take a hit. Once, in a game against the Lions, Detroit defensive tackle Dave Pureifory came plowing over the line unscathed and tattooed Tark square in the melon. Fran crumbled. Then, after realizing that three of his front teeth had popped out, he jumped up, put his arm on the giant tackle's shoulder and sarcastically whispered: "No hard feelings, Dave. I'm OK already...". And, just to spite him, he even came back in the second half to lead the Vikes to a 47-7 blow-out. After the game, Tark received nearly 60 stitches and endured several days of oral surgery.

From 1973-78, Fran led the Vikings to an amazing 62-22-2 record, and guided them to three Super Bowls. Then, in 1978, after 18 incredible seasons in the NFL, 13 of which were with Minnesota, Tark decided to call it quits. At the time of his retirement, he owned nearly every one of the NFL's major passing records: most passing attempts (6,467), most completions (3,686), most passing yards (47,003), most games played (246), and most touchdown passes (342). He had also rushed for 3,674 yards en route to scoring 32 touchdowns, a stat that made him the ultimate double-threat. And, for 15 consecutive seasons, he threw for more than 2,000 yards. He was also a four-time All-NFL selection, played in nine Pro-Bowls, and was named as the league's MVP in 1975. Fittingly, in 1986, Fran was proudly inducted into the Pro Football Hall of Fame.

Fran was an A-typical quarterback who's dogged determination to keep trying in the face of failure made him a huge fan-favorite. Back in the 1970s, the Vikings "golden era," he was every Minnesota kids' hero. Because he tried as hard as he did, sacrificed as much as he did, and, at times, carried the team on his back, we loved him. Without question, Fran should be regarded as the best signal caller ever to wear the purple. He was just simply that good.

Today Fran resides in the Atlanta area, where he has four children and several grandchildren. After football Fran tried his hand at just about everything. After hosting TV's "That's Incredible," Fran became a very successful businessman. In fact, he started and built more than a dozen businesses with varying degrees of success. A highly sought after motivational speaker, Fran is also a board member of several major companies and has countless personal business interests throughout the world. "I'm a capitalist without apology," he would say.

1975 RUNNER-UP: MIKE POLICH

The hockey Gophers make it back to the NCAA Frozen Four, only to lose to Michigan Tech in the Finals, 6-1. (The Gophers had beaten Tech the year before in the Finals, 4-2.) Incidentally, Warren Miller's hat trick was the difference in the team's 6-4 semifinal win over Harvard. One of the stars of the team that season was All-American center **MIKE POLICH,** who led the team with 19 goals and 33 assists for 52 points. The Hibbing native would go on to play in the NHL with his hometown North Stars from 1978-81, scoring 53 points.

HONORABLE MENTION: CINDY NELSON

The amazing year of Minnesota's greatest skier, *CINDY NELSON*. The Lutsen native earned Alpine Skier of the Year honors in 1975 and then parlayed that success into a bronze medal the following season at the 1976 Winter Games in Innsbruck, Austria, where she was honored by serving as the U.S. flag-bearer during the Opening Ceremonies. Affectionately called the "Old American" by her European counterparts, Nelson was a member of the U.S. Ski Team from 1971 to 1985, and remains the only woman to ski on four U.S. Olympic teams. One of the most decorated skiers in U.S. history, she won nine World Cup races and skied for the International Skiing Federation world championship team in 1974, 1978, 1982 and 1985.

The Vikings had every reason to come out feeling sorry for themselves in 1976. With memories of the "Hail Mary" still fresh in their minds, they chose instead to come out and try even harder that season. With that, the team posted a tremendous 11-2-1 regular season record, and earned yet another trip to the post-season. On November 21st, with a 17-10 win against the Packers, the defense, which allowed only three teams to score more than 13 points that season, led the team to its eighth division title in nine years. One of the bright spots for the defense was the addition of cornerback Nate Allen, who loved to tear it up and make big hits. He even posted three of the team's 15 blocked kicks or punts that season.

Foreman, who had his best rushing year with 1,155 yards, and Tarkenton, who, with 2,961 passing yards, surpassed Johnny Unitas as the all-time leader in virtually every major passing category, were again the heroes on the offensive side of the ball. But they were joined that season by a couple of receivers who would make for a wonderful a one-two punch. Sammy White, who would earn Rookie of the Year honors, and veteran Ahmad Rashad, who, after a couple of stints with St. Louis, Buffalo, and Seattle, finally found a home in Minnesota. The team's core group of stars were aging though, and played with a sense of urgency that year. Key players such as Tarkenton, Marshall, Eller, Tingelhoff, Hilgenberg and Krause, all knew that this might be their last chance to get that elusive Super Bowl ring.

The season had its share of highlights, including Foreman's amazing 200-yard game against Philadelphia, as well as the nail-biter in Detroit, where the Vikes hung on to beat the Lions, 10-9, on a blown second half conversion. And then there was the 17-6 win at Pittsburgh, where the Vikings' defense played like they were possessed. They owned the Steelers that day, as Page blocked a field goal and a conversion; Eller blocked a field goal; and Nate Allen picked off a pair of Terry Bradshaw passes — one of which came on the heels of Page's forced fumble which later led to Foreman's game-winning touchdown.

It was now off to the playoffs, where the purple squared off against the Washington Redskins at Met Stadium. This one proved to be a wild one right out of the gates as Brent McClanahan rumbled 41 yards on the first play from scrimmage. Just three plays later, Tarkenton found Stu Voigt, who plowed his way over two Redskin defenders en route to an 18-yard touchdown. After a Washington field goal by Mark Mosely, Tark hit Sammy White on a key third-and-nine play for a 27-yard touchdown to make it 14-3. From there, Chuck Foreman capped a pair of 66 and 51-yard drives by scoring a pair of two and 30-yard touchdown runs. White added another TD of his own in the third, this one being a nine yarder following a 76-yard drive. Washington quarterback Billy Kilmer rallied his squad back late but came up on the short end of a 35-20 ballgame. With the win, the Vikes had earned themselves another title bout with the Rams for the NFC championship.

The Rams flew in to Minneapolis on Christmas Eve for the NFC title tilt with a business-like attitude. Pro Bowl L.A. defensive end Jack Youngblood vowed that this time his team was not going to be psyched-out by the frigid weather. Just how much did they want to make a statement to the Vikings on that 12-degree below zero wind-chilled day? They came out for their pre-game warm-ups in T-shirts, thoroughly impressing the grounds-crew workers who were out trying to soften up the frozen turf with flame

throwers. It didn't do much for the Viking's players though, who just thought that they were nuts.

The Rams came out swinging early in this one, driving the length of the field on the opening series behind the running of Lawrence McCutcheon. Then, after the Vikes held the Rams out of the end-zone on several key defensive stops, Rams kicker Tom Dempsey came in to attempt a 26-yard field goal. That's when Nate Allen flew over the pile and blocked the kick, leaving Bobby Bryant to scoop up the bouncing ball and race 90 yards for a touchdown.

It was at this point in the game where Vikings linebacker Matt Blair took over. First he recovered a John Cappelletti fumble to kill a Ram's drive at the Minnesota 21-yard line, and then proceeded to block a Rusty Jackson punt midway through the second. Freddy Cox gave Minnesota a 10-0 lead at the half on a 25-yard boot, which was then followed by Chuck Foreman's third quarter 62-yard scamper off the right tackle to get down to the Rams two-yard line. From there, he simply ran it in to make it 17-0. The Rams didn't lie down though, as cornerback Monte Jackson intercepted a Tarkenton offering and got his squad back in the game. They rallied behind McCutcheon's 10-yard score, followed by quarterback Pat Haden's five-yard TD pass to Harold Jackson to make it 17-13. A monster rush by the Purple People Eaters forced Dempsey to rush his extra-point though and it missed the uprights, wide left.

The Rams kept coming and reached the Vikings' 33 and 39-yard lines on their next two possessions. Wally Hilgenberg blitzed and sacked Haden to end the first threat, and with 2:31 to go, Bobby Bryant killed the Ram's final drive by nabbing his second interception of the day deep in Minnesota territory. A few minutes later, after Tarkenton found Foreman on a critical third down play, reserve running back Sammy Johnson ran it in to ice the 24-13 victory for Minnesota.

With that, and to the dismay of millions of football fans across America (much like the Buffalo Bills of the '90s), the Vikings were going back for a fourth shot at the Lombardi Trophy against the perennial AFC playoff bridesmaids, the Oakland Raiders, in Super Bowl XI. Grant said that he felt his team was as prepared for that game as they could have been for any game he had coached, but he knew that this was getting to be the end of the line for many of the players.

The Vikings would attempt to seek redemption from the Super Bowl gods under the scrutiny of an estimated 81 million television viewers, along with the 103,438 fans at the Rose Bowl in Pasadena, Calif. Minnesota got the first break, when Fred McNeill blocked a Ray Guy punt, and the Vikings recovered at the Raider three-yard line. But the momentum shifted quickly when Oakland linebacker Phil Villapiano ducked under Minnesota's offensive line and stuck his helmet on the ball Brent McClanahan was carrying, popping it out of his arms and into the awaiting hands of his teammate Willie Hall just two plays later. (Incidentally, the player who made the defensive call which helped cause the McClanahan fumble was Oakland linebacker and Bloomington native, Monte Johnson, who grew up worshiping the Vikes — even selling programs at the Met as a kid.) The Raiders, long known for their physical, hard-hitting and even dirty cheap-shot style of play, took it to the Vikes early and often that afternoon. Minnesota hung in there early, but faltered down the stretch.

Led by quarterback Ken Stabler, who completed 12 of 19 passes for 180 yards, and running back Clarence Davis, who gained 137 yards rushing, the Raiders quickly drove the length of the field to set up an Errol Mann 24-yard field goal. Before half-time they added a one-yard touchdown pass from Stabler to Dave Casper as well as a one-yard Pete Banaszak touchdown run. They were dominating the Vikings, holding them to a mere 86 total yards of offense in the first half, compared to 288 of their own.

In the second half, after another Mann field goal, Tarkenton finally put Minnesota on the board, capping a 68-yard drive by connecting with Sammy White on an eight-yard touchdown pass. However, two Raider interceptions led to another 13 points for the silver and black — one set up a two-yard Banaszak touchdown run, and the other was a record 75-yard pick-off return by Willie Brown to pay-dirt. Minnesota rallied to get to within 18 points when back-up quarterback Bobby Lee hit Stu Voigt on a 13-yarder. But it was way too little way too late, as the Raiders went on to crush the Vikes, 32-14. Thanks to the blocking up front by future Hall of Famers Art Shell and Gene Upshaw, Oakland amassed a Super Bowl-record 429 yards, while Fred Biletnikoff, who caught four passes for 79 yards, earned MVP honors.

Nine years after getting spanked by the Packers in Super Bowl II, 33-14, the Raiders had won football's biggest prize. But their victory would be obscured by the shadow of Minnesota's Super Bowl futility — a record four losses in eight years. Sadly, it would mark the last time that the Vikings would get back to the big dance.

To add insult to injury, Raider Coach John Madden (a native of Austin, Minn.) said that his team had played tougher games in the conference playoffs. Afterward, Tarkenton tried to make light of the obviously painful situation: "What we're trying to do is run through all the American Football League clubs to see if there's one we can beat...".

"I still don't have good feelings about it," said Rashad, who caught 53 passes for 671 yards and three touchdowns that season. "It was one of those things where I thought we changed everything that we did well during the season to try to do something different for one game, and when it didn't work it was just too late. In retrospect, I guess when you lose a game you don't have many good memories about it. For me, I figured that I had joined a team that had gone to four Super Bowls, so I thought that we'd be back three or four more times. The next thing you know, your career is over. There's something to be said about losing. It teaches you things, and everybody's got to lose at some point. It keeps you going."

As Smooth as Silk
Formerly known as Bobby Moore (He converted to Islam in 1972 and changed his name to Rashad, which means "Admirable One Led to Truth."), Ahmad Rashad grew up in Tacoma, Wash., and attended the University of Oregon on a basketball and football scholarship. After being drafted in the first round by the St. Louis Cardinals in 1972, Rashad was traded to the Bills two years later. Then, after missing his second season in Buffalo due to an injury, he was acquired by Minnesota in a 1976 trade for, among others, Bob Lurtsema.

In Minnesota Rashad gelled immediately with Fran Tarkenton and became a superstar. Rashad still ranks on the Vikings all-time receiving list with 400 career receptions and 5,489 yards receiving. He had 13 100-yard receiving games from 1976-82, won NFC receptions titles in 1977 and 1979, and from 1978-81 was named to the Pro-Bowl. Perhaps his best season with the Vikings was in 1979, when he caught 80 balls for nine touchdowns and had 1,156 yards receiving.

For his career, Rashad caught 495 passes for 6,831 yards and 44 touchdowns. However, one catch stands out in his career. In a December 1980 game vs. the Cleveland Browns, Vikings quarterback Tommy Kramer threw a last-second bomb to Rashad that resulted in a thrilling come from behind 28-23 victory which ultimately gave the Vikings the Central Division title. In addition, Rashad also holds the NFL record for the longest non-scoring pass reception, when he hooked up with Cardinal quarterback Jim Hart on a 98-yarder in 1972.

Today Rashad is one of America's most respected sports journalists. A star in the world of television, he hosts several weekly sports and variety shows In addition he does NFL, NBA and Olympic broadcasting for several networks as well. Rashad still has a summer home in Lakeville and once here, he often goes out with his best friend, Bill Murray, either golfing or to watch the St. Paul Saints, of which Murray is a part-owner. Among his many honors, Rashad was inducted into the College Football Hall of Fame in 2007. Ahmad, has four children and currently resides in both New York City and Connecticut.

What Did it Mean for You to Be a Viking?
"Minnesota will always be my home because that's where I had the chance to blossom as a player. I had the perfect coach in Bud Grant, the perfect quarterback in Fran Tarkenton, and it was just an ideal situation for me. It was the first time that I had gotten someplace where I felt like I had a kinship with the players and was a part of the team. Anytime you play a sport, you want people to respect your performance. I feel like my years in Minnesota were great, and I was on a real run there. I can't remember ever having too many bad games. I played some pretty good Sundays in Minnesota. Overall, I am a Minnesota Viking. When I look back on my career, I remember only playing for the Vikings. The love affair went both ways I felt. I really enjoyed playing there, and I enjoyed the people. It really felt good to actually feel that love from the people because very few athletes get a chance to do that in their careers."

TRIBUTES
"He was the Baryshnikov of wide receivers," said Chuck Foreman. "I remember watching him run patterns, and he was just like a gazelle — smooth and fast. He was a great addition to the Vikings and played a very important role on our last Super Bowl team. He is somebody that I admire and respect. He is a great player and a great person."

"He found a home in Minnesota," said Bud Grant. "He was one of the finest receivers I ever coached. He and Sammy White were a great pair together."

"Ahmad was a great receiver and made a lot of amazing plays for us," said Jim Marshall. "He could catch anything thrown to him. He was unbelievable."

"Ahmad had great hands, great speed, and a great ability to get open," said Alan Page. "He was just a great wide receiver."

1976 RUNNER-UP: REED LARSON
The hockey Gophers rally from being down 3-0 to beat Michigan Tech, 6-4, and win the NCAA National Championship. Minnesota got to the Finals after winning a 7-6 triple-overtime thriller over Michigan State in the WCHA playoffs (goalie Jeff Tscherne had an NCAA record 72 saves in this one), followed by a 4-2 win over B.U. in the Frozen Four semis. One of the leaders of that squad was All-American defenseman *REED LARSON*, who tallied 13 goals and 29 assists that season. The Minneapolis Roosevelt grad would go on to play in the NHL for 16 years, scoring 685 points. Among his many honors, in 1996 he was inducted into the U.S. Hockey Hall of Fame and in 2007 the three-time All-Star received the NHL's Lester Patrick Award.

HONORABLE MENTION: ALAN MERRICK
The Denver Dynamos of the North Atlantic Soccer League relocate to Minnesota, where they are renamed as the Kicks. The team made history in its first season by advancing all the way to the NASL Finals, where, after upsetting Seattle and San Jose, they ultimately lost to Toronto, 3-0. The captain of the team was *ALAN MERRICK*, a former 10-year English League player, who played in the NASL for seven seasons. Merrick, who also played on the U.S. national team, was a real fan favorite. He would later serve as the head coach of the Minnesota Strikers of the MISL, and then as the coach of the University of Minnesota men's soccer club.

The baseball story of the year in 1977 was that of Rod Carew, who flirted with .400 and became a bonafide superstar before the eyes of the nation. More than a million fans passed through the Met's turnstiles, that year, mostly to see Rod Carew win the American League's MVP award. He led the league in average (.388), hits (239), runs (128) and triples (16), and also knocked in 100 RBI's to boot.

Carew carried the Twins on his back that year, willing them into a tough pennant race with Kansas City, Chicago and Texas, who were all battling for first place until after Labor Day, when the Royals ran away with it. Carew's hitting was infectious too, as Glenn Adams, Lyman Bostock and Larry Hisle (this group was affectionately known as the "Lumber Company"), also played great, posting .338, .336 and .302 averages, respectively. Hisle led the AL with 119 RBI's as well. In addition, Minnesota native Dave Goltz won 20 games, while Tom Johnson added 16 of his own. As a team, the Twins posted a league best .282 batting average, while tallying nearly 5.5 runs per outing.

Twins Manager Gene Mauch seemed bound and determined to shake things up at the beginning of the season. So, he brought a bunch of candidates into training camp that year and came out with 10 new players on his roster. The motivational tactic seemed to work, as everybody got fired up to not only play better, but also to keep their jobs. In the end, however, the team's solid hitting couldn't make up for pitching depth, and they faltered down the stretch to finish at 84-77, fully 17 games behind first-place Kansas City.

Perhaps the highlight of the season came on June 26th, when 46,463 fans, the largest regular season crowd ever to cram into the Met, showed up to watch the Twins destroy the White Sox, 19-2, and jump into first place in the West. While Glenn Adams led the way that afternoon with a record eight RBI's, the big story was the amazing hitting of Rod Carew, who raised his batting average to .403, teasing Ted Williams' legendary record in the process.

"When I went four-for-five against the White Sox and broke .400, that was probably the most memorable game of my career," said Carew. "During that game I received six standing ovations. Their response, by standing up every time I got a base hit, showed me that they cared and appreciated what I was doing."

The Greatest Twins Hitter of All-Time

The son of a Panama Canal tugboat worker, Rod Carew came into the world in a very unique way. On October 1, 1945, in Gatun, Panama, Olga Carew went into labor on a speeding train. As luck would have it, a physician, Dr. Rodney Cline, just happened to be on that same train along with a nurse by the name of Margaret Allen. They delivered Olga's baby boy right there on the train. A grateful Olga then named her son Rodney Cline Carew, after that doctor, while the nurse, Margaret Allen, became the baby's godmother.

As a boy Rod loved playing baseball. He used to listen to Major League games on his radio and dreamt of coming to the U.S. to become a big leaguer. One day, Rod's godmother wrote a letter to his mother from New York City. She encouraged them to pack-up and move to New York to pursue a better life. So, in 1962, at the age of 16, Rod, his mother, brother, and sisters, picked up and moved to Harlem, where his mother supported the family by working in a factory.

Speaking little English, young Rod had trouble fitting in at school. He was also wary of the many drug dealers and thugs operating in his neighborhood. Rod spent his afternoons working in a grocery store to help support his family and, in doing so, dearly missed his passion, playing baseball. His luck then changed when he tried out for a weekend sandlot baseball team, the Cavaliers, which played in the shadows of Yankee Stadium in the Bronx.

There, he played shortstop and second base, hitting consistently and with power — and finishing with a whopping .600 average. Word of Carew's skill soon reached Herb Stein, a New York transit detective, who also scouted young talent for the Minnesota Twins. Stein watched Rod play in several games and was impressed. "He was spraying hits all over the place," said Stein. "He had a pair of wrists that just exploded." Stein told Hal Keller, head of the Twins' farm system, to come see Carew play. That day, Rod went 6-for-7 with two singles, three doubles, and a grand-slam. Rod had officially been discovered.

When Minnesota came to town to play the Yankees, team officials invited Carew inside for a pre-game tryout. After easily putting two balls into the Yankee Stadium seats, Twins Manager Sam Mele looked around nervously to see if any of the Yankees players had seen the young phenom in action. Then the cautious Mele ordered, "Get that kid out of here before somebody else sees him!"

A month later, in June of 1964, Rod signed his first big-league contract with the Twins. Minnesota agreed to pay him an immediate bonus of $5,000, a minor league salary of $500 a month, and a future bonus of $7,500 when (and if) he made the Major League roster. Although other big league teams had started to show some interest in him, Rod was anxious to sign with the Twins. He took the $5,000, gave some money to his mother, bought some new clothes, and put the rest in the bank.

He would go on to spend the next two years in the Twins farm system before being called-up for the start of the 1967 season. The 21-year-old was thrilled to finally get to show his stuff. He didn't waste any time making a name for himself either. In fact, by the end of the season he would be named Rookie of the Year and get selected to the All-Star team. From there he just kept on going, leading the Twins in nearly every offensive category for years to come.

Without question, Carew's best season was in 1977, when he was simply the biggest story in all of sports. After switching over from second base to play first base, Rod had the greatest season of his incredible 19-year big league career, nearly becoming the first hitter since Ted Williams to break baseball's magic .400 mark. Carew even appeared on the cover of Sports Illustrated with the "Splendid Splinter" himself during the season. Rod also appeared on the cover of Time magazine with the headline, "Baseball's Best Hitter." He would come close, batting over .400 for the first half of the season, but then slowing down to finished at .388.

The number was good enough to earn him his sixth batting title, while his 239 hits proved to be the most in the Majors since Bill Terry hit 254 nearly 50 years earlier. He also scored 128 runs, hit 14 homers and stole 23 bases. In addition, he struck out just 55 times in 616 at-bats. He also had 38 doubles, 16 triples, and drove in 100 runs as well. At season's end Carew won the MVP award and for the 11th straight year was selected for the All-Star team, this time with the biggest number of fan votes ever recorded. Further, he also received the coveted Roberto Clemente Award for distinguished service to his community.

Afraid that he was going to lose Carew to free agency, Calvin Griffith traded Carew to the California Angels on February 3, 1979, for outfielder Ken Landreaux and some prospects. And, so it went that Carew would finish his career in California some eight years later.

No true Twins fan will ever forget the graceful power of Rod's smooth hitting style. Carew was a career .328 hitter in 19 big league seasons and won seven batting titles (second only to Ty Cobb and Honus Wagner). He hit .300 or better for 15 consecutive seasons, finished with 3,053 hits, scored 1,434 runs, belted 92 homers, knocked in 1,015 RBIs, and stole 353 bases. (His 3,000th hit came on August 4,

1985, against Twins pitcher Frank Viola in Anaheim Stadium.) He was also named to 18 consecutive All-Star teams. Rod's No. 29 was retired by the Twins on July 19, 1987, and then, on January 8, 1991, Rod was elected to the Baseball Hall of Fame. He would later come back to Minnesota in 2005 to serve as a special hitting instructor at Spring Training. Rod Carew was the greatest pure hitter of his era, and a true wizard with the bat. He is also one of Minnesota's all-time fan favorites.

Some Lesser Known "Carewisms…"

There were some oddities to Carew's brilliant baseball career that maybe you weren't aware of. For instance, did you know that he treated his bats with extreme tender love and care, putting them in a hot closet next to the clubhouse sauna to "bake out the bad wood." He also washed his bats in alcohol to clean off the sticky pine tar, because he "loved to use a clean bat." Like a lot of ballplayers, Rod chewed tobacco during games. He said that a big plug of chew would stretch his facial muscles so he could squint more, and as a result, see the ball better. He also used to drink Coca-Cola almost non-stop, sometimes gulping down more than a dozen glassfuls per game. Sometimes. he would ride his bicycle from his home to the ballpark, a distance of some 15 miles. He loved to chase balls for the pitchers during practice too, and once, during a game, he even fined himself when he quit running after giving up on a foul ball that blew fair. An amazing bunter, he used to impress his teammates by putting a handkerchief at various spots throughout the infield and then dropping bunts onto it.

What Did it Mean For You To Be a Twin?

"I enjoyed the Twin Cities, and I really enjoyed the people. I came there as a young kid, still learning a lot about playing the game. In the years that I was there I really matured as a person and as a baseball player. I appreciated the Twins organization, Mr. Griffith, and the way the fans there treated me and responded to me."

On Minnesota:

"Minnesota to me is still home and I have a lot of fond memories there. The people are what is important. I will always remember the way that they embraced me, even after I went to play for the Angels and came back to Minnesota in a different uniform. They still kept me as one of their own."

When Were You Happiest?

"I think it was after my first two seasons with the Twins. I was a little bit of a hot-headed kid. I played for Billy Martin, and he taught me how to stay on an even keel and not get upset at every little thing or every person that made a remark or comment about me. I started mellowing out when I met my wife, got married, and had children. I found that coming home from road trips or ball games or just a bad day, it didn't really matter, because my daughters didn't care that I was Rod Carew, the baseball player. For them, it was just dad coming home."

Twins Tombstone:

"I came to Minneapolis and played the game hard. I gave people enjoyment, and they responded by showering me with love and respect."

TRIBUTES

"We were roommates for 10 years," said Tony Oliva. "Between the two of us I would tell people that our room was hitting over .700, even though his average was always higher than mine. Rod was a remarkable ballplayer, a great person, and a good friend."

"He was one of the finest hitters I ever saw and the best bunter ever," said Harmon Killebrew. "He used to come out early to the park and practice his bunting. He could drop that ball down the third base line and, with the speed he had, nobody could throw him out. He was just outstanding and just a great, great hitter."

"I followed Rod Carew's career when I was growing up, and I thought he had the best pair of wrists of anybody I ever saw," said Paul Molitor. "The way he could wait and put the ball out to left field was incredible. He was a very gifted hitter who studied the game, knew how to take advantage of pitchers and their weaknesses, and had a remarkable, outstanding Major League baseball career."

"In California, we had as close a relationship as any player and manager ever had," said Gene Mauch. "He knew how much I respected him and I felt like he felt the same way about me. It was a great privilege for me to manage Rod Carew. Watching him almost bat .400 was a season of the greatest hitting that I ever saw, and I played with Ted Williams. Watching him operate with the bat was incredible."

"He was such a talented hitter, and I really enjoyed watching him do what he could do," said Jim Kaat. "He was a real magician with the bat. I have a warm relationship with him to this day."

"I remember when I got my first hit, it was against the Angels, and Rod was playing first base," added Kirby Puckett. "I stood on base and said to him: 'How ya doin' Mr. Carew? I just want to tell you that I've been a big fan of yours, and it's my pleasure to meet you, man, because you're awesome, and I'm a rookie so I'm gonna shut up now and be quiet!' 'Please, call me Rod,' he said to me. 'I know you're a rookie, and I just want to tell you to just keep playing, keep enjoying yourself, and keep playing the game the way you know how. And, the most important thing you should know, is to learn how to play when you're hurt, and you'll be just fine.' I will always remember that. Rod Carew is the very best there is."

"He was one of the toughest outs to get," said Jack Morris. "I would have to say that he would be in the top five of the all-time best hitters. Aside from Carl Yastrzemski, Rod was my toughest out in all of baseball. I felt that every time that he wanted to get a hit off me, he could. It was scary that Rod was so good."

1977 RUNNER-UP: MICK TINGLEHOFF

The 9-5 NFC Central Division champion Vikings beat the Rams, 14-7, in the divisional playoffs, only to lose to the hated Cowboys in the conference championship, 23-6. One of the stars of the team was center **MICK TINGLEHOFF**, a six-time Pro Bowler and five-time first-team All-Pro. The Nebraska native played his entire 17-year career with the Vikings, from 1962-78. Tinglehoff also started an amazing 240 consecutive games, second in NFL history (at the time of his retirement) only to teammate Jim Marshall.

HONORABLE MENTION: MARION BARBER JR.

The football Gophers lose to Maryland in the Hall of Fame Bowl, 17-7, in Birmingham, AL. The Gophers had a great season in 1977, finishing with a 7-4 record — complete with wins over Rose Bowl participants Michigan and Washington. With that, the team was invited to play in its first bowl game since the Rose Bowl in 1962. Minnesota got on the board first when freshman running back **MARION BARBER JR.** scored on a one-yard plunge. The Terps rallied for 17 unanswered points though and got the win. Barber, a two-time All-Big 10 honoree, would go on to play in the NFL with the Jets from 1982-89. (Incidentally, his two sons would also go on to play in the NFL: Marion III, a Pro Bowl RB with Dallas; and Dominique a DB with Houston.)

1978

JANET KARVONEN
The New York Mills Girls High School Basketball Dynasty

Janet Karvonen is one of the greatest athletes to ever hail from the state of Minnesota and is considered by many to be the modern matriarch of women's basketball in our state. Back in the late 1970s, she single-handedly put the tiny town of New York Mills on the map. And, in 1978, Janet led her Eagles to their second straight Class A title — confirming a true basketball dynasty was in the works.

After an unbelievable 22-1 regular season record, the defending champions from "The Mills" went on to beat the Perham Yellowjackets, 78-58, at the Sauk Centre gym to win the Region 6A title. In that game, Karvonen, then a sophomore, scored 51 points, pulled down 16 rebounds, and was totally unstoppable. Next, it was off to the Twin Cities and the Girls State High School Basketball Tournament for the Eagles, where they would face the Fertile-Beltrami Falcons in the first round quarterfinals. There, behind Karvonen's 31 points, New York Mills crushed Fertile-Beltrami, 80-33.

Next up were the Minnesota Lake Lakers in the semis, and the Eagles waltzed to a 59-40 victory in this one behind Karvonen's 21 points. At 6:43 of the first period, she made history when she hit a soft 15-footer to pass Morton's Mary Beth Bidinger and take over the all-time girls scoring record with 1,474 points. She was averaging around 30 points per game and she was only 15-years-old! So, it was back to the Finals for the Eagles, where they would meet the undefeated Redwood Falls Cardinals, who had won the title two years earlier.

The Cards jumped out to a 14-9 lead after the first period in this one, only to see the Mills score 16 straight points to start the second quarter and gain a 33-20 halftime lead.

"I knew we were going to come back," said Janet. "Everyone on the team was hitting really well. I think that's the best we've played all year, in the second and third quarters."

Led by six-foot-one center Jenny Miller, who grabbed 21 boards, the Rutten sisters, and all-state point guard Kim Salathe (who would go on to later become the school's head hoops coach), the Eagles increased their lead to 52-36 after three periods. The Cardinals hung in there and even trimmed the lead to nine at one point, but the Eagles were too tough down the stretch. They went on to win the game, 64-55, earning their second title in as many years.

Peggy Zimmerman's squad had out-rebounded their opponents 46-20, and she set up a zone defense that forced the Cards to shoot from long range. "We knew how to stop them," said Karvonen, "and we did."

Jean Hopfenspirger led the Cards with 19 points while her sister Joan added 10. The 7,000-plus fans were in awe of "Janet the Great," as the six-foot forward scored a game high 24-points and added 10 rebounds of her own. The team also set a tournament record, tallying 203 points.

It was a special time for New York Mills during that magical three-year title run from 1977-79. Just like in the movie "Hoosiers," Janet recalled how the town "emptied out at tournament time," with many of the local farmers driving more than three hours back home from St. Paul each night to milk their cows. It was a big experience for everyone, including the girls themselves, who made the most of their time in the big city by "watching planes take off and land at the airport and going to Southdale Mall."

Minnesota's Finest

Janet Karvonen grew up in New York Mills, a small Finnish community of just 800 souls near Wadena, approximately 180 miles northwest of the Twin Cities. She was taller than most of her classmates for as long as she could remember, already standing five-foot-nine in the sixth grade. Janet started playing sports at a young age, but was extremely well-rounded. It was no wonder that she would excel at basketball and tennis, seeing as she had a tennis and basketball court in her back yard. But growing up she also was an accomplished pianist, she played the saxophone in the school band, and even she rode Arabian horses raised by her father. Janet also helped out at her father's funeral home and worked at his furniture store as well.

Janet loved to play basketball, and her father often took her to Milwaukee to see the NBA's Bucks play. Before long, she started to take the game very seriously. She attended summer camps and, with a lot of hard work, made the varsity basketball team in 1976 as an eighth grader. That same year, girls basketball finally got the respect it deserved in the state, when it was officially recognized by the Minnesota State High School League and given a tournament format that featured two classes: AA and A. New York Mills would compete in the Class-A bracket, even though there were schools with much larger enrollments in the same class.

In 1977, as a freshman, Janet led the Eagles past Mayer Lutheran High School by one point in the title game to win the state championship. It was an amazing feat for the small town, but the Eagles didn't stop there. They won it all the next year against Redwood Falls and just kept on rolling. In 1979, New York Mills would three-peat as state champs, this time beating Albany, 61-52. Karvonen scored 98 points for the tournament, a new record. As a senior, the Eagles again went to the state tournament to defend their title, only this time it would not have the same outcome. In 1980, New York Mills was upset by Austin Pacelli in the semifinals, 55-43. Although they rebounded to beat East Chain, 59-54, for third place honors, it signified the end of one of Minnesota sports' greatest dynasties. Karvonen set the single season scoring record her senior year with 845 points, averaging nearly 33 points per game.

When it was all said and done, Janet, who was also her class valedictorian, had completely rewritten the record books. She had scored 3,129 points over her high school career, the most ever scored by either a boy or girl in the history of Minnesota basketball. Norm Grow of Foley had previously held the all-time career scoring record with 2,852 points, back in the 1950's. (Janet held the career girls' scoring record for 17 years, until 1998, when Roseau's Meagan Taylor scored 3,300 points. The boys' record was broken in 1991 by Chisholm's Joel McDonald, who put in 3,292 points over his career. To this day, they are the only a handful players — boys or girls — in state history that belong to the prestigious 3,000-point fraternity.)

A four-time all-stater, Karvonen was also a Parade All-American first-teamer as well as the U.S. National High School Player of the Year. She even got to appear on the Good Morning America TV show as a guest with O.J. Simpson.

It all happened like a blur for Janet, but she handled her newly-found celebrity with class, never letting it go to her head.

"You have to understand that when I was 14, reporters were asking me what I thought of the ERA and Rudy Perpich — and I'd only just stopped playing with my Barbie dolls! I grew up fast, because I became very mature for my age."

After sifting through more than 150 college offers, Karvonen opted for perennial women's basketball powerhouse, Old Dominion University. Old Dominion had just won back-to-back national championships under one of the greatest female basketball players of all-time, Nancy Lieberman, who had just graduated. Lieberman, who made the Olympic team when she was 16 years old, was also a two-time Wade Trophy winner — women's college basketball's Heisman equivalent. The pressure was on, as some felt that Janet was pegged to be her heir-apparent.

Janet jumped right in and absorbed as much as she could.

She made a big contribution that first year and was rewarded when her Lady Monarchs made it all the way to the NCAA Finals. After two years at Old Dominion, however, Janet decided that the college wasn't right for her, so she left the school to enroll at ODU's biggest rival, Louisiana Tech University. She said it was a very difficult decision for her to leave, but one she felt good about nonetheless.

"I left Old Dominion as a starter and had to start over at Tech," she said. "I had to sit out a year, and it took that long before many of the Tech players accepted me."

She eventually cracked the starting line-up and once again helped to lead the school to the 1984 Women's Final Four, this time losing to USC. While there, Karvonen developed a great rapport with her coach at Tech, Leon Barmore.

"I had a lot of respect for him," she said. "He was a great role model and a positive influence in my life."

Life wasn't always a picture postcard there for her though. "I remember a game against UCLA," she remembered. "There was this guard I just couldn't handle. She blew by me at every turn and finally my coach called a time-out. He screamed at me to keep an eye on her and later took me out of the game." That UCLA player turned out to be a Jackie Joyner-Kersee, who would go on to become a gold medal winning Olympic sprinter.

Janet graduated with a B.A. in Journalism from Louisiana Tech University in 1985 and then came home to Minnesota. At first she worked as a reporter at a Duluth television station, and later worked in the legislature for Minnesota Commerce Commissioner Mike Hatch. During this time, Karvonen was doing some serious soul-searching and was trying to figure out how she could somehow combine her love of basketball with her newly-found love of public speaking.

"I felt on a gut level that there was a need for female motivational speakers," Janet said. "There were voids that could be filled."

So, in 1988, Karvonen went into business for herself as a public speaker and basketball-camp director — ironic for someone who had dropped out of her college speech class because she was "scared to death" of public speaking. She then established her own educational and sports-oriented company called, Janet Karvonen, Inc. She even established a joint-venture relationship with Reebok and began one of the most successful dual careers in the local sports scene.

As a national public speaker and leadership workshop director, Janet appears in school, corporate, and civic engagements focusing on areas of drug-free choices, self-esteem and motivation. She also runs the largest girls basketball camps in the Upper Midwest, appropriately called the Janet Karvonen Basketball Camp, now in its third decade of operation. In addition, she has become a household name serving as a television analyst for the high school basketball tourneys as well as Women's Big Ten Basketball games.

"I want to be a friend to youth, a great mother, and someone who leads the way and opens doors for more young women for them to discover their worth," she said. "I want to help girls in their teens as they struggle with sense of self, with issues such as suicide, eating disorders, alcohol and drug abuse, and teen pregnancy. In my speaking, I am able to make a difference, and that's been rewarding."

Karvonen was inducted into the National High School Hall of Fame in 1987, the Minnesota Sports Hall of Fame in 1989, and the Minnesota High School Hall of Fame in 1996. Today, she is also recognized as one of the all-time great female basketball players. She has spent the better part of her life playing and promoting the game and has had a significant role in increasing the popularity of it in the state. From the French-braided naive teenager that Minnesota fell in love with, to the mega-powerful, successful businesswoman today, she is a wonderful role-model for young girls everywhere.

What Did it Mean For You To Be a Pioneer of Sorts?

"At the time, I really didn't think about it; you just enjoy what's happening. Obviously, I brought a lot of positive attention to a very small and relatively unknown Minnesota community, which, prior to girls basketball, was famous for being the home of Lund boats. When I look back now it's really surprising how many people remember my high school days. It was real special not only for the Eagles, but for the community of New York Mills as well."

On Teaching Young Girls Today and Making a Difference:

"My philosophy is that we're developing young women and young women's skills in life. We're not just limiting it to girls basketball. We want them to feel good about themselves and send them home feeling more confident — ready to take on new challenges and start applying themselves. Academics are really the foundation, but athletics enhance who you are."

On Women's Professional Basketball Today:

"I think it's a really exciting time for women in basketball right now. Girls growing up now can be drafted into the professional ranks and can have something tangible to look forward to. I think it's great."

Minnesota Sports Tombstone:

"As someone who brought girls sports to a new level in Minnesota and who helped people across the state gain a greater appreciation for girls' talents and the importance of opportunities for girls in sports. Also, people knew that I could play. I had a jump shot, I had skills, and I was worthy of being appreciated. Girls basketball isn't a joke anymore. In the early days, it was pretty rough going, and I think it will be the same way for girls hockey now. Girls hockey is a much slower game, and it takes time to appreciate it, but more and more people will like and appreciate the sport as time goes by."

1978 RUNNER-UP: MYCHAL THOMPSON

The basketball Gophers finish second in the Big Ten with a 17-10 overall record. Leading the charge was center *MYCHAL THOMPSON*, who averaged 22.1 ppg that season en route to earning All-American honors for the second straight season. From there, Thompson, the school's all-time leading scorer with 1,992 points, would go on to become the program's only No. 1 overall draft pick when he was selected by the Portland Trail Blazers that year. He would later be traded to the Los Angeles Lakers, where he would win a pair of NBA titles. In all, he played in the NBA for 12 seasons, averaging 13.7 ppg and 7.4 rpg. His No. 43 jersey was retired into the rafters at the Old Barn on March 4th, 1978.

HONORABLE MENTION: MATT BLAIR

The Vikings finish first in the NFC Central Division with a record of 8-7-1, ultimately losing to the Rams in the first round of the playoffs, 34-10. Leading the charge that season was linebacker *MATT BLAIR*, who wore the purple from 1974-85. A second round draft pick out of Iowa State in 1974, Blair played his entire 12-year NFL career with the Vikings. Playing in six consecutive Pro Bowls and two Super Bowls, Blair finished second on the team's all-time list for tackles with 1,452; and holds the record for blocked kicks with 20.5.

1979

NEAL BROTEN
The Hockey Gophers are Back on Top

In 1979 Herb Brooks' Gophers got back to the promised land yet again. It was smooth sailing in the early going of the season as the Gophers found themselves ranked No. 1 in the country. They hit a slump in January, losing five of six, but rebounded to win six of eight in February. The final series of the season featured a tough North Dakota team coming to town in what would prove to be a WCHA championship showdown. The Gophers took the opener, 5-2, but the Sioux rallied to take the title in one of the best series ever witnessed at Williams Arena.

In the playoffs, the Gophers went on to sweep both Michigan Tech and then the University of Minnesota-Duluth at home. They then knocked off Bowling Green, winners of the CCHA, earning a trip to Detroit and the NCAA Frozen Four.

In the first game of the tournament, led by Eric Strobel's hat trick, Minnesota held on to beat New Hampshire, 4-3. It was now on to the Finals, where they would meet their neighbors from North Dakota. Minnesota jumped out to an early lead in this one on goals from Steve Christoff, John Meredith and team captain Bill Baker, to make it 3-1 after the first period. The Sioux then rallied in the second, narrowing the gap to 3-2. Then, early in the third period, Neal Broten, the freshman sensation from Roseau, scored on a fabulous, sliding chip shot in what would prove to be the game winner. (Most Gopher fans would agree that the shot was arguably the greatest in Gopher history.) UND added another goal late, but the incredible goaltending of Gopher senior netminder Steve Janaszak proved to be the difference as the Gophers held on to win, 4-3, and claim their third national crown.

With 35 saves, Janaszak, fittingly, was voted as the tournament's MVP. Three other Gophers also made the all-tournament team including, freshman defenseman Mike Ramsey and forwards Steve Christoff and Eric Strobel. Additional honors would cascade down to a couple of other future Gopher legends as well. Billy Baker, who scored a then single-season record of 54 points, most ever by a defenseman, was selected as an All-American; while Broten was named as the WCHA's Rookie of the Year. As a team, the Gophers won 32 games and simply rewrote the record books that season, scoring an amazing 239 goals in 44 games. Leading the charge were Steve Christoff and Don Micheletti, who both tallied 36 goals apiece that year.

"We were playing against a tremendous North Dakota team," said Coach Brooks. "I think they had 13 guys that turned pro that next year. Broten scored a dramatic goal, sliding on his stomach and hitting a chip-shot over the goalie. It was incredible. I remember speaking at a Blue Line Club meeting the year before and saying that we were going to win it all that next season. It leaked out in the press and went across the country, putting a lot of pressure on our team. I kind of wish I wouldn't have said it now. But I just felt really strong about that team.

I put a lot of pressure on those kids and I really raised the bar. But, because of their mental toughness and talent, we won the championship."

"I remember playing at the old Olympia Arena in Detroit," said Broten. "Just being in there and thinking about Gordie Howe and all those old Red Wings teams that had played there was really neat. North Dakota was our biggest rival back then and beating them in the Finals was a great win for us. That year was great, and I have a lot of great memories of my teammates from that season. It was special."

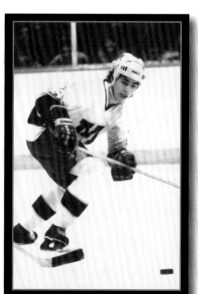

The Pride of Roseau

Neal Broten was born on November 19, 1959, in the hockey-crazy town of Roseau, and grew up loving hockey with his two brothers, Aaron and Paul. Roseau, which is located just south of the Canadian border, is a town of just 3,000 people, yet the city has three hockey arenas. Roseau has also sent more teams to the State High School Hockey Tournament than any other in the state (32) and has somehow won seven state titles along the way — not to mention five second place finishes as well. This tiny community has one of the richest hockey traditions of anywhere in the country, and much of that can be attributed to the three Broten brothers: Neal, Aaron, and Paul — who each played for the Roseau Rams, Gophers, and then in the NHL.

For the Broten brothers, it started at sun-up, when their parents would awaken before sunrise on frigid winter mornings to drive them to hockey practice.

"When he was a pee-wee, he was scoring five, six, seven goals a game," said Gary Hokanson, Broten's coach. "You could see then that he was going to be something special. He was a little guy who could handle the stick and put it in the net like nothing I'd ever seen."

"Roseau is such a great town, with so much hockey tradition," said Neal. "We used to always watch Hockey Night in Canada on TV, and basically all we did was go to school and play hockey. Mom used to make us grilled cheese sandwiches after school, and then it was off to the rink. High school hockey was the biggest thing to do up there. We'd pack all 3,000 people in that arena, and the whole town would root us on. With so many people involved in hockey up there, it was a really special place to grow up."

From there, Neal opted to head south, to the U of M, where he quickly took Gold Country by storm. In 1979, as a freshman, Broten easily exceeded everyone's expectations when he broke John Mayasich's 25-year-old school assist record by dishing out 50 helpers to his teammates. In the process, he led the Gophers past North Dakota en route to winning the national championship.

The next chapter of Neal's life story proved to be the one that may very well have linked his name to the sport of hockey forever. That off-season, he was selected to be a member of the fabled 1980 gold medal winning U.S. Olympic Team that shocked the world. Neal would play center and finish as the teams' fourth-leading scorer.

After the Olympics, Neal could've easily turned pro, having been drafted by the Minnesota North Stars. Instead he returned to the U of M to be reunited with his two former linemates from Roseau, his brother Aaron, and his high school pal Butsy Erickson, who had recently transferred to the U of M from Cornell.

"I needed to work on the weights and get a little stronger before I started pro hockey," Broten said. "Besides, the North Stars had a lot of centers at the start of the year, and I didn't think my chances of breaking in right away would be so good. And, I thought it would be fun to play with Aaron and Butsy again."

New Gopher Coach Brad Buetow quickly assembled the three to make up one of the most feared scoring lines in all of college hockey. In 1981 the trio led the Gophers to the NCAA championship game for the second time in three years. There, at the Duluth DECC, the Gophers came up short against Wisconsin, losing 6-3 in the Finals. Neal went on to earn All-America honors that year and was also selected as the first-ever recipient of the Hobey Baker Memorial Award, which recognized the nation's top collegiate player.

"I felt terrible winning the Hobey Baker over my brother Aaron," said Neal. "He deserved it more than I did. I mean he had 106 points and had a lot better year than I did. Aaron had always been in my shadows growing up, and he had a great year that season. He deserved the award way more than I did, and I still feel bad about it to this day."

While that season marked the end of Broten's collegiate career, for Minnesota hockey fans it would only be the beginning of his professional career. Neal left the U just in time to join the Cinderella North Stars as they were heading into the Stanley Cup playoffs that year. The Stars had even traded center Glen Sharpley, freeing up Neal's lucky No. 7 jersey. The Stars made it all they way to the Finals that year, before losing to the New York Islanders in five games.

"Glen Sonmor was a great coach, and he just let us play the game," said Broten. "It all happened so fast, I had only played three games for the Stars' when we went to the Stanley Cup Finals. I was so wet behind the ears, I didn't really know what was going on. Things happened so fast and the next thing I knew I was playing with guys like Bobby Smith, Steve Payne, Al MacAdam and Freddy Barrett. It was a great experience and I will always remember that first run at the Cup."

For 11 seasons Broten dazzled the Minnesota faithful as a member of the North Stars. He later led them to their only other Stanley Cup Finals appearance in 1991, where they ultimately lost to Mario Lemieux and the Pittsburgh Penguins. Neal was a legend. Period. He became the first U.S.-born player to score 100 points in a season when he tallied 105 in 1986, and never slowed down. The perennial All-Star also led the Stars in scoring from 1982-86, and went on to set the team records for games played (861), points (793) and assists (544).

When the North Stars moved to Dallas, Broten played two seasons in Texas before being traded to the New Jersey Devils during the 1994-95 season. There, Broten became the final piece in the Devils' Stanley Cup puzzle. He ignited New Jersey's offense by scoring seven goals, including four game-winners, while dishing out 12 assists during their amazing playoff run to become the first Gopher player ever to have his named inscribed on Lord Stanley's Cup.

"I can remember sitting there in the locker room with him after they won it," said Neal's father Newell. "He looked at me and said, 'Dad, can you believe it, after all these years?'"

Neal went on to play with the L.A. Kings and Dallas Stars yet again before finally retiring for good in 1997. His career numbers are outstanding, and should warrant him a place in the Hall of Fame someday. In 1,099 games he scored 289 goals and dished out 634 assists for 923 career points. He also added 98 career playoff points as well.

For the kid Herb Brooks called "The best player I ever coached at the U of M," the circle was now complete. Three trips to the high school tournament, a Gopher title, a Hobey Baker, an Olympic Gold medal, two Stanley Cup runs with his native Stars, and finally winning a Cup of his own with New Jersey. Broten lived out a hockey dream as only John Mariucci might have dared to imagine it. Known and loved by every hockey aficionado in the "State of Hockey," Neal will forever be the measuring stick against which all others will be judged. Neal Broten has become synonymous with Minnesota hockey.

Among his many honors, on February 7, 1998, Broten's No. 7 jersey was retired by the Dallas Stars. In 1998 he received the Lester Patrick Trophy for his contributions to American hockey, and in 2000 he was inducted into the United States Hockey Hall of Fame.

As for the "where are they now?", Neal and his wife Sally have two daughters and live in scenic River Falls Wis., where they have a 75-acre horse farm. He recently became a grandpa, believe it or not, and he is loving life. When he's not golfing, hunting or doing charity work for the many causes that he tirelessly supports, Neal is talking about hockey — something that will remain near and dear to his heart for the rest of his life.

What did it mean for you to be a Gopher?

"They way I feel about the Gophers can be summed up in two words: pride and tradition. There is just so much class there, and to be a part of that was really a humbling experience. Just the feeling of putting on that big 'M' sweater with all those other Minnesota kids, and to play in front of such great fans was something I will always cherish. Then, getting the chance to play on the 1980 Olympic team was an experience I will never forget as well. Just making that squad was an accomplishment. It's something that I always look back on proudly, because there were 12 of us Minnesotans on the team. That just showed the world what kind of kids come from Minnesota, and we were all really proud of the way we represented our state."

What Did it Mean For You to Be a North Star?

"It meant a lot to be playing for my home state team. It was pretty special for me to have been able to have played with all those great players in front of all the great Minnesota fans. I feel spoiled that I got to be here for so long, and that the fans for some reason treated me like a king. I just can't thank them enough. To come home and retire, and to be treated so well by the people here is something I can't explain. I am so humbled by everyone's generosity and am just proud to have been able to have brought joy to their lives through the game of hockey."

Most Memorable Game?

(In 1990, on the weekend when Roseau won the state high school hockey tournament, the North Stars had a "Broten Brothers Day," at a game against the New York Rangers at the Met. Neal and Aaron were both playing for the Stars, and Paul was playing for the Rangers.) "It was great supporting the Rams, the town of Roseau, and to see them win the championship like that was incredible."

On the Stars' Move to Dallas?

"It was tough for me to take. A lot of people took it pretty rough, and it was a real big deal. I remember this strange feeling and thinking that this can't be happening to me. You didn't really think it was going to happen until it happened, and then you're moving to Texas."

Gopher & North Stars Tombstones:

"I just want to be remembered as an unselfish team player who thought of his teammates before himself."

1979 RUNNER-UP: ALLEN WILLEY

The Kicks win the NASL's Central Division crown with a 21-9 record. Despite the fact that the team scored a franchise record 184 goals that season, they wound up getting upset by Tulsa in the first round of the playoffs. One of the stars of the team was *ALLEN WILLEY*, who came to the U.S. on loan in 1976 from the English Football League and ended up staying in the U.S. for nine seasons. He played primarily for the Kicks from 1976 to 1981, followed by a two-year stint in Montreal. One of the highlights of Willey's career came in a playoff game against the New York Cosmos, where he scored five goals in a 9-2 Kicks victory. After playing with the Kicks, Willey later returned to Minnesota and played for the Strikers. He finished his career as the second leading scorer in NASL history with 129 goals in 234 games, and was later inducted into the National Soccer Hall of Fame in 2003.

HONORABLE MENTION: JOHN CASTINO

The Twins finish at 82-80, good for just fourth place in the division. One highlight, however, was the play of third baseman *JOHN CASTINO*, who hit .285 and earned American League Rookie of the Year honors. Castino played with the Twins for his entire six year MLB career, hitting .278 with 41 homers and 249 RBI.

The 1980 basketball Gophers were all about a kid from Hibbing by the name of Kevin McHale, who would help lead this young team all the way to the N.I.T. Finals. McHale, the team captain, had taken the young group under his wing the year before when he found himself starting alongside of four freshmen: forward Trent Tucker, center Gary Holmes, and guards Mark Hall and Darryl Mitchell. In addition, Lake City's Randy Breuer, a seven-footer, was on the squad and getting better by the day.

The Gophers opened their non-conference schedule by reeling off four straight wins before losing to both Tennessee and Florida State. After beating Kansas State, Minnesota won the Pillsbury Classic tournament. Then, they dropped their conference opener, 71-67, at Michigan, but rebounded two nights later with an impressive 93-80 win over the defending Big Ten and NCAA champs from Michigan State. It was up and down for the young Gophers though, as they lost several close games on the road after that. Included were three rough overtime defeats at the hands of the Illini, Buckeyes, and Boilermakers, as well as a 73-63 loss to Iowa. Minnesota did, however, go on to beat Indiana, 55-47, as well as Ohio State, 74-70, Purdue, 67-61, Illinois, 79-75, and Michigan, 68-67.

All in all, it was a good season for the Gophers and a great senior season for McHale. Minnesota would ultimately finish the regular season with a 17-10 record, tied for fourth place in the Big Ten with Iowa at 10-8. Although they didn't make the NCAA Tournament, the Gophers did get an invitation to the 43rd annual post-season National Invitational Tournament, or N.I.T. There, in the first round at Williams Arena, the Gophers rolled over Bowling Green, 64-50, and followed that up with wins over Mississippi, 58-56, and Southwestern Louisiana, 94-73, thanks to Tucker and Breuer, who had 18 points apiece, while Hall and McHale added 16 and 15, respectively. Next, it was off to the N.I.T.'s version of the Final Four at New York City's famed Madison Square Garden.

In the semifinals, behind Breuer's 24 points, the Gophers avenged their overtime loss to Big Ten rival Illinois in a nail-biter, 65-63. In so doing, they now set the stage for the championship game against seven-foot sensation Ralph Sampson and the Virginia Cavaliers.

The Gophers jumped out to a 21-12 lead in the first 10 minutes of the title game behind the strong play of McHale, Tucker and Breuer. But, thanks to Sampson, who had 15 points and 15 rebounds, the Cavs took the lead at halftime.

It was a back and forth affair for both squads throughout the second half. Then with 1:31 to play, Sampson sank two free throws to put Virginia ahead, 54-53. Now, with 1:06 remaining in the game, McHale's pass to Breuer was intercepted. So, with only 33 seconds on the clock, Minnesota fouled Virginia's Terry Gates. Gates missed the one-on-one, but the Cavaliers came up with the rebound. Jeff Lamp, a Cavalier guard, was then fouled and proceeded to sink both shots and put his squad up by three. With 11 seconds left, McHale, in desperation, drove for a dunk on Sampson and was fouled. He made both shots to get the Gophers within one point. Minnesota was then forced to foul immediately. It was Lamp who would go to the line again, only this time he sank them both to ice it for Virginia, 58-55.

"We just got too cautious," said Dutcher, whose squad finished the year with an impressive 21-11 record. "We

didn't push the ball down the floor and look for any fast breaks. And we got so conscious of getting the ball inside that we didn't take the outside shots we had."

"I remember the game very well," added McHale, who scored eight points in the game. "We got all the way to the Finals and, unfortunately, we didn't play particularly well that night. I was sad on a lot of levels. Besides losing the game it was also my last game as a Gopher. I felt a lot of anxiety at that moment because there were some big, big changes coming my way in a hurry."

Mitchell, who had a game-high 18 points, along with Breuer, were both named to the all-tournament team. McHale, meanwhile, who averaged 17.4 points and 8.8 rebounds per game that season, was named to the All-Big Ten team.

"Kevin is one of the premier big men in the nation," said Dutcher. "He has the ability to score inside or outside. We feel he is one of the most complete players in the country. He can rebound, score, block shots and run well."

From Hibbing to the Hall of Fame

Kevin McHale is without question the greatest basketball player ever to hail from the state of Minnesota. With his patented fade-away jumper and silky smooth touch, he was simply unstoppable in the low post. His hoops legacy was in fact a rather unique form of basketball artistry. From jump-hooks to baseline reverse lay-ins, McHale was a true artist whose canvas was the hardwood.

After an amazing Hall of Fame career with the NBA's Boston Celtics, Minnesota was blessed when its most prodigal of native sons decided to return home for good to begin his second career as an executive with the upstart Timberwolves in 1993. An avid outdoorsman, Kevin couldn't wait to get back to the Land of 10,000 Lakes to resume fishing and hunting, which, outside of the basketball court, is where he probably feels most at home.

McHale's story is a long and fascinating one, which has roots that extend all the way up to Hibbing, where he grew up learning the values of a strong work ethic from a father who was a miner on the great Missabe Iron Range. It was up in the northwoods where this kid learned to love and appreciate the power of sports. At first, Kevin played them all. And who knows? Had it not been for that lanky six-foot-ten frame of his, perhaps he would've gone on to greatness as a winger for the North Stars instead!

Fortunately for us, he decided to pursue his calling on the hardwood, where he has certainly made us all so very proud. From what began as a hobby at the Green Haven Elementary School, became an obsession for a kid who dreamt of one day playing for his beloved Golden Gophers. As a youngster, Kevin would oftentimes go down to the Hibbing library to read about the Gophers in the Minneapolis Newspapers. He had to have his fix, and every time he read about guys like Jim Brewer, Corky Taylor, Ron Behagen, and Clyde Turner, it made him even hungrier to pursue his dreams.

Kevin worked hard as a prepster and went on to earn All-State honors as a junior at Hibbing Senior High. He led his club to the post-season that year as well, only to get upset in the first round of the section playoffs by Little Falls. Then, as a senior, he led his Blue Jackets to the 1976 Class AA State Basketball Tournament title game against Bloomington Jefferson. They ultimately lost that big game to the Jaguars, but not before making believers out of every "David vs. Goliath" fan in the state. And, when Kevin outplayed Jefferson's All-State big man, Steve Lingenfelter, many of the nation's top collegiate recruiters knew that they were witnessing something special.

Kevin, who went on to win the coveted "Mr. Basketball Minnesota" award after his senior season, modestly turned away all of the scholarship offers, and opted to instead pursue his dream of wearing the Maroon and Gold at the U of M. Gopher fans everywhere rejoiced when they heard the news, and quickly tabbed him as the savior of a program that was on the rebound. McHale then came in and simply took Gold Country by storm, becoming an instant fan-favorite at

Williams Arena.

Kevin became synonymous with Minnesota basketball, and from 1977-80, he averaged 15.2 points and 8.5 rebounds per game, while accumulating an incredible 1,704 points – then second all-time in school history. A two-time All-Big 10 selection, McHale was also the U's career record holder for blocked shots with 235, and had also amassed the second most rebounds of all-time with 950 as well. An extremely unselfish player, McHale wasn't afraid to get physical down in the paint and do the dirty work that most players tend to shy away from. He took just as much pride in his rebounding as he did in his scoring, which said a lot about the type of player he was.

After his illustrious career in Gold Country, McHale was selected with the third overall pick of the first round of the 1980 NBA Draft by the Boston Celtics. Before he joined the club though, he played on a pair of gold medal-winning U.S. Pan-Am teams in both Puerto Rico and Mexico.

McHale then headed east to join one of the greatest franchises in all of sports, the Celtics. There, he would help make up one of the most formidable front-lines in the history of the game, alongside Hall of Famers Larry Bird and Robert Parrish. He made an impact his rookie season too, garnering All-Rookie Team honors en route to leading the team to the NBA title. He led Boston to two more championships in both 1984 and 1986, as well as five Eastern Conference titles and eight Atlantic Division crowns. He was given the NBA's Sixth-Man Award both in 1984 and 1985, and among his seven trips to the All-Star game, he was selected to the All-NBA First Team in 1987. He was also named to the NBA All-Defensive First Team in 1986, 1987 and 1988.

Over his incredible 13-year NBA career he scored 17,335 points, while averaging 17.9 points, 7.3 rebounds, and 1.7 assists per game. At the time of his retirement in 1993 he ranked 10th all-time in the NBA in career field goal percentage with .554. In fact, twice he led the league in field-goal percentage, and he remains the only player in NBA history to shoot over 60 percent from the field and 80 percent from the free throw line in the same season when he did it in 1987. In addition, his 56-point effort against the Detroit Pistons on March 3, 1985, still ranks in the top-five all-time in Celtics' single-game history.

In 1993 Kevin quietly retired from the game. Perhaps famed Boston Globe writer Bob Ryan put it best: "The long-armed wonder from Minnesota's Missabe Iron Range won his way into the hearts of Beantowners with his lunch-bucket approach to the game and his uncanny ability to play Tonto to Larry Bird's Lone Ranger."

Danny Ainge, McHale's former teammate jokingly referred to his buddy as "the black hole," because once you got a pass to him inside, the ball was not coming back out. "He just struck fear in the hearts of the defenders," said Ainge.

"During the height of his career he was easily the best power forward playing the game, and I'd rate him in the top three of all time," said Celtic great Bob Cousy.

"Kevin was a great college player but I think he turned out to be a better pro," added Larry Bird. "As a low-post player he's the best I've ever seen."

Kevin came home to his beloved Minnesota in 1993 and

began working with the Minnesota Timberwolves. For two years he worked as the assistant GM and also served as a TV analyst for Wolves games. In May of 1995, he took over the team, becoming the general manager as well as vice president of basketball operations. In that role, McHale has become responsible for the franchise's entire basketball operations department – overseeing player personnel decisions, scouting and the coaching staff. One of his first moves with the Wolves was selecting high-school phenom Kevin Garnett with the fifth-overall pick in the 1995 NBA Draft. Mchale wasted little time in retooling the entire Wolves roster and soon made his presence felt. In 1997, the team made its first-ever playoff appearance under McHale's former Gopher teammate and pal, Coach Flip Saunders. From there, the Wolves would make eight consecutive post-season appearances, with the highlight coming in 2004, when the team made it all the way to the Conference Finals before losing to L.A.

McHale's legacy will include many things. Most importantly will be his reputation as the most unstoppable NBA low-post scorer of his era. His hard work and desire to win, coupled with his creativity with the ball down in the paint truly revolutionized the game for generations to come.

Among his many honors and accolades, in 1997 McHale was named as one of the NBA's Top 50 Players for the league's first half-century, and in 1999 he was immortalized forever when he was inducted into the Basketball Hall of Fame. In addition, in 1995, Kevin was honored as the best player in 100 years of Gopher Basketball, as his No. 44 was officially retired up into the rafters of Williams Arena.

Today Kevin continues his never-ending quests of shooting that perfect round of golf, landing a 10-pound Walleye, watching and hoping that his Vikings will someday win the Super Bowl, and most importantly, leading his Timberwolves to that elusive NBA championship. He is happy to be home though, pursuing both of his passions of the great outdoors and basketball. He and his wife have five kids and presently live in North Oaks.

What Did it Mean For You To Be a Gopher?
"This was a great time in my life. I had a ton of fun going to school at the U and met so many good people. I still have a lot of great friends from my years there. We had such a good time playing ball. At that time I didn't even think about a future in the NBA. I was just happy to have fun and get an education. It was the whole atmosphere at the U that I just loved."

1980 RUNNER-UP: THE "MIRACLE ON ICE"

Led by coach Herb Brooks, the *1980 U.S. OLYMPIC HOCKEY TEAM* makes history by winning the gold medal at the Winter Games in Lake Placid, NY. Fully 13 Minnesotans were on the fabled squad, including: Bill Baker, Neal Broten, Dave Christian, Steve Christoff, John Harrington, Steve Janaszak, Mark Johnson, Rob McClanahan, Mark Pavelich, Mike Ramsey, Buzz Schneider, Eric Strobel and Phil Verchota. After beating the heavily favored Soviets in the semifinals, the Americans topped Finland to claim gold. The epic event would later earn the honor of being named as the "Sports Achievement of the Century."

HONORABLE MENTION: SCOTT LEDOUX

Heavyweight boxer *SCOTT LEDOUX* gets his shot at the belt, only to come up short against the reigning world champ, Larry Holmes. The match takes place on July 7th at the Met Center in Bloomington, with Holmes scoring a TKO over LeDoux midway through the seventh round to retain his WBC title. During the late 1970s and early '80s, the Crosby-Ironton native was ranked among the top heavyweight contenders in the world. During that time he was in the ring with 11 world champions — from Muhammed Ali to George Foreman to Frank Bruno. While LeDoux didn't win any titles, he did manage two draws against Leon Spinks and Ken Norton. Another highlight came in 1978, when he beat Pedro Soto at Madison Square Garden.

1981

BOBBY SMITH
The North Stars Take a Shot at the Cup

The 1981 North Stars season will forever be remembered as one of the all-time greats in Minnesota sports history. It was our first taste of Stanley Cup Finals hockey, and it literally took the state by storm. A combination of youth and veteran experience played a big role in the Stars compiling a solid 35-28-17 record that season, and leading the way was Center Bobby Smith, who scored 93 points on 29 goals and 64 assists.

The team had advanced all the way to the conference finals the year before, beating Toronto and Montreal before losing to Philadelphia, and was hungry to take that next big step in 1981. They had a great regular season and then also got a late boost that post-season when Neal Broten, who had just completed a Hobey Baker Award winning season with the Gophers, was added to the roster, adding even more quickness to an already speedy squad. The Stars had even traded away Glen Sharpley, thus freeing up Neal's lucky No. 7 jersey.

Much to the approval of the Minnesota fans, the Stars opened the first round of playoffs on the road against rival Boston. Now, coming in to this best-of-five playoff series, the Stars were a collective 0-28-7 in Boston, having never won a game in the Garden. There was clearly no love-loss between these two clubs, who, earlier in the year had beaten the hell out of each other at Met Center for a combined 406 penalty minutes (a record that still stands today!). So, the Stars headed to Beantown expecting another blood bath. Coach Glen Sonmor had prepared his boys to hope for the best, but to prepare for the worst. What they found, however, was that Boston wanted to play some serious hockey, and with that, the fans were treated to a great series.

In Game One, with the score tied at 4-4 the end of regulation, Steve Payne scored the dramatic overtime game-winner at 3:34 of the extra session to give the Stars a 1-0 lead in the series. With the Boston "monkey" now finally off of their proverbial backs, Minnesota followed it up with a 9-6 victory in Game Two. The series then shifted back to Bloomington for Game Three, and in what would play out to be a classic, the Stars, brimming with confidence, beat the Bruins 6-3 to sweep the series. "That had to be the biggest upset in Stars history," said legendary radio play-by-play analyst Al Shaver after the game.

Next up for Minnesota were the Adams Division champion Buffalo Sabres, who were sporting a gaudy .619 winning percentage. Steve Payne once again set the tone by scoring yet another overtime game-winner in Game One. The Stars didn't look back from that point on, winning both Games Two and Three, only to drop a Game Four double-overtime heart-breaker by the score of 5-4. They rolled on to win the series four games to one.

In the semis, the Stars found themselves pitted against another surprise team, the Calgary Flames. With Goalies Gilles Meloche and Donny Beaupre trading off in net, the Stars were proving to be a for-

midable force. Minnesota made a statement in the series opener by crushing the Flames, 4-1. Calgary came back to win Game Two on a late third period goal, only to see Minnesota win the next two games, 6-4 and 7-4. The Flames rallied to win Game Five, 3-1, back in Calgary. But the Stars hung in there and behind Brad Palmer's game-winning wrister in the third, took Game Six, 5-3. Protecting their home ice throughout the series, the Stars simply outplayed the Flames and ultimately won the series four games to two. With that, after several disappointing semifinal losses over the past

decade and a half, the North Stars, for the first time in franchise history, had finally made it to the Stanley Cup Finals.

"Getting the opportunity to play in the Stanley Cup Finals was incredible," reminisced Bobby Smith years later. "I can still remember standing on the bench as the conference finals game against Calgary was winding down, and Brad Palmer had just scored an insurance goal for us. Just realizing that you had spent your whole life watching the Stanley Cup Finals and now you were going to be playing in them, was tremendously exciting."

The Finals would prove to be a classic case of Cinderella vs. Goliath. Goliath, in this scenario, was the defending Stanley Cup champion New York Islanders, whose path to the Finals went through Edmonton, and then the Big Apple, where they swept their cross-town rival Rangers, in the semis. The Stars were now in uncharted territory as they geared up for the Isles, who were no strangers to the hoopla surrounding Lord Stanley's Cup.

Minnesota, primed on speed and enthusiasm, opened the best-of-seven series in New York. There, in front of some 15,000 fans, the Stars prepared to make history. It wouldn't be easy. The Stars, visibly nervous and looking scruffy (from not having shaved their "playoff beards" in weeks), took the ice with aspirations of winning professional hockey's most coveted prize. Things got off to a bumpy start for Minnesota as New York jumped out to a quick 1-0 lead on a goal by Anders Kallur. The Stars then caught a break when Bob Bourne was assessed a major penalty for spearing. Unfortunately, however, the Islanders jumped right back as Kallur and Brian Trottier scored two unanswered shorthanded goals during the five-minute disadvantage, and the Stars were never able to recover. A pair of third-period New York goals on only three shots secured an easy 6-3 Isles victory.

Game Two got off to a better start for the Stars as Dino Ciccarelli scored a power-play goal to go ahead early. (Dino emerged as a star in the playoffs, scoring 14 goals and 21 points in 19 games — both NHL playoff records for a rookie.) Then, just one minute later, Mike Bossy tied it up for New York. Shortly thereafter, both Potvin and Nystrom each scored one of their own as well. But the Stars rallied and came back to tie it at three apiece in the second, on goals from Palmer and Payne. The defending champs got nervous, but their experience prevailed as Potvin, Ken Morrow, and Bossy each scored in an eight-minute stretch to mirror the result of the 6-3 series opening win.

Game Three brought Stanley Cup mania to Bloomington. The Met Center was the site of countless tailgate parties as the adoring North Star fans welcomed home their heroes from the Big Apple. The Stars jumped out to a 3-1 lead after the first period in this one, and the crowd went crazy. But Butch Goring tallied twice in the second as the Islanders took a 4-3 lead into the final period. Again, the Stars rebounded, tying the game at the 1:11 mark of the third, only to see the Islanders regain the lead less than a minute later. With New York up by one, Goring put the final dagger in the collective hearts of Minnesota, scoring again at the six-minute mark for the hat-trick to all but seal it up. The Isles added an empty-netter and came away with the 7-5 victory.

Refusing to lie down and be swept, Minnesota played brilliantly in Game Four. Utility man Gord Lane opened the scoring for the Isles to silence the crowd early in the first. But then, midway through the period, controversy struck. With Minnesota on a power play, Brad Maxwell tallied on a blistering slapshot from the blue line. Or so he thought! Referee Andy Van Hellemond apparently never saw the shot, which was later seen on the replay to rip right through the goal netting. The crowd went nuts over the no-goal call, but they were eased just seconds later when Craig Harstburg's shot from the point beat Billy Smith to tie it up. This time the red light was turned on and the crowd went berserk. With the score tied up at two apiece, Minnesota took the lead on Steve Payne's top-shelf slapper midway through the third. Bobby Smith then added an insurance goal late in the game to insure a 4-2 victory for the Stars. The arena nearly erupted.

The 19-year-old phenom goaltender, Donny Beaupre, played

huge, turning away shot after shot against the mighty Islanders, who had been held to fewer than five goals on only three occasions in 18 post-season games that season. The Stars kept their cool during the game and it paid off. Of the four North Star goals scored in the game, two came on power plays and a third was scored three seconds after an Islander penalty had elapsed.

With the win, the Stars had lived to skate yet another day. The series once again shifted back to Uniondale, Long Island, for Game Five. Unfortunately for the Stars though, New York came out flying. And, once again it was Butch Goring who would do most of the damage. At 5:12 of the first period a North Star clearing pass deflected off referee Bryan Lewis and right onto the stick of Bob Bourne, who promptly fed the rushing Goring for the goal. Then, less than a half a minute later, John Tonelli and Bob Nystrom dug the puck out from behind the Minnesota net and fed it to a wide open Wayne Merrick, who beat Beaupre to make it 2-0. That line was amazing. It was their 18th goal of the playoffs — all of which came while at even strength against their adversaries' top lines. A few minutes later, Goring, who would capture the Conn Smythe Trophy as the playoff's MVP, scored again on a wrister, putting the game out of reach. Behind legendary coach Al Arbour, the Isles went on to win the game, 5-1, and the series. It would be the second of four-straight Cups in the Islander's amazing dynasty.

The Savior

Bobby Smith grew up playing hockey in Ottawa and went on to play major junior hockey for the Ottawa 67s in the Ontario Hockey Association. In the 1978 he scored 69 goals and 123 assists for an amazing 192 regular season points, and then added another 30 points in the playoffs. He topped the OHA in both assists and points that season, and was named as the Canadian Major Junior Player of the Year. His stock rose quickly from there and before long was projected to be the No. 1 player selected in that year's upcoming NHL draft.

For the Stars, finishing dead last in the Smythe Division at the conclusion of the 1978 season may have been a blessing in disguise, for they were rewarded with that very No. 1 overall pick in the draft. It was a tumultuous time for the organization. Against the background of several losing seasons, there were serious financial problems facing the struggling franchise. As a result, management decided to merge their franchise with the Cleveland Barons. The move, controversial at the time, would save the franchise from extinction. Now they needed to get the fans excited about hockey again in Minnesota. They needed a savior, and his name was Bobby Smith. Lou Nanne, the long-time North Star who had moved from the ice up to the front office, was overjoyed to obtain the rights to select the 20-year-old, six-foot-four phenom.

Smith established a torrid scoring pace in his first year, scoring 30 goals and 44 assists en route to winning the Calder Trophy, as the NHL's Rookie of the Year. The Stars also improved by 23 points under the tutelage of veteran coach Glen Sonmor, who had previously guided the WHA's St. Paul Fighting Saints. Bobby instantly became a fan favorite in Minnesota, leading the Stars in scoring four of his first five years with the club. Perhaps his finest season with the team, however, came during the 1981-82 campaign when he notched career highs in games played (80), goals (43), assists (71), and points (114).

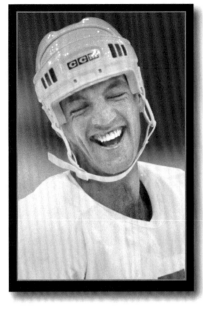

In 1984, Smith was involved in one of the team's most talked-about trades ever, when be was dealt to the Montreal Canadiens for Keith Acton, Mark Napier and a third-round pick. Smith played seven seasons north of the border, recording 70-plus points in five of those years. In 1986, he led the Canadians to a Stanley Cup victory, even scoring the game-winning goal in a 4-3 win over Calgary. It was truly a dream-come-true.

Then, in 1991, Smith, now a 33-year-old veteran, returned to Minnesota to lead the Stars back the Stanley Cup Finals, this time against the Pittsburgh Penguins. Unfortunately the series had all too familiar results, as Mario Lemieux and Jaromir Jagr beat the Stars in six games. Nevertheless, Smith's leadership and guidance, both on the ice and in the locker room, was immeasurable. He contributed eight goals and eight assists in that playoff run after a 46-point regular season, proving that he hadn't lost the edge that had always made him special in the minds of Stars fans.

For 15 seasons Bobby ruled the red line. He played in 1,077 games with the North Stars and Canadiens, scoring an amazing 1,036 points. Smith also played in 184 playoff games, where he scored 64 goals and 96 assists for 160 points, ranking him 12th on the NHL's all-time playoff point leaders list. Smith also played in four NHL All-Star Games (1981,1982, 1989 and 1990), and from 1981 to 1990 served as the vice president of the NHL Players' Association.

When the North Stars were hijacked to Dallas in 1993, Bobby promptly retired, ending two wonderful chapters of Minnesota hockey. After retiring from the game Smith fulfilled a lifelong dream and went back to college at the U of M to obtain his MBA. That experience would pay quick dividends, when, in 1996, he became the Phoenix Coyotes' first Vice President of Hockey Operations and later the GM. Smith would later become the majority owner of QMJHL's Halifax Mooseheads, for whom his son Daniel played.

Bobby was one of the greatest hockey players to ever lace up the skates representing a Minnesota team. He had incredible instincts, an amazingly accurate shot, and a great passing touch. He was the ultimate competitor and team player, always putting his teammates first.

North Stars Tombstone:

"I would like to be remembered as a guy who always competed to the best of his ability and became as good a hockey player as he could have become. And, as a guy who played his best hockey in the playoffs, when it was the most important, as well as when it was the most difficult to play your best."

1981 RUNNER-UP: AARON BROTEN

The hockey Gophers come up short in the 1981 NCAA Finals, losing to rival Wisconsin, 6-3. Minnesota advanced to the Finals after beating Michigan Tech in the semis, 7-2. What made the event even more exciting was the fact that the Frozen Four was held at the Duluth Entertainment and Convention Center (DECC) that year. Leading the charge for the Maroon and Gold was *AARON BROTEN*, who narrowly lost out on winning the inaugural Hobey Baker Award (emblematic of the nation's top college player), to his big brother, Neal. Aaron led the nation in scoring that year with 47 goals and 59 assists for 106 points. The Roseau native would go on to play in the NHL for 11 seasons, tallying 515 points in 748 career games.

HONORABLE MENTION: DICK BEARDSLEY

Marathoner extraordinaire *DICK BEARDSLEY* wins the inaugural Grandma's Marathon in Duluth with a time of 2 hours, 9 minutes and 37 seconds — a record that still stands. The Rush City native would go on to make history that next year as well when he finished second in what still remains the closest Boston Marathon ever, narrowly losing to Alberto Salazar. Beardsley was cut off by a TV motorcycle in the final stretch, causing him to lose the race by just two seconds. Incidentally, both runners set course and U.S. records in the process.

1982

TRENT TUCKER
The Gophers Win the Big Ten Title

The Minnesota faithful had good reason to be optimistic for the upcoming 1981-82 hoops season. After all, the team was returning all of its starters and even opened the year ranked in the top-10 in the nation. Led by Trent Tucker, Randy Breuer, Darryl Mitchell, Mark Hall, Gary Holmes, Jim Petersen and Tommy Davis, the Gophers won their first five non-conference games that year, including victories over San Francisco State, Dayton, Loyola, Drake and Marquette. After losing to Kansas State, they returned home to the friendly confines of Williams Arena, where they first crushed Army, 79-37, and then the Arizona Wildcats, 91-62, en route to capturing their eighth consecutive Pillsbury Classic holiday title.

In their final non-conference game, the brilliant Trent Tucker led the way with 22 points, as coach Jim Dutcher's contingent easily handled Cal State Long Beach, 75-67. With an impressive 8-1 record, the stage was now set for the start of the 1982 Big Ten Conference race. Unfortunately though, the Gophers lost the opener to a very tough Ohio State team, 49-47, in Columbus. Minnesota bounced back two nights later, however, with a 64-58 victory against Michigan State at East Lansing. The next stop was Williams Arena and the hated rivals to the south, the Iowa Hawkeyes. There, more than 17,000 zealous fans jammed the barn to watch the Gophers upend the Hawkeyes. Behind Randy Breuer's 22 points, Minnesota won the game, 61-56. Two nights later, Tucker stepped up by pouring in 21 points en route to leading his Gophers past the Michigan Wolverines, 67-58.

Minnesota continued to build its confidence throughout the season, with Tucker and Breuer shouldering much of the load. Fans from across the state suddenly started to hop on the bandwagon as the Gophers began to show signs that they were for real. That next week, the now 5th ranked Gophers simply outplayed the Badgers in Madison, winning in a blow-out, 78-57. Their next opponent, Illinois, would give them trouble all season. The Illini came to town on January 23rd and knocked off Minnesota, 64-57. The loss could have been a turning point for the team, but they would have little time to dwell on it as they traveled to Evanston, Ill., and Bloomington, Ind., the following week. But, in what was starting to become a trend for the squad, they rebounded from the Illinois loss by beating the Northwestern Wildcats, 61-53, and Bobby Knight's Indiana Hoosiers, 69-62, in a game where all five Minnesota starters scored in double figures

They followed this up with a 73-50 drubbing of the Purdue Boilermakers at home, but stumbled against the Hoosiers at Williams Arena, losing a squeaker, 58-55. Unfazed, the Gophers sucked it up and won three in a row against the Badgers, Boilermakers, and Wildcats, to set up the much anticipated rematch with the Illini in Champaign. There, in a game that was closer than the final score would reflect, the Gophers once again fell to Illinois, 77-65.

It was now crunch time for the Gophers as they headed into the final two-week stretch of the season. The Gophers, of course, were still very much in contention for the Big Ten title. First, they invaded Michigan, where they hadn't beaten the Wolverines since 1963. That 0-16 record fell in a big way on that day though, as Minnesota prevailed, 60-51. With their confidence higher than ever, the Gophers then traveled to Iowa City to do battle with the Big Ten front-runners, in what turned out to be the biggest game of the year. The implications were enormous as Iowa led Minnesota in the conference standings.

This one was back and forth throughout the entire contest. It seemed that everytime Minnesota struggled to gain the lead, the Hawkeyes found a way to pull ahead. It was a thriller that went down to the wire, and the two teams ultimately wound up going into overtime. Then another overtime and amazingly, one more. Finally, in the third exhausting extra session, Darryl Mitchell, who led the Gophers with 21 points, sank two huge free throws with no time showing on the clock to clinch a stunning 57-55 Minnesota win.

"That triple overtime game against Iowa was probably the most memorable game I ever played in — it was just unbelievable," said team captain Trent Tucker. "It was a really tough situation in a very hostile environment, but we got a total team effort to win it. I'll always remember Randy Breuer's big blocked shot to save us to get us back into it, and then Darryl Mitchell's two free throws to seal it. The whole thing was just incredible!"

The Gophers, now deadlocked with Iowa for the Big Ten lead, returned home to host Michigan State the following Thursday. In front of a packed mob of excited fans, the Gophers did not disappoint. Despite only shooting a paltry 35 percent from the floor, they upended the Spartans, 54-51, in another nail-biter, highlighted by a pair of Gary Holmes free throws with 11 seconds remaining to seal the win. Mitchell led the way with 16, while Breuer added 14 and Tucker added 13. In an interesting side-bar, Illinois beat Iowa to put Minnesota in the driver's seat on the road to the championship. Then, in the final regular season game of the year, Breuer lit it up by scoring a career high 32 points and 12 rebounds while Tucker added 23, as the Gophers beat Ohio State, 87-75, to win the 1982 Big Ten title.

"For me, it was seeing all my expectations and goals come true," said Tucker. "I came to Minnesota in 1978 as a part of the biggest and most celebrated recruiting class in the history of the program. So the pressure was there from day one, and we were expected to someday win a championship. Now, it was year four, and we had matured to a level where we could win it all. To hear the final horn go off and to see the jubilation of the fans, the coaches, and the players was just great."

"It was a tight race all season long, but we held on to win it," added Breuer, who led the team in scoring, rebounding, and blocks. "It was amazing. It was tremendously gratifying because we were the team that was predicted to win it all from the beginning. We had a lot of seniors on that team, but it was a tough fought battle all season long. You couldn't relax for one game because the whole season was tight all the way."

Minnesota ultimately finished 14-4 in the conference that season, good enough to win their first Big Ten title in 10 years. For Dutcher, the 1981-82 team was his third team in seven years to win 20 or more games. And for the first time ever, his squad also earned an NCAA post season tournament bid.

After receiving a first-round bye, the team flew to Indianapolis to play the University of Tennessee-Chattanooga in the Mideast Regional. There, the Gophers, who were led by 20 points from Tucker, 17 from Breuer, and 16 from Mitchell, squeaked by UTC, 62-61, in a thriller. Next it was off to Alabama, where they would have to take on Denny Crum's tough Louisville Cardinals. There, despite 22 points apiece from Breuer and Tucker, the Gophers lost down the stretch, 67-61. (Perhaps the team fell victim to the "Sheraton Jinx." You see, the Gopher basketball team was staying at the Sheraton Hotel in Birmingham, the same hotel that the Gopher football team stayed at when they were beaten by Maryland in the Hall of Fame Bowl only five years earlier.) At any rate, it was a disappointing loss and a sad ending to a fabulous season for the Gophers, who finished with an impressive 23-6 overall record. (They should also be given credit for being a "Sweet 16" team, because back then the "Tourney" featured only 32 teams.)

Post-season honors were highlighted by the naming of Tucker to the All-American and All-Big Ten teams. He would go on to be drafted in the first round by the New York Knicks, who took him sixth overall. Breuer and Mitchell were also named to the 1982 All-Big Ten team as well. Breuer was selected in the first round of the NBA draft by the Milwaukee Bucks and later played for the Minnesota Timberwolves. And, in a testament to Gopher basketball success, Hall, Holmes, Peterson, and Davis also went on to be drafted too.

Tuck

Born December 20, 1959, in Taraboro, NC, the youngest of four children, Trent Tucker grew up in Flint, Mich., and went on to play basketball and baseball at Flint Northwestern High School, just north of Detroit. There, the six-foot-five guard averaged 29 points and 12 rebounds per game, good enough to be named as a high school All-American. Out of high school he was heavily recruited throughout the Big Ten, especially by his home state Wolverines at the University of Michigan. Tucker had always been a big-time Michigan Football fan. But, luckily for us, he was recruited by Jesse Evans, an assistant coach with the Gophers who was his junior high school coach. And, as luck would have it, when Trent came to Minnesota on a recruiting trip, he watched the Gophers upset his Wolverines at Memorial Stadium, and from that point on he knew that he wanted to be a Gopher.

Tucker wore the Maroon and Gold from 1978-82. He went through a lot during his tenure in Gold Country, including learning the game from a couple of pretty good teammates — Mychal Thompson and Kevin McHale. For his career, he remains at or near the Top 10 all-time in nearly ever offensive category, including scoring, with 1,445 points, assists with 219 and steals with 153. He averaged 12.5 points and 3.4 rebounds per game over his four-year career, while shooting 50 percent from the field and nearly 80 percent from the charity stripe.

After his brilliant career at the University, Tucker went on to play 11 seasons in the NBA, nine of them with the New York Knicks, but also with Michael Jordan and the Chicago Bulls, where he won a championship ring in 1993. He retired from active competition after that season and went on to become a TV analyst for the Timberwolves. For his career in the NBA, Tucker averaged 8.2 points, 2.0 assists and 2.0 rebounds per game. A solid two-way player, he also tallied 6,236 career points, of which 1,725 were from three-point range. He still ranks fifth in 3-point field goal percentage in the history of the NBA.

Tucker was one of the greatest pure shooters ever to have come out of Minnesota. His jump-shot was legendary, and one could only imagine what he would have done if they had a three-point line back in those days. He will always be remembered not only for being an incredible basketball player who led the school to a Big Ten title, but also because he is a genuinely nice person who always played team basketball. Today, in addition to running his basketball camp, Trent cohosts a popular sports radio show on KFAN and also gives back to the community through his "Trent Tucker Non-Profit Organization," which is dedicated to empowering youth to make positive choices.

What Did it Mean For You To Be a Gopher?

"As a freshman, I didn't understand what it really meant to be a Gopher because I was too young to understand. But as I progressed and got older, the significance of being a Gopher and what it meant to the community became apparent to me. It was an unbelievable experience and something I will always treasure. I looked upon my teammates just like

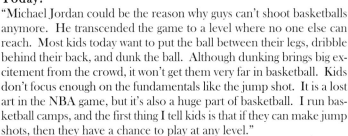

we were a family. You'd go through the ups and downs with your teammates and when the last game was played, all you have is memories. I miss those moments of guys pulling together, trying to overcome all the adversity, and then finding a way to win as a team. Aside from furthering my education, the University of Minnesota also afforded me the opportunity to fulfill my lifelong childhood dream of playing in the NBA. Knowing that all that hard work had paid off was very gratifying to me."

Where Are the Pure Shooters in the NBA Today?

"Michael Jordan could be the reason why guys can't shoot basketballs anymore. He transcended the game to a level where no one else can reach. Most kids today want to put the ball between their legs, dribble behind their back, and dunk the ball. Although dunking brings big excitement from the crowd, it won't get them very far in basketball. Kids don't focus enough on the fundamentals like the jump shot. It is a lost art in the NBA game, but it's also a huge part of basketball. I run basketball camps, and the first thing I tell kids is that if they can make jump shots, then they have a chance to play at any level."

On That Patented Tucker Jumper:

"I was born to shoot a basketball, like some guys are born to hit a baseball. I had the knack from day one. I had the proper technique and the proper balance as a player to shoot the jump shot. I was a natural shooter and I honed the skills that I was given."

Gopher Tombstone:

"Trent Tucker was a guy who came out and gave everything he had every night and played the game the way it was supposed to be played."

TRIBUTES

"Trent is such a nice guy," said Willie Burton. "He is someone you could look up to and follow and was a heck of a competitor. We played against each other a few times in the NBA, but I had already developed a tremendous amount of respect for him back when I was in college. Off the court he was the nicest guy around, but on the court, whoaaa!"

"He is a great guy and was a great basketball player," said Randy Breuer. "He also had a great family. I remember his parents and brothers coming up to Minnesota to watch us quite often when we were playing, and I thought that was really neat. I enjoyed playing with him a lot, and, boy, we had a great time."

1982 RUNNER-UP: DINO CICCARELLI

The North Stars win the Norris Division crown with a 37-23-20 record. Led by superstar **DINO CICCARELLI**, who tallied 55 goals and 51 assists for 106 points, the Stars met up with Chicago in the first round of the Stanley Cup Playoffs, only to get thumped by the Blackhawks, three games to one. The goaltending tandem of Gilles Meloche and Don Beaupre played well that year, but the club just came up short in the post-season. As for Ciccarelli, the scrappy winger would go on to score 608 goals and 592 assists for 1,200 career points over the next 20 seasons. The Hall of Fame is the next stop for this Minnesota fan-favorite.

HONORABLE MENTION: NANCY BAKER

The Gustavus women's gymnastics dynasty finally comes to an end. Led by legendary coach **NANCY BAKER**, the lady Gusties won seven NCAA Division III national championships from 1982-92. In addition, the Baker-led Gusties won 15 state championships in a 17-year span as well. Baker led 29 of of her 30 teams to the national tournament, and that was during a time when Divisions I, II and III all competed against one another at the same venue. The four-time NCAA Coach of the Year also coached five all-around national champions, 14 individual national champions and 34 All-Americans.

1983

BUD GRANT
A Coaching Legend Retires

In 1983, Bud Grant, possibly the greatest athlete ever to play and coach in the history of Minnesota sports, retired as the head coach of the Vikings. The gray-haired, crew-cutted warrior's exit from the game signified an end to one of the greatest sports eras of all time.

The early 1980s were a tumultuous time for the Vikings. Much of the teams' infrastructure, personnel and personality were about to change. The Purple People Eaters were all gone, and in 1982, the Vikings lost much of their mystique when they moved indoors to the Metrodome, something Bud could never really get used to. The cold weather had always given Minnesota a unique psychological advantage.

"The things that bothered me about going into the dome is that it took some of the coaching out of it," said Grant. "Outside I could use the elements to my advantage. Things like the wind, sun, rain, snow or a even a frozen field."

Bud never allowed his players to use heaters on the sidelines or even wear gloves or turtlenecks under the jerseys either. He wanted them to stay focused, and theorized that if his players were thinking about getting warm then they weren't thinking about football.

"We knew we could play with numb fingers and frozen feet, which gave us an edge," said receiver Ahmad Rashad. "A lot of times I caught passes without ever feeling the ball, just this heavy thump against my frozen hands."

"The Vikings always ran out for the warm-ups with this big facade, like we weren't cold," said Rashad in his book of the same name. "Of course, we were freezing. But the other teams didn't know that, not for sure. They would be looking at us out of the corners of their eyes, thinking 'How come these guys look so warm?' They must be some bad dudes."

At the end of the 1983 season, the Vikings had finished with an 8-8 record, good enough to place second in the NFC Central. Shortly after the season, Bud announced his resignation as the team's head coach. Not only was the entire state of Minnesota shocked by his announcement, but so too was the entire world of football. Bud simply decided it was time to get out. He wanted to spend more time with his family and enjoy more of the outdoors in the summer and fall, hunting and fishing. Those were his true passions.

"In my mind, timing is the most important thing," said Bud. "I decided this was the time to quit. There wasn't any pressure on me. There are a lot of things I want to do while I still have my health."

Grant was happy to be getting out on his terms, and he could now enjoy life from the stands, rather than from the sidelines. He was replaced by assistant Les Steckel, who had a drill sergeant's mentality and, unlike Bud, ran preseason training like boot camp. Steckel had issues and the team struggled, big-time.

Steckel's Vikings would rack-up an embarrassing 3-13 record in 1984, something that was hard for Grant to take. So, after helplessly sitting by and watching the team he had built crumble before his eyes, Bud decided to do something about it.

So, on December 18, 1984, fully 327 days after calling it quits, and after owner Max Winter and G.M. Mike Lynn begged him to resuscitate some life back into their franchise after its' disastrous season, Grant promptly un-retired. With Lou Holtz packing the Dome for Gopher games, Lynn needed a sure-thing. He needed a savior.

"It's unusual, but we're in an unusual business and you have to have the opportunity to be unusual," said Bud. "I think I'm old enough now to claim a little senility."

Grant's team rebounded in 1985 by going 7-9 and finishing third in the Central Division. Bud wanted to rehabilitate his team and get it back on track. He succeeded. So, on January 6, 1986, only 384 days after his return, Bud shocked the world yet one more time by announcing his re-retirement for the second time in as many years.

"I've been in professional sports for 36 years," said the 58-year-old Grant. "I think I'd like to enjoy the fruits of those endeavors."

His replacement this time was long-time assistant coach and friend, Jerry Burns. Determined to hang em' up for good, he even turned down several other high-buck offers to coach in the NFL. It was truly the end of an amazing era in Minnesota sports history.

From Superior Upbringings
Harry "Bud" Grant was born on May 20, 1927, and raised in Superior, Wisconsin. His father was the Superior Fire Chief. Bud grew up playing sports and became a tremendous prep athlete. After playing football, baseball and basketball at Superior's Central High School, Bud joined the Navy in 1945 and was stationed at the Great Lakes Naval Station outside Chicago. Bud continued his athletic prowess at Great Lakes, where his team played Big Ten clubs under football Coach Paul Brown and basketball Coach Weeb Ewbank, both hall of famers. In 1946, Bud was discharged and enrolled at the University of Minnesota.

There, even without a scholarship (because he was in the service, the G.I. bill paid for his tuition), he would excel in three sports, earning nine letters from 1946-49. He was a two-time All-Big Ten end on the football team, he starred as a forward and was the team MVP on the basketball team, and also played centerfield and pitched for the baseball team — where he even led the team in hitting as a freshman. On the gridiron under coach Bierman, Bud played with Gopher greats such as Leo Nomellini, Clayton Tonnemaker, Gordie Soltau, Billy Bye, Jim Malosky and Vern Gagne. Then, to earn spending money in the summers throughout college, Grant became creative. Since he could pitch three days a week and bat clean-up, he played baseball as a "ringer" for several small town-teams around Minnesota and Wisconsin, where he could mop up as much as $250 bucks in a good week.

"Being a Gopher kind of grows on you a little bit," said Bud. "It wasn't anything that I felt particularly strong about when I got there, but now it means a lot. Back then, the Gophers were the only game in town and we always played before a packed house. It was a tough time, with no scholarships and little money, but we had a lot of fun."

By 1950, Bud had finished his tenure at the U of M, and was considered by most to have been the most versatile athlete ever to compete there. (That was affirmed when he later beat out Bronko Nagurski and Bruce Smith to be named as the "Top Athlete at the University of Minnesota for the First 50 Years of the Century.") From there, he joined George Mikan and Jim Pollard as the newest member of the Minneapolis Lakers dynasty. In joining the Lakers, Bud also became the NBA's first "hardship case," meaning he could leave college early and play professionally. (Lakers GM and longtime friend Sid Hartman petitioned the league and made it happen for him.) As a Laker, Grant averaged 2.6 points per game in each of the two years he played for the club, both of which were NBA championship teams.

Anxious to try something different, Bud left the Lakers and joined the NFL's Philadelphia Eagles, who had made him their No. 1 draft pick that year. So talented was Grant, that in 1952, after switching from linebacker, where he led the team in sacks, to wide receiver, he finished second in the league in receiving and was voted to the Pro Bowl. After two years in Philly, he decided to take a 30% pay-raise and head north of the border to play for the Winnipeg Blue Bombers of the Canadian Football League. In so doing, Bud became the first player in NFL history to play out the option on his contract. He dearly missed hunting and fishing, something he figured he could readily do in up in Winnipeg.

There, he played both ways, starting at corner and at wide receiver. He led the league in receiving for three straight years and also set a record by intercepting five passes during a single game. Then in 1957, after only four years in the league, and in the prime of his career, the front-office offered the 29-year-old the team's head-coaching position. He accepted and proceeded to lead the Blue Bombers to six Grey Cups over the next 10 years, winning four of them.

On March 11th, 1967, Grant came home again, this time to take over the NFL's Minnesota Vikings. "I enjoyed Winnipeg very much, but coming to Minnesota was coming home for me," said Grant. It was a position that former Lakers owner, Max Winter, who now ran the Vikings, had originally offered to him, but had declined back in 1960. Bud took over from Norm Van Brocklin, and although he only won three games in his first season, that next year he led the purple to the division title. The year after that, in 1969, they made it to the Super Bowl, and Bud was named the league's Coach of the Year. It would be his first of four.

That was the beginning of one of the greatest coaching sagas in all of sports. Bud could flat out coach, and his players not only respected him, they also liked him. Bud treated them like men. He didn't work them too hard in practice and his players always knew they could count on that post-season playoff check. He was tough, but fair.

Grant, who coached for 28 years, won a total of 290 regular season and post-season games, 122 as coach of the Winnipeg Blue Bombers of the CFL from 1957-66, and 168 as coach of the Vikings from 1967-83 and 1985. At Minnesota, his teams made the playoffs 12 times, and won 15 championships: 11 Central Division (1968-71, 1973-78, and 1980), one NFL (1969) and three NFC (1973, 1974 and 1976). In 1994 Bud was inducted into the Pro Football Hall of Fame. With it, he became the first person ever to be elected to both the NFL and the Canadian Football League Halls of Fames.

"It's something that they can't take away from you," said Bud, whose presenter at the event was his old pal, Sid Hartman. "Usually in sports there is a new champion crowned every year, but this is forever."

Today, Bud and his wife Pat live in Bloomington. They have six children and many grandchildren. And, although he is officially retired from football, he maintains an office at the Vikings headquarters in Eden Prairie and still consults with the team from time to time.

Now, when he is not spending time either with his family or in the great outdoors, hunting or fishing, he has championed many causes that are near and dear to his heart. Among them is the fight against commercial fishing with nets and spears on Minnesota lakes. Bud is a zealous activist when it comes to preserving our natural resources and does all that he can to help preserve them for future generations.

Gophers/Vikings/Lakers Tombstones:

"There were people who could run faster, jump higher, throw harder and shoot better than me, but I don't think anybody competed any harder than I did. I felt that I always had an advantage over my opponents because I never got tired. The longer we played, the stronger I got. Then I could beat you. And I applied that same theory to coaching. That was the type of player who I was always looking to get to play

for me. Also, one thing that most coaches can't say, is that I've never been fired. I've always left whatever I was doing on my own accord, and I am proud of that. Every dollar I have ever made was from professional sports. I've had no other business or profession, and the only investments that I've got are six kids with college education's. Other than that, I don't have much."

TRIBUTES

"Bud should go down as one of the most intelligent coaches in the game," said Jim Marshall. "He understood how to deal with men. He had a unique sense about him that he could get the best out of every one of his players. He was a great organizer, he put together the team, ran a tight ship, and he brought true discipline to the team. He knew how to harness the talent and the energy that we as players had. I feel very respectful towards him for understanding that and not trying to change that part of what we had. He was not an egotist. He was a winner."

"Bud was the greatest professional coach that I have ever been around, he treated you like a man," said Ahmad Rashad. "He never wasted words. Bud was one of these guys that used to say: 'You practice, you prepare, you play, you go home, you have dinner.' He was a no-nonsense guy and just a great person."

"I came to know, understand, and appreciate Bud much later in life," said Carl Eller. "My affection for Bud has actually grown more since I left football. He was not a person to get close to his players, yet he cared deeply for his players. He had a great charisma, knowledge, and skill of the game. I appreciate his strengths and qualities much more now."

"He commanded respect as well as anyone I've ever known, and he did it without yelling or intimidating or chewing people out," said Fran Tarkenton. "He never put himself up as an offensive or defensive genius. But everybody knew that he was the leader. He just wasn't overbearing. He's a very wise man."

"I played football the old fashioned way, and I believe I was a great student of Bud Grant," said Joe Kapp. "He didn't coach a lot about X's and O's, but rather with an attitude. There was a deep fire in Bud that you never saw."

"He was very tenacious, a great defender, and he could shoot from the outside," said Laker great George Mikan. "He was always assigned to guard the opposing team's best scorer. One of his great talents was his ability to throw me the ball into the pivot. I loved him."

"Bud didn't tell you what you wanted to hear, he told you what you needed to know, and that's a big difference," said Chuck Foreman.

1983 RUNNER-UP: CURT GILES

The North Stars finish with a 40-24-16 overall record, good for second place in the Norris Division. From there, the Stars beat Toronto in the divisional semifinals of the Stanley Cup Playoffs, three games to one. They then went on to face rival Chicago in the divisional finals, where they got beat four games to one. One of the stars of the team was defenseman **CURT GILES**, who tallied 23 points from the blue line. Giles first hit the Minnesota hockey scene as a two-time All-American with the UM-Duluth Bulldogs. He was drafted by the Stars in 1978 and ultimately had two tours with the team (1979–86 and 1987–91). Giles also played for the Rangers and Blues, scoring 242 points over his 14 year NHL career. Giles would go on to coach at Edina High School.

HONORABLE MENTION: SCOTT BJUGSTAD

The hockey Gophers win the WCHA title and advance on to the NCAA Frozen Four. Led by center **SCOTT BJUGSTAD**, who paced the nation with 91 points that year, Minnesota posted a 32-12-1 record. The team beat New Hampshire in the playoffs, but then lost to Harvard in the Frozen Four semifinals, 5-3. The Irondale High School grad would go on to play on the 1984 U.S. Olympic team before joining his hometown North Stars that same year. He would play professionally for the next 10 years, ultimately scoring 76 goals and 68 assists in 317 career games.

TOM KURVERS & BILL WATSON
The Duluth Bulldogs Lose a Heartbreaker

Since its first official game back in 1931, the University of Minnesota Duluth has established a hockey tradition that has become synonymous with success. For many, hockey is a form of religion in northern Minnesota, and the UMD Bulldogs have gained a tremendously loyal following. There have been a lot of Bulldog hockey stars over the years, including the likes of: Tom Kurvers, Bill Watson, Bret Hull, Norm MacIver, Curt Giles, Derek Plante, Chris Marinucci, Jim Johnson, Chad Erickson, Tom Milani, Mark Pavelich, Murray Keogan, Chico Resch, Dave Langevin, Walt Ledingham, Ron Busniuk, Dennis Vaske, Bob Mason, Dan Lempe, Jim Toninato, Brett Hayer, Pat Boutette, Keith Christianson, Shjon Podein and Junior Lessard, to name a few.

There have been many great teams to play in the port city over the past 80 years, but none was better than the team that hit the ice in 1984. That year the Dogs finished with an impressive 29-12-2 overall record, the best in school history. They also posted a 19-5-2 mark in the WCHA, good enough to win their first-ever conference title in the 20 years that they had been in the league. Then, led by All-Americans Tom Kurvers and Bill Watson, the Dogs came as close as a team could possibly come to winning a national championship, only to come up just short. That national championship game was, by most accounts, the greatest ever played in college hockey history.

UMD Coach Mike Sertich's team, fresh of their first-ever showing in the NCAA playoffs against Providence the year before, started out their magical season by receiving a lesson in humility when they got spanked by the U.S. Olympic team, 12-0. Winger John Harrington of Virginia and goaltender Bob Mason of International Falls were both former Bulldogs who played on that 1984 squad. Another highlight that season came in December, when the Dogs split a two-game exhibition series with the Junior Red Army Team in Leningrad and in Moscow to become the first American collegiate ice hockey team to tour the Soviet Union.

UMD settled down after that and kicked off the WCHA season by sweeping Colorado College. From there, the Bulldogs won eight of nine and finished the regular season losing only four of their final 16 games. They swept Wisconsin at the season's end to win their first McNaughton Cup, signifying the conference title.

Forced to host a "home" series at Williams Arena in Minneapolis, due to a scheduling conflict with the Duluth Arena, the Dogs slaughtered North Dakota, 8-1 and 12-6, before near-capacity crowds in the WCHA championship series to advance to the NCAA quarterfinals at home against Clarkson. There, they split with Clarkson, and in so doing, earned themselves a trip to Lake Placid, NY, to face North Dakota in the NCAA Frozen Four. UMD did not disappoint either, beating the Fighting Sioux, 2-1, in an overtime thriller when two-time All-American right wing Bill Watson scored off a Bob Lakso feed in front of the net at the 3:09 mark of the first extra session.

Their opponents in the title game were the champions of the CCHA, Bowling Green, who had knocked off Michigan State in the other semifinal. Bowling Green, whose line-up was dominated by Canadians, had only four Americans on the squad. Duluth, on the other hand, comprised mostly of home-grown Minnesotans, had only four Canadians. The sell-out crowd of nearly 8,000 people had no idea that they were about to be a part of college hockey history when the opening puck dropped. They were though, and this one was noth-

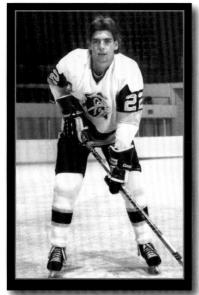

ing short of spectacular.

For the first time in two games, UMD fell behind early when Bowling Green defenseman Garry Galley crashed into Bulldog goalie Rick Kosti, and roofed a backhander at 5:58 of the first. The Dogs came back, as they had done so often that season, when Aurora's Bob Lakso stole the puck in the Bowling Green zone and slipped a pass to Chisholm's Mark Baron, who flipped the puck under the crossbar to tie it up at one apiece.

Then, after being stymied on their first three power-play attempts, Hoyt Lakes' Matt Christensen directed a face-off to the left point where Bill Watson proceeded to tip in a Kurvers blast to put UMD up by one. In the third, Lakso, who would be named to the all-tournament team, spurted between two Falcon defensemen and fired a low wrister to beat goaltender Gary Kruzich on the short side. Things were looking pretty good for UMD as they were now up 3-1. It didn't last long though, as Falcon forward Jamie Wansbrough, pressured by Bulldog defenseman Jim Johnson, drove in and went five-hole on Kosti. UMD answered right back, however, at 11:55 on a wrister by International Falls' Tom Herzig to make it 4-2.

As it went back and forth throughout the third, Bowling Green scored once again at 12:42. Kosti stopped a blue line blast by Mike Pikul, but got caught up in traffic in front of the net as he tried to recover. Forward Peter Wilson put in the garbage goal to make it 4-3, still in favor of Duluth. Then with 1:37 to go, Bowling Green tied it up on a fluke goal. With their goalie pulled, the Falcons dumped a long, off-target shot into the zone from beyond the red line that many people felt was off-side. Oddly, the puck bounced off the end boards and past Kosti, who had stepped behind the net to control a puck which would never arrive. The puck hit a crack in the dasher board, deflected to the net, hit the left post and stopped in the crease. With Kosti way out of position, John Samanski, who had sprinted down the slot, tapped in a "freebie" to tie it up.

"I've never seen it happen, but I've heard of it happening," said the goaltender of the tough-luck bounce that completely caught him off guard. "However, it never happened to me. It happened so fast that I didn't know what to do. I felt helpless."

From there the teams went to sudden death. And not just one overtime, in fact, there would be a total of four! Save after save, both goalies battled to stay alive. In the blur of the overtimes, Kruzich and Kosti, both freshmen goalies, played out of their heads. Kruzich stopped three UMD break-aways while Kosti stopped 19 shots in the final 37 minutes. Time stood still. It was unbelievable. Both teams were visibly fatigued and seemed to be skating on pure adrenaline.

Finally, at 7:11 of the fourth overtime, it ended, breaking the collective hearts of UMD hockey fans forever. Falcon winger Dan Kane sped into the Bulldog end from the neutral zone and, from the high slot, threaded a pass to Gino Cavallini, who broke in all alone on Kosti. Cavallini took the puck from the left to the right and buried a back-hander to make history. Sadly, UMD's dream season was over.

Kosti, who tied a tournament record with 55 saves, really had no chance on the game-winning goal. Kane made the perfect pass, and Cavallini made the perfect shot. That was it. As soon as the puck hit the back of the net, Kosti skated straight to his bench, where he was met by his teary-eyed teammates, who sat motionless in disbelief.

The Bulldogs and Falcons had skated for 97 minutes and 11 seconds at Olympic Arena, in a game that took nearly four hours, while taking part in the (then) longest and most memorable game in college hockey history. The historic arena in Lake Placid that housed the famed "Miracle on Ice" Olympic team four years earlier, had now played host to the "Marathon on Ice."

"The thing I remember most about the overtimes was being really tired and gasping for air during the whistles," said team captain Tom Kurvers. "I think we only played four defensemen for most of the game. After a while, you didn't take any chances. You just played your position and tried not to make a mistake. The whole overtime was confusing. I hardly remember any of it. I was hugely disappointed at the loss, but it was an incredible game."

"Just to be going into overtime was a huge letdown, and we didn't feel that we had to be there," added Bill Watson. "It's one thing to score late to get into overtime, and it's another thing to squander the lead to get into overtime. The excitement level was incredible. The overtimes went on and on and on, and it just became a situation of survival and mind over matter as to just how much you wanted to win. It was tough playing on the much bigger Olympic ice surface too. It was probably my toughest loss ever as a hockey player."

UMD turned the corner that night in the world of college hockey though. No longer were they just the second-best team in Minnesota. Bulldog hockey had officially arrived.

Then, in an ironic twist, UMD returned to the Final Four again the following year. This time, led by a young freshman named Brett Hull, they lost a 6-5 triple overtime heart-breaker to RPI, in Detroit. They rebounded to finish third in the nation by winning the consolation game, 7-6, over Boston College, in, you guessed it... overtime. For his team's efforts, Coach Mike Sertich was selected as the WCHA's Coach of the Year for an unprecedented third season in a row.

A Pair of Hobeys

Over those two fantasy seasons, two Bulldog players: Tom Kurvers and Bill Watson, each stood out above all others and were rewarded with college hockey's highest honor, the Hobey Baker Memorial Award. Kurvers won it in 1984, while Watson won it in 1985.

Tom Kurvers was born on September 14, 1962, and grew up skating in the shadows of the Met Center in Bloomington. In 1980, his Bloomington Jefferson Jaguars were knocked off in the State High School Hockey Tournament by Grand Rapids, who were led by future North Star goalie, John Casey.

During his tenure in the Duluth, Kurvers scored 43 goals and 149 assists for 192 total points. For his efforts he was named as a first-team All-American. He went on to play for seven teams over 11 seasons in the NHL where he scored 93 goals and added 328 assists for 421 career points. He retired from pro hockey in 1995, but has remained close to the game as a scout and team executive.

Bill Watson, meanwhile, was born on March 30, 1964, and grew up playing hockey in Powerview, Manitoba. He would go on to star on back-to-back national junior hockey championship teams in Prince Albert, Sask. He came to UMD in 1982, and by the time he had left, the right-winger had scored 89 goals and 121 assists for 210 points. He still holds the record for most assists in one season with 60. For his efforts he was twice named as a first-team All-American in 1984 and 1985. Watson then went on to play with the NHL's Chicago Blackhawks for five seasons, scoring 59 career points, before retiring in 1990 because of a shoulder injury.

What Did it Mean For You To Be a UMD Bulldog?
Kurvers: "I love the connection that I feel towards Duluth. There's a pride and bond there because of all the success that we had."

Watson: "There is such great hockey pride and tradition there. Duluth has always had a reputation of producing great players. We have

had not only great individuals, but we had some great teams as well. We went out there every night under the lights and play hard to win. Great players make great programs."

Bulldog Tombstones:
Kurvers: "He was one of the best hockey players to come out of Minnesota. Obviously not the best, but I am honored when my name gets tossed around with a Mike Ramsey, Reed Larson, Neal Broten, or Phil Housley — not as a comparison, but just in the group. It means so much to me to be thought of in the same breath as those guys, who I have a lot of respect for."

Watson: "My career was more than the Hobey Baker Award and the individual trophies. It meant a great deal to play in Duluth. It was very tough for me that we didn't win that national championship. As close as we came, we probably should have won back-to-back national championships. I felt that I was on a team that was probably as good as any team that college hockey has ever seen — and that was probably the biggest honor that I could ever have bestowed upon myself."

Both of Watson and Kurvers remain loyal Bulldog fans and both are still heavily involved in the game of hockey. After receiving his Masters in Business Administration from the University of St. Thomas in 1997, Kurvers went on to became a radio broadcaster and scout with the Phoenix Coyotes, later serving as the team's Director of Player Personnel. Watson, meanwhile, went into coaching, first at Duluth's St. Scholastica, and then at Western Michigan University. He later moved back to Duluth, where he currently has a successful insurance and financial planning business. Tom and Bill remain friends and still reminisce about those glory days back in the early 1980s when they came oh so close to winning it all.

"As a teammate, he really evolved into a great leader," said Watson of Kurvers. "When our class came in, I think it helped Tommy a lot that we could take a little bit of the burden off of his shoulders. Our friendship grew more and more as the team kept on winning. He is a great guy and a tremendous hockey player."

"Billy Watson was our best player," said Kurvers. "Even the year that I won the Hobey Baker, he was our MVP and go-to guy. If he had played another year at UMD, he could have possibly scored the most points ever for a college player. I've always said that if we were playing a pond hockey game and I could draft anybody in the universe to be my teammate, Bill Watson would be the one — he was that good of a hockey player."

1984 RUNNER-UP: JOEL OTTO

Bemidji State wins its first Division III hockey national championship, posting a perfect 31-0 record — becoming just the second team in NCAA history to go undefeated. Led by legendary coach Bob Peters, the No. 2 winningest college hockey coach (any division) of all time, the Beavers defeated Alaska Fairbanks, 9-6 and 4-2, in a two-game total-goal series format, and then went on to beat Merrimack, 6-3 and 8-1, for the title. The star of the team was *JOEL OTTO*, a three-time All-American who was named as the 1984 NCAA D-II Hobey Baker winner (emblematic of the nation's top player). The Elk river native would go on to play in the NHL for 14 seasons, recording 195 goals and 313 assists for 508 career points. The All-Star forward played on several U.S. Olympic and National teams, and also won a Stanley Cup in 1989 with the Calgary Flames.

HONORABLE MENTION: TRACY CAULKINS

Winona's *TRACY CAULKINS*, arguably Minnesota's greatest swimmer, makes history at the 1984 Summer Olympics in Sarajevo, winning three gold medals. Caulkins won a record 48 national titles — more than any other U.S. amateur athlete — and set 66 world or U.S. records. In addition, Caulkins also won the Sullivan Award as the top U.S. amateur athlete in 1978, becoming the youngest recipient ever to receive the honor.

RICKEY FOGGIE
The Gophers Win the Independence Bowl

In 1985 the upstart Gophers greatly improved to finish with a 7-5 record, which included the program's first post-season bowl appearance in nearly a decade. Leading the charge once again was Rickey Foggie, who tore up the Big Ten that year. There have been quite a few memorable T-formation quarterbacks at the University of Minnesota, but none of them was as versatile a performer as was Rickey Foggie. Foggie could run, pass, scramble, and wreak havoc on opposing defenses — seemingly making up the rules as he went along.

Led by Foggie, who scored three touchdowns on 140 yards rushing while throwing for another 157, the Maroon and Gold kicked off the season with a 28-14 win over Wichita State. From there, the Gophers crushed Montana, 62-17, as Foggie again played masterfully. The Gophers piled up over 500 yards of offense in this one as Valdez Baylor rushed for 89 yards and a pair of touchdowns, while Foggie scored three TDs of his own and passed for another to Mel Anderson.

Minnesota, despite Foggie's TD pass to Kevin Starks late in the game, then lost a heartbreaker to the top-ranked Oklahoma Sooners, 13-7, in Week Three. The team rebounded though by pouncing all over Purdue, 45-15, as Foggie threw for 212 yards and a TD, while rushing for 47 yards and another touchdown. The Gophs went on to beat Northwestern in Week Five, 21-10, behind nearly 300 yards of total offense from Foggie, in addition to 102 yards receiving and a TD from tight end Kevin Starks. In Week Seven they beat Indiana, 22-7, in a game that featured Valdez Baylor rushing for a career high 141 yards and a TD, along with three Chip Lohmiller field goals.

Minnesota then lost a pair of nail-biters, one to Ohio State at Homecoming, 23-19, and the other to Michigan State, 31-26. Foggie scored the only two touchdowns in the Buckeye game, and then sat out the Spartan game with a pulled groin, as backup QB Alan Holt came up just short in leading the team back from a huge deficit. In Week Nine, the Gophers beat Wisconsin, 27-18, in a game that was highlighted by an 89-yard record-setting TD bomb from Foggie to Mel Anderson. The Gophers finished out the season on a huge downer, getting pummeled by Michigan, 48-7, and then by Big Ten champion Iowa, 31-9. Despite finishing only fifth in the Big Ten with a 4-4 record, the Gophers were invited to once again go "bowling," something that hadn't occurred since 1977, when they played in the Hall of Fame Bowl.

With that, Minnesota was off to Shreveport, La., to meet the Clemson Tigers in the 10th annual Independence Bowl. Nearly 43,000 fans, many of whom made the trip from the Gopher State, crowded into Independence Stadium to watch the big game.

Now, in a bit of off-the-field drama, Coach Lou Holtz controversially opted to exercise a little-known secret clause (which would later become known affectionately as the "Notre Dame Clause") in his contract which entitled him to step down to take the head coaching position at Notre Dame, should it become available. It did, and he went, leaving his defensive coordinator, John Gutekunst, to take over as head coach of the team. "Gutie," who had served as an assistant at both Duke and Virginia Tech before joining Holtz at Arkansas and then Minnesota, was eager and excited to make the most of his "golden" opportunity.

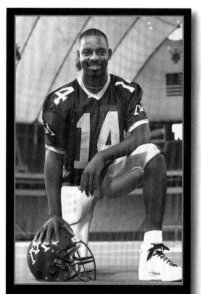

"Lou's got to be one of the top five greatest college coaches of all time, without question," said Foggie of Holtz's decision to leave. "Everywhere Holtz has been, he's won. He turned our football program around and got people in the stands. He was able to recruit good athletes to come in and make us competitive again. His greatest asset was to be able to recruit and to motivate his players to go out and win at all costs. I just wish he would've stayed at Minnesota longer, because there's no telling where the program would be today if he had."

"It was a big change for us, but, because Gutie was already on the staff, we were familiar with him, and we kind of knew what to expect," Foggie added. "But, going from Lou Holtz, who was a fiery, up-tempo guy, to Gutie, who was a more laid-back kind of coach, was a big change. Gutie wasn't the motivator that Coach Holtz was, but he knew the X's and O's of the game, and he was a good guy."

With "Gutie" at the helm, the Gophers took to the field and made a statement on the game's first play from scrimmage. That's when Clemson QB Rodney Williams hit wide receiver Ray Williams on a screen pass. Williams, upon being tattooed by Gopher defender Doug Mueller, then proceeded to cough up the ball at the Tiger 39-yard line. Minnesota then took over and began to drive downfield behind Ed Penn's 25-yard run, which got the Gophers down to the Clemson five-yard line. But after a holding penalty, they could only muster a field goal attempt. Kicker Chip Lohmiller came in, but was wide-right on a 22-yarder, keeping the score at 0-0. Then, two plays later, Clemson again fumbled on their own 26-yard-line. After a failed attempt to get the ball in the end-zone, Lohmiller came in and this time drilled a 22-yarder straight through the uprights to put the Gophers up 3-0.

In the second quarter, after forcing the Tigers to punt, the Gophers put together an impressive drive that started with two David Puk nine-yard scampers up the middle. Foggie then hit tight end Craig Otto on another nine-yarder to get to their own 43, followed by 15 and 20-yard runs by Baylor. Finally, on third-and-four, at the Tiger nine, Foggie hit Anderson on a nine-yard scoring strike to put the Gophers up 10-0. Clemson rallied back in the third though, thanks to a pair of Jeff Treadwell field goals to make it 10-6. Then, behind the running of Clemson tailback Kenny Flowers, the Tigers drove and scored on a Jennings touchdown catch to take a three-point lead, 13-10.

The valiant Gophers came back in the fourth, behind their leader, Rickey Foggie, whose running and passing sparked an 85-yard drive that was capped by another Lohmiller "Chip-shot" to tie the game at 13 apiece. After the Gopher defense forced the Tigers to punt, Foggie came out and lined up in the shotgun formation. He started out the drive with a 10-yard pass to Anderson, followed by a 16-yard Baylor run to the Clemson 36. Foggie then hit flanker Gary Couch on a 14-yarder, quickly followed by a Baylor run that gave him 12 more of his team-high 98 yards. Then, with the Gophers at the seven-yard line, fullback David Puk rumbled down to the one. That was all Baylor needed to launch himself into the end-zone as the Gophers took a seven-point lead.

The Gophers weren't out of the hot water yet. Faced with a fourth-and-six at their own 39, Clemson faked a punt to stay alive. Then on fourth and 12, Williams completed a 21-yarder to Jennings to reach the Gopher 31-yard line. So, with 90 seconds left in the game, the Tigers tried a trick play. Williams tossed a long, backward pass to receiver Ray Williams, who then turned around and lofted a pass of his own to tight end Jim Riggs near the goal line. That's when cornerback Donovan Small dove, and just barely got his finger on the ball, deflecting it out of bounds and preserving the Gopher victory.

"When they first threw that ball out wide," said Small, who was named as the Defensive Player of the Game, "I was going to come up to try to tackle the guy. I thought it was a screen pass. But just out of the corner of my eye I saw this Clemson guy running really hard downfield. I wondered why that guy was running so hard, so I decided I'd better try to catch up to him."

"I have fond memories of that game because I always wanted to attend Clemson," added Foggie, who threw for 123 yards and a touchdown in the game. "But the Clemson coach told my high school coach that I was too slow to run their offense. So there was a definite revenge factor there for me personally. I knew a lot of the guys that played for Clemson, and to go out and play well and to beat those guys was just really satisfying for me. Minnesota hadn't been to a bowl game for a while, so to win it was a special experience for everyone."

For the season Foggie accounted for 1,821 yards of total offense and was named to the All-Big Ten team. Baylor led the team in rushing with 680 yards, while Lohmiller led the team in scoring with 75 points. In addition, linebacker Peter Najarian was the team's top tackler (for the third straight season) with 133 total hits.

The most versatile quarterback in Gopher history, Rickey Foggie could do it all. He could pass, run, scramble, and wreak havoc on opposing defenses, all while leading his club to victory. When his tenure was over in Gold Country, there were quite a few pages in the record books that had to be rewritten. Not since the days of Sandy Stephens had Gopher fans seen a quarterback who could play like that.

The Fog
Rickey Foggie was born on July 1, 1966, in Waterloo, S.C., and grew up as one of nine siblings in a family that loved sports. At Laurens High School he was an all-conference and all-state performer in both football and basketball. As a senior, he led his high school football team to the South Carolina state championship.

After being heavily recruited in both sports, Foggie came to Minnesota in 1983, following the disastrous 1-10 Gopher season under Joe Salem. As a freshman, he led the team in both rushing and passing, and showed great promise by redefining the conventional rules of the quarterback position. For his career he was twice named as the team's MVP and twice he earned All Big Ten honors. He accounted for nearly 2,000 yards in offense in his senior season alone, passing for 1,232 yards and 8 TDs, while rushing for 714 yards and 6 TDs.

Foggie left Minnesota as the school's all-time leader in total offense with 7,312 yards. In addition, he ranks in the top 10 all-time in rushing with 2,150 yards and 25 TDs as well. He also scored 160 points, threw a record 34 touchdowns, and ranked No. 2 all-time behind only Marquel Fleetwood in career yards passing, with 5,162. He was also later named as the Outstanding Offensive Player in the 1986 Liberty Bowl. Considered a threat every time he touched the ball, he became only the third quarterback in college football history to run for more than 2,000 yards and pass for more than 4,000 yards.

When Rickey finished his tenure at Minnesota, he headed north of the border to play in the Canadian Football League, first with the British Columbia Lions, then the Toronto Argonauts, and lastly with the Edmonton Eskimos. From there, he headed to Memphis, when the CFL expanded to the United States, and then to the Hamilton Tiger Cats. Then Rickey had a homecoming of sorts when he came home to Minnesota in 1996 to play for one season in the Target Center with the upstart Fighting Pike of the Arena Football League.

"I felt like I had a good reception from the fans, and it was great to be able to come back to the Twin Cities," said Rickey of his time with the Pike. "We had a lot of fun that year, but it was unfortunate that we didn't get to win any games at home. I was disappointed that my Pike experience wasn't a successful situation, but I was glad to get back into the atmosphere of having the fans come out and watch me

perform again."

When the team folded that next season Foggie headed east to play with the New Jersey Red Dogs of that same arena league. He would go on to play with the Florida Bobcats, Detroit Fury, Toronto Phantoms and Carolina Cobras. All in all the Fog spent 10 years in the CFL and another seven in the AFL. He finished his AFL career with 17,921 yards passing, 325 touchdowns and a 96.38 quarterback rating. From there, he got into coaching with the AFL, where he has been ever since. Foggie lives in Minneapolis, during the offseason and even finds time to help coach at Burnsville High School.

With his amazing ability to run the option attack like no other before him, Rickey will go down as one of the best Gopher quarterbacks ever. He electrified the fans in Minnesota and was pivotal in turning a shattered football program around. When Foggie left Gold Country the Gophers had not only gone to two bowl games, but they had also returned to a semblance of their former glory.

What Did it Mean For You To Be a Gopher?
"Once I learned the great tradition of the school and its winning success, it all kind of sunk in. Coach Holtz brought back a lot of the tradition. To be able to play in front of sell-out crowds for our first two years was great. I felt that we brought a college football atmosphere back to the U of M. The fans were great, and it always meant a lot to me that they supported me the way that they did. Maroon and Gold is something that I will never be able to get out of my system, and I am always proud to say that I am a Gopher."

Gopher Tombstone:
"I would hope to be remembered as a guy who went out and just had fun playing the game, was part of rebuilding a program that had been down for a couple of years, and helped bring the excitement and respectability back to Gopher football."

TRIBUTE
"Rickey is a really good guy," said teammate Darrell Thompson. "I remember that when I was a freshman, he was so nice to me and really helped me through a lot. Throughout all the pressures of the games, he was good at keeping things fun and light. He even used to give me little gifts before games and, when he wasn't joking around with me in the huddles, he was giving me tips on how to improve my game. I appreciated it and we still keep in touch today."

1985 RUNNER-UP: BRETT HULL
The University of Minnesota-Duluth comes up just short yet again in the NCAA Frozen Four Finals in Detroit. Led by future NHL MVP winger **BRETT HULL,** the Bulldogs lost a triple-overtime heart-breaker, 6-5, to RPI. They rebounded to finish third in the nation, however, by winning the consolation game, 7-6, over Boston College. As for Hull, he would go on to play in the NHL for 20 seasons, scoring an amazing 741 goals (3rd all-time) and 650 assists for a total of 1,391 points in 1,269 career games. The 1991 league MVP also won a pair of Stanley Cups with the Dallas Stars in 1999 and the Detroit Red Wings in 2002. He would get into broadcasting and later become an executive with the Dallas Stars. Already a member of the U.S. Hockey Hall of Fame, the eight time All-Star's next stop is undoubtedly the Hockey Hall of Fame in Toronto.

HONORABLE MENTION: TOM BRUNANSKY
The 1985 Major League Baseball All-Star Game is played at the Metrodome, with the National League beating the American League, 6-1. Representing the Twins was right fielder **TOM BRUNANSKY**, who hit a team-high 27 homers and 90 RBI with the Twins that season. "Bruno" would play for the Twins from 1982-88, until being traded to St. Louis for second baseman Tommy Herr. He would ultimately play another six years in the big leagues before retiring in 1994 with 271 home runs and 919 RBI in 1,800 career games.

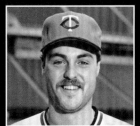

1986

DARRELL THOMPSON
The Gophers Come Up Short at the Liberty Bowl

The Golden Gopher football program has a long and epic history that has been dotted with many peaks and valleys. Minnesota has always been known to represent the "three yards and a cloud of dust" mentality of Big Ten football, which was anchored by a sound running game. There have been so many outstanding running backs through the years in Gold Country, including the likes of Bronko Nagurski, Bruce Smith, Paul Giel, Pug Lund, Bill Daley, Bob McNamara, Marion Barber, Rick Upchurch, , Chris Darkins, and even Marion Barber III and Lawrence Maroney, as of late. All were great in their own right, but none of them could run like Darrell Thompson, who rewrote the record books during his tenure at the U of M. In 1986, Thompson, as a true freshman, led the Maroon and Gold to the Liberty Bowl in Memphis, where the Gophers lost a heart-breaker to the Tennessee Volunteers.

In 1986 the Gophers were anxious to show the world that their Independence Bowl victory over Clemson the year before was no fluke. It was John Gutekunst's first full season as head coach, having taken over the reigns from Lou Holtz, who left to coach at Notre Dame just prior to the 1985 Independence Bowl. Gutie was a "player's coach," and had earned the respect of his men over the past couple of seasons as a quiet but tough leader.

The beginning of the 1986 season brought more hype and hoopla to campus than perhaps every before. That season a kid from Rochester hit campus by the name of Darrell Thompson, and by the time he was done four years later, he would own most every rushing record in the books. "Darrell and Rickey" (Foggie) became quite the dynamic duo that year, as the upstart Gophers earned their second straight post-season trip to a bowl game.

The season got underway against Bowling Green, as Thompson made an immediate impact by rushing for 205 yards and scoring four touchdowns en route to a 31-7 victory. The Gophers hit a few bumps in the road after that, including a giant pothole in the shape of the University of Oklahoma, who crushed the Gophers by the ugly score of 63-0. Minnesota followed that up with a 24-20 loss to tiny Pacific University, despite two more touchdowns by Thompson. From there, the Gophers rebounded and went on a roll, first beating Purdue, 36-9 (as quarterback Rickey Foggie scored three rushing touchdowns and hit Mel Anderson for another), then Northwestern, 44-23 (led by Thompson's 176 yards rushing and two touchdowns, as well as Mel Anderson's 90-yard kickoff return for another), and finally Indiana in a squeaker, 19-17. Thompson ran wild for 191 yards in this one and also set up Chip Lohmiller's game-wining 21-yard field goal with two seconds to go on the clock.

Minnesota ran into some more trouble in Week Seven when they got shut-out by Ohio State, 33-0, thanks to the Buckeye's defense, which was led by future NFL star, Chris Spielman. The squad then

lost to Michigan State that next Saturday by the final of 52-23. But the Gophers rebounded as they had done all season long in Week Nine, this time defeating the Wisconsin Badgers, 27-20, to retain Paul Bunyan's Axe. In that game, Foggie threw a 27-yard strike to Dennis Carter for the go-ahead touchdown, while Thompson rushed for 117 yards to become the first Gopher frosh to run for 1,000 yards in a single season.

Next up, No. 2 ranked Michigan, who had beaten Minnesota the past eight meetings. The Michigan game, in all of its pomp and circumstance, would prove to be one of the greatest ever for the University of Minnesota. After back and forth scoring the entire game, it all came down to the wire in this one. Down 17-16 with just over two minutes to go in the game, Michigan coach Bo Schembechler opted to go for the tie instead of a two-pointer to win. He succeeded, and with the game now all tied-up, Minnesota drove the ball downfield. Then with 47 seconds left, Foggie took off from the Michigan 48 and ran for 31 yards to the Michigan 17. The stage was now set for Woodbury kicker Chip Lohmiller, and the "Chipper" came through in a big way. He nailed the 30-yarder as time ran out to give the Gophers a dramatic 20-17 victory. With the big win came the annual rights to the coveted Little Brown Jug, which hadn't spent much time in Minnesota over the past decade. Leading the way was linebacker Larry Joyner, who sparked the defense with 11 tackles and forced two fumbles, en route to earning Defensive Player of the Week honors.

"I knew once we got it inside the 40, Chip could put It through," said Foggie. "He's got a great leg."

The Gophers finished out their season by losing to Iowa, 30-27, despite Lohmiller's record 62-yard field goal. It didn't matter though, as the Gophers still earned a berth to the Liberty Bowl, where they would face the University of Tennessee, right in the Vols' own backyard of Memphis. Droves of Minnesota fans would road-trip it down to Dixie to root on their beloved Gophers as they tried to make it two straight bowl game victories in a row.

The game got underway with the Volunteers jumping ahead 14-0 on two Jeff Francis touchdown passes. The first came to Joey Clinkscales in the left flat as he beat both cornerback Matt Martinez and safety Steve Franklin to scoot into the end zone for an 18-yard touchdown. After a second quarter Foggie fumble at midfield, Francis dumped a screen pass to fullback William Howard, who promptly took it to the house to make it 14-0. The Gophers came close twice in the half – once getting to the Vols' six-yard line, where Foggie came up short on a sneak, and then again when Thompson fumbled on the Vols' 33-yard line. Minnesota's only points came on a Lohmiller 27-yard field goal that capped a 70-yard drive at the end of the half.

When the third quarter opened, Foggie appeared to be a man on a mission. The junior quarterback led Minnesota on a 10-play, 88-yard drive that was highlighted by an 11-yard quarterback-keeper for a touchdown. Then, Thompson added a two-point conversion to make the score 14-11. Still in the third, behind 38 of Thompson's game-high 136 yards, the Gophers started a long march down to the Tennessee 14. But, a holding call nullified their touchdown hopes, and Minnesota had to settle for another field goal by Lohmiller.

Tied at 14-apiece in the fourth, the Vols cruised upfield on a 67-yard drive that was capped by Clinkscales' second TD catch of the game less than two minutes later. So, with Tennessee up, 21-14, the Gophers tried to mount a rally. Their next drive got stalled on their own 49-yard line, but after an exchange of punts Minnesota got the ball back at midfield largely because of two great plays by freshman linebacker Jon Leverenz – who forced a two-yard loss on a first-down play, and then broke up a key third-down pass.

So, with Foggie and Thompson poised for the upset, they tried one last drive to win it all. The final push, a seven-play drive, started out well, but unfortunately ended near midfield when Foggie's fourth-down pass to Waconia's Ron Goetz fell incomplete. Tennessee took over with 16 seconds left and simply ran out the clock to win it. Minnesota out-gained Tennessee in the game 374-324, but, in the end, the final score read 21-14 in favor of the Vols.

The Gophers played well, despite having to do battle deep inside enemy turf. For the season, they finished at 6-6 and tied for third in the Big Ten with a very respectable 5-3 record. Thompson, who led the conference in rushing that year, also set a new Gopher single-season rushing mark with 1,240 yards.

"It was a big deal because you grow up watching the bowl games on TV, and when you finally get to play in one, it is a very special event," said Thompson, who was named to the All-Big Ten team following the season. "I mean, only the year before I was playing for Rochester John Marshall High School, and now here I was starting at running back in the Liberty Bowl, it was an exciting time."

"Daaaa-rrrr-ellll!" — "Daaaa-rrrr-ellll!" — "Daaaa-rrrr-ellll!"

Darrell Thompson was born on December 23, 1967, and grew up playing several different sports in Rochester. His parents encouraged their children to play a lot of sports and to be well-rounded athletes. After all, his dad played basketball at Clark College in Atlanta and his mom was a three-sport star at Alcorn State University in Mississippi. Thompson's younger brother and sister also went on to earn scholarships playing volleyball as well.

At Rochester John Marshall High School, Thompson was a three-sport star. Along with being a forward on the basketball team, he also earned all-state honors in track. There he ran the 100, 200, and 400 meters, and even anchored the 1985 state championship mile relay team. Football, however, was his main sport and clearly his passion. His senior year he rushed for over 1,000 yards, scored 102 points and averaged an amazing 9.7 yards per carry. Not only was he all-state in football, he was also an All-American. In fact, Darrell was the state's most highly recruited football player ever, and was wooed by nearly every major college in the country. He grew up loving the Gophers though and considered it to be a dream come true when he accepted his scholarship to wear the Maroon and Gold.

For his career at the University of Minnesota, Darrell rushed for 4,654 yards on 936 attempts and scored 40 touchdowns, making him the school's all-time career rushing, attempts, and touchdowns leader. He also scored 262 total points, placing him second on the all-time scoring list behind only teammate Chip Lohmiller — a kicker. From 1986-89, his teammates voted him as the team MVP. He is also the only running back in Big Ten history to go over 1,000-yards as a freshman and a sophomore. In 1987, he became the first player ever to gain more than 200 yards in a game against Michigan. In that same game he dazzled the sell-out Metrodome crowd as well as the national TV audience with a 98-yard touchdown run, the longest run from scrimmage in Big Ten history. He also threw two passes for the Gophers, both good for touchdowns.

After a phenomenal senior season, he was selected in the first round of the NFL Draft by the Green Bay Packers. He went on to play for five seasons with the Pack before retiring in 1995. Because he was hampered by injuries throughout much of his pro career and was often forced to play out of his natural position, at fullback, he was never able to truly showcase his talents in the NFL.

Statistically speaking, Darrell was the greatest running back that has ever played at the University of Minnesota. With his six-foot-one, 220-pound frame combined with his 4.4 speed and acceleration, he was an elusive yet punishing back.

"Darrell can get into another gear at any time," said coach Gutekunst. "It's phenomenal. He has quickness and shiftiness laterally. He can step out of things, change direction, and get back to full speed in a hurry."

Perhaps the only things tougher than trying to tackle Darrell was trying to get him to talk about his amazing accomplishments. "I

don't see it as that big a deal," said Darrell of his gridiron talents. "I can run a football, but some other guy can hook up a stereo. God gave everybody their own thing."

Darrell was not only an incredible athlete, he was also one of the nicest guys you could ever meet. He was definitely the big man on campus, but when you got to know him, it became readily apparent that he was just a modest guy from Rochester who happened to be pretty darn good at carrying a pigskin.

What Did it Mean For You To Be a Gopher?
"I took a lot of pride in it. I really enjoyed playing for the U, and I'd like to see more kids from Minnesota experiencing the same pleasure that I had there. Athletes can carve out a real nice niche in the community here."

Why Did You Select the U of M?
"At the time I didn't think that pro football was a very realistic expectation, so I figured that I would rather end up working in Minneapolis when I was through playing at the U. When I was being recruited, I went to schools like Nebraska, Wisconsin, and Iowa, but I didn't think that I would want to live in those towns after my football career was over. They were all great football towns, but Minneapolis is a great city to live in. I see a lot of Big Ten football players from all over the country living here now because it's just a great place to live."

On Being the Packers' First-Round Draft Pick:
"I was really happy and I was blessed. It was something that I never thought was even that realistic, but when it happened it was special. We were a pretty close knit family, and it was neat that they could all drive up to Green Bay from Rochester to see my games."

On Giving Back to Kids and On the Future:
Thompson currently lives in the Twin Cities with his wife and children and serves as the director of Bolder Options, a Minneapolis-based early intervention youth mentoring program. "I tell kids today that they can play in the pros if they work really hard at it — but I tell them to be realistic," he said. "Since there's only a one-in-10,000 chance of making it in the pros, I tell them that they need to study and make other plans in life so that they can be successful even if they don't make it."

Gopher Tombstone:
"I'd want to be remembered as a guy who played hard, loved to compete, and was someone that commanded respect from his teammates."

1986 RUNNER-UP: TINO LETTIERI

The Minnesota Strikers finish second in the Eastern Division with a 26-22 record and make it all the way to the Major Indoor League Soccer (MISL) Finals, where they ultimately lose to the San Diego Sockers, four games to three — after being up three games to one. The star of the team was goalie *TINO LETTIERI*, who earned Goalkeeper of the Year honors the following season. Incidentally, the franchise came to Minnesota in 1983, when the Fort Lauderdale Strikers relocated here. The team played that season in the Metrodome, in the NASL, before moving the next year to the indoor MISL at the Met Center. The franchise played in Minnesota for four seasons, posting a 107-97 record before folding in 1988.

HONORABLE MENTION: BRETT HEDICAN & MATT CULLEN

The St. Cloud State Huskies make the leap from Division III to Division I thanks in large part to legendary coach Herb Brooks, who took over as the team's head coach in 1986 after coaching the NHL's New York Rangers for four seasons. Brooks led the team to the D-III Final Four, lobbied the legislature to get a new state-of-the-art hockey arena built, and then passed the torch to assistant coach Craig Dahl. The program has since flourished, as evidenced by two of its more prominent alumni *BRETT HEDICAN* and *MATT CULLEN*, who won the Stanley Cup as teammates with the Carolina Hurricanes in 2006.

The 1987 Minnesota Twins were, in a word, awesome, and their story is perhaps one of the greatest in all of sports. It all began during that off-season when GM Andy MacPhail set the early tone by acquiring ace reliever Jeff Reardon. Was he the missing piece of the puzzle? Heck, most baseball pundits predicted another season of mediocrity for these Twinkies, probably no better than fourth in the AL West. Boy were they wrong!

The Twins took baseball by storm in 1987, featuring a line-up that was comprised of Minnesota's own "fab-four," the quartet of Herbie, Kirby, Bruno and the G-man (Kent Hrbek, Kirby Puckett, Tom Brunansky and Gary Gaetti). They even added a new kid by the name of Dan Gladden, a hard-nosed left fielder who was full of grit and determination. Add to that an outstanding pitching staff which included Frank "Cyola" Viola, and it was off to the races for these kids. The team was up and down that season but overall, played solid fundamental baseball under manager Tom Kelly.

One of the highlights (or lowlights) that year came on August 3rd, when pitcher Joe Niekro was ejected from the team's 11-3 win in Anaheim. Niekro, a crafty old veteran, got caught with his hand in the cookie jar in this one as he coughed up a five inch emery board out his pocket after being accused of doctoring knuckle-balls. Busted!

The Twins finished the regular season with a modest 85-77 record, which was good enough to win the American League Western Division. Pitcher Frank Viola began to show great consistency as a starter, as did veteran Bert Blyleven, who, believe it or not, was with the Twins the last time they were in the American League Championship Series back in 1970. Leading the charge offensively was Kent Hrbek. After being stiffed for the All-Star Game, Herbie took out his anger on opposing teams that season, finishing with a career-high 34 home runs and adding 90 RBI's to boot.

The Twins would open the pos-season against the Detroit Tigers. Detroit, with the best overall record in the big leagues, was predicted to crush the Twins. The Twins thought differently though and took the first two in Minnesota and then went on to win two of the final three in Detroit. Tim Laudner's double off Tigers ace Jack Morris was the difference in Game Two, and in Game Four they took the lead for good on Greg Gagne's fourth-inning home run. The star of the series was third baseman Gary Gaetti, who was named as the ALCS MVP.

From there, it was on to the World Series, where the Twins would face the National League champion St. Louis Cardinals. The first two games weren't even close. In Game One at the Dome, the first World Series game ever played indoors, the Twins blasted St. Louis, 10-1, thanks to Dan Gladden's grand slam. The second game was another cakewalk, an 8-4 victory, highlighted by homers from both Gary Gaetti and Tim Laudner. Then, just when it looked like a series

sweep for Minnesota, the Cards came back and took the next three games in St. Louis. The Twins hung in there in Game Five on Gaetti's eighth-inning, two-run triple, but the Cards held on for a 4-2 win. Down three games to two, the series now shifted back the Metrodome.

Game Six was a wild one. Down in the fifth, the Twins retaliated behind DH Don Baylor's three-run homer, and then slammed the door on the Cards thanks to Kent Hrbek's childhood dream-come-true. With the Twins up 6-5 in the sixth, Herbie made history when he proceeded to hit a 439-foot grand

slam over the center field wall, and into a sea of white homer hankies. The series was now even at three games apiece. As the Bloomington native circled the bases with his fists pumping and his mouth wide open, he remembered playing out that very play a million times before in his own back yard – just a stone's throw from the old Met. The Twins, behind Puckett's four hits and four runs, went on to take Game Six, 11-5, to even up the series at three games apiece.

Said teammate Roy Smalley after Game Six: "Before Kent went up to bat I looked at Frank Viola and said, 'You watch... This is too set up. This is too much like a storybook. It's too perfect.' "

"It is something I will never feel again," said Herbie after the big game. "People talk about thrills in baseball. Just making the big leagues was a thrill. Hitting a home run at Yankee Stadium in my first game in the big leagues was a thrill. Hitting a grand slam in the World Series in your home state — that is indescribable."

Game Seven had all the drama you could ask for. The Cardinals scored first in this one with a pair of runs in the second, but the Twins rallied with runs in the second and fifth, and then took the lead on three walks and an infield single in the sixth. Frankie Viola held St. Louis scoreless on just two hits after the second inning, and ace reliever Jeff Reardon came in to retire the Cards in order in the ninth to bring Minnesota its first world championship.

It was truly a wild one. Three Twins were thrown out at home plate. Greg Gagne drove in the winning run on an infield hit. Frankie "Sweet Music" Viola pitched eight beautiful innings, giving up only two runs early on. And fittingly, Jeff Reardon came in for the ninth to close the door, getting the final out on Willie McGee's ground ball to Gary Gaetti. When the G-man threw the ball across the diamond to Herbie at first, the Twins had won the game, 4-2, earning the title of baseball's World Champions. As Carl Spackler (alias: Bill Murray from the classic movie "Caddyshack") put it so prophetically, this was truly a "Cinderella-Story."

In the series finale, the fans had actually grown quite fond of the parachute-topped edifice better known as the "Homerdome," a true testament to its' inexplicable magic it had provided the Twins. Frank Viola would earn Series MVP honors, and for Herbie, there would be ticker-tape parades, presidential meetings, and even Late Night with David Letterman.

"I just step back and think of the guys that I played with back then," Hrbek would later recall. "Great guys, like Viola, Gaetti, Brunansky, Laudner and Bush. We grew up in the big leagues together, we lost in the big leagues together, and then, in 1987, we were the best in the world together. I can still remember sitting on the clubhouse floor after the game. Everybody thought we all were drunk as pigs, but we weren't, we were all just mentally and physically spent. It was something that we had all worked so hard for, and had so much fun doing. And when it was over we just soaked it all in and enjoyed it."

"That team was the closest-knit group of guys I've ever been around," added Kirby Puckett. "It was unbelievable. I mean win or lose, every night you could find at least a dozen of us eating together at a restaurant. We hung out together and we won together. I still remember, after we won Game Seven, a bunch of us were just sitting there on the floor in the clubhouse, drinking champagne, and staring at each other like, 'What did we just do?' I've had a lot of people ask me since then, 'How did it feel?' And you know what? I can't tell them. It's something you have to experience for yourself to get it. It was something only the people in that room could understand."

Herbie

Kent Hrbek was born on May 21, 1960, and grew up in the shadows of Metropolitan Stadium in Bloomington. He would go on to star at Bloomington Kennedy High School, where he hit .480 his senior year.

"He was an excellent fielder," said Buster Radebach, his high school coach. "He was a student of the game and he studied it."

As good as he was in high school, it was in American Legion ball that summer where he started to get noticed for his massive home runs. "He could handle the glove and could run for a big man," said former Twins owner Calvin Griffith, who went to see one of Kent's American Legion games. "I could see that his stroke alone was sufficient to gamble on him." So, in the 17th round of the 1978 draft, Herbie became a Twin, accepting a $30,000 offer.

After a brief stint in Visalia, where he was voted the MVP of the California League, he got the call to come up to the "Show." After batting .301 with 23 home runs and 92 RBIs, he finished second to Cal Ripken in the Rookie of the Year voting, and was the lone rookie on the All-Star team that year as well. "My sister probably sent in 10,000 votes on her own!", Kent quipped regarding that year's All-Star balloting. He even made the cover of Sports Illustrated with the title: "Best of the Worst," and also appeared on the ABC-TV's Good Morning America show. He had arrived.

While Herbie was most appreciated by his teammates and the fans for his upper-deck power and agility, he will also be remembered as one of the best fielders ever to play first base. A .282 lifetime hitter over his 14-year career, Hrbek finished second in the 1984 MVP race when he hit .311. At the time of his retirement in 1994 he ranked among club leaders in nearly every offensive category: 2nd in homeruns (293), 2nd in RBI's (1,086), 4th in hits (1,749), 4th in runs (903), 5th in total bases (2,976), 2nd in walks (838), 3rd in total games (1,747), 5th in at-bats (6,192) and 3rd in doubles (312).

Fittingly, Hrbek's No. 14 was retired on August 13, 1995, in an emotional ceremony at the Dome. Since then he has enjoyed retirement to its fullest. He launched his own TV show "Kent Hrbek Outdoors," which features interviews and stories about local sports personalities and celebrities. In addition, Kent also hosts an annual bass fishing tournament up on Island Lake in Duluth for a cause that is near and dear to his heart, ALS. An all-around great guy, Herbie will go down as one of the all-time greatest fan-favorites in Minnesota sports history.

What did it mean for you to be a Twin?
"I thought being a Twin was just about the greatest thing in the world. Being from Minnesota, and being just a huge sports fan, I have always rooted for our teams, whether it was the Twins, Vikings, North Stars, Timberwolves, or Gophers — I just wanted our teams to win. I don't think there is anybody that wanted to win a ball game more than Kent Hrbek, and there probably never will be."

On Minnesotans:
"I just think the people up here are great. I don't know, and people might think I'm a dink for saying this, but I think East Coast people could care less about family, and West Coast people, they don't even know if they have a family! When you can walk into a mom and pop restaurant in the middle of Iowa while you're out pheasant hunting, and everybody knows everybody, and they all care about each other, that to me is home."

Twins Tombstone:
"I had a great time playing. I liked to put on a show and have a good time and make people think that I wasn't so much different than they

were, just because I was a Major League baseball player. People always thought that I had too much fun on the field, but having a good time was the only way I played well. I'd like to think that I was a fun-loving guy who felt like 'Hey, don't look at me badly because I could drink a beer and I was a Major League baseball player.' There are too many guys now that thought they were so much better than others because they were Major Leaguers, and I could never stand that! Let me tell you, you're not better than me because you can hit a 90 mph fastball, and because you make $6 million a year! Don't think that your sh-- doesn't stink, because it does!"

On retirement:
"I just want to be Kent Hrbek, have a family, and be able to stop at Super America and pump my gas without worrying about signing this or that. I want to be able to walk around with my fly down, or with spit dribbling off my chin, because I'm human, and everybody else has done that before. I don't want to be Kent Hrbek, the Minnesota Twin, I just want to be 'Joe Blow,' because that's who I am."

TRIBUTES
"He was awesome," said Kirby Puckett. "He was the best first baseman that I ever played with. He was one of the best teammates that I ever had. He was a great person, fun to be around and he made every day special coming to the ballpark. I always felt that he should have won several gold gloves and been on more All Star teams. He's like me, just care free and just wanting to play the game. He loved what he did and he played hard every day. He got hurt a lot at the end, I think he separated that shoulder like three or four times, but they were all tough injuries during the call of duty. You knew that whenever you had Herbie and me in the same clubhouse, it was going to be loud and something would always be going on. Herbie always made me laugh, and he didn't even have to try."

"Kent is a fun-loving guy and he always played and conducted himself that way whether he was on or off the field," said Tom Kelly. "He was such a talented hitter and player, and he enjoyed playing the game. He probably wanted to win more than any other player I have managed. He had such a desire and will to win. He was a home grown athlete who was just a great player."

"He grew up with me," said Tony Oliva. "I coached him all the way through the minor leagues and into the big leagues. He was a wonderful player and a great person."

1987 RUNNER-UP: ANTHONY CARTER

The 8-7 Vikings finish second in the NFC Central, but make the post-season as a wild card team. After crushing New Orleans in the first round, 44-10, the Vikings upset San Francisco in the divisional playoff game, 36-24. From there, the red hot Vikings suddenly found themselves in the NFC Championship game, where they wound up losing a heart-breaker to Washington, 17-10. Minnesota got down to the Redskin 6-yard line with under a minute to go in the game, but quarterback Wade Wilson's fourth down pass, intended for running back Darrin Nelson in the end zone, was batted away by cornerback Darrell Green. One of the stars of the team that season was Pro Bowl wide receiver *ANTHONY CARTER*, who hauled in an NFL playoff record 10 receptions for 227 yards in the win over the 49ers. The acrobatic Carter played with the Vikings for six seasons and finished his illustrious 11 year NFL career with 486 receptions for 7,733 yards and 55 touchdowns.

HONORABLE MENTION: JOHN ANDERSON

The baseball Gophers win the Big Ten Division title with a 36-25 record. The team then advanced on to the post-season, only to lose to Stanford and Oral Roberts in NCAA tournament. Steering the ship for the Gophers was coach *JOHN ANDERSON*, who, over the course of 26 seasons, has led the Gophers to a record of 946-591-3 (.615). The Nashwauk-Keewatin High School grad is now the school's all-time winningest coach.

By the start of the 1988 season all of Minnesota was still dizzy and hungover from all of the World Series hoopla that had swept throughout the state just six months earlier. As a result, people were more interested than ever to see if the club could repeat as world champs that next season. Fans turned out at the Metrodome in droves. In fact, the Twins became the first American League team ever to draw three million fans, as 3,030,672 people passed through the Metrodome turnstiles to watch the reigning champs defend their title. They wanted to see the action live and in person and to be a part of the history that for many of them had unfolded before their eyes only on television.

On the field, the 1988 Twins finished with a quite respectable 91-71 record, en route to a second place finish in the American League West. In fact, it was the team's first 90-win season since 1970. Minnesota battled Tony LaRussa's Oakland A's for the better part of the season, but in the end the Athletics were too tough and won the AL crown with an amazing 104 wins.

As a group, the Twins placed second in the Major Leagues with a collective .274 batting average. Kirby Puckett had another monster year, batting .356 (the highest by a right-handed hitter in the A.L. since Joe DiMaggio's .357 back in 1941), while leading the league in hits with 234. Gary Gaetti hit .301, Hrbek hit .312, and previously-unheralded pitcher Allan Anderson, who was called up from Portland (AAA), won 16 games — while producing the league's lowest ERA at 2.45. In addition, closer Jeff Reardon notched a club-record 42 saves, good for second in the Majors as well.

As for their skipper, the remarkable Tom Kelly, he reaped the benefits of leading his ballclub to the 1987 World Series and was honored by managing the 1988 All-Star game. He was joined at the All-Star festivities in Cincinnati by Kirby Puckett, Tim Laudner, Gary Gaetti, Jeff Reardon, and Frank Viola — who also just happened to be the starting and winning pitcher for the AL, as they beat the NL, 2-1.

Viola's heroics weren't confined to the 1988 All-Star Game though. He picked up right where he left off in 1987, when he won the World Series MVP. The 1988 season was a dream for Viola as he led the league with 24 wins, posted a 2.64 ERA, and struck-out 193 batters. He also set the Twins record for the all-time best winning percentage that season at .774. For his efforts, he won the Cy Young award as the league's best pitcher.

The man ultimately responsible for the success of the team was manager Tom Kelly. The Twins skipper never made a lot of noise in the dug-out, yet was able to lead his team all the way to the promised land. Kelly's soft-spoken, "lead-by-example" attitude filtered throughout the club-house and became infectious with all of his players. He was a stickler for the fundamentals, and it was no coincidence that his team committed a league record for the fewest errors (84), while posting a gaudy .986 fielding percentage. Kelly had a reputation for being a big fan favorite, a media darling, and all-around good guy. Perhaps the biggest compliment paid to him though was that he was commonly referred to as a "player's manager." He had certainly earned their respect, both on and off the field.

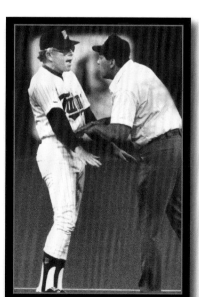

T.K.
Tom Kelly's career has been a long and winding one, with roots that begin right here in Minnesota. Jay Thomas Kelly was born on August 15, 1950, in Graceville, Minn. Baseball had always played a big role in his life because his father, Joe, was a Northern League pitcher during the 1940s and later played in the New York Giants system. His family ultimately moved east, where Tom grew up in New Jersey. He would go on to become an outstanding ballplayer at St. Mary's High School in South Amboy, N.J. From there, he went on to attend Mesa Community College in Mesa, Ariz., and also Monmouth College in West Long Branch, N.J. Baseball remained a big part of his life as he continued to get better and better at each level that he played at. By now he was getting looked at by scouts and knew that he had a good shot at making it in the big leagues if he was just given the opportunity.

Kelly fulfilled a boyhood dream in 1968 when the expansion Seattle Pilots selected him in the fifth round of the Major League Baseball free agent draft. With that, he reported to the club's minor league team in Newark to begin his quest of one day playing in the big leagues. In his first year he hit an impressive .317, led the league in stolen bases and became an All-Star. From there it was off to Clinton and then Jacksonville, until 1971, when he was signed as a free agent by the Minnesota Twins. After spending a year in Charlotte, he began a four-year stint in Tacoma, the Twins triple-A club.

Then, in 1975, Kelly got the call he had been waiting for his entire career — he was going to the Show. On May 19th, he got his first Major League hit when he singled off Detroit's Joe Coleman. It wasn't a very long stint in the bigs, 127 at bats in 49 games to be exact. But it was something he had dreamed of during his entire career as a ballplayer. So, for a career minor leaguer, the entire big league experience was pretty special to him. He ended up with 23 hits, while driving in 11 batters, scoring another 11 runs and batting a buck-eighty-one. Kelly's lone dinger of his career came off Tigers Pitcher Vern Ruhle.

"It's something you always dreamed about, to play at the Major League level," said Kelly. "As a minor leaguer, you were always working towards that goal. I got the opportunity, but I wasn't good enough to stick around. At least I did have a chance which was great for me, and it is something I will always remember."

After a season at triple-A Rochester, Kelly caught another break. This time he found his calling as he would spend the next three years in Tacoma and Toledo as a player/manager. In 1979 and 1980, he managed a Twins' farm team in Visalia, where he led the club to two consecutive divisional titles. He was also named the California League Manager of the Year for two years in a row. He was then promoted by the Twins to Orlando, where he was named as the Southern League Manager of the Year after guiding his team to the league championship.

In 1983, he got another call to the Majors, this time as the new Twins third base coach, becoming the first Minnesotan to ever become a member of the team's managerial staff. Then, near the end of the 1986 season, T.K. took over the Twins' managerial duties from a faltering Ray Miller. The team was underperforming and management wanted to shake things up. They decided to give the kid a shot. They wouldn't be sorry. It would be the start of an historic ride.

In 1987, Kelly became only the fifth manager in baseball history to win a pennant as a rookie when his Twins beat the Cardinals in the World Series. For his efforts the 37-year-old was named as the American League Manager of the Year. It was a tremendous victory for all of Minnesota and T.K. was given much of the credit. And deservedly so, for it was he who acted as the glue which held those players together.

Kelly's heroes won their second World Series over the Atlanta Braves just five years later. Tom thus became first Twins manager ever to lead his club to two divisional titles (and subsequent world championships), and the third manager ever in baseball history to have won two World Series while losing none. In 1991, Kelly again was again named as the American League Manager of the Year. In 1992, Kelly managed the American League All-Star team to a 13-6 victory in San Diego. Fittingly, Kirby Puckett was named as the game's MVP.

In 2001 T.K. stepped down as the Twins manager and handed the reigns to his long-time assistant coach, Ron Gardenhire.

When the dust had finally settled, Kelly's career resume was simply amazing. Very quietly he became entrenched as baseball's longest-tenured manager, managing 2,385 games in his nearly 20 years behind the bench in Minnesota. In addition, he became the all-time winningest manager in Twins history, having won 1,140 games. He also won a pair of World Series in a span of five years. This may not sound impressive until one realizes that the Chicago Cubs have not won a single World Series since 1908. Kelly will no doubt go down in history as the greatest Twins manager of all time. Period.

Presently, Kelly continues to work with the team as the Special Assistant to General Manager Bill Smith, who took over the role in 2006 when longtime GM Terry Ryan stepped down. Kelly still very much enjoys coming to the ballpark. At his core, TK is a teacher, and loves to teach the fundamentals to the young players. Most importantly, he is happy being a part of the organization on his own terms.

"In 1975, I was just so happy to be in the big leagues that it didn't mean much to me right away," said Kelly. "But after being in the organization for 20-some years, I think it's very special, and I put more credence to it now than I did then. The Minnesota Twins have been good to me and my family. I feel like a part of the organization, maybe not an intricate part, but a piece. I feel like it's more of an honor now. We try to convey that point to the players, that it is an honor to wear the Twins uniform. We think it's important that they represent the uniform as well as they represent themselves and their families."

On his longevity as Twins manager, T.K. was humble: "It just shows that I have had a lot of good players here over the years, and good players make managers look good. You have to remember that a manager is only as good as his players, and I've been very fortunate. I think it's the result of a good Twins minor league system, good scouting and good coaching. It's not just one person, there are a lot of people involved. The game itself can beat you up. All the time I spent playing and managing in the minor leagues with the bus rides, the traveling, and the wear and tear was tough. I am starting to feel the 'longevity' of the game maybe a little more — it's catching up to me. But I am grateful to be where I am, and I do think it is an honor to be the manager of the Minnesota Twins."

On the 1987 World Series:
"Being it was my first full year as a manager, it was a very special thing. It was a new experience for me getting into the playoffs and into the World Series. Typically, we are somewhat afraid and apprehensive about new experiences because we don't know what to expect. There was a lot of cautious optimism surrounding the whole experience. The playoffs were a little more nerve-racking than the Big Dance, but, all in all, it was an incredible experience."

On the 1991 World Series:
"By 1991, we knew what to expect, so I think I enjoyed that one a little bit more because I knew what was going on. I wasn't as nervous this go around as I was in 1987. I frequently use the phrase 'storybook-like' to describe the games that series, because each game was like turning a page in a book to find out what was going to happen. Having the

games come down to the ninth inning and the last at-bat was incredible. We were very fortunate to win, because either team could have easily won. What was really rewarding was the fact that we went from last place in 1990 to first place in 1991. It was also very special to me because we proved that smaller market teams could still win it all."

Twins Tombstone:
"He was someone who worked hard to get where he got, all the time knowing that good things can happen to someone who works hard."

TRIBUTES
"T.K. will always be my favorite manager," said Kent Hrbek. "He's such a great guy. He was like my mother at the ballpark. He knew how I was feeling when I walked in the door just by looking at me. I just think he is an awesome manager, and I just love the guy."

"I consider Tom to be the most fair manager that I ever played for," said Jack Morris. "He let everybody know that there were no superstars on his team, and the players respected that."

"We go way back," said Kirby Puckett. "I played for T.K. back when I was in the instructional leagues, and we always got along well. All he ever asked of me was that I gave a 100 percent, and I've always listened to whatever he had to say."

"Even before I came here I had the greatest respect for Tom Kelly," said Paul Molitor. "The way that his teams would perform in last-place seasons, or in championship seasons, was remarkably consistent, and that definitely relates to the manager's control and leadership. Coming to the Twins, he surpassed my expectations as a manager in the manner of how he handles teams, rosters, and the ups and downs of a typical season."

"We played together for a season, and we had a very good relationship," said Rod Carew. "I liked him then, and I like him today. I like the way that he goes about getting his players ready to play. He's a player's manager, and all of the players that have played for him, speak very highly of him. He allows his players to enjoy playing the game, and I think that is important. Tom goes about handling all the personalities on the team in a very professional and fun way, and that's why he is successful."

"He is a great person," said Tony Oliva. "He wants you to work hard, and he knows a lot about baseball. I don't have enough good words for Tom Kelly, he is just a great man."

"I have the utmost respect for him, and I think he was the best manager in the game," said Jim Kaat. "I think the way he molded that 1987 team was incredible."

1988 RUNNER-UP: AMY PETERSON

Minnesota's greatest short-track speed skater, **AMY PETERSON**, begins her incredible Olympic saga, representing the USA in the 1988 Winter Games in Calgary. The Maplewood native would go on to compete in an unprecedented five Olympiads (1988, 1992, 1994, 1998 & 2002), later winning a silver in Albertville in 1992 and a pair of bronzes in Lillehammer in 1994. At the 2002 Olympic games in Salt Lake City, Peterson was honored by being voted by her teammates to be the flag bearer in the opening ceremonies. She is one of just two Minnesotans (Winona swimmer Tracy Caulkins) to have won three individual Olympic medals.

HONORABLE MENTION: JILL TRENARY

In 1988 Minnesota's greatest figure skater, **JILL TRENARY**, finished second at the U.S. National Championships; fifth at the World Championships. and placed fourth at the Winter Olympics in Calgary. The Minnetonka native won an amazing four U.S. National Championships in 1987, 1989, 1990 and 1992. In addition, Trenary also won a World Championship in 1990, in Halifax, Nova Scotia, by defeating the reigning champion, Midori Ito. Trenary would go on to perform professionally with several high profile celebrity shows and later got into TV broadcasting as a figure skating analyst.

1989

DOUG WOOG
The Hockey Gophers Come Up Just Short

Doug Woog is a coaching icon at the University of Minnesota. Perhaps the Minnesota equivalent to the Notre Dame football coach, so too is the program's hockey coach. Woog achieved great success in Gold Country, and he did it all with Minnesota kids. That alone may have been the single greatest tradition in all of college sports, yet it was something that was constantly used against him as the reason why his teams never won the NCAA championship. Always the bridesmaid, never the bride. Woog sent six Gopher squads to the NCAA Frozen Four, but none was able to bring home the hardware. One thing is for certain though, the closest the Wooger ever came to getting that monkey off of his back came in 1989, when his Gophers lost a heart-breaker to Harvard at the Civic Center in St. Paul. Despite the fact that Minnesota lost, the game ranks right up there as one of the greatest NCAA Finals in college hockey history.

The Gophers were coming off of their first WCHA championship under Woog that season and were expected to finish even better than the previous year's Frozen Four semifinal loss to Maine. Things looked promising for the team at the start of the season. Dave Snuggerud and Tom Chorske had returned from the Olympics and led the team in scoring; the reigning Hobey Baker Award recipient, Robb Stauber was in goal; and returning leadership could be found in such players as: Randy Skarda, Todd Richards, Lance Pitlick, Luke Johnson, Jason Miller, Ken Gernander, Dean Williamson, Peter and Ben Hankinson, Larry Olimb, Sean Fabian, Grant Bischoff, Jon Anderson and David Espe. In addition, there were two highly regarded freshmen in Tom Pederson and Travis Richards, who would both contribute to the cause.

The Gophers opened the season by winning 12 of their first 14 games, including sweeps over Wisconsin, Denver, North Dakota and Colorado College. The team was awesome that year, losing back-to-back games only once. They went on to win the WCHA crown by a seven-point margin over Michigan Tech, making it back-to-back Mc-Naughton Cups for the first time in the history of Gopher hockey. With an impressive 34-11-3 overall record (26-6-2 in conference play), they then went on to meet Colorado College in the first round of the WCHA Playoffs. There, they swept the Tigers, 5-4 and 7-1. Then, at the WCHA version of the Final Four at St. Paul's Civic Center, Denver and Wisconsin both upset the Gophers, each winning by a goal.

Minnesota then swept the Badgers in the ensuing NCAA playoffs, which were held at Mariucci Arena, by a pair of matching 4-2 scores. This now set up a rematch with their old adversaries from the East — Maine, in the NCAA Frozen Four semifinals which were conveniently being held at the St. Paul Civic Center. Revenge was sweet for the Maroon and Gold, as they crushed the Black Bears, 7-4, behind Jon Anderson's hat trick.

With that, the stage was set. The Gophers would now face Harvard for all the marbles in the championship game. Minnesota jumped out to a 1-0 lead when Jon Anderson went downstairs, stick-side, off a sweet Benny Hankinson pass at 6:24 in the first. Then Harvard's Ted Donato and Lane MacDonald each scored in the second to pull ahead by one. Bloomington's Jason Miller evened it up at two apiece when he scored his fourth goal in three games, off a Lance Pitlick rebound. In the third both teams exchanged power-plays until Ted Donato tallied again to put the Crimson back on top, 3-2.

But, like so many times before that season, the Gophers came back. This time on a Pete Hankinson wrister to make it three apiece. The buzzer sounded and with that, both teams headed to overtime.

Now, just as the fourth period got underway, Randy Skarda skated down, made a move and took a slapper at Harvard Goalie Chuckie Hughes. All you could hear was a dull plunk, which could've only meant one thing: Skarda hit the pipe. "Half an inch and we're champions," said Woog afterward. Then, at 4:16 of sudden-death, Harvard's Ed Krayer got a gift. After Stauber stopped a shot that took him out of position, Krayer picked up the rebound that landed on his stick and slid a back-hander under his sprawled out pads. It was a dagger sent right into the collective heart of Gopher fans everywhere.

Stauber, who stood on his head the entire game, stopping 24 shots, sat motionless on the ice in utter disbelief. As the nearly 16,000 Minnesota fans sat in silence, shock set in as they pondered just how close they had come to finally winning it all. Many in the large crowd thought that the 4-3 decision might have been the best college hockey game that they had ever viewed.

"I don't like to think about it," said Stauber, who led the WCHA in goaltending that season. "I remember the shot, and I reached for the rebound but missed it. There were so many things in that game I would've done differently. Sometimes in big pressure games you tend to be more reserved and play more conservatively than you'd like to. But, that was a great year, and we had nothing to be ashamed of at all."

Randy Skarda had come within one inch of getting that 900-pound gorilla off Doug Woog's back on that fabled day in April. "It was probably the most crushing defeat of my life," said Skarda. "Kenny Gernander set me up, and I hit the inside of the pipe. Afterwards I couldn't leave my house for two weeks, I was devastated."

As for the Wooger, the thought of coming that close was something he will never forget. "We had the advantage of being at home in St. Paul that year, and the disadvantage of not getting to bed the night before until 3:00am because of all the fans," he said. "I remember Hankinson scoring late and tying it up for us as we came back, and I can still see Randy Skarda making a rush on their goalie and the sound of that puck hitting the pipe. That one pipe changed the history of Gopher hockey forever. It delayed the inevitable that we will win a national championship. There is always something that puts humility into the pot, and that's the one you gotta answer every week: 'When will we win the big one?' "

The Wooger
Doug Woog grew up playing hockey in St. Paul. Before graduating in 1962 from South St. Paul High School, he earned all-state hockey honors for an amazing three consecutive years. He also starred in football and was a good student to boot. From there, Doug fulfilled a life-long dream by accepting a scholarship to play for John Mariucci at the University of Minnesota.

Woog went on to a fabulous career in Gold Country, earning All-American honors his junior season after leading the team in scoring. He was named as team captain for his senior season en route to leading the team to a 16-12-0 record, and a second place finish in the WCHA. For his efforts he was named the team's MVP. From 1964-66 the speedy center scored 48 goals and 53 assists for 101 career points. Doug graduated with honors from the U of M in 1967.

He would on to play for the 1967 U.S. National Team before entering the real world as a Geography teacher and coach (football and hockey) at Hopkins West Junior High School. Then, in the fall of 1968, he took a job at his high school alma mater, where he became the head soccer coach as well as an assistant on both the hockey and baseball teams. While coaching at South St. Paul, his soccer program won six conference titles and twice finished as runner-up's for the state championship.

From 1971 through 1977 he branched out to coach the St. Paul Vulcans and the Minnesota Junior Stars, which he led to two U.S.

Junior National titles. During that time, in 1973, Woog fulfilled another dream when he earned his Master's Degree in guidance and counseling from St. Thomas University.

With aspirations of becoming a college coach, Woog got as much experience as he could get over the next couple of decades. In 1978 Woog was chosen to lead the West Team in the U.S. Olympic Festival, where his squad won the gold medal. (He would win another gold at the 1989 Olympic Festival as well.) He was the assistant coach of the 1982 U.S. National Junior Team, and then served as an assistant coach on the 1984 Olympic team that competed in Sarajevo, Yugoslavia. In 1985 Woog coached the U.S. National Junior Team; in 1987 he served as the assistant coach for Team USA in the 1987 Canada Cup; and in 1989 he was the head coach of the of U.S. Select 17 team.

In 1985 the "Wooger" got the call he had been waiting for, to take over as the head coach of his college alma-mater. There, he guided the Gophers to seven league championships (four regular season and three post-season) over what would turn out to be an illustrious 14-year career. During his tenure in Gold Country the Gophers were among the nation's very best, garnering WCHA Final Four/Five and NCAA appearances in 12 of 14 seasons, posting seven 30-win seasons, and appearing in six NCAA Frozen Fours. In 1999 Woog resigned as the University of Minnesota's head hockey coach to take an assistant athletic director position at the school. He would leave as the program's all-time winningest coach with a 389-187-40 record (.664).

Today, in addition to his work with the Gopher Athletics Department, Woog is a television analyst for Gopher Hockey games and also runs his own summer hockey camp in Breezy Point, Minn. In addition, he has been instrumental in initiating and maintaining youth athletic organizations in his community and beyond. A tireless promoter of the game he loves, the Wooger continues to carry the torch for John Mariucci. Further, he has been involved with amateur hockey, his community, as well as numerous local charities at all levels throughout his career. He is a solid coach, a wonderful person, and a great supporter of Minnesota hockey. In 2002 he was honored by being inducted into the U.S. Hockey Hall of Fame. Presently, Doug and his wife Jan reside in St. Paul. They have three children and many grandchildren.

What Did it Mean For You To Be a Gopher?

"It was a life-long dream come true for me to be able to play for the Gophers. The fact that we had scholarships was just a means to an end. Back then there weren't that many opportunities for us after college as far as hockey was concerned, with only six NHL teams and all. So, we played for the love of the game and were happy to get to school to be able to make a living. Yeah, being a Gopher was pretty special."

On Coaching the Gophers:

"To see how it has grown and prospered and how the people of Minnesota have grasped on to hockey is unbelievable. People realize that Gopher Hockey is associated with quality, and to be the coach of that was a real honor. There's a pedigree and an aura for kids to play Gopher hockey. Starting with Herbie in the 70's, our program has been consistent and we have had a lot of wins. This program was doing fine

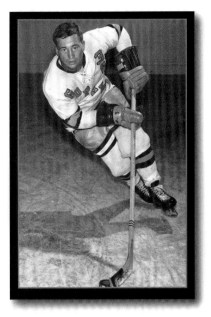

as far as their ability to win before I got here, and it didn't need me to come over.

"What I gave the program was a level of respectability in terms of how I communicated to the public. I think I gave some consistency to the educational value of the sport and brought some credibility to the program in terms of the media and television. It has also become very profitable for the University in terms of dollars, and our program alone generated television revenues that probably exceed the entire WCHA put together. The new rink was a statement to the people and to thank them for their support."

On Only Recruiting Minnesota Kids:

"I was committed to going with the Minnesota kid as long as I was the coach. We provided opportunities for Minnesota kids to get professional jobs, and we got more kids than any other school in the country playing professionally. I'm proud of the fact that kids in Minnesota grow up dreaming about being Gophers, and they have great role models to look up to and watch. But, it got tougher with Duluth, St. Cloud, Mankato and Bemidji all competing for Minnesota kids. A kid might rather have played on the first line somewhere else rather than to play on our third or fourth. That's how we were recruited against, but I wouldn't change a thing."

Gopher Tombstone:

"I want to be thought of as someone that won with dignity and performed with dignity."

TRIBUTES

"I coached Doug on the Gopher freshman team, and he was a great player," said Lou Nanne. "Doug has been a very successful coach at the U and he's a guy that's really committed to the program. He had his own feelings on how he wanted to develop it with Minnesota kids, but he was successful for the most part and he had a wonderful run."

"They don't have to win the title to be successful," said John Mayasich. "I would say there are American born players out there who could help him. I wouldn't say don't go out and get them to have them contribute, but I think we can be competitive with the Minnesota kids. It takes 20 players and a hot goalie to win it."

"I played for Doug with the Vulcans," said former NHL star Paul Holmgren. "He was a terrific coach as well as a tremendous player. For a small guy, he could be really intimidating. I enjoyed playing for him, and I think he's done a great job with his teams."

1989 RUNNER-UP: POOH RICHARDSON

Nearly three decades after the Lakers left us for Los Angeles, the NBA returns to Minnesota with the expansion Timberwolves. In the end the team finished the season with a modest 22-60 record, good for 6th place in the Midwest Division. Minnesota wound up setting an NBA single-season attendance record that season, however, by drawing more than one million fans to watch them play at the Metrodome. The team's first ever draft pick was a point guard out of UCLA by the name of **POOH RICHARDSON**, who averaged 11.4 points and 6.8 assists per game that season, and was named to the NBA All-Rookie Team. Richardson would play for 10 seasons in the NBA, averaging 11.1 points and 6.5 assists per game.

HONORABLE MENTION: KEVIN LYNCH

The basketball Gophers make it to the Sweet 16 thanks in large part to the efforts of Bloomington native **KEVIN LYNCH**, who averaged 10.3 points per game that season. The Gophers finished fifth in the Big 10 with a 19-12 overall record and then went on to beat Kansas State, 86-75, and Siena, 80-67, in the opening round of the NCAA Tourney, but then got beat by Duke, 87-70, in the NCAA East Regional to end the season. Lynch played for the Gophers from 1988-92, averaging 11.4 points and 3.1 rebounds per game. He went on to play for three seasons in the NBA with the Hornets, before becoming a Gopher basketball TV analyst.

Expectations were running at an all-time high for the 1989-90 Gophers, a team which entered the season ranked 20th in the nation — the program's first national ranking since finishing seventh back in 1982. After a summer exhibition tour of Australia, the team, which was pretty banged up, returned home to begin its non-conference schedule. They also returned home to face another distraction — this one from the ever-probing NCAA, which this time alleged that former University administrator Luther Darville had misappropriated University funds by issuing payments to both football and basketball players. The case lingered on and proved to be a real distraction.

Moving on, the team went out and posted a 9-1 non-conference record that year — losing just their season opener on a buzzer-beater, 66-64, to the Bearcats of Cincinnati. From there, the Gophers, led by Melvin Newbern's 27 points, went out and crushed the No. 4-ranked Illini, 91-74, in the Big Ten opener. They dropped two straight after that to both Purdue, 86-78, and Michigan, 87-83, but rebounded to spank Northwestern, 97-75, and Ohio State, 83-78. Their momentum was short-lived though, as the team got upset that next week in Madison, 77-75, on a last-second Badger dunk. Back at the Barn three nights later, Minnesota upended Iowa, 84-72, thanks to Willie Burton's 21 points and 10 rebounds, and Richard Coffey's 14 points and 13 rebounds. They followed that up with a huge 108-89 home win over the Hoosiers on Super Bowl Sunday, with Willie Burton, Richard Coffey, Kevin Lynch, Melvin Newbern, Jim Shikenjanski and Walter Bond, all scoring in double figures. It was the most points ever scored against a Bobby Knight-coached team.

After losing to Illinois, Minnesota came home to the old Barn where they knocked off Purdue in one of the season's best games. Newbern was the hero du jour, nailing a turn-around jumper in the final seconds to seal a 73-72 victory for the nearly 17,000 Gopher faithful in attendance. The Gophers then climbed up to the No. 17 spot in the AP poll after beating Michigan State, 79-74, but once again fell to earth following a 99-72 spanking by the Illini. After edging Purdue, 73-72, on yet another Newbern jumper in the game's final seconds, Minnesota was beaten by Michigan, 77-73, to abruptly end their impressive 12-game home winning-streak. They rebounded to beat Northwestern, 90-72, followed by Iowa, 102-80, and Indiana, 75-70, to make it 20 wins for the season. But, they wound up losing their final two conference games of the year to eventual Big Ten champion Michigan State, on Senior Night, in an overtime heartbreaker, 75-73, and also to Ohio State, 93-83, despite a career-high 31 points from Willie Burton. (The five Gopher seniors — Burton, Richard Coffey, Connell Lewis, Newbern, and Jim Shikenjanski took a farewell lap around Williams Arena on Senior Night, and Willie whooped it up big-time by getting up on a chair and waving a towel to all the fans for his final curtain call.)

With that, the No. 6 seeded Gophers received another NCAA bid for the Big Dance. Their first opponent: the University of Texas-El Paso, at the Southeast Regional in Richmond, Virginia. There, behind Kevin Lynch's 18 points and Coffey's 11 rebounds, the Gophs hung on to win ugly, in overtime, 64-61.

"It was awesome because everything that Coach Haskins had said and told us began to really come true," said Burton. "The hard work, running in the mornings, being put down all the time by the fans at the other schools, it was tough. But it all came together and we were a force to be

reckoned with."

Two nights later the team faced the Northern Iowa Panthers in the round of 32. There, behind Burton's 36 points and 12 rebounds, Minnesota rolled to an 81-78 victory — earning their second trip to the "Sweet 16" in as many years. With the loss of Duke still fresh in their minds from the year before, the Gophers then headed to the New Orleans Super Dome that next week, to take on the mighty Syracuse Orangemen. Led by future NBA stars Billy Owens and Derrick Coleman, the Gophers knew they would have their hands full.

"My club has come a long way," Haskins said before the game. "They've shown great improvement and they remember getting to the Sweet 16 a year ago only to get whipped by Duke. They haven't forgotten that and they'll carry that memory into the Syracuse game."

What happened next though, was pure magic. Down by four at half-time, the Gophs came back and shot nearly 80% from the field in the second half, en route to an impressive 82-75 victory. Five players scored in double figures, including 20 from Newbern, 18 from Lynch, and 10 from seven-foot Center Bob Martin of Apple Valley. Even the ex-paratrooper, Richard Coffey, got into the act, snatching 12 boards as well.

The next step for the Cinderella Gophers was their first-ever appearance in the Tourney's "Elite Eight," where they would face off against the Georgia Tech Yellow Jackets, and their "Lethal Weapon Three" trio of sharpshooters: Kenny Anderson, Dennis Scott and Brian Oliver. In what would go down as one of the greatest games in Gopher history, Minnesota came out and played valiantly.

"I finally realized, in my heart, that if we lost, we would never play together again as a team," said Burton. "We didn't want it to be over, so we went out there with destruction on our minds. We just didn't want the ride to end."

It was a back and forth contest all day, but in the end, the Jackets came out on top — thanks in large part to the fact that the referees wound up issuing an unbelievable 35 free throws to Georgia Tech, compared to just 11 for the Gophers. That disparity would ultimately cost the Maroon and Gold the game. Despite that fact though, the team battled down to the wire, and refused to roll over.

Willie led the Minnesota attack, and the Gophers jumped out to a 12-point lead. But the Yellow Jackets closed the gap and trailed by only two at halftime, 49-47. Later in the fourth, now down 93-88 with just seven seconds left on the clock, Burton dribbled down and pulled up from the top of the circle to nail a dramatic three-pointer to make it 93-91. Then, when Tech got the ball in-bounds, the Gophers quickly fouled Guard Kenny Anderson. Anderson, who would go on to NBA stardom, stepped up and nervously missed the front end of the one-and-one free-throw.

With that, Richard Coffey, the rebounding machine, grabbed the ball and heaved it to an awaiting Mario Green, who in turn, tossed it to a streaking Kevin Lynch at mid-court. Lynch then dribbled down to the right corner of the court, and with time running out, stopped and fired an off-balanced three-pointer over the top of the outstretched Johnny McNeil's fingertips. At that moment, it was like slow-motion. The ball just hung in the air for what seemed like an eternity. Then, as the buzzer sounded, the ball bounced harmlessly off the front of the rim — crushing the collective dreams of the millions of Gopher fans who were tuned in across the nation. Minnesota's Final Four dreams were over as the team watched in disbelief.

It was a sad ending for an otherwise brilliant season. The improbable 23-9 Gophers had shocked the world and emerged as a real contender. And, for seniors Willie Burton, Melvin Newbern, Jim Shikenjanski, Richard Coffey, Connell Lewis, as well as Coach Haskins — the collective group of newcomers who came into a program in shambles back in 1986 — it was the end of an amazing ride. They had joined a ravaged and ragged Gopher program, and as seniors they left as saviors, giving Gold Country fans two magical back-to-back trips to the Big Dance.

For Burton, who emerged as one of the program's most

beloved all-time players, it was a very sad and emotional ending to an incredible career in Gold Country.

"It almost went in and it really bothers me because it was a good shot, he barely missed it," said Burton, who, after averaging 24.4 points per game, was named to the All-Big Ten Team and received honorable mention All-American honors. "Personally, I think that the last shot was just too much pressure for him (Lynch) to take. I mean at the time he was open, going top speed and he had a look at the hoop, but it was a lot of pressure to deal with. When Kevin missed, I was so bummed out because I didn't want it all to end like that. I remember, after the game, I stopped and looked hard at everyone. I took a picture of everybody together in my mind for one last time."

"They shot 25 more foul shots than we did, and they won by two," added Burton, when asked about the blatantly lopsided refereeing during that game. "I had 35 points and never took a foul shot the entire game. Maybe it was because those refs were from the ACC, Georgia Tech's home conference? We just couldn't get a break that night, and it was frustrating because the referees just wouldn't blow their whistles for us."

Several thousand fans showed up at the Twin Cities International Airport following the Georgia Tech loss to show their appreciation for an unbelievably entertaining and exciting season. The Gophers had captured the hearts and imaginations of the state of Minnesota that season, finally putting the program back on track and into the national spotlight. Going to games at Williams Arena that season was an event, an outing that was looked forward to and cherished. They had brought back the pride that the program had briefly lost, and made us all very proud.

Willie B.

Born on May 26, 1968, Willie Burton grew up in inner city Detroit playing baseball, basketball, football and track. Solid in both athletics and academics in high school, he graduated with a 3.6 GPA. His prep athletic credentials were also impressive. He earned three letters in basketball and two in baseball. In basketball, where he averaged 22 points and 12 rebounds per game his senior year, he was a two-time All-Stater as well as an All-Detroit selection.

From there, Willie decided to attend the U of M, where, after four glorious years, he was named to the All-Big Ten Team, received honorable mention All-American honors, and for three straight years was voted as the team MVP. Willie finished his Gopher career averaging 19.3 points per game with 6.4 rebounds. Upon graduation, he ranked ninth in career rebounding (705), sixth in career blocks, (79) and was third on the all-time scoring list, with 1,800 points, behind only Mychal Thompson and Voshon Lenard.

"The reason I went to the University of Minnesota was because it had more to offer after basketball," said Burton. "I took a recruiting visit to the Twin Cities and just fell in love with the region. I thought it was a beautiful place. The people got along, I loved the mix of the cultures that were there, and it was just a dream place as far as where I would like to live once my basketball days were over. I knew in my heart that it was the place that I wanted to be. I signed a letter of intent for Coach Dutcher one month before the program's troubles in

Madison. But, through it all, I never said I would leave because my goal was to be a Gopher and to live in Minnesota. Coach Haskins and I started out together and we just started the basketball program over. All of us seniors came in together when Clem took it over, and that's why we were so close to each other. We went through a lot of scrutiny after all that happened, but when it was all over we showed the world we could go a long way."

After his memorable career with Minnesota Burton went on to be selected with the ninth overall pick of the first round by the NBA's Miami Heat. He would later find himself playing for the Philadelphia 76ers, where he scored a career high 53 points during a game against the Heat on December 13, 1994. He bounced around with several teams after that, including Atlanta, San Antonio and Charlotte, before retiring in 1999 with a career scoring average of 10.3 points per game. His quick first step and outstanding post-up ability made him a solid NBA player for nearly a decade, and one of the best-ever to hail from Minnesota.

What Did it Mean For You To Be a Gopher?
"Playing at the University of Minnesota was the most meaningful thing in my life. The time I spent on campus was the best four years of my life. My teammates and I were like brothers who all genuinely cared about each other. I loved it there. I lived in Centennial Hall for all four years that I was there, and it was great. I still proudly wear a University of Minnesota baseball cap because I've earned the right to wear it. I can't put into words what the University of Minnesota meant to me. The experience was just awesome."

On Minnesota Fans:
"My relationship with the Gopher fans was incredible. I think I bonded with them because they genuinely cared. When I came to Minnesota, in my freshman year, we were getting clobbered, but the fans still came and filled up Williams Arena. I will never forget that, and neither did my teammates. That was the reason we went out and we played the way we played."

Gopher Tombstone:
"I want to be remembered as being a good person with a good heart. Someone who genuinely appreciated the game, the fans, and the everyday people of the Twin Cities. You could say that I was one of the nicest guys in the world until the game started, and then I had a hockey player's mentality. I didn't want the spotlight, I just wanted to play."

1990 RUNNER-UP: GREG LEMOND

Minnetonka native **GREG LEMOND** wins his third Tour de France title. Minnesota's greatest cycler first made history in 1986 when he became the first American to win the largest single annual sporting event in the world. Then, after recovering from a nearly fatal gunshot wound he suffered in a hunting accident in 1987, LeMond worked himself back into shape and won the race again in 1989. This time he overcame a seemingly insurmountable lead by Frenchman Laurent Fignon to win by just eight seconds, the narrowest margin of victory ever in the Tour's 87-year history. For his efforts he was named as the 1989 "Sports Illustrated Sportsman of the Year."

HONORABLE MENTION: JOHN ROETHLISBERGER

The Gopher gymnastics team wins the Big 10 title but comes up just a tenth of a point short to Nebraska in their bid to claim the NCAA national championship. Leading the way was **JOHN ROETHLISBERGER**, who was without question the greatest gymnast ever to compete for the U. The four-time Big Ten Athlete of the Year was a five-time NCAA champion, 10-time conference champion, 15-time All-American and three-time Olympian. John's dad, Fred, was the program's long-time coach and his sister, Marie, was also a Gopher. Incredibly, all three represented the USA as Olympians. They are truly Minnesota's first family of gymnastics.

1991

JACK MORRIS
The Twins are World Champs Once Again

The good thing about finishing in last place is that the only place to go from there is up. And that is exactly what the 1991 "worst to first" World Series champion Twins did. These Twins were a full-circle success story that will forever be remembered for Jack Morris' amazing Game Seven heroics.

After the team's best pre-season ever at their new spring training facility, the Lee County Sports Complex in Ft. Myers, Fla., (they moved after playing 55 years in Orlando), the squad got off to a pathetic 2-9 start, courtesy of a pair of ugly west coast swings. They rebounded though, and played solid fundamental baseball under manager Tom Kelly. Early on, many Twins fans had a good feeling about this new bunch of kids. The team just got better and better as the season went on and they continued to close the gap on first-place Texas. The highlight came when they reeled off 15 wins in a row en route to winning the American League West. One of the reasons for the clubs' success was the unbelievable pitching of Scott Erickson, who, at one point, won a club-record 12 consecutive games.

The 95-67 Twins then went on to easily win the American League Championship Series, beating the Toronto Blue Jays four games to one, to earn a trip back to the World Series. One of the highlights of the ALCS came in Game Three, when pinch-hitter Mike Pagliarulo won it for the Twins on a home run to right in the 10th inning. Kirby Puckett also homered in Games Four and Five to seal the deal for Minnesota.

Now, in the World Series, the Twins would face another cellar-dwelling team from 1990, the resurrected Atlanta Braves, who had beaten the Pittsburgh Pirates, 4-3, in the NLCS. The World Series got off to a great start for Minnesota. The Twins won Games One and Two at the Metrodome, 5-2, and 3-2, respectively. Game Two was highlighted by Kent Hrbek's now infamous all-star wrestling tag-out of Atlanta's Ron Gant on first base. In addition, Chili Davis hit a two-run homer in the first inning, while Scott Leius added one of his own in the eighth. The Homer Hankies were back and so were the Twins.

The series then shifted south, to "Hot-Lanta" where the Braves won three straight, highlighted by a 14-run shellacking of the Twins in Game Five. Up three games to two, the Braves then returned to the Dome to try and wrap it up. Kirby Puckett thought differently though and played the game of his life in Game Six. First, Puck robbed Braves outfielder Ron Gant of a home run in the third on a Ringling Brothers-like grab off the center field Plexiglas. Then, after a Terry Pendleton homer to tie it up, Puckett regained the lead for his Twins on a sacrifice fly. Atlanta knotted the score again in the seventh to send it into extra innings, only to see Kirby take over in the 11th. There, with the game tied at three, Kirby stepped up and hit a towering shot off Atlanta's Charlie Liebrandt that was without question the greatest home run in Twins history, giving Minnesota a thrilling 4-3 win and evening the series at three games apiece. "We'll see you tomorrow night!", said legendary broadcaster Jack Buck following the big hit.

The locker room was surprisingly calm before Game Seven. In fact, the clubhouse television sets were all tuned to football games when the players arrived — so they could set their fantasy football line-ups, believe it or not. Manager Tom Kelly had named Jack Morris as his starter in the most important baseball game of 1991, while Atlanta's Bobby Cox countered with John Smoltz, a Detroit native who grew up worshipping that very Jack Morris.

The game was a back and forth pitching duel that went scoreless into the top of the eighth. That inning would prove to be one of the most tense of the series. With Lonnie Smith on first, Terry Pendleton hit a liner to the gap. Then, Smith, who was running on the pitch, mysteriously eased up and slowed down as he was rounding second. Replays showed that Twins second baseman Chuck Knoblauch put on a fabulous deke, faking that he was going to catch the ball coming in from the outfield. Little did Smith know, however, was that the ball was, in reality, still rolling around in the outfield at the time. By the time he realized what was going on though, he could only advance to third. Had he looked, he would have certainly scored what would have been the game-winning run. Gant then hit a squibber to Hrbek for an easy out, followed by Sid Bream, who hit into a 3-2-3 double play to end the inning. Morris leaped into the air pumping his fist up to the sky as the Twins had dodged a huge bullet.

Through the tenth, the Twins and Braves matched donuts on the scoreboard. It had now become only the second Game Seven in World Series history to reach extra innings. Kelly would later say: "There was no thought of changing pitchers. Morris could rest in November; the outcome of October was his to decide."

Dan Gladden then led off the last of the 10th with a broken-bat base-hit that he somehow managed to stretch into a double. Knoblauch, who would be named Rookie of the Year that season, had just one sacrifice bunt all year. He got his second on that night though by moving Gladden to third. The Twins were now 90 feet from their second title in just five years. After intentionally walking Kirby and Herbie to load the bases, Gene Larkin now stood at home plate for the at-bat of his life. Larkin jumped on the first pitch and hit a fly ball to left-center. Atlanta left fielder Brian Hunter, who was playing way in, could only look on helplessly as the ball flew over his head and landed harmlessly on the turf. The rest, they say, is history.

"The Twins are gonna win the World Series!", shouted announcer Jack Buck after the huge hit. "The Twins have won it!"

Fittingly, Morris was the first to grab Gladden as he touched the plate. Two mobs of players, one at home and the other at first base, eventually merged in the center of the diamond in a sea of chaos. The Atlanta Braves had been "tomahawk-chopped" by the Minnesota Twins in one of the greatest World Series' ever.

With five games decided by a single run, this series was, in a word, incredible. In front of 55,118 rabid fans under the teflon tent, Morris had pitched a seven-hit, 10-inning, 1-0 shut-out gem. Jack won two pivotal games for his Twins in the Series, and they were the most important — the first and the last. His performance in Game Seven will go down in baseball lore as possibly the greatest ever. His two wins coupled with an amazing 1.17 ERA, earned him Series MVP honors.

"I wasn't really aware of what was going on historically when I was in that game, because my focus was strictly on getting out the Atlanta Braves and making sure that the fans at the stadium and everyone else watching would not go away disappointed," said Morris. "I've only watched the replay of Game Seven a few times because I get kind of choked up. I've recognized and realized that as soon as the game was over that it was probably my best day ever. Nothing else would compare in my career, and I recognize that I could never do any better than that, so I should just take it and appreciate it."

Amazingly, when Jack was asked just what was going through his mind when he took the mound in that 10th inning, it was something all Minnesota sports fans could relate to: "I don't mean this in any derogatory way," he said, "but Fran Tarkenton had a big influence in that game. I remember growing up in Minnesota and watching the Vikings lose their third Super Bowl. I know that it is unfair for me to say that Fran was the reason they lost, because obviously it's a team sport. But you know, I think there were so many people that were disappointed in the Vikings, and particularly in Tarkenton, because he was the leader. The quarterback and the pitcher are considered to be the team leaders, and they are the people with the most influence on the outcome of a game. As I sat there, and the game progressed, I just couldn't help but think of the Vikings and those Super Bowl losses. During that seventh game, I looked up in the Metrodome crowd and saw all these people, just exhausted from screaming and cheering, but going absolutely berserk, wanting a winner so bad, and a sort of calmness came over me. It was like something was driving me from that point on, and I just refused to let the fans of Minnesota go home disappointed. I knew that we were going to win, if it took all night long. We weren't going to be losers, we weren't going to be the Vikings."

Tiger Jack

From the sandlots of St. Paul, Jack Morris attended Highland Park High School and then went on to play college ball in Utah, at Brigham Young University. From there he was drafted by the Detroit Tigers and would go on to become one of baseball's all-time greatest pitchers. He was the only pitcher to have won 14 or more games in each year of the 1980s and three times he won 20 or more. Although some were critical of his perennially high ERA, Jack would shrug and say that he was paid to win games, and that his contract did not stipulate that the margin of victory be by a shut-out or by a score of 6-5.

The winningest pitcher of the 1980s, Morris was a workhorse, notching double-digit wins in 14 of his 16 full seasons in the Majors, while finishing in the top 10 in Cy Young Award voting seven times. He won a trio of World Series titles as well, winning his first in 1984 with Detroit, his second in 1991 with his hometown Twins, and his third in 1992 with Toronto. He was also very durable, being relegated to the disabled list just twice in his 18-year career. He had a solid fastball, a hard slider, and excellent split-finger to make his pitching arsenal one of the game's best. Morris even hurled a no-hitter against the Chicago White Sox on April 7, 1984, matching the earliest date in a season a no-no was thrown. Among the most reliable pitchers in history, he holds the AL record with 515 straight starts, once going more than 10 seasons with just one missed start. An excellent all-around athlete who was often used as a pinch runner, he also holds the Major League career record for put-outs by a pitcher, with 387.

"Every ballplayer whether they signed out of high school or college probably has some kind of dream of playing with their hometown team," said Jack of his return home to Minnesota. "And I was no different. After being drafted by Detroit and playing there through the years, I thought I might finish my career there. But as the political football of baseball goes, you gotta do what you gotta do, and when the opportunity arose to come play for Minnesota, it was like a dream come true. The 1991 season was a fairy tale."

Jack had spent 14 seasons with the Tigers before coming back to Minnesota — where he wound up staying for just one year.

"As players, we don't always recognize what points of light come across our paths until after they're gone," said Jack. "I never had any intention of leaving Minnesota when I was here. I never wanted to, but I understand what happened. Mr. Pohlad had to save his money for a guy named Kirby Puckett. He lost several great players and really the nucleus of a ballclub because of the fan appeal of one player. I'm not blaming anybody, Kirby did what he had to do, and he was justified in doing it. Carl Pohlad did what he had to do, and all of us players who

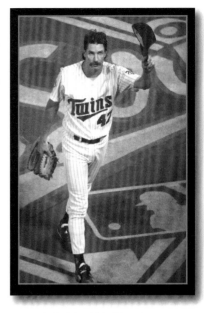

left the Twins did what we had to do. It was just unfortunate that we couldn't have kept it together because I wanted nothing more than to win it all again with that same group of guys."

After his heroics with the Twins, Jack signed with Toronto, followed by stints in Cleveland and Cincinnati before finally hanging up his spikes at the tender age of 40. Then, in 1994 Jack opted to come home yet again to become the ace of the Northern League's St. Paul Saints, where he ended up leading the league with a 2.61 ERA. He retired during that season in St. Paul though, to spend more time at his ranch in Montana. Jack finished his illustrious career with 254 victories and 175 complete games. One of the game's all-time greats, Jack's next stop will hopefully be the Baseball Hall of Fame.

Twins Tombstone:

"I think people need to know that I loved the game of baseball. I really appreciate and respect the game and had fun playing it. I realize that I am rough around the edges. I've never really been well versed enough to be smooth and sensitive to everybody, because I was so driven in one direction — and that was to win. I blocked out a lot of distractions. It was the price of winning. In the process I turned off a few people. I just want people to know that I gave it all I had, and winning was most important to me. I think that when you are a perfectionist like myself, the only way you're justified in your effort is to win. It creates a huge burden on you — and you become your own worst enemy as well as your own worst critic."

TRIBUTES

"Jack was a very competitive player," said Tom Kelly. "He was intense about his job and was very workman-like. He knew how to win and took the ball every four or five games. He was a great pitcher."

"His Game Seven performance was the most jacked up I have ever seen a pitcher pitch in a ballgame, and I don't think there will ever be another game pitched like it," said Kent Hrbek. "To me that was the single most gutsy performance by a pitcher that I have ever seen."

"Tiger Jack was probably one of the most intense people that I have ever been around," said Kirby Puckett. "He was a warrior and gave you everything he had. Whatever he had going, he would use it to get it done, and that's the mark of a great pitcher. He protected us as well. If another pitcher threw at us, he would throw at their players — and that is the way the game is supposed to be played. He took the ball no matter what and wouldn't miss a start. I respected that."

1991 RUNNER-UP: MIKE MODANO

The Cinderella North Stars go on a post-season tirade, upsetting Chicago (four games to two), St. Louis (four games to two), and Edmonton (four games to one) in the Conference Finals — earning a trip back to the Stanley Cup Finals against Pittsburgh. Minnesota split Games One and Two in Pittsburgh, and then won Game Three back at the Met. Penguins Hall of Famer Mario LeMieux took over from there, however, and the Pens went on to win the next three straight to take the series in six games. Leading the way for the Stars was second-year winger **MIKE MODANO**, who tallied 28 goals and 36 assists that season. The Michigan native would go on to superstardom, scoring 528 goals and 755 assists for 1,283 points in just 1,320 career games. Now in his 20th NHL season, in Dallas, the future Hall of Famer is the top-scoring U.S. born player in league history.

HONORABLE MENTION: DAVID WHEATON

Deephaven's **DAVID WHEATON** attains a No. 12 world ranking after reaching the semifinals at Wimbledon and then winning the largest prize money event in tennis — the Grand Slam Cup. Wheaton played on the Tour from 1988-2001, won more than $5 million, and reached the semifinals or better in singles or doubles of every grand slam event. He also represented the U.S. as a member of the Davis Cup Team in 1993.

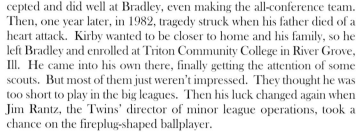

The Twins made big news even before the 1992 season got underway when they signed Kirby Puckett to a new contract during a live, made-for-TV extravaganza. There had been Kirby sightings in Boston, New York, and even one in Des Moines. Would he stick around and finish his illustrious career with Minnesota, or would he go? That suspenseful question was answered on December 4th, when, in a circus-like atmosphere, he inked a five-year, $30-million deal that made him the highest paid player in baseball. (Incidentally, that dubious honor ended just a few hours later when Barry Bonds signed an even bigger deal with the San Francisco Giants.)

The '92 season was, by all accounts, a success. The Twins went 90-72 and finished the year in second place in the American League West. They played well, but just couldn't catch the Oakland A's down the stretch. They did, however, achieve several record-setting individual and team accomplishments. Among them was Tom Kelly winning his 523rd game, the most of any Twins manager in team history. There was also Kirby Puckett's fabulous year which included reaching 200 hits for the fifth time; knocking in 100+ runs and 100+ RBI's, and hitting over .300 for the seventh time in nine seasons. In addition, he also belted out three grand slams en route to twice being named as the AL Player of the Month. Other Twins to notch the 100-run plateau included Shane Mack and Chuck Knoblauch, who each had good years as well. In addition, reliever Rick Aguilera got his 109th save to become the Twins' all-time saves leader as well.

The Puck

Kirby Puckett was born March 14, 1961, in Chicago. He grew up in the Robert Taylor Homes, a public housing project on Chicago's tough South Side, just down the road from Comiskey Park, the home of the the White Sox. Kirby's dad, William, was a postal worker, and his mom, Catherine, stayed at home in their 14th floor apartment to take care of Puckett's nine brothers and sisters. Kirby usually came home from school, did his homework, and then went out to play ball.

"It was a long haul, coming from where I came from," said Kirby. "I can remember as a kid I broke up so many lamps and windows up in my room hitting the ball around — even with a wadded up sock ball. I was just playing baseball, just doing what I loved to do."

In 1973, his family moved out of the projects and into a better neighborhood outside of the city. Kirby would attend Calumet High School, where he would emerge as a star third baseman. He found it hard to get noticed by any scouts or college recruiters though.

"Not too many scouts came to the ghetto to see me play." he said. "We didn't even have a field, so we just played in a forest preserve that didn't have any fences or anything."

Kirby persevered through it all though and graduated in the top 20 percent of his class. That summer, Kirby took an assembly line job working at the Ford Motor plant on 130th street in Chicago.

"There were only two buses a day that went out there," he said, "so if you missed one, you were done for. It took 90 days to get into the union, and I remember I was there for like 89 days, and then they laid me off."

Kirby's luck would soon change. At a Kansas City Royals free agent try-out camp, amongst several hundred hopeful kids, Bradley University Coach, Dewey Kalmer, offered him a scholarship. Puckett enthusiastically ac-

cepted and did well at Bradley, even making the all-conference team. Then, one year later, in 1982, tragedy struck when his father died of a heart attack. Kirby wanted to be closer to home and his family, so he left Bradley and enrolled at Triton Community College in River Grove, Ill. He came into his own there, finally getting the attention of some scouts. But most of them just weren't impressed. They thought he was too short to play in the big leagues. Then his luck changed again when Jim Rantz, the Twins' director of minor league operations, took a chance on the fireplug-shaped ballplayer.

"He stood out," Rantz said. "It wasn't because he had a home run, a double, stole two bases, threw a guy out at home, or had a shaved head, either. What stood out was the enthusiasm he had for the game on a miserably hot night, when everybody was dog tired. That was the thing you noticed."

Once he was in organized baseball, Kirby tore up the minor leagues — first in Elizabethton, then in Visalia, and finally in Toledo. Virtually everywhere he went, he won the league's MVP award. The Twins soon realized that they had themselves a diamond in the rough.

Then, while playing for Toledo in a game up in Maine, Kirby got the call he'd been waiting for, to come up to the "Show." Mud Hens manager Cal Ermer called him in to tell him the good news and that he had to get on a plane to Los Angeles right away.

"I was called up, and I was so nervous," he said. "The plane was five hours late and by the time I finally got to the airport, there was nobody there to meet me. I had no idea how far the stadium was, and I only had $10 to my name. So when I got in a cab and told the driver that I needed to get to Anaheim for my first game, the driver gave me a funny look. By the time we got there, the fare was $60. So, I left all my stuff in the cab, and he waited for me to run in and get some money. I ran in and got my meal money from the Twins, telling them it was $85, so I could tip the driver $25 bucks. I still wish I had remembered to get the taxi driver's name because I was really grateful."

Kirby would make the most of his opportunity. On May 8, 1984, Puck became the sixth player in AL history to get four hits in his big league debut. He had arrived. Puckett's career would prove to be a long and storied one. There were two World Series wins, two ticker-tape parades down the streets of Minneapolis, and two pretty incredible Game Sixes. There was Game Six in the 1987 "Cinderella-Series," against the Cardinals, when he got four hits and scored four runs to carry the Twins. And there was the "Worst-to-First Series" of 1991, when, in that Game Six, Kirby first robbed Braves outfielder Ron Gant of a home run on a circus-like grab off the plexiglass, which was then followed by his game-winning home run in the 11th inning off Atlanta's Charlie Liebrandt — arguably the greatest moment in Twins history.

His bat didn't always make for heroics though. There was the Tony Oliva-inspired home-run epiphany during spring training in 1986, when, during batting practice in Orlando, Puck hit 10 consecutive balls over the fence. However, after each hit, he heard a strange sound. "Little did I know that they had some kind of auto show going on next door," said Puckett. A motorcycle cop then drove out onto the field where he told Kirby, "Swing at one more pitch, and I'll throw you in jail!" Turned out his monster shots had been smashing windshields!

Kirby was incredible. Only Willie Keeler had more hits in his first 10 years in the big leagues (2,065) than Puckett (2,040). In 12 seasons and 7,244 at-bats with Minnesota, Kirby finished with a career batting average of .318, which included 2,304 hits, 1,071 runs, 1,085 RBIs and 207 homers. He won a league MVP, played in 10 All-Star games, was named an All-Star game MVP, finished with a .989 fielding percentage, and earned six Gold Gloves. He was also awarded the treasured 1996 Roberto Clemente Man of the Year Award by Major League Baseball for his outstanding community service work.

Tragically, in 1996, Kirby's career was ended due to irreversible retina damage in his right eye. Amazingly, his last trip to the disabled list was also his first. "I knew that baseball wasn't going to last forever," he said. "It was great living in a fairy tale for 12 years, and I enjoyed every minute of it. I just thank God that I got the chance to live out the dream I had since I was five years old. Isn't that the way life's supposed to be?"

Puckett found it remarkable that anyone could feel sorry for a man who, in 1997, despite not being able to play, was in the final year of a $6-million contract. He grants himself but one regret, he would have liked to have reached 3,000 hits.

In August of 2001, Kirby, who went on to serve as the Twins' Executive Vice President of Baseball, was inducted into the Baseball Hall of Fame in Cooperstown, N.Y., alongside his teammate and friend, Dave Winfield. It was an amazing day for all of Minnesota baseball as the Gopher State was thrust into the national limelight for all to see. For Kirby, it was a fitting tribute to one of the game's best ever.

"My first love was always baseball, and it still is baseball," he said. "I've lived a dream, man, and being a Twin means everything to me. I was a gamer, and I came to play every day. I never took the game for granted. Not for one day. I had a smile on my face, but when I stepped between the white lines, I tried to hurt you because that was my job, man. I took my job very seriously because I knew that people paid their hard earned money to come see me play, and I wanted to give them the best possible show that I could every time I stepped onto a baseball field. I always did the little things that could give my team the edge, and that's why my teammates loved me."

"No matter what, with the game on the line, I wanted to be the man," he added. "I thrived on that, and that's what made me the player that I was. I never thought of myself as a superstar or anything like that, I'm just Kirby. My mom used to always tell me what goes up has to always come down, and sooner or later, all those people that you treated badly on the way up, you see again on the way down. I've remembered those words."

Tragically, Kirby Puckett died on March 6, 2006, after suffering a massive stroke at his home in Scottsdale, AZ. He was survived by his children, son Kirby Jr. and daughter Catherine. The news hit baseball fans everywhere extremely hard. Shock and disbelief quickly set in as the nation mourned one of our nation's true heroes. On March 12 (declared "Kirby Puckett Day" in Minnesota), a ceremony was held in his honor at the Dome, which was attended by family, friends, ballplayers past and present, and thousands of adoring fans. It was one of the saddest days in Minnesota sports history, bar none.

With his trademark smile, goatee, cartoon-like physique and shiny bald head, Kirby was without question the most popular athlete in Minnesota sports history. His boyish enthusiasm for the game was his greatest trait and his positive attitude not only inspired his teammates but also the fans. From his patented after-the-hit "bat-flip," to his in-depth explanations on his hitting style, which included: "I'm just trying to get my hacks man..." and "I'm just seeing the ball good man...", he was simply the best. Kirby truly was the face of this franchise and will forever be dearly missed.

TRIBUTES

"I loved to play against him because he would be your friend just before the game, but when you got on the field he would do everything he could to try to stop you," said Paul Molitor. "That's what I liked about him. That and because he had fun doing it. I could see the positive ef-

fect that he had on other players who he had played with over the years. For him to have to retire was such a strong disappointment for me, knowing that I wouldn't have the chance to play with him. He was just a great player and a tremendous person."

"He is one of the most energetic, giving, influential playmakers that I ever played with," said Dave Winfield. "He was a dynamite player, who was ready to go every day. He was always up and always a positive influence. I think it hurt me more when he couldn't play than when I couldn't play any more. He was one of my best friends in the game, and I really enjoyed working with him. I understand now why he was able to carry that franchise over all these years."

"I have played with a lot of great guys and a lot of great players over the years, but never have I played with anybody more popular than Kirby," said Jack Morris. "Pitching against him you always felt a sense of accomplishment if you got him out because he wanted to hit you every time. Just by his actions he could show the whole world his love and appreciation for the people and the game of baseball."

"He's in a class by himself," said Tom Kelly. "He added more charisma on and off the field to the game than any player, maybe ever. He is such an outgoing and friendly person, and always had time to say hello to everybody he had contact with, and I think that is a very special quality. He was a terrific player, worked very hard and had a lot of good things happen for him. He has a magical quality about him that will always be remembered."

"He loved to play the game," said Kent Hrbek. "I watched him hit for 12 years from the on-deck circle, and I don't care what they threw at him, he could hit everything. He was definitely the best hitter I ever saw in baseball. Kirby is a great friend, and what more can I say about a player who was the greatest there ever was?"

"He is just a great person, and it was a real pleasure and a gift from him for me to be his coach," said Tony Oliva. "He would always come to the ballpark ready to work, smiling all the time. He is great, just great. I don't have enough words to describe Kirby because he is so special to me."

"Kirby and I have developed a very good friendship over the years," said Rod Carew. "He's made a name for himself on and off the field, and he does so much for the community. He is such a happy-go-lucky, fun-loving guy, and he went out and enjoyed playing the game of baseball. Kirby is the type of individual who never forgot who he was or where he came from. He never thought he was better than anyone else because he was a baseball player and an athlete."

1992 RUNNER-UP: JOHN RANDLE

The Vikings win the NFC Central Division title with an 11-5 record. After beating Pittsburgh and Green Bay to round out the season, Minnesota then went on to get upset by Washington in the first round of the playoffs, 24-7, to end the season. Leading the way for the purple was defensive tackle *JOHN RANDLE*, who posted 56 tackles and 11.5 sacks that year. Randle joined the Vikings in 1990 as an undrafted free-agent out of Texas A&I and played with the team for 11 seasons, becoming a seven-time Pro Bowler and six-time first-team All-Pro. He signed with Seattle in 2001 and retired in 2004, tied for fifth in career sacks with 137.5 — the most by a defensive tackle in NFL history. He was elected to the College Football Hall of Fame in 2008 and is a sure bet for the Pro Football Hall of Fame as well.

HONORABLE MENTION: SUPER BOWL XXVI

Super Bowl XXVI is held at the Metrodome on January 26, 1992, where the Washington Redskins defeated the Buffalo Bills by the final score of 37-24. The leading scorer for the Skins that night was Woodbury native *CHIP LOHMILLER*, who tallied 13 points via three field goals and three extra points en route to leading his squad to victory. Lohmiller, who kicked for the Gophers from 1984-88, played in the NFL for nine seasons, tallying 913 career points, and earned Pro Bowl honors in 1991.

DAVE WINFIELD
Winny Comes Home to Hit No. 3,000

In 1993 Minnesota saw the return of one of its most beloved native sons, Dave Winfield. The greatest all-around athlete to ever hail from the Gopher State, "Winny" came home that year to get the 3,000th hit of his illustrious career. Fresh off his World Series run north of the border in Toronto, Winfield was the lone bright-spot on an otherwise mediocre Twins season. The big day came on September 16th, when he got hit No. 3,000 off Oakland's ace closer, Dennis Eckersley, becoming only the 19th player in Major League history to achieve that coveted plateau.

"It was great," said Winfield. "I was so glad to come home and to have been able to accomplish such a major milestone in front of my home crowd in the Metrodome. That was definitely a special event for me in my career, and it's something that I will always remember."

Winfield's achievement wasn't the only highlight of 1993, however, as Kent Hrbek reached 1,000 RBI's, and Brian Harper became just fourth catcher in more than four decades to hit .300 in three consecutive seasons as well. To top it off, on July 13th, in Baltimore, Kirby Puckett earned All-Star Game MVP honors by hitting a homer and an RBI double in the mid-summer classic. Closer Rick Aguilera also pitched well in the bullpen. It wasn't all roses though, as evidenced by Scott Erickson's 19 losses — tops in the big leagues that year. Overall, Minnesota finished with a 71-91 record, which left them tied for fifth place in the American League West with the Angels.

Winny

Dave Winfield grew up in St. Paul loving sports. After a phenomenal prep career at St. Paul Central High School, Winfield opted to stay close to home and attend the University of Minnesota. There, he would pitch for legendary Coach Dick Siebert on a baseball scholarship. He was eventually "discovered" by Gopher basketball coach Bill Musselman while playing in an intramural basketball league on campus. The Gopher junior varsity basketball team needed some tough competition to practice against, and since Winfield's intramural team, the "Soulful Strutters" were campus champs, a scrimmage was arranged. There, upon seeing Winfield's incredible athleticism, Musselman immediately made the six-foot-six forward a two-sport star at the U of M.

"I switched from a baseball scholarship to a basketball scholarship," he recalled. "Baseball was only a partial, and I needed a full ride. A poor kid from St. Paul... so I switched, and the rest is history."

Making the jump to the hardcourt, Winfield played two seasons with the Gopher basketball team, becoming a starter on the 1971-72 team that went 18-7 and won the Big Ten championship — the school's first in 53 years. His big break though, ironically enough, came on the heels of the now infamous "Ohio State Brawl," in which several players were suspended from the team. Thrust into the starting line-up as a member of the notorious "Iron-Five" squad, Winfield went on to average 6.9 points per game that season. Then, in 1972-73, he averaged 10.5 points per game en route to leading the Gophers to a 21-5 record — good for second in the Big Ten.

"Dave is one of the most extraordinary athletes that I have ever been around in my life," Coach Musselman later recalled. "He is one of the hardest working people, and one of the most sincere athletes that I have ever seen. For 20 years, the first thing that I checked every day during the baseball season was Dave's box score from wherever he was playing. We are good friends, and I think the world of Dave. I have so much respect for him, because he was on a Gopher baseball scholarship and didn't have to play basketball. What he sacrificed knowing that he had a career in baseball was incredible. I mean he could have gotten injured. I have never seen anybody play harder than Dave Winfield. He had the most incredible endurance and was the best rebounder I have ever seen. When he was 28, he told me he was going to play baseball until he was 45, and I think he finally retired at 44. He took great care of himself, and his combination of speed and strength was just awesome."

Winfield's Gopher sports career was nothing short of incredible. On the diamond Winfield was a three-time All-Big Ten pitcher and was a career .353 hitter. In 1973, he led the Gophers to the Big Ten title, and was selected as an All-American as well as the MVP of the College World Series. As a pitcher, his 19-4 career record afforded him an amazing .826 winning percentage. He finished with 229 career strikeouts, second only to Paul Giel's 243, and his single season record of 109 strikeouts stood for nearly 25 years. (The University of Minnesota baseball program has since honored the former great by giving the Dave Winfield Pitcher of the Year Award to the team's top annual hurler.)

"For me, I was a baseball player first," said Winfield. "But I loved playing basketball for the Gophers as well, and I was lucky enough to play both sports. I really liked all the guys on the basketball squad, and we had a lot of good competitors on that team. Mentally and physically I thought I was ready, and each game I thought I got better. It was here and now, and we just had a good time. That's why we were successful."

"He is truly an amazing athlete and, as our captain, he was a strong team leader," recalled Dick Siebert. "I don't know of any sport he can't excel at. I remember when David asked for a half-hour off from baseball practice to compete with his buddies in an intramural track meet. He had never before high jumped, and all he did was place first, going 6-foot 6-inches while still in his baseball uniform. He may be the finest all-around athlete I have coached, or for that matter to ever compete for Minnesota. To top it all off he was also a fine student."

Upon graduating from the U of M in 1973, Winfield found himself with several post-graduate options. He is one of the few persons in the history of sports to be drafted in all three professional major sports. He was taken in baseball by the San Diego Padres, in basketball by the NBA's Atlanta Hawks as well as the ABA's Utah Stars, and in football by the Minnesota Vikings. Three professional sports, four teams — a simply amazing feat that will never be equalled again.

"In football, they drafted me strictly as an athlete," said Winfield. "I was six-foot-six and 230 pounds with good hands, speed, and strength. The Vikings officials figured they could make me into a tight end. Who knows? It would have been great to have caught some of those Fran Tarkenton passes! There's no question that I made the right choice though, and I would have had a short career playing football."

Not surprisingly, Winfield chose baseball, going directly to the big-leagues to join the Padres, where he batted .277 in his first year. (Not bad for a guy drafted as a pitcher!) In 1979, he became the first Padre voted to the All-Star Game starting line-up. Then, in 1980 he signed with the New York Yankees and became the richest man in professional sports. He stayed with the Bronx Bombers until being traded to the California Angels in 1990. He signed with the Toronto Blue Jays in 1991 and won a World Series with that club in 1992. Then, in 1993, he came home to join his hometown Twins, where, he would remain for two seasons before retiring that following season as a designated hitter with the Cleveland Indians.

"He was just a super athlete and a classy human being," said Tom Kelly. "He was very, very athletic, and the things he could do at his age were remarkable. He conducted himself and carried himself with such class. He has such a wonderful attitude and so much professionalism. I really enjoyed having him here as a Twin. His 3,000th hit was another new experience for me. We were trying to get him to get it at home by spacing out his at-bats, and when it finally happened, it was a thrill for all of us."

And, while Winfield opted to leave that next season to pursue another pennant with Cleveland, he certainly made Minnesota proud. Spanning nearly a quarter of a century, two countries, two leagues, and six cities, Winfield has done it all. The 22-year veteran of six teams and 12-time All-Star won seven Gold Gloves and six Silver Bat awards. He amassed more hits (3,110) than Babe Ruth, more home runs (475) than Joe DiMaggio, and more RBIs (1,833) than both Mickey Mantle and Reggie Jackson. He is one of only five players with over 3,000 hits, 450 homers, and 200 stolen bases.

In the summer of 2001, Winfield was finally given his due when he was inducted into the Baseball Hall of Fame, alongside fellow Minnesota sports icon Kirby Puckett. It was a special day for all of Minnesota as Winfield spoke eloquently about his life and the game of baseball. His amazing career had finally come full circle and his good teammate and friend, Kirby Puckett, was right there by his side. An All-Star and fan-favorite who played hard well into his forties, Winny will always be remembered as one of the game's great ones.

"I always looked at baseball three ways," said Winfield. "It was a game, a science, and a business. I used it as a springboard to do the other things that I am doing in life such as the Dave Winfield Foundation. I met a lot of people, traveled the world, and have done a lot of great things. I have become a role model, if you will, for a lot of young people. I think I have become someone that people listen to and they respected the way I went about my work, and I am proud of that. It seemed that the better I played, the more I was able to accomplish."

Off the field, his accomplishments are equally impressive: He served on the board of President Bill Clinton's National Service Program. He was a Williams Scholar at the U of M. He received the first Branch Rickey Community Service Award, and he was given baseball's coveted Roberto Clemente Award. Nowadays he devotes much of his time to what might be considered to be his crown jewel of achievements, the Winfield Foundation — a non-profit foundation, which for several decades now has been a reflection of his commitment to children. Winfield has always been a very popular athlete and role model and has given of himself long before it became fashionable. His foundation's message to kids isn't "be a superstar" but rather "be the best that you can be." His generous monetary gifts, contributions of time, creativity, and commitment are immeasurable. He has traveled coast to coast to conduct drug-prevention seminars. His organization has generated and distributed millions of dollars, and worked with four presidential administrations, government, organizations, corporations, media, celebrities, and every-day people to bring forth grassroots programs that have touched countless thousands on a one-to-one basis.

One of Minnesota's most precious of native sons, Dave Winfield is a true living legend. As for his whereabouts these days, he lives in southern California with his family and currently works as an executive vice president with the San Diego Padres. He also recently wrote a book entitled "Dropping the Ball: Baseball's Troubles and How We

Can and Must Solve Them."

On Coming Home:
"It was a real pleasure to play for the Minnesota Twins. Minnesota is a place that I really wanted to play at during some point in time over my baseball career. I just didn't know if it would ever happen, but luckily it worked out. It was easy playing and working there, and I was really glad that I got a chance to do it."

TRIBUTES
"When I was in 8th grade, Dave was a senior in high school," said Paul Molitor. "I saw him play, but I never had a chance to play with him. I think in a lot of ways I owe him a lot, because as a member of the Gophers when he was drafted, he opened some eyes about Minnesota baseball. That gave kids like myself a lot more opportunities to get some exposure. The parallels of our careers are somewhat remarkable in that we grew up on the same playgrounds, played for the same American Legion team, competed at the same university, and we both had to go north of the border and wait until the latter stages of our careers to win a World Series championship. For two guys who grew up five blocks apart in St. Paul to end up both accumulating 3,000 hits with their hometown teams is pretty remarkable, I think. I marveled at Dave's play for many years. He was a tremendous, tremendous athlete. I consider him to be a good friend, and whenever we see each other, we always reminisce about our past and growing up in St. Paul."

"When I was a rookie, Winny took me under his wing," said Kirby Puckett. "I'll never forget going to New York City and talking to him. I remember saying 'Hello Mr. Winfield,' and I remember him saying to me, 'I've heard a lot about you, rook.' I was just in awe. He's like six-foot-six and so intimidating. Then he sent me a note in the clubhouse inviting me to dinner with him that night after the game. I remember just talking to him. He was so nice to me. That was really special to me."

"It was fun playing with him toward the end there," said Kent Hrbek. "I know that playing against him I was scared to death of him. He could hit a baseball as hard as anyone ever has. I was always afraid that he was going to kill somebody out there when he hit the ball. I remember one time when he hit a line-drive bullet right between shortstop Lenny Faedo's legs, and poor Lenny didn't even have time to get his glove down on the ball. For a big, huge, opposing figure-of-a-guy like he is, he's very gentle at heart and is really a super-nice, sweet guy."

"Dave is a first-class gentleman," added Jim Kaat. "He has so much professionalism and was just a great athlete. He used his great athleticism to turn himself into a Hall of Fame hitter."

1993 RUNNER-UP: VOSHON LENARD

The basketball Gophers win the N.I.T. championship behind All-Big Ten guard *VOSHON LENARD*, who averaged 17.3 points, 4.3 rebounds and 2.6 assists per game that season. Minnesota, which won 17 games that year, opened the tourney with a 74-66 win over Florida; followed by an 86-72 victory over Oklahoma. Minnesota then shut down USC in the N.I.T. quarterfinals, 76-58, to earn a trip to the Final Four in New York. There, behind Lenard's 25 points, the Gophers downed Providence, 76-70. They then beat Georgetown in the Finals, 62-61, thanks to Chad Kolander's dramatic blocked shot with 2.7 seconds to go. Lenard, the tournament MVP, would finish as the leading scorer in Gopher history with 2,103 career points. He then went on to play in the NBA for 11 seasons, where he averaged nearly 12 points and 3 rebounds per game.

HONORABLE MENTION: JEFF SWENSON

Augsburg college wins the Division III national championship in wrestling behind legendary coach *JEFF SWENSON*. Swenson, who coached the grappling powerhouse program for 25 years, led the Auggies to a record-10 NCAA D-III national titles (not to mention seven second place finishes) and produced a career dual-meet record of 321-44 (.879%). The 13-time MIAC Coach of the Year also won 20 MIAC team titles as well.

CRIS CARTER
CC Breaks the NFL's Single-Season Receptions Record

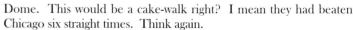

In 1994, the Minnesota Vikings finished with a respectable 10-6 record, good enough to stay ahead of the Packers, Lions, Bucs, and Bears to win the NFC Central Division. The team's hopes of getting past the first round of the playoffs, however, something coach Denny Green had yet to do, were dashed when they were beaten by the hated Bears, 35-18, at the Metrodome.

One of the team's bright spots that season was the spectacular play of Vikings wide receiver Cris Carter. In 1994, Carter had the biggest season of any wide receiver in the history of the National Football League, snagging a then league-record 122 balls, shattering Sterling Sharpe's record of 112 catches set with Green Bay the year earlier. Carter also set a team record for receiving yards in a season with 1,256, breaking former teammate Anthony Carter's record of 1,225 yards in 1988. The 1,256 yards receiving were fourth best in the NFC and seventh in the NFL. He averaged 10.3 yards per catch that year while finding the end zone seven times to boot. It was truly a season to remember for the man simply known as "C.C."

With the addition of wide receiver Jake Reed's 85 catches, the dynamic duo set an NFL record for receptions by a receiving tandem with 207, breaking the previous record held by Houston's Haywood Jeffries and Drew Hill of 190 back in 1991. Interestingly, both tandems had the luxury of quarterback Warren Moon throwing them the ball. Moon wasted little time in torching the competition in 1994, shattering nearly every one of the team's major single-season passing records in the process. His league-leading 4,264 yards and 371 completions were simply mind-boggling.

Carter emerged as a superstar that season, leading the team in 100-yard receiving games, with five, and at times carrying the team on his back. On September 9th, C.C. caught three touchdown passes in the first half of a game against the Dolphins. Less than a month later, on October 2nd, he single-handedly took care of the Phoenix Cardinals when he caught a team record 14 passes for 167 yards. Then, against the Bears, Carter had two touchdown catches, including the overtime game-winner on a 65-yard bomb from Moon, thus earning NFC Player of the Week honors. He also scored the first ever two-point conversion in team history on September 18th against those same Bears. Carter became the first Vikings player in history to have three seasons with 70-or-more receptions, and at season's end, he had caught at least one pass in 54 consecutive games, including the playoffs. For his efforts, No. 80 was selected to the Pro Bowl for the second straight season, his first as a starter, while also earning All-Pro and All-NFC recognition.

"It was nice to break the NFL record, but I wasn't all that wrapped up in it," said Carter. "It was a great year for us as a team, and winning the NFC Central was a great accomplishment for everyone. It was especially great to have Warren Moon with us as well. It was Warren's first year and we were experimenting and getting used to one another on the field. We put together 244 balls, which is still a record for back-to-back seasons. Our timing and cohesiveness was just great. Warren was just a phenomenal quarterback."

Just how tough was the Central that year? With Minnesota being joined by Chicago, Detroit and Green Bay in the playoffs, it marked the first time in league history that a division had placed four teams in the post-season. And, it would be those same gritty Bears that the Vikes would host in their first-round wild-card playoff game at the Dome. This would be a cake-walk right? I mean they had beaten Chicago six straight times. Think again.

Despite their fourth-place conference finish, Chicago was not to be taken lightly. They were led by quarterback Steve Walsh, a Cretin High School alum who would play inspired football in front of his home-town fans, completing 15 of 23 passes for 221 yards and two touchdowns. Minnesota jumped out to a quick 3-0 lead in the first on Fuad Reviez's" 29-yarder. But the Bears, who had turnovers on their first two possessions, came back with a pair of second quarter scores from both Lewis Tillman, who capped a long drive with a one-yard dive, and by Walsh, who hit tight end Keith Jennings on a nine-yarder in the end-zone. The Vikings then cut Chicago's margin to 14-9 just 19 seconds before the half on Moon's four-yard touchdown pass to Carter.

Down but not out, the Bears roared back in the third on Raymont Harris's 29-yard touchdown run. After another Reviez field-goal, Walsh made it 28-12 late in that same quarter when he found Jeff Graham with a 21-yard touchdown pass. Vikings' third-down specialist Amp Lee came in and tried to mount a late rally when he caught an acrobatic 11-yard TD pass from Moon midway through the fourth, but when Bears cornerback Kevin Minniefield scooped up a fumble and raced 48 yards the other way for a touchdown, the 35-18 upset was complete.

The Vikes had really stunk up the joint. Their defense, which logged seven touchdowns and had held its opponents to only 68 rushing yards per game up to that point — the fourth lowest in NFL history — simply couldn't shut down Walsh. Even Pro Bowl defensive tackle John Randle, who registered 13.5 sacks that year, was neutralized. They just couldn't capitalize — as evidenced by their two turnovers which produced just three points in the ball game. Conversely, the Bears shut down Minnesota's running game, and forced Moon, who was playing injured, to go to the air far too frequently — 52 times to be exact.

So, with three straight playoff defeats in as many seasons, including a pair at home in the Metrodome, everyone began to wonder if coach Green simply had what it took to get this team on to the next level. That would be the million dollar question as this squad moved forward.

C.C.

Cris Carter was born in Troy, Ohio, on November 25, 1965. He went on to graduate from Middletown High School in 1983, where he caught 80 passes for over 2,000 yards, and earned Parade All-American honors as a senior. He also excelled as an all-state basketball player, scoring over 1,600 points during his prep career. (His older brother Butch went on to play for seven years in the NBA and later served as the head coach of the Toronto Raptors.)

Heavily recruited out of high school, Carter chose to go to Ohio State, where he earned first-team All-American honors in 1986. When it was all said and done, Carter would finish as the Buckeyes' all-time leader in receptions, with 168, and touchdown catches, with 27, while ranking No. 2 in receiving yards, with 2,725.

He went on to be selected in the fourth round of the 1987 supplemental draft by the Philadelphia Eagles. After three productive years in Philly, then-head coach Buddy Ryan, for some insane reason, released Carter, citing irreconcilable differences. C.C. was then immediately claimed off the waiver wire by the Vikings. Philadelphia's blunder was Minnesota's gain. Now the purple had two receiving Carters, Cris and long-time Viking great, Anthony, to form one of the most lethal receiving tandems in the league. Cris got some sweet revenge against his old mates on November 15th that year as well when he nabbed six receptions for 151 yards, including a 78-yarder for a TD.

"I was really excited about the possibility of playing in Minnesota because I knew about the tremendous tradition that the Vikings had built over the years," said Carter. "But I was most excited about the opportunity to play with Anthony Carter."

In 1991, Cris led the Vikings in receptions with 72 and added 962 receiving yards to go along with his five TDs. That next year, after leading the club in receptions, receiving yards and TD's, he knew he had made it to the big-time when he was selected as a member of John Madden's notorious "All-Madden" team. In 1993 he played in his first Pro Bowl, and in 1994 he set the NFL's all-time receptions record, with 122. Showing that 1994 wasn't a fluke, Carter went on to catch another 122 balls for the second consecutive year in 95', giving him the most catches ever in the NFL over a two-year span.

"I think that season I accomplished even more than in 1994 by catching 122 again, as well as catching 17 touchdowns," he said. "That might be the best year that I have ever had as a pro."

In 1996, Carter made his fourth Pro Bowl team in his eighth season with the Vikes. Perhaps his biggest accomplishment that season came during the off-season, however, when he was ordained as a minister. Inspired, Carter went on to simply dominate the world of professional football. Week in and week out he continued to amaze fans everywhere by making spectacular one-handed finger-tip catches. He had a sixth sense as to where the sideline was, and always seemed to somehow drag both feet in order to make sure he was in-bounds.

In 1998 the Vikes took a gamble on drafting a wide receiver with some baggage by the name of Randy Moss. Carter took on the role of tutoring the rookie, showing him the ropes along the way about what it took to make it in this league. As a result, they would go on to become the most feared duo in the NFL. In 1998 the team made it to the NFC Championship game, only to lose a heart-breaker to the Falcons, and in 2000 they made it back to the title game, only to get embarrassed by the New York Giants, 41-0. Nonetheless, the Carter/Moss tandem was simply unstoppable during that stretch run.

Carter retired from the Vikings following the 2001 season holding most of the team career receiving records. The team was on the downside and C.C. had simply had enough. From there, he would go on to become a very successful TV analyst on the HBO show, "Inside the NFL." Then, in October of 2002, Carter un-retired when the wide-receiver depleted Miami Dolphins came calling. Carter makes his home in South Florida, so it was a good fit for him to be close to his family while still being able to play the game he loved. And why not? Jerry Rice was still going strong in Oakland at the time, and he was 40 years old — fully four years older than Cris.

As for his time with the purple, the eight-time Pro Bowler and three-time All-Pro ranks among the very best of the best, scoring 129 touchdown, catching 1,093 passes and racked up 13,833 receiving yards. In fact, he ranks second in NFL history only to Jerry Rice in those same stats. He was named to the NFL 1990s All-Decade Team and is a virtual lock for the Hall of Fame. A truly gifted athlete, Cris Carter will go down as one of the all-time best ever.

Aside from his on-the-field stats, Carter is also very proud of his achievements off of the field. In 1999 he was honored by being named as the NFL's Man of the Year — receiving the coveted Walter Payton Award. He was also honored for his efforts in the community with his Cris Carter's CAUSE (Christian Athletes for Spiritual Empowerment), as well as for his tireless work with inner-city schools, the Special Olympics, the Boy Scouts and the Make-A-Wish Foundation. In addition, Carter frequently speaks to kids about drug awareness and is actively involved in the Big Brother-Big Sister program.

Presently, Carter is the owner of Cris Carter's FAST Program, a sports training center in South Florida which facilitates several high profile NFL players during the off-season. In addition, Carter also works for ESPN as a studio TV analyst during the football season.

On the Vikings Records:
"It's really nice because those records are pretty substantial, and the players who played before me were phenomenal. That gives the records a lot of credence and value in my mind. It's always nice to be compared to great people of the past and also with people who are still playing in the league. Growing up and watching Ahmad (Rashad) and Sammy (White) catch passes in those blustery days at old Metropolitan Stadium, to me is unbelievable. It's nice to have been able to have seen some of their incredible careers, along with guys like Anthony Carter, and know that I was be able to pass them up. This means a lot to me."

On Minnesota's Fans:
"I really enjoy the fans in Minnesota. They're great, and I loved playing for them. It seems that they warmed up to me as my performances got better. I feel that they have shown their appreciation towards me and have always been very respectful of me. It has always given me a sense of confidence in my ability knowing that during tough situations, the fans are behind me. Because a lot of times in certain situations, they know that I'm going to get the ball, and it's nice knowing they are behind me. In Minnesota, the fans really know their sports, are very knowledgeable, and they know the history of their sports heroes. There is just a great football tradition there — which makes rivalries like against the Packers even better."

On Minnesota:
"I'm not a big fan of the Minnesota weather, and I only lived there during the season, but I can definitely see the appealing aspects of guys wanting to live there as far as the quality of life goes. When my family and I were there, we definitely loved it, and we became very comfortable in our second home. The people are very cordial, and it was a pleasure for my family and I to be with Minnesotans."

Vikings Tombstone:
"I would like to be known as a strong competitor and for my ability to compete. I think that would be the thing that would make me the most proud."

1994 RUNNER-UP: JEFF NIELSEN

The 25-13-4 hockey Gophers notch their second straight WCHA Tournament title and make another run to the NCAA Frozen Four. One of the stars of the team was All-WCHA senior co-captain *JEFF NIELSEN*, a Grand Rapids native who led the team with 29 goals and 16 assists. The Gophers first headed to East Lansing, Mich., to face Lowell. There, behind Nielsen's dramatic game-winner in double overtime, Minnesota advanced back to the NCAA Finals — which were being held at the St. Paul Civic Center. With the bad memories of the 1989 NCAA Finals overtime loss to Harvard in that same arena still fresh in their minds, the Gophers hit the ice against Boston University with high hopes. Goalie Jeff Callinan came up with 29 saves that evening, but wound up on the wrong side of a 4-1 loss. Nielsen, meanwhile, would finish his career in Gold Country with 141 career points before going on to play in the NHL for five seasons with the Rangers, Ducks and Wild.

HONORABLE MENTION: SCOTT ERICKSON

SCOTT ERICKSON becomes the third pitcher in Twins history to throw a no-hitter when he beat the Milwaukee Brewers, 6-0, on April 27, 1994. Erickson played with the Twins from 1990-95 before being traded to Baltimore. He would pitch in the Majors for 15 seasons, posting a career record of 142-136 and a .459 ERA.

1995

KEVIN GARNETT
The Timberwolves Draft a High School Phenom

In 1995, the Minnesota Timberwolves astonished the basketball establishment when they became the first NBA team in more than 20 years to draft a player directly out of high school. With the fifth overall pick of the first round, Wolves GM Kevin McHale gambled on the raw talent of a 19-year-old kid out of Chicago by the name of Kevin Garnett. Less than a month removed from his senior prom, Garnett, the most highly recruited prep player of maybe all-time, became Minnesota's lottery prize. The Wolves, who were entering their seventh sad year of mediocrity, had always seemed to be just one ping-pong ball away from drafting a superstar. Minnesota simply had nothing to lose by drafting a high schooler, so they rolled the dice.

To fully understand why this gamble was so big, and why the story was equally as big, one has to go back to the franchise's infancy and look at the evolution of mishaps and draft-bungles that put the team in a position to take such a risk.

After a 29-year hiatus (the Minneapolis Lakers moved to L.A. in 1960), the NBA returned to Minnesota in 1989 in the form of the expansion Minnesota Timberwolves. The team's first draft pick was UCLA point guard Pooh Richardson and its first coach was Bill Musselman, who had previously been with the Gophers in the early '70s. The Wolves played their first two seasons in the Metrodome, and at the end of their inaugural season, had set a new all-time NBA attendance record with well over a million customers walking through the turnstiles. Unfortunately, that was the only worthwhile record the franchise would set. From 1989-95, the Wolves won only 126 games and lost 366. By 1995, the honeymoon had clearly worn off, and the fans were growing weary of being the league's doormat. Minnesota's sporting public wanted a winner and were growing inpatient. NBA expansion teams were notorious for slow starts and growing pains, but, by that time, the three other expansion franchises that came into the league around the same time that the Wolves did had all made the playoffs, with Orlando even making it to the Finals.

The Timberwolves had experienced more than their share of tough luck, but much of the blame had to be put on poor drafting and inadequate management. Along with two ownership groups and an aborted move to New Orleans, the head coaching position had been a regular revolving door. After Musselman came Jimmy Rodgers, then former Wolves Guard Sidney Lowe, followed by Bill Blair who was succeed by Flip Saunders. The Wolves had also chosen six consecutive lottery picks without hitting the jackpot — Richardson, Felton Spencer, Luc Longley, Christian Laettner, Isaiah Rider and Donyell Marshall. It was time to shake things up.

The word on Garnett come draft day was that he was a seven foot beanpole with terrific all-around talent. Sports Illustrated even went as far as saying that he just might be the best athlete in the draft.

He was described as a cross between Indiana guard Reggie Miller and a kinder, gentler version of Miami center Alonzo Mourning. He could run, leap like crazy, block shots, monster-dunk, handle the ball like a guard, and shoot 20-footers with ease. He represented the most elusive of all commodities for the league's bottom-feeder's, and that was hope. Some members of the media even hyped him up as a "savior," while others quickly tabbed him as the "next Michael Jordan."

Garnett had been wooed by nearly every Division I college in the country. Early reports had him going to either Michigan or North Carolina. But, because he hadn't achieved the necessary college admission test scores and because the big money was there, he bypassed it all and made himself available for the draft.

Drafting a 19-year-old was no easy task. The nay-sayers were out in force, and if the Wolves wanted to keep up any fan base at all, Garnett would have to deliver big-time. The Minnesota fans were skeptical because few had ever seen the lad play, which only added to his mystique. Garnett also carried some baggage with him that would raise some questions. The move from South Carolina his senior year to Chicago came in large part as a result of an incident in which he and several friends were charged with assaulting a student. His police record was later cleared though, because he participated in a pretrial diversion program for first-time offenders.

There were genuine concerns about his maturity, social skills, stamina, sense of responsibility, friends, and even his diet. He was more than a typical NBA "project," and he needed a lot of T.L.C. As one reporter put it, "People in Minnesota hear the word project, and they break out in a Luc Longley-sized rash."

There had only really been four players who had successfully made the leap from high school directly to the NBA — Moses Malone in 1974, Darryl Dawkins and Bill Willoughby in 1975, and Shawn Kemp in 1989 (who played only briefly at the collegiate level). At the same time, Sports Illustrated fed the media frenzy by featuring Garnett on the cover of their pre-draft issue with the headline: "Ready or Not."

Would he dominate and revolutionize the game of pro basketball? Or would he join a long line of NBA casualties crushed by fame, too much money, and groupies? Sure, there are countless young men who play pro hockey and baseball at even younger ages. But this was different — this was the NBA, where size definitely matters.

"Is he a franchise player?" retorted former Timberwolves coach Bill Blair at a press conference. "I can't say that but this kid does some things that excite you. From a maturity level? No way he can be ready. He's not ready for the airplanes, the four games in six days, and for the free time he's now possessing. Those things we have to help him with. You just hope he's so interested in basketball, you hope he wants to be the best player in the league."

Reaction around the basketball world was mixed. "He's a genetic freak," said Detroit coach Doug Collins. "All the great ones are." Said McHale: "Garnett is a basketball junkie. He's the kind of guy we'll have to chase off the court, rather than worry he's not spending enough time on it." University of Minnesota Gopher basketball coach Clem Haskins added: "You won't find athletes with more raw talent than Garnett. He has great upside with great enthusiasm for the game." Former Seattle GM Bob Whitsitt, who drafted Shawn Kemp said: "The team that takes Garnett has to commit its entire organization. Ownership, coaches, other players, everyone has to realize this is a 24-hour-a-day process. You have to be willing to spend the years, not the days, the years, to make this work." Russ Granik, the NBA's deputy commissioner, even put in his two cents worth: "If it were up to us, we'd prefer not to see someone come into the league at that tender age, but the courts say otherwise."

On June 28, 1995, in Toronto's SkyDome, the Wolves, after patiently watching Joe Smith, Jerry Stackhouse, Antonio McDyess, and Rasheed Wallace go in the first four picks, held their breath and selected Garnett. As McHale presented him with his new No. 21 jersey, Garnett just smiled proudly.

"I'm not gonna rush nothing," said Garnett. "I'm not going to do anything I know I can't do. I can't wait to get in the gym with Mr. McHale and learn some of those dazzling moves he has."

"The one thing that bothers me is everybody thinking I just got into this without thinking it over," he added. " I thought about it a lot, and I think I'm ready."

Knowing that it was going to be a full-time job, developing and grooming the young player into his new surroundings, the Timberwolves took some steps to protect their investment. Then-GM Flip Saunders called the steps "safety nets," and laid out the groundwork to ease his transition during his rookie season. Plans were even made for his mother to move to the Twin Cities to help support him that year.

The Wolves were building for the future and, in 1995, big things were happening at the Target Center. Shortly after the season got underway, coach Bill Blair was replaced by Flip Saunders. Later in the season, Christian Laettner was dealt to the Atlanta Hawks. Laettner had complained about the extra treatment the rookie was receiving and as a result, got shown the door. And, at seasons' end, Isaiah Rider and all of his baggage were sent packing as well. The Wolves were going to have to weed out the bad apples if this was going to work out.

The team finished at a dismal 26-56 that season, good enough for fifth in the Midwest Division. Garnett struggled at first, but then did all right that rookie season, averaging a modest 10.4 points, 6.3 rebounds and 1.8 assists per game. For his efforts he was named to the NBA all-rookie second team. Cudos to the organization for easing him along and making the transition a smooth one.

There was no question as to whether or not Garnett was going to be a remarkable NBA player. Following his second season, a poll of league coaches and general managers asked who they thought was going to be the star player of the next decade. Garnett was their overwhelming choice. They were right too, because "KG," as he is affectionately known, would go on to become one of the league's elite players over the ensuing years.

As for his time with the Wolves, it was both wonderful as well as frustrating. In 1997 Garnett signed a six-year contract extension with the Wolves worth an amazing $125 million, or nearly $21 million per season. The Wolves ownership clearly sent a signal to the fans of Minnesota that K.G. was the future of the franchise, and that they were willing to spend some pretty big bucks to be a contender in the league. The contract was so big, however, that it actually prompted the league to institute a revenue-sharing "salary cap" of sorts, that Garnett would ultimately be grandfathered into.

Now, Garnett lived up to his end of the bargain, putting up All-Star numbers year in and year out, while keeping the Target Center seats pretty much full. Garnett would lead the team to the post-season for eight straight seasons from 1997-2004, with the highlight coming in 2004, when the team made it all the way to the Western Conference Finals before losing to the Kobe Bryant and Shaquille O'Neal-led Lakers. The team's achilles heal though, was its inability to come together in the post-season. The Wolves struggled in the playoffs, year in and year out, losing in the first round for seven straight seasons. Garnett would sign another contract extension in 2002, which was both good and bad for the franchise. It was good because he was by far the team's best player and biggest draw. It was bad, however, because his huge salary was handcuffing the team with regards to them being able to sign any other All-Star players to compliment him out on the court.

The team missed the playoffs in 2005, 2006 and 2007, prompting GM Kevin McHale to finally take drastic measures. Knowing that he was damned if he did and damned if he didn't, McHale did the unthinkable in the Summer of 2007 when he dealt the "Big Ticket," to the Boston Celtics in exchange for several players and draft picks. The Minnesota fans were devastated. McHale couldn't risk Garnett playing out his contract year and then leaving as a free-agent the fol-

lowing season, leaving the Wolves with nothing to show for their investment. To make matters worse, Garnett would lead the Celtics, McHale's former team, to the NBA title in 2008 – where he finally got the championship ring that had eluded him for 12 seasons in Minnesota.

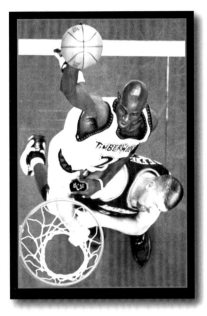

Da Kid

Kevin Garnett was born on May 19, 1976, and grew up in Mauldin, S.C., just outside Greenville, as a die-hard Lakers fan. A four-time all-state player, Kevin was named Mr. Basketball for the state of South Carolina as a junior in 1994. For his senior year, the young phenom moved to Chicago, where at Farragut Academy, he was once again selected as Mr. Basketball, this time for the state of Illinois. As a senior he averaged 25.2 points, 17.9 rebounds, 6.7 assists, and 6.5 blocks per game. For his efforts, he was tabbed the National High School Player of the Year by USA Today and also earned All-America first team honors. He capped off his prep career by being named as the MVP of the 1995 McDonald's All-Star Game. It was there where he dominated the country's best college prospects and gained the reputation of being an NBA "sure thing."

Since joining the NBA in 1995, Garnett has established himself as one of the game's premier all-around players. Now in his 14th NBA season, Garnett has averaged an amazing double-double for his career, with 20.4 points and 11.2 rebounds per game. In addition, he has averaged 4.4 assists and 1.4 steals per game as well. His accomplishments include being voted Most Valuable Player of the 2003-04 season, NBA Defensive Player of the Year of the 2007-08 season, being named to 11 All-Star teams and being named to eight All-NBA and All-Defensive Teams. In addition, he won an Olympics gold medal as a member of Team USA at the 2000 Summer Games in Sydney.

From his "poster-dunks" to his animal-like cleansing of the boards, this 6'11" forward is the complete package. (He is actually taller than that but doesn't want to be known as a seven-footer.) Full of high octane energy and high flying slam dunks, he has become the prototypical NBA forward. He is the rarest of big men with an incredible array of skills, making him the most complete all-around player in the league. Garnett is a freak of nature. He can play like a small forward, yet can be just as dominant in the post-up game underneath the basket. He can also handle the ball, pass off the dribble and shoot from the perimeter. Defensively, he is a perfectionist who can rebound, block shots, and guard much quicker players who are half his size. He is truly the complete package. He is also a fun-loving kid, raw with passion and emotion, and full of charm and wit. He truly is "The Franchise."

1995 RUNNER-UP: BRIAN BONIN

The 25-14-5 hockey Gophers advance to the NCAA Frozen Four. Leading the charge for the Maroon and Gold was junior center **BRIAN BONIN**, who led the team and WCHA with 32 goals and 31 assists. Minnesota started its post-season run with a 3-0 win over RPI in Madison, followed by a 5-2 win over Colorado College. From there, the team advanced back to the Frozen Four, this time in Providence, where they wound up losing to Boston University, 7-3. As for Bonin, he would be named as the WCHA Player of the Year and earn All-American honors to boot. The White Bear Lake native only got better from there the following season, as he led the nation in scoring with 34 goals and 47 assists en route to winning the coveted Hobey Baker Award, as the nation's top player. He would go on to play professionally for eight seasons before retiring in 2005.

HONORABLE MENTION: CHAD KOLANDER

The 19-12 basketball Gophers make it back to the NCAA Tourney's "Big Dance," only to lose in overtime to the St. Louis Billikens in the opening round, 64-61. One of the stars of the team was Owatonna native **CHAD KOLANDER**, whose dramatic lay-up tied the game with just seconds to go to send it to overtime. Kolander scored 737 points and collected 461 career rebounds from 1991-95. In addition, he led the team in blocked shots for three straight years and was also voted as the Gopher's best defensive player in both 1993 and 1994.

PAUL MOLITOR
Molly Comes Home to Hit No. 3,000

In 1996, while Twins fans were mourning the retirement of Kirby Puckett, another local hero came home to fill the void and make a little history, Paul Molitor. The former Cretin High School and Gopher star had established himself as one of the game's greatest all-time hitters by now, and was anxious to play in front of the legions of home town fans who had supported him over the years.

The Twins, who chased a wild card spot that year, finished with a modest 78-85 record — good for fourth place in the Central Division. The real story, however, was the amazing play of the 40 year old Molitor, who led the team as a designated hitter that season with an outstanding .341 average, as well as a league-leading 225 hits. The highlight of the season came on September 16th, in a road game against Kansas City, with Jose Rosado on the mound. With the entire state of Minnesota seemingly waiting in anxious anticipation, Molitor became the 21st player in Major League history to notch 3,000 hits. He did it in style too, becoming the first player ever to reach the milestone with a triple. In an otherwise ho-hum Twins season, Paul Molitor had not only made history, he had also made Minnesota proud.

"I definitely tried to put it on the very back burner," said Molitor of the big hit. "When that ball got into the gap and I got to third, it finally sunk in. I found out afterwards that no one had ever hit a triple on their 3,000th hit, and that made it kind of special too, because it adds to the uniqueness of joining what is already a pretty small group of people. It's my most memorable game in baseball and just having it happen to me as a member of the Minnesota Twins was amazing."

Molly

Paul Molitor was born on August 22, 1956, in St. Paul. One of eight children, he grew up loving the game of baseball. A huge Twins fan, his favorite player was Harmon Killebrew. Molitor was a natural athlete and his talents became readily apparent as a high schooler for the Cretin Raiders, where he developed his lifelong passion for the game.

"I first thought of Molitor as having the potential to become a professional when he was in the ninth grade," said Bill Peterson, his high school and American Legion team coach. "He was always an exceptional player and had a very strong arm."

Believe it or not, he missed his entire senior year at Cretin due to a bout with mononucleosis. "He wasn't even supposed to practice," Peterson added, "but he begged and begged to let him hit. He must have had a month's worth of energy stored up because he put on a hitting exhibition like I've never seen."

Molitor rejoined the Raiders for the playoffs and led his team to the 1975 Catholic League High School title. In the state tournament championship game, he pounded a 380-foot grand slam, en route to helping Cretin repeat as state champs. Molitor would garner All-State honors that year in baseball as well as in basketball.

At this point, Molitor had drawn the interest of both college and Major League scouts, who had recently focused their attention to the state of Minnesota. You see, in 1973 the San Diego Padres drafted another kid out of St. Paul by the name of Dave Winfield, so they knew that there was some talent hidden away up in those northwoods. As a result, he was heavily recruited, even as a junior.

Molitor was getting mixed reviews from the scouts, however, particularly those representing the Twins. They thought he was too small and

would have a difficult time making it at the next level. The St. Louis Cardinals didn't see it that way and decided to take a chance on the young shortstop, selecting him in the 25th round of the 1975 entry draft. The Cards offered him a $4,000 contract, which was just the kick in the rear he needed to opt for a free university education instead.

With that, Molitor accepted a scholarship to the University of Minnesota to play baseball under legendary coach Dick Siebert. Siebert, who had a special eye for talent, would later say that Paul had the best base-running instincts of any player he ever saw in amateur or professional baseball, and that he was, without a doubt, the best Major League prospect he'd ever seen.

Molitor was a quiet, lead-by-example type of player, who was an aggressive yet patient hitter. As co-captain, he would lead the Gophers to the Big Ten title in 1977. Then, as Molitor and his teammates prepared for the 1977 College World Series, he heard the news that he had been drafted by the Milwaukee Brewers as the third overall player chosen, after the White Sox took Harold Baines and Expos took Bill Gullickson. The Twins, who had made it clear that they were now interested in drafting him, had missed their chance at the young slugger.

"It took me a little while to get down to the ground," he said after hearing the news. College baseball's hottest prospect, and newest cheesehead, went ahead and signed with the Brewers for $85,000. By the time Molitor turned pro after his junior season, he had established himself as one of the greatest all-around baseball players in Gopher history. He had become the Gophers' career leader in runs-scored, hits, RBI's, triples, home-runs, total bases and stolen bases. In his three seasons, he set five single-season records and seven college-career records. The Gopher shortstop's best year was his sophomore season, in which he batted a career-best .376, earning himself first-team All-American honors for the second straight year. He would finish his college baseball with an impressive career batting average of .350.

"Growing up in the St. Paul, as I did, I knew that the Gophers had a tremendous baseball tradition," said Molitor. "I remember in high school, following the Gopher baseball team and, in particular watching Dave Winfield lead the club to the College World Series, before they ended up losing some heart-breakers down in Omaha. When Coach Siebert offered me a scholarship to be a Gopher, I realized how much pride the program had in representing the state's baseball abilities. Back then, it was a very rare occasion when the Chief would recruit outside the state to bring in players, so almost everyone in uniform was home-grown. I think that when you played for his teams, you realized that it wasn't just the U, but the type of baseball that Minnesota kids played, that was being represented. It carried a lot of significance for me, and it meant a great deal for me to be a Gopher."

"I thought he had more ability than any player I have ever coached, and I coached Dave Winfield, so Paul's accomplishment is a pretty tall order," said coach Siebert of Molitor's Gopher career.

Molitor was then sent to Milwaukee's Class-A farm team in Iowa, the Burlington Bees. It soon became apparent that he was the best player in the Midwest League. He could have gone up to Triple-A after only three weeks with Burlington, but he asked to stay with the Bees to help them win the league championship. They agreed, and sure enough, he not only led the Bees to the Midwest League title, he also won the batting crown with a .348 average. From there, it was off the "Show," where he would embark on an epic journey that would ultimately bring him full circle back to Minnesota 21 years later.

In Milwaukee, Robin Yount was the Brewers everyday shortstop. Even though he was less than a year older than Molitor, he was already a seasoned pro, having gone straight to the Majors in 1974. Drafted as the shortstop of the future, Molitor was quoted years later on his memories of that first visit to County Stadium: "I remember Sal Bando coming over and throwing Robin an outfielder's glove and saying to him, 'Well, I guess this will be your last year at shortstop, kid...'. "All I wanted was to get out of there!"

Profoundly modest, Molitor doesn't care about personal accolades, rather, he always preferred to be a team player. He was an explosive athlete with an ability to attack with the sudden element of surprise, whether at the plate or on the bases. He was a hitting machine, able to swing so late, stretching time until that optimum instant for contact seems to have passed. His eyes could evaluate a pitch, calculate its curve, its spin, its velocity, and then measure it, to precisely drive the ball exactly where he wanted it to go, all in about the same time it would take the average person to blink. That was his signature, and his knowledge of the physics of the game allowed him to just get better with age. A true student of the game, Molitor was also known as a master sign decoder, able to detect opposing pitchers' every subtle moves and use that information to his advantage. That was why he was such a feared and respected hitter.

Molitor played 15 seasons with the Brewers, making it to the World Series in 1982 before losing to the Cardinals in the so-called "Suds Series." In 1987, Molitor put together a 39-game hitting streak, the seventh-longest in Major League history. Molitor left Milwaukee to go north of the border in 1993 where he led the Blue Jays to the World Series championship, earning MVP honors along the way. Following this accomplishment, many felt that Paul could have run for Prime Minister in Canada, and they weren't kidding. He was that popular.

On December 5, 1995, Molitor came back to Minnesota. He fulfilled a lifelong, childhood dream by getting the opportunity to play for his hometown Twins. He would ultimately spend the final three seasons of his career with the Twins, playing like he was a rookie all over again. And just what was the secret of this 40-something's success? Explanations for his longevity included a regiment of common sense, zen, and staying in great shape, combined with a daily focused routine of discipline and thoroughness. Maybe it was just the water? Whatever it was, it worked. He was awesome.

"When the opportunity finally came up where I was available, and they had an interest, I couldn't pass up the opportunity to finally be a Twin in spite of a lot of interest from elsewhere and probably more money from some other teams," said Molitor of his move back to Minnesota. "To have a chance to return home and to kind of complete the cycle, so to speak, was something that goes back to that dream as a kid. Now, to have it happen so far down the road was a little bit ironic, but also a real nice way to end my career."

"I think at least for Dave Winfield, Jack Morris, Terry Steinbach, and I, after growing up and playing high school baseball here, we had a certain pride about being from Minnesota that maybe people from other parts of the country might not easily understand," he added. "This has to do with the lifestyle and priorities of family — it's a Midwestern thing. I'm not sure if just that on its own would've been enough to entice us back, but when you factored the status of the team under manager Tom Kelly, it became even more appealing. Combine that with the chance to return home to friends and family, and then to play for the team we followed as youngsters was just an irresistible package for me."

Molitor finally hung up the cleats for good in 1998. The 21-year veteran played his last game on September 27th at the Dome, where he singled and then scored in his last at-bat. The crowd went nuts. It was an appropriate ending for an amazing player and person.

At the time of his retirement, Molitor had become just one of only four players in Major League history with at least 3,000 hits, a .300 lifetime batting average, and 500 stolen bases. The other three are Hall of Famers Ty Cobb, Honus Wagner and Eddie Collins. Molitor's lifetime statistics include 2,683 games played, 1,782 runs scored, 3,319 hits, 234 home runs, 1,307 runs batted in, a .306 batting average, and 504 stolen bases. In addition, the seven-time All-Star batted .368 in five post-season series. For his efforts, on January 6, 2004, he was elected to the Baseball Hall of Fame in Cooperstown on his very first ballot.

Gopher and Twins Tombstones:
"I hope that people will have seen in the way that I played that I had a certain passion and, yet, respect for the game. Whatever I have accomplished, I have tried to do with humility and when I failed, I tried to maintain a certain level of consistency about my demeanor. I think that's important because in a lot of ways sports reflects life. How you handle your ups and downs says a lot about your character. That's what I hope has left an impression, and particularly on young people."

TRIBUTES
"I grew up with Paul in St. Paul," said Jack Morris. "We played Babe Ruth ball, city ball, and American Legion ball against each other. Finally we played with each other in Toronto and won a pennant together. Paul is a great, great player. He is one of the greatest hitters I have ever seen and easily in the top five of all time. I've never seen a guy with better hands than Paul. He is truly a hitting machine."

"He is such a classy and professional individual," said Tom Kelly. "He plays the game at a higher level than anybody that I've ever seen. Paul was on a mission (in 1996) to get that 3,000th hit out of the way, and it was quite an experience that capped off a fabulous season for him."

"I played against Paul in the 'Suds Series' of 1982 and have gotten to know him over the years," said Jim Kaat. "He is a solid individual and one guy that I appreciate very much. He seems to know everyone, calls them by their first names, and has the time for them. He has great respect for the game, and as a result of that, I have great respect for him."

"We always had that local tie together and felt that since we were both Minnesota boys, we should like each other," said Kent Hrbek. "He is a super-nice guy, and I would have to say that if Kirby Puckett is the best right-handed hitter ever, Paul would have to be right behind him."

1996 RUNNER-UP: TOM LEHMAN

TOM LEHMAN, Minnesota's most celebrated golfer, wins the 125th British Open by shooting a 271 at Royal Lytham and is named as the 1996 PGA Tour Player of the Year. Lehman, who grew up in Alexandria and went on to golf at the University of Minnesota, turned pro in 1982. The 2006 U.S. Ryder Cup team captain has 22 professional wins, including five career PGA Tour victories: Memorial (1994), Colonial (1995), British Open (1996), The Tour Championship (1996) and the Phoenix Open (2000). Lehman will always be know for his amazing run of U.S. Opens from 1995-97, in which he held the 54-hole lead, only to come up short in the end. He is without question the greatest men's golfer ever to hail from the state of Minnesota.

HONORABLE MENTION: BRIANA SCURRY

Led by goalie *BRIANA SCURRY*, who let in just three goals the entire tournament, the U.S. Olympic women's soccer team wins gold at the 1996 Summer Games in Atlanta. An outstanding all-around athlete, Scurry was an all-state basketball player and earned national goalie of the year honors as senior at Anoka High School. She then went on to star in net at the University of Massachusetts, before joining Team USA. In addition, Scurry also led the U.S. team to victory at the fabled 1999 World Cup tournament as well. Further, her career total of nearly 170 international appearances ranks her in the top 10 in American soccer history.

The 1996-97 basketball Gophers came into the season with high expectations of making a serious run at winning the Big Ten title. They had their nucleus back and were the buzz of the Twin Cities. Coach Clem Haskins had convinced his players that they had been jobbed the season prior by not getting an NCAA tourney bid, and the kids responded by working hard that summer during the off-season. They played basketball every day, lifted weights, got into shape, and hung around each other — building the chemistry that would take them farther than any Gopher team in history.

Led by Bobby Jackson, the talented transfer from Western Nebraska Community College, Sam Jacobson, Courtney James and John Thomas, who all received honorable mention All-Big Ten honors the year, these Gophers set out to make history. The team opened its season by winning its first five non-conference games before getting beat by a pesky Alabama team that nailed a three-pointer with just seconds remaining to win, 70-67. They rebounded to post an impressive 11-1 non-conference record, even crushing lowly Alabama State along the way, 114-34 (the program's largest all-time margin of victory).

The Gophers then won their Big Ten opener against Wisconsin, 68-43. From there the Maroon and Gold headed to East Lansing, where they spanked the Spartans, 68-43, shooting 53% from the floor. The team then beat Indiana and Michigan as Bobby Jackson was named as the Big Ten Player of the Week. After falling to Illinois, the Gophers procceded to beat Ohio State, 73-67. The now 15th-ranked Gophers hosted the 23rd-ranked Iowa Hawkeyes at Williams Arena. There, in front of a national television audience, Sam Jacobson poured in a career-high 29 points to lead Minnesota to a 66-51 victory.

Next, the Gophers cruised past Purdue, 91-68, Northwestern, 75-56, and then returned home to beat Penn State, 85-70. They then went back to Purdue to beat the Boilers, 70-67. At Iowa, Eric Harris and John Thomas each hit key free throws down the stretch to lead the team to a 68-66 victory. Against Ohio State, back at the Barn, the Gophers held the Buckeyes to just 34% shooting in a 60-48 win. By now the team was on cruise-control and had a chance to clinch at least a share of the Big Ten crown by avenging their earlier loss to the Illini, this time at home. There, behind Thomas' two free throws with just four seconds remaining, the Gophers sealed a 67-66 victory to clinch the title. The Williams Arena crowd went nuts in this one, truly giving the team a distinct home-court advantage.

Jackson again led all Minnesota scorers that next outing, this time with 18 points, in a big 55-54 win over Michigan at Crisler Arena — a building that had not surrendered a victory to the Gophers since 1982. The next game, a 75-72 win over the Indiana Hoosiers, at the Barn, was a classic. Nearly 15,000 Gopher fans showed up to cheer on the Maroon and Gold in this one as Courtney James dished in 14 points, Charles Thomas added 13 and Trevor Winter grabbed a career-high 10 rebounds. The team's home season concluded with an 81-74 victory over Michigan State on Senior Night to round out an amazing 15-0 home record. Before the game, the senior foursome of Bobby Jackson, John Thomas, Trevor Winter and Aaron Stauber, hoisted the 1997 Big Ten championship banner up to the old Barn's rafters for all to see.

They wound up losing their final game of the year in Wisconsin, 66-65, as Sam Jacobson was stripped of the ball while he was attempting a last-second shot which could've won the game. As a result, the team's 12-game winning streak was snapped, but they still managed to finish the regular season with the best record in school history at 27-3. And, believe it or not, that was just the beginning of one of the greatest rides in Minnesota sports history — it was going to be a "March to Madness."

The Big Ten champion Gophers were then rewarded with a coveted No. 1 seed in the NCAA's Midwest Region, in Kansas City. Thousands of Gopher fans made the trip to KC to watch the Gophers open the 64-team tourney against Southwest Texas State. And, thanks to Charles Thomas' 14 points off the bench, Minnesota cruised to a 78-46 victory. Next up was a tough Temple squad, known for their trapping defense. But, thanks to double-figure scoring from Harris, Jacobson, Jackson and Thomas, the Gophers cruised to a 76-57 victory, and a trip back to the "Sweet 16," this time in San Antonio.

Next up for the Gophers was Clemson, a team that would test the very moral fiber of their being. This one came down to a dramatic double-overtime thriller with Minnesota somehow emerging victorious with a 90-84 win. Jacobson and Jackson combined for 65 points, posting career highs of 29 and 36 points, respectively, as the team rallied for its biggest win of the season. With the huge win the team was now headed to the "Elite Eight," to face the mighty UCLA Bruins in the regional final.

With a Final Four berth on the line, guard Eric Harris, who had gone down with a shoulder injury in the Clemson game, stepped it up and decided to play hurt. The Gophers would need him in this one, the biggest game in the history of the program. The game was a back and forth affair, with Minnesota finding itself down 33-28 at halftime. But, behind a 52-point barrage in the second half, highlighted by Midwest Regional MVP Bobby Jackson's 18 points, the Gophers hung tough and pulled off an amazing 80-72 victory — garnering the school's first-ever Final Four appearance. After the game the players climbed a ladder to proudly cut down the net, a truly amazing site for everyone to see back in Minnesota.

It was now off to the Final Four at Indianapolis' RCA Dome for the Gophers to take on the defending national champions from Kentucky. While no other Gopher hoop squad had ever made it as far in the NCAA tournament, there was nothing Cinderella-like about this team. The Gophers had won the Big Ten title outright and had deservedly earned a No. 1 seed in the tournament. No. 1 seeds are given that designation for a reason. What was unexpected was the active support of all the Minnesota fans. When the team came back to Minneapolis, they arrived to a homecoming celebration at the Barn, which was filled well beyond its seating capacity.

Now, there was all kinds of drama leading up the big game against Kentucky, especially with Clem Haskins, who grew up in the Blue Grass State and was a big prep star there. But because of segregation issues back in the early 1960s, Haskins, who wanted to attend the University of Kentucky to play for legendary coach Adolph Rupp, opted to instead attend Western Kentucky University, where he became the program's first African American player.

Finally, in Indy, as the team made its way to the RCA Dome, nearly 10,000 Gopher fans turned out for a rally before the big game to support their team. It was going to be a battle. Things didn't start out so hot for the Gophers either against the Wildcats in the opening game of the semifinals. In fact, it would be safe to say that it would be a tale of two halves. In the first 20 minutes, a tense Gopher squad turned the ball over 15 times, and the stalwart bench that usually delivered the goods was nowhere to be found. Further, Kentucky's relentless defense was clearly presenting problems for Minnesota.

Then, with 14:31 remaining in the second half and Kentucky leading 47-43, James went down the lane and scored on a monster dunk. Everybody in the dome, including droves of North Carolina and Arizona fans (the other semifinalists), who by now were rooting for the underdog Gophers, went berserk. The deafening roar of the crowd was drowned out, however, by the sound of the referee's whistle, as he negated the basket and called a charging foul on James. At that point

Clem went berserk and his suit coat went flying. But, before the Armani jacket could even hit the floor, the referee slapped Clem with a "T." It was just one turning point in a game that had many. The resultant six-point swing put the Wildcats up 51-43.

The Gophers came back as they had done all season long though. First, Jacobson floated in mid-air to hit a jumper. Then, Jackson proceeded to hit a leaning double-pump lay-up, and then popped in a three-pointer. The RCA Dome erupted when the Gophers finally fought their way back from all the pesky turnovers and fouls that hindered them early on to take a 52-51 lead with 10:45 to play.

Then it got ugly for the Maroon and Gold. With the the game tied at 54, the Wildcats, led by All-American forward Ron Mercer, reeled off 14 of the next 17 points. The fat lady was, regrettably, warming up her vocal chords. Unable to play at Kentucky's torrid pace, the Gophers ran out of gas down the stretch and lost the game, 78-69. In the end, Minnesota, the escape artists of college hoops, had succumbed to great coaching, a blown charge call, and a terrific Kentucky defense. Throw in the fact that Sam Jacobson, Charles Thomas and Eric Harris were all playing hurt, and it all started to add up. The previously mistake-free Gophers had yielded to the relentless Kentucky press that caused them to turn over the ball to the Wildcats a sick 26 times.

The Golden Gophers gave us all some great memories during that magical 1997 season though, and renewed our pride in Minnesota basketball. Bobby Jackson, who finished the game with 23 points, had a once-in-a-lifetime season. For his efforts in the tournament, he was named to the All-Final-Four team

"Words can't describe how great that season was for me," said Jackson. "We worked really hard to get where we went, even when it seemed everybody doubted us. We just wanted to play hard and show everybody what we were about. I had never been in a Final Four situation, and it felt so good to accomplish that much. The Gopher fans played a major part in our success, and I would like to thank them for being there for us."

All in all, it was a storybook season that Gopher fans will never forget. The basketball team finished with an amazing 31-4 record en route to winning its first Big Ten title in 15 years. Led by the NCAA Coach of the Year, Clem Haskins, the Gophers made it all the way to their first-ever Final Four and were ranked as high as No. 2 in the nation for much of the season.

After the season, the awards started to roll in. Bobby Jackson, a consensus second team All-America selection, was named as both the Big Ten Player of the Year and Big Ten Defensive Player of the Year. Power forward John Thomas was named as a second team All-Big Ten selection, Eric Harris was third teamer and Courtney James earned honorable mention honors too. Jackson and Thomas were also both chosen in the first round of the NBA draft that June, while several of the other players went on to play pro ball as well.

Action Jackson

Bobby Jackson was born on March 13, 1973, in Salisbury, N.C. He grew up in basketball country, dreaming of playing college hoops. Jackson went on to average 22 points per game over his junior and senior seasons at Salisbury High School, earning all-conference and all-state

honors in those same two seasons. From there, the speedy guard went to Western Nebraska Junior College in Scottsbluff, Neb., where he garnered second team All-American honors in 1995.

Jackson then transferred to Minnesota for the 1996 season, and although he was only in Gold Country for two years, he made the most of his time here. With his patented long white socks, he finished his illustrious tenure in Minnesota with a career scoring average of 14.4 points, 5.5 rebounds, and 3.5 assists per game.

"Coming out of junior college, I could've gone to Wake Forest, Cincinnati, or Minnesota," recalled Jackson. "I chose Minnesota because of their team concept. I was looking for an opportunity to come in and help my team out right away and make an impact. I wanted to come in and win a conference championship, and that's exactly what we did during my last year. Being a Gopher really means a lot to me. There are only a certain amount of people that get to wear the Maroon and Gold and I am just happy that coach Haskins let me be a part of it all."

After receiving his degree in sports management, Bobby was selected by the Seattle SuperSonics in the first round (23rd pick overall) of the 1997 NBA Draft. Jackson was then immediately traded to the Denver Nuggets, where he emerged as one of the league's top young players. Two years later he was dealt to the Timberwolves, where he rekindled his relationship with Minnesota fans. In 2000 he was sent packing to Sacramento, where, in his fifth year in the league, he surpassed the coveted 2,000-point plateau. After spending six seasons with the Kings, he would bounce around the league as a veteran role player, with stops in Memphis, New Orleans and Houston through the 2008 season. The former Sixth Man Award winner has averaged 10.0 points, 2.6 assists and 3.1 rebounds per game over his 11-year NBA career.

Bobby Jackson could just flat out play and that was why the Gopher fans adored him. He was an amazing scorer, who could light it up at any time during the course of a game. He possessed unbelievable speed, quickness, and an explosive first step. With his fantastic court vision and unselfish passing abilities, Bobby went on to become a very productive NBA player.

Gopher Tombstone:

"I would hope to be remembered as a guy that went out and played hard every day, and always smiled and had fun every time he stepped on to the court."

1997 RUNNER-UP: JOHN HARRIS

Roseau native **JOHN HARRIS** wins his second U.S. Amateur Golf Championship. (His first title came in 1993.) Harris was named as a member of the coveted U.S. Walker Cup team for the second time that year as well (amateur golf's version of the Ryder Cup). Harris, who played hockey at the University of Minnesota in the early 1970s and won an NCAA championship in 1974 under Herb Brooks, also earned All-American honors as a golfer for the Gophers. After a brief minor league hockey career, Harris went on to earn a spot on the PGA Tour in 1976. He left the Tour shortly thereafter, however, to start a successful insurance business. In 1983 he regained his amateur status and went on to dominate on the local golf scene, winning four state titles and five mid-amateur titles. Turning 50 in 2002, Harris joined the Champions Tour, where he has won nearly $3 million in prize money. His first title came in 2006, when he won the Commerce Bank Open.

HONORABLE MENTION: KHALID EL AMIN

Minneapolis North wins its third straight state high school basketball title. Leading the Polars was guard **KHALID EL AMIN**, who paced the team to an amazing 81-4 record from 1995-97. El Amin would lead U-Conn to the NCAA title that next year before going on to play professionally in the NBA and in Europe.

The Vikings made a very bold statement in 1998 by selecting Marshall University Wide Receiver Randy Moss with their first-round pick of the NFL Draft. The six-foot-five former sprinter would make an instant statement in Minnesota, however, earning Rookie of the Year honors en route to leading his team all the way to the NFC Championship Game. It was one wild ride that year, that was for sure.

Moss wasted little time in letting everyone from Minnesota know that he had officially arrived. He caught his first NFL regular season pass against Tampa Bay on the third play of the game, an 11 yard bullet from Brad Johnson. His next catch, two drives later in the first quarter, went for a 48-yard touchdown. Throughout the game the Buccaneer defensive backs were visibly intimidated by Randy's size and speed. While most rookies got jacked-up off the line of scrimmage, in order to slow them down before they could get open running their routes, Randy was getting a 10-yard cushion. They were giving the rookie the kind of respect usually reserved for All-Pro's. He added another score in the second quarter as well, as the Vikes went on the crush the Bucs by the final score of 31-7.

From there, the Vikes just dominated their opposition. In Game Two Randall Cunningham came in for the injured Brad Johnson, and hit Cris Carter for a 19-yard game-winning TD to secure a 38-31 victory. Cunningham and Moss connected immediately, hooking up for a pair of touchdowns in wins over both Detroit and Chicago the next two weeks. Against the Lions Moss caught five balls for 37 yards, including a five yard touchdown pass in between double-coverage in the back of the end-zone. Then, against Chicago, Moss somehow leaped and hovered above a trio of Bear defenders only to come down with a miraculous 44-yard come-from-behind game-winning touchdown strike from Cunningham. The kid was legit.

Week Five saw Minnesota traveling to rival Green Bay, where Moss put on a show that left the cheese-heads utterly speechless. Moss used the nationally televised Monday Night Football game as his coming out party as he torched the defending NFC champions for 190 receiving yards and a pair of touchdowns. (It would've been three had it not been for a 75-yard TD negated by a holding penalty.) Green Bay's sold-out Lambeau Field was as quiet as a Sunday mass after Cunningham threw for a record 442 yards, including a couple of 52 and 44-yard bombs to Moss, as the Vikes rolled to a 37-24 win.

After pummeling the Redskins, 41-7, behind Robert Smith and LeRoy Hoard's three scores in Game Six, the Vikings traveled to Detroit for a rematch against the Lions. Minnesota got ahead early and was able to use its running game to tire the Lions defense. Robert Smith rushed for 134 yards in this 34-13 blow-out, while cornerback Jimmy Hitchcock returned a 79-yard interception for a touchdown. Oh yeah, Cris Carter and Jake Reed each tallied as well. By now the receiving trio of Moss, Carter and Reed were known simply as "Three Deep."

The undefeated Vikings then hit a bump in the road in Week Eight, getting upset by Tampa Bay, 27-24. After rebounding to win their next two games over both New Orleans and Cincinnati, Minnesota was off to its best start since 1975 and looking good. Moss was playing out of his head, Carter was as steady as ever and Robert Smith was having a career year. The defense was also looking good, having allowed the second fewest points in the NFC (170), and Cunningham, who was named as the NFC's

Player of the Month for October, had emerged as the catalyst for this high-octane offense.

No one knew how to handle this potent air attack, which was scoring at a record pace. Not even Brett Favre and the Green Bay Packers, who got lit up by the Vikings yet again in Week 11 by the final of 28-14. As if to prove that his two touchdowns weren't a fluke back in Week Five, Moss wowed the Metrodome crowd with eight catches for 153 yards that afternoon, including a 49-yard touchdown with 3:17 left on the clock to seal the win.

Then, on Thanksgiving weekend, Moss gave Minnesotans a whole bunch to be thankful for — a nationally televised 46-36 drubbing of the hated Dallas Cowboys, in Texas. While Randy had performed well all season long in the clutch, this game would stand out as his official "break-out" game. In an offensive explosion, Moss tortured the Cowboys for three 50-plus yard touchdown strikes, not to mention drawing a 50-yard interference penalty that set up another score. While Dallas, which did get three TDs from Emmitt Smith, cried that the loss was simply because their Pro Bowl cornerback Deion Sanders was out with a sore foot, fans from around the country knew better.

With the division crown now in hand, and the home-dome field playoff advantage secure, the Vikes went out and tried to have fun in their remaining couple of games. With the pressure off, Minnesota routed Chicago 48-22, behind Moss' three touchdowns. From there the Vikes cruised to victories over Baltimore, 38-28, Jacksonville, 50-10, and Tennessee, 26-16, to finish out the franchise's best-ever regular season record at 15-1. (The team's only loss came in Week Nine against the Bucs, losing a close one, 27-24.) For the season, Minnesota's offense had set a new NFL single-season record for total points, with 556 — a statistic that scared the daylights out of any team that would have to face this offensive juggernaut in the playoffs.

After a well deserved playoff bye-week of rest, the Vikes hosted the upstart Arizona Cardinals in the NFC divisional semifinals at the Dome. Feeling the pressure, Minnesota came out and dominated the young Cards. While quarterback Jake Plummer played heroically for Arizona, his two first-half interceptions, which each led to Vikings scores, rattled his confidence. Minnesota came out and built a 24-7 half-time lead and never looked back. Cunningham threw for 236 yards and tossed three touchdown passes on the day — one to tight end Andrew Glover, another to LeRoy Hoard and a third to Moss. Robert Smith added 124 yards on the ground, and Kicker Gary Anderson continued his perfect season with a pair field goals and five extra points. Running back Mario Bates tallied three touchdowns for the Cardinals, but it wasn't nearly enough as the Vikes cruised to a 41-21 blow-out victory. With the win Minnesota had earned themselves a ticket to the final-four of pro football, the NFC Championship Game.

Next up for the Purple were the high flying Atlanta Falcons, who, like Minnesota, were used to playing on artificial turf in a deafening domed stadium. The game got underway with Minnesota starting out slow, but then looked like they were going to blow it wide open. After Atlanta's Pro Bowl running back Jamal Anderson scored on a five-yard pass from Chris Chandler to give his club a 7-0 lead, the Vikes rallied. Cunningham was on fire, hitting Moss, Carter and Reed all over the field. Robert Smith and LeRoy Hoard were carrying the load up the middle, and the defense was holding its own. Minnesota made it 20-7 thanks to Cunningham's one-yard TD run, a pair of Anderson field goals, and Moss' 31-yard touchdown strike. Atlanta then battled back behind wide receiver Terrence Mathis' 14-yard touchdown pass from Chandler to make it 20-14 at half-time.

After a Morten Andersen 27-yard field goal made it 20-17 in the third, things heated up in the fourth. Cunningham found Matthew Hatchette on a five-yard slant to give the team some breathing room. After another Morten Andersen field goal, the game came to a climax when the Vikings had a chance to ice the Falcons once and for all. All they had to do was kick a 30-yard field goal and put the game out of reach. The good news was that Minnesota Kicker Gary Anderson had set an amazing NFL record that year by not missing a single field goal during the entire season. The bad news was that his luck unfortunately ran out right then and right there in the biggest game of his life. Incredibly, they lined up and he somehow missed the kick. Atlanta, behind Chandler's amazing downfield drive in the game's final minutes, then rallied back. When he tossed his second TD pass of the day to Terrence Mathis with just 49 seconds left in the game, the score was suddenly tied at 27-27.

Then Minnesota did something that no one could figure out. Knowing that they had lost a couple of key players to injuries, Green, despite having a time-out left, opted to play it safe by instructing Cunningham to simply take a knee on both third and fourth downs, instead of going for a long bomb to win the game. The home crowd boo'd to no avail and the grudge-match went into overtime. There, after both teams failed to score in their opening drives, Atlanta quarterback Chris Chandler, hobbling on a bad leg, drove his club deep into Minnesota territory. Then, as the clock ran down to just a few seconds, they called a time-out, brought in Morten Andersen and said a prayer. Anderson, the old veteran war-horse, calmly came in and kicked the 38-yard game-winner with ease. As the ball sailed through the uprights, the Falcons stormed the field. With that, the "Dirty Birds" had upset the Vikings, 30-27, thus earning themselves a trip to Super Bowl XXXIII in Miami.

The 64,060 Metrodome fans stood in complete and utter disbelief, shock and horror. With the exception of the "Hail Mary" back in 1975, it was probably the worst loss in the history of the franchise. It was also a brutal ending to an otherwise brilliant season. While Cunningham stepped it up huge that year, passing for 3,704 yards and 34 touchdowns, the big story was the incredible rookie season of No. 84, Randy Moss. Moss, who finished with 69 receptions for 1,313 yards and a league leading 17 touchdowns (10 of which came on plays of over 40 yards), was named as the Rookie of the Year. In addition, he also became the only rookie to be named as a starter, alongside teammate Cris Carter, for the NFC in the Pro Bowl.

Simply Amazing
Born on February 13, 1977, Randy Moss grew up loving sports in the small West Virginia town of Rand. He later attended DuPont High School in the neighboring town of Belle, where he played football, basketball, baseball and ran track as a sprinter. A three-time all-stater and 1994 West Virginia Player of the Year, Moss, who scored 40 touchdowns, led his DuPont Panthers to a pair of state football championships. He also teamed up with Jason Williams (who would go on to star in the NBA), to win a state hoops title as well. He averaged better than 30 points and 12 rebounds per outing that season, earning a pair of Mr. Basketball Player of the Year awards to boot.

After the season the lottery for Randy's athletic services heated up. He ended the suspense though when he announced that he had accepted a scholarship to play football at Notre Dame under Coach Lou Holtz. But, a controversial fight during his senior year turned into a criminal charge. And as a result, the Irish said "no thanks." Shortly thereafter, Florida State coach Bobby Bowden called to tell him that there was a scholarship waiting for him at FSU. The only catch would be that he would have to red-shirt his freshman year and keep his nose clean. He agreed, and impressed them all with his blistering speed.

That next summer, however, Randy got busted for allegedly smoking pot. This didn't sit too well with Bowden though, and as a result, he was released from his scholarship.

Moss finally got back on the field that next summer, when Marshall University, a Division I-AA school in West Virginia, said he could play there. He obliged and went on to smash nearly every collegiate receiving record over the next few years. He led the Thundering Herd to a national championship in 1996 and then, after the program switched to Division I that next year, led them to the inaugural Motor City Bowl in 1997. When the smoke had finally cleared, Moss was being touted as the greatest college football receiver, maybe ever. In just two short college seasons he had amassed 168 receptions, 4,528 all-purpose yards and 53 TD catches. For his efforts, he was named as a unanimous first team All-American, and also finished fourth in the Heisman Trophy voting.

Despite his amazing talent though, his off-the-field baggage caused his draft stock to plummet. Twenty NFL teams passed on Moss in that first round before NFL Commissioner Paul Tagliabue announced: "With the 21st pick of the 1998 NFL Draft, the Minnesota Vikings select Randy Moss, Wide Receiver from Marshall University...". Minnesota thought that they had died and gone to heaven when they looked up at the draft board and saw that he was still available so late. Vikings coach Dennis Green felt that he was just a misunderstood kid who had made some bad decisions, and was willing to give him a shot. He felt that the Vikings, with their veteran roster, would be a great place for the youngster to mature and develop into a complete player. Minnesota also acquired Randy's brother, Eric, a Tackle, which they felt would ease his transition as well.

Moss played with the Vikings from 1998 to 2005, when he was traded to Oakland for linebacker Napoleon Harris and a No. 1 draft pick. He would remain with Oakland for two seasons, before joining the New England Patriots in 2007. For his career, the six-time Pro Bowl and four-time All-Pro receiver has registered 774 receptions for 12,193 yards and 124 touchdowns.

Today Randy Moss is one of the NFL's biggest superstars. An amazing offensive threat, he is that rare talent who can take a game over almost single-handedly. And, while Randy does and says things from time to time that are too stupid to comprehend, he is a phenom. From squirting refs with water bottles, to "Randy-Ratios," to leaping, one-handed circus catches in triple coverage — there is never a dull moment with him. And, perhaps, that is why we love him. A future Hall of Famer, he will no doubt go down as one of the all-time great ones.

1998 RUNNER-UP: SAM JACOBSON

The 20-15 basketball Gophers win the N.I.T. tournament. After getting snubbed for the NCAA Tourney, the Gophers went on a magical run, beating Colorado State, UAB and Marquette, all at Williams Arena, before heading off to New York's Madison Square Garden for the N.I.T. Finals. There, Minnesota won a thriller over Fresno State in the semis, 91-89, before beating Penn State in the championship game, 79-72. Leading the charge for Minnesota was Cottage Grove native **SAM JACOBSON**, who tallied 23 points in the title game. Jacobson earned Honorable Mention All-America honors that season after averaging 18.2 points and 5.2 rebounds per game. The guard/forward would go on to play professionally in the NBA and in Europe.

HONORABLE MENTION: ILA BORDERS

Duluth Dukes pitcher **ILA BORDERS** makes history when she becomes the first female pitcher to record a win in a professional men's baseball game. The historic event happened on July 24, 1998, when her (independent) Northern League Dukes beat the Sioux Falls Canaries, 3-1. That night Borders went six innings, giving up just three hits, walking two, and striking out two. Borders made headlines the year before as well, when she signed with the St. Paul Saints, thus becoming the first woman since St. Paul native Toni Stone (who played in the Negro Leagues) to be integrated into mens pro ball. She retired in 2000 at the age of just 26.

DAUNTE CULPEPPER
Another Playoff Run Comes Up Short

The Vikings went into the 1999 season with expectations running high. The team had made big news that off-season by trading quarterback Brad Johnson to Washington for its No. 1 draft pick (11th overall). And with it, they surprised everyone by selecting Daunte Culpepper, a six-foot-four, 265-pound gun-slinger from little known Central Florida University. Nobody would have guessed that Minnesota would pick a quarterback at this position in the draft, let alone an unproven kid from a small school that had just transitioned from Division I-A status. Would he learn under the tutelage of Randall Cunningham, or would coach Green throw the rookie to the Wolves to fend for himself? It was going to be a wild ride that season in Minnie.

The Vikings opened the season by traveling to Atlanta for the much-anticipated rematch against the same Falcons who had so mercilessly upset them that last January in the NFC title game. With the hype running high, Minnesota hung its pride on the line and rallied to beat the "dirty birds" by the final score of 17-14. It wasn't pretty, but it was a "W," as the Falcons were done in, ironically, by the man who drove the dagger through the hearts of Vikings fans everywhere, kicker Morten Andersen — who missed two field goals in the loss.

While Game Two may have officially been billed as Minnesota vs. Oakland, the media had hyped it up as the Randy Moss vs. Charles Woodson show. The meeting between the two second-year phenoms didn't produce any afternoon of fireworks — rather, just one amazing play. It happened midway through the second quarter when Cunningham dropped back from the Raiders 34-yard-line and lofted a hanging spiral to Moss on the right sideline. Moss, who was running back towards to ball, leaped over Woodson and somehow made a miraculous one-handed 29-yard grab to give the Vikings a first down at the five yard line. The Vikes fell apart after that big play though, as the Raiders scored on their next four consecutive drives to turn a 10-3 deficit into a 22-17 victory.

The purple traveled to Green Bay that following week to face the Pack, who incidentally, in an effort to give themselves a fighting chance against Moss that season, selected three tall cornerbacks with their first three picks of the draft. Moss, who capped an 80-yard drive by catching what appeared to be the game-winning touchdown with just under two minutes on the clock, was out-done by Green Bay quarterback Brett Favre, who completed a miraculous 23-yard game-winning touchdown with 12 seconds left to give his club a 23-10 victory.

With a 1-2 record, and Tampa Bay in town for Week Four, Moss caught a pair of 61 and 27-yard touchdown passes on the Vikings' first two drives of the game, as Minnesota went on to beat the Bucs 21-14. The Vikings went into a slump after that though, losing their next two by just two points each to conference rivals Chicago and Detroit. In the Detroit game, Cunningham just wasn't getting it done. So Denny decided to put in the newly acquired Jeff George at quarterback. While many were rooting for the rookie Culpepper to get the nod, George, baggage and all, would produce. Daunte would have to wait in the wings.

That next week George came in and torched the once mighty San Francisco 49ers by the score of 40-16. In Week Eight the Vikes headed west to Denver to face the two-time defending Super Bowl champion Broncos. This one was a wild one, with the game coming down to a defining moment on a pivotal third-and-10 play late in the game. That's when Moss somehow caught a loose ball that had just been deflected off of both Cris Carter and Denver cornerback Ray Crockett. The incredible play saved the drive and led to an emotional 23-20 Minnesota victory.

Next up for the purple was a hyped-up Monday Night Football matchup against the Dallas Cowboys, and the best cover corner in the game, Deion Sanders. Dallas jumped out to a quick 17-0 first-half lead, but when All Pro running back Emmitt Smith was forced to leave the game with an injury, the Vikes mounted a comeback. Moss, whose second TD of the day, a spectacular 47-yard bomb from George with 5:10 remaining in the game, helped to rally the team back to an amazing 27-17 victory. But the real excitement came on Cris Carter's game-winning TD grab amidst the back-drop of some premature pyrotechnics. That's right, the dude who shoots the cannon after touchdowns got excited and blew it off as the ball was in mid-air. It was no problem for C.C though, who stayed focused and made it look easy.

With the momentum on their side the Vikes went on a roll. Against the Bears Moss was absolutely phenomenal, posting a career-high 12 catches for 204 yards. Carter added nine catches of his own for 141 yards and three touchdowns as well, as the Vikings hung on to win a wild one, 27-24.

After getting a much needed rest over their bye week, the team's high-powered offense revved up and produced a season-high 485 yards in a 35-27 victory over the Chargers. While the offense of old had seemed to be back on track for the purple, it was the team's shaky defense that was causing the fans to get nervous. The Vikings then hit a couple of road blocks in both Tampa Bay and Kansas City. Down, but not out, Minnesota came back in Week 15 to beat the Packers at the Metrodome, 24-20, thanks to a pair of Moss TDs, including a dramatic 57-yard bomb from George late in the second quarter.

With their playoff lives in jeopardy, the Vikings traveled to the Big Apple, where they took on the New York Giants. The highlight of the game came late in the third on a razzle-dazzle play called "Z-Pass-Right." George handed the ball off to Moss on a reverse. Moss then faked the run and instead pulled up for a flea-flicker, tossing a perfect strike to a streaking Cris Carter for a 27-yard TD. Minnesota held on for a 34-17 win, thus guaranteeing them a shot in the post-season.

In the final regular season game of the year, the Vikes went on to beat a very good Detroit team by the final score of 24-17. Minnesota would now host the Cowboys in the first-round of the playoffs. The Dallas game went back and forth, but behind Robert Smith's team playoff-record 140 yards rushing, and Randy Moss' 127 yards receiving, the Vikings dug out of an early 10-3 hole, scored the game's final 24 points, and advanced to the NFC's final four for the third straight season. With the victory, the Vikings would now face the upstart St. Louis Rams for the right to go to the NFC Championship Game. It would be a tough battle playing in St. Louis' noisy domed stadium, but the purple embraced the challenge.

The Rams, much like the Vikings, were an explosive team with an explosive offense. All predictions were that it was going to be a shoot-out, and that was a huge understatement to say the least. When the smoke had cleared after this one was over, the Rams were declared the victors by the final score of 49-37. The Vikes, despite going into the lockerroom at half-time up 17-14, were completely thrashed in the second half. St. Louis came out of the gates smoking and inflicted a 35-0 second-half run that started with Tony Horne's 95-yard momentum-swinging kickoff return for a touchdown. The Vikes rallied, but it was too little way too late as they came up short. It was yet another ugly season ending loss, as the Vikings found themselves with an early post-season exit for the second frustrating year in a row.

Something drastic needed to be done that next year. It was the beginning of the new millennium, and several of the team's veterans were on their last legs. So, Jeff George hit the road for Washington and Denny made the announcement that his prized pupil, quarterback Daunte Culpepper, was going to be his guy. He wouldn't disappoint.

Daunte's Inferno

Born on January 28, 1977, Daunte Culpepper grew up in the small northern Florida town of Ocala. His childhood wasn't like most other kids though. You see, Daunte's birth mother was an unmarried prison inmate who was serving time in a Miami jail for armed robbery. In fact, she gave birth to Daunte while behind bars. Fearing that her child would be trapped in the social services system, she decided to give him up for adoption with the hopes that he would get a better life than she could offer. So, she turned to an elderly housemother named Emma Culpepper, who had befriended her a few years earlier when she was in juvenile detention. At 62 years of age, Emma was well-known in those parts as a real-life saint, having already raised 14 children — with none of them being her own. Daunte was going to be No. 15.

Before long, Daunte began to thrive in his new environment and playing sports quickly became his favorite thing to do. By his junior year at Ocala's Vanguard High School, college recruiters were all over him. There was one problem though. Daunte had poor grades. So, he sucked it up and decided to go back and re-take several of his freshman classes over again. And, because he couldn't take them during summer school, he had to sit in with the little freshman all year long. Daunte wanted a scholarship and knew that this was the only way. On the gridiron, Daunte was awesome, passing for 3,074 yards and 31 touchdowns while rushing for 602 yards, en route to earning All-American honors and the prestigious title of "Mr. Football Florida."

That next season Daunte set the school record for both career passing yards, with 6,107 and touchdowns, with 57. He rushed for 927 yards and 26 more touchdowns as well. That winter Daunte also lit up the hardwood by averaging 19.5 points, 11.3 rebounds and 5.1 assists per game on his basketball team. He was even being recruited by several major college basketball powerhouses, including the University of Kentucky. Then, in the spring, he tore up the baseball diamond by hitting nearly .500. So good was he in baseball that he was even selected by the New York Yankees in the 26th round of the Major League Baseball Draft. Daunte had a lot of options at that point, but was set on playing college football.

With that, the school year ended and Daunte's plan had finally worked itself out. His grades were up to an impressive 3.0 that year and just like that, all of those colleges which had ignored him earlier in the year, suddenly started calling again. Nearly every major university in the nation wanted him, but Daunte was particularly grateful to the University of Central Florida, which had stuck with him through his academic troubles, and he wanted to reward them. He did and what a ride it was. When it was all said and done, Daunte ended his amazing career at UCF with more than 30 school records and garnered All-American honors to boot. He became just the third player in NCAA history to pass for more than 10,000 yards and rush for more than 1,000 yards in a career.

Shortly after the season, Daunte began working out diligently to prepare himself for the upcoming NFL draft. The scouting report on him read like that of a superhero. He could run the 40-yard-dash in just 4.42 seconds, he had a 36" vertical leap and could throw the ball an incredible 80 yards. He could also bench-press over 400 pounds while squatting 500 — stats better than some linemen.

The NFL scouts knew he could dominate the college boys, but they weren't totally convinced that he could handle the much bigger and faster professionals. The Minnesota Vikings rolled the dice though and drafted him with the No. 11 overall pick. Daunte then signed a whopping five-year contract which included a $5 million signing bonus. The first thing he bought was a beautiful new home for Emma.

After learning the ropes in 1999, Daunte came out in 2000 and led the Vikings back to the NFC Championship game, and was even named as the starting quarterback in the Pro Bowl that year. Sure, they got humiliated by the Giants, 41-0, but they had established themselves as one of the premier teams in the league. Despite the loss, it was an outstanding season for Daunte. He finished the year with a nearly perfect quarterback rating of 98.0 as he threw for 3,937 yards and 33 touchdowns. In addition, he also ran for 470 yards while rushing for seven more TD's.

Culpepper would play for the Vikings through 2005, before being traded to Miami after suffering a serious knee injury during the 2005 season. The three-time Pro Bowl selection would play with the Dolphins for one season before joining the Oakland Raiders in 2007. Never fully recovering from his knee injury, Culpepper retired prior to the 2008 season. His career stats were impressive: 21,091 yards passing yards, 137 touchdowns and a career quarterback rating of 90.8. In addition, he also rushed for 2,496 yards to go along with 30 rushing touchdowns.

At six-foot-four and 265 pounds, Daunte Culpepper truly redefined the position of quarterback. In his prime, he was arguably the game's most versatile and respected offensive threat. In addition to being a fabulous athlete, Daunte has also become an outstanding role-model and citizen in his community.

"Being a Viking makes me feel very proud," said Daunte. "All of the great players — the Alan Pages, Carl Ellers Jim Marshalls and Ahmad Rashads — to play in the same organization as them means a lot to me. Knowing the history and tradition of the team, it just inspires me to go out and try to be the best player that I can be, and to represent the organization proudly."

"The fans are great up there too," he added. "They are real die-hards and I respect that. They have so much support for the team and that makes us as players try hard to get them victories. They really show me their appreciation and for that I am very grateful. Everyone is so nice and that makes it a very fun place to live and work. I just want to show them my appreciation by being the best I can be."

1999 RUNNER-UP: TYRONE CARTER

The football Gophers go 8-3 and make it to the Sun Bowl, where they ultimately lose to Oregon. It was the first post-season bowl game for the program in 13 seasons. The game was one of missed opportunities for the Gophers, as they turned the ball over three times and gave up the winning touchdown with just under two minutes to go in the game. The team also made history that season when they beat No. 2 ranked Penn State, 24-23, on the road. One of the stars of the team was two-time All-American safety *TYRONE CARTER*, who won the Jim Thorpe Award as the best defensive back in college football that season. Carter was drafted in the fourth round by the Vikings and has since gone on to play in the NFL for nine seasons, with New York and Pittsburgh.

HONORABLE MENTION: KATIE SMITH

Women's professional basketball comes to Minnesota when the expansion Lynx hit the local sports scene as members of the WNBA. The Lynx, which are owned and operated by the NBA's Timberwolves, played to large crowds that inaugural season at the Target Center and finished with a very respectable 15-17 record. One of the team's first stars was All-Star forward *KATIE SMITH*, who averaged nearly 12 ppg in 1999. Smith would spend seven seasons with the Lynx (averaging nearly 18 ppg) before being traded to Detroit in 2006.

To the delight of countless Minnesota hockey fans, the NHL's expansion Wild finally hit the ice in 2000. It was a long and arduous journey that finally came to fruition after several years of very hard work and determination. It had been a long hangover from that cold day back in 1993 when a jerk named Norm hijacked our North Stars to Texas, and Minnesota hockey fans everywhere were eager to get back on the ice. On June 25, 1997, the NHL Board of Governors voted unanimously to award an expansion franchise to the state of Minnesota for play to begin in the year 2000. Just hours later a celebration erupted in downtown St. Paul, where a parade of some two dozen Zambonis took to the streets. Team owner Bob Naegele, himself a high school and collegiate goaltender, later unveiled the plans for a new state-of-the-art arena which was to be located on the site of the St. Paul Civic Center.

The team's new $130 million arena, named as the Xcel Energy Center, would be first class. Complete with 74 luxury suites, and all the extras, this 18,600-seat "X" would truly mark the spot.

Shortly thereafter, a state-wide name search was conducted with six finalists emerging: Blue Ox, Freeze, Northern Lights, Voyageurs, White Bears and Wild. The latter, of course, was chosen, and was officially unveiled at a naming party in front of a sell-out crowd at historic Aldrich Arena.

By now the team had begun assembling a front-office and hiring key members of its staff. Former NHL star Doug Risebrough was named as the team's first-ever GM and he would later hire the legendary Jacques Lemaire to serve as his head coach. The pieces were starting to come together.

In June the league held an Expansion Draft for the two new kids, the Wild and Columbus Blue Jackets. There, the Wild selected several players who would make the roster, including: goalie Jamie McLennan; defensemen Filip Kuba, Curtis Leschyshyn and Sean O'Donnell; and forwards Jim Dowd, Sergei Krivokrasov, Scott Pellerin, Stacy Roest and Cam Stewart. In addition, a couple of Gophers were added to the mix — Darby Hendrickson and Jeff Nielsen. Shortly thereafter, the 2000 NHL Entry Draft took place with the Wild selecting winger Marian Gaborik from Slovakia with the No. 3 overall pick. Several other players were selected on that day as well, including defenseman Nick Schultz, winger Maxim Sushinsky and defenseman Lubomir Sekeras, all of whom would pay dividends.

Risebrough wanted to assemble a team that that would not only be a winner, but would also be entertaining and exciting for the fans.

"We are going to build this team through the draft, waivers, free agency, by trades and through our farm system," said Risebrough. "It will be a real fun time, and also a real testing time for these guys who are going to have to come in here and perform. It is a honeymoon so to speak. History will be made as we go, and that is a very exciting prospect."

In September of 2000 the Xcel Energy Center was completed for the Wild's inaugural NHL season. With the team wrapping up its training camp at Minneapolis' Parade Ice Garden, the opening day roster was starting to take shape. On September 19th the Wild played their first-ever preseason game, tying San Jose, 3-3, at the Rose Garden in Portland, Oregon. That next week the team finally returned home to play their first-ever preseason home game, beating the Mighty Ducks of Anaheim, 3-1.

The club, which was slotted to play in the newly realigned Northwest Division of the Western Conference, along with the Calgary Flames, Colorado Avalanche, Edmonton Oilers and Vancouver Canucks, opened the season on the road in Anaheim. There, rookie Marian Gaborik scored the first-ever goal in Wild history in the second period, but the team wound up on the short side of a 3-1 game. Finally, on October 11, 2000, the Wild made their home debut vs. the Philadelphia Flyers. Richfield native Darby Hendrickson scored the first Wild goal at Xcel Energy Center and helped guide the team to an impressive 3-3 tie. The crowd went nuts. Hockey was back.

"It was a great pass and I was just in the right place in the right time," said Darby of that first goal. "But that was fun and very memorable. It was a huge thrill. At the time it didn't register. Trust me, at the time I was not thinking about making history and scoring the first ever goal at the X, but it happened and it was very special. We played Philly to a tie that night, which was a real positive, and it was the beginning of a great season that just got better and better. The entire atmosphere in the Twin Cities that night was incredible. Hockey was back and it was great to just be a part of it. It was truly awesome."

From there the team just kept on rolling and the highlights followed. On October 22nd goalie Jamie McLennan recorded the first shut-out in team history, stopping 24 shots in a scoreless tie at home against Florida. A few weeks later the team notched its first-ever road victory by beating Calgary, 3-2, on Antti Laaksonen's thrilling overtime goal. On November 26th Laaksonen tallied the first-ever hat-trick in franchise history in a 4-2 home win against Vancouver. The team then got hot in January, extending its unbeaten streak to eight games at one point when Filip Kuba scored the franchise's first home overtime goal to defeat Detroit, 3-2. The sell-out crowds at the X were loving it.

The unequivocal highlight of the year, however, came on December 17th, when the former North Stars, now the Dallas Stars, came to town. The atmosphere in the X was absolutely electric that night and the fans were looped. How would the Wild respond? They shined, spanking the Stars, 6-0, in front of an emotional record sell-out crowd. Minnesota natives Darby Hendrickson and Jeff Nielsen combined for three goals and an assist as the Wild scored a pair in each of the three periods to ice it. The Wild peppered Dallas goalie Eddie Belfour all night while his former back-up, Manny Fernandez, stopped all 24 shots he faced to earn the amazing shut-out victory.

"That was just unbelievable drama that night," said Hendrickson. "The fans were still chanting 'Norm Sucks!' from the old North Star days. I mean I grew up here and understood the entire saga, but most of the guys on the team had no clue about just how much the North Stars meant to this area. So, when we came out and crushed the Stars that night it was huge. The fans were so into it and I think I was even a fan that night. The atmosphere in there was unbelievable and everything just went our way. The fans really deserved that after all they had been through over the years."

Through it all the fans were loving every minute of it. In fact, on March 28th the Wild established an NHL expansion team attendance record with their 39th consecutive sell-out against Phoenix. The team would ultimately finish the season with 41 consecutive regular season sellouts — good for an NHL Expansion Team record of 751,452 fans and an average of 18,329 per game. Throughout the year the fans got to know the players and the players got to know the fans. One player, however, stood out — rookie Marian Gaborik, who became the first Wild player to be named NHL Player of the Week, after scoring eight points in early March.

Finally, on April 8, 2001, the Wild completed their inaugural season with a tough loss to Colorado, 4-2, at home. In the process, Wes Walz scored his seventh short-handed goal and ninth short-handed point of the season to set the individual expansion team record. Darby Hendrickson also scored his career-high 18th goal in this one as the Wild finished their inaugural debut with an impressive record of 25-39-13-5, good for 68 points. The leading scorers for the Wild that season were Andrew Brunette (69 points), Marian Gaborik (67 points) and Jim Dowd (43 points), while goalies Dwayne Roloson and Manny Fernandez won 14 and 12 games, respectively, between the pipes. Lemaire's infamous "neutral zone trap" had worked its magic and the rest of the league stood up and took notice that these guys were not going to lie down for anybody. The defensive-minded coach had instilled a solid system that the players genuinely liked, which gave them a good foundation to build on.

By all accounts that first season was a huge success. From top to bottom the organization was just first class. The fans couldn't get enough of their wild and the team even threatened to make the playoffs at one point before slowing down at the end. It was also a rejuvenation of sorts for St. Paul, which embraced the team by redeveloping Kellogg Boulevard and West Seventh Street, complete with new restaurants, bars and even a new children's museum. The fans came out in droves and really embraced the entire experience.

The Pride of Minnesota

Darby Hendrickson grew up learning to love the game of hockey on the lakes of south Minneapolis at the age of just three. He went on to become a prep star at Richfield High School, where he led his team to the state tourney in 1991, only to lose to Duluth East in the quarterfinals. Darby won the Mr. Hockey Award that same year as a senior and from there went on to the University of Minnesota. At the U of M Darby lit it up, garnering WCHA Rookie of the Year honors that very next season. The speedy winger would play just two seasons in Gold Country, scoring 82 points in just 75 collegiate games, before going on to play on the 1994 U.S. Olympic team in Norway. From there, he opted to turn pro and sign an NHL contract.

Hendrickson would go on to play in the NHL for 11 seasons, scoring 65 goals and 64 assists for 129 career points in 518 games with Toronto, New York (Islanders), Vancouver, Minnesota and Colorado. With his hometown Wild, Hendrickson had a rebirth of sorts, establishing career-highs in goals (18) and points (29) in the 2000-01 season alone. In addition, he was named as the team captain for the second half of that season — an honor befitting of his determined play.

Overall, it was a wild year for Darby, literally. He suffered a bad eye injury at the end of the 2001 season and then missed several months of the 2002 season after breaking his wrist early in preseason. He persevered though and made us proud. For him to be thrust into the home-town superstar role on a new expansion team, and then have the pressures of being home with the friends and family was a lot to ask of anyone. The pressure would always be on him as the lone Minnesotan on the club, but he handled it with grace — always representing his team and himself with class. A great player and a great guy, Darby Hendrickson is a great friend to Minnesota hockey. Period.

As for Darby today, he is back home working as a Wild TV analyst for Fox Sports North. He had spent two seasons playing in Austria before finally deciding to retire from the game he loves in 2007. Darby and his family presently reside in Inver Grove Heights. They also have a cabin up on Island Lake near Duluth as well, where they love to get away in the summer to go fishing and golfing. And, while Darby might have been the go-to guy on the ice, he doesn't mess with his wife out on the links, she used to play college golf!

On Coming Home
"I knew that the expansion draft was coming up and that I wasn't going to be protected by Vancouver. I was optimistic at that point and hopeful that it was going to happen. Then, when I got the call I was sort of numb. I was so excited about coming back to play for my new home-town team and knew it was going to be a great opportunity for me in my career. Looking back I guess it was just meant-to-be and I am now really grateful that it all worked out the way it did."

On the Team's Success:
"I think the success of this (2000-01) team can be traced back to a couple of places. First, the leadership of Jacques Lemaire and his coaching staff has been outstanding. They picked a whole bunch of solid players who were hungry and that was nice to be around. Secondly, the ownership has just done everything right, from the marketing on down. And thirdly, the new building is just first-class and that has made it the 'place to be' in Minnesota sports. We just have great fans here who really understand the game and want to get behind us. That entire situation is a great recipe for success. From there, the team has kind of formed its own identity. I mean we were all disappointed on not making the playoffs, but we were a part of building something and that was special. Jacque's system is a good system for us and we play well in it. Plus, we have been very competitive and I think the fans really appreciate that. Give us some time, we will be there."

What Does it Mean For You To Be With the Wild?
"I grew up wanting to play for the North Stars. I mean Neal Broten was my idol and I followed them so closely. But when they left town, that dream left too. Now, to get the chance to come home and play for Minnesota's newest team is just amazing. It has been more than anything I ever could've asked for. It has been a great ride and everything about it has been so positive. Being home is special, in more ways than one, and I can't thank the fans enough for all their support and encouragement. I really appreciate it."

What Did it Mean For You To Be a Gopher?
"That was a dream-come-true for me. As a kid I dreamt of being a Gopher and to be able to achieve that was amazing. It just meant everything to me."

Gopher and Wild Tombstones:
"I just want to be known as a good teammate both on and off the ice and an overall team guy who thought about the team first."

2000 RUNNER-UP: ROBERT SMITH
The 11-5 Vikings win the NFC Central Division. From there, the purple go on to beat the Saints in the playoffs, 34-16, only to get crushed by the New York Giants, 41-0, in the NFC Championship game. (The game is actually played on Jan. 14, 2001.) One of the stars of the team was two-time Pro Bowl running back *ROBERT SMITH*, who, in eight seasons with Minnesota, tallied 32 touchdowns on 6,818 yards rushing, and caught 178 balls for 1,292 yards receiving. Despite rushing for 1,521 yards in 2000, the most in the NFC that season, Smith decided to go out on his own terms while he was still on top and promptly retired.

HONORABLE MENTION: TELLIS REDMON
Led by running back *TELLIS REDMON*, the football Gophers finally beat Ohio State, by the score of 29-17, an accomplishment 50 years in the making that left the nearly 100,000 Buckeye faithful in Columbus speechless that afternoon. The 6-6 Gophers earned a trip to the post-season that year, only to lose a heartbreaker to North Carolina State in the Micron PC.com Bowl, 38-30. Redmon rushed for a pair of touchdowns on a record 246 yards that day, only to see his team surrender a 24-0 lead. The Wolfpack, meanwhile, were led by future NFLers QB Philip Rivers and WR Koren Robinson, who tallied four times in the big rally.

In 2001 the Golden Gophers won their first ever NCAA Wrestling Championship. It was as good as it gets for longtime head coach J Robinson, who brought home the hardware from arguably the toughest venue in all of team sports, Iowa's Carver-Hawkeye Arena. It was truly a storybook ending to a fairytale season.

The Gophers broke several school and national records along the way to this historic team crown, as all 10 members of the squad made significant contributions along the way. Prior to the national tournament, the Gophers breezed through the 2000-01 season, going 19-1 in dual meets. They also won team titles at the Midlands Championships, National Duals and Big Ten Championships. Overall, Minnesota outscored its opponents in dual meets on the season by the whopping margin of 573-170.

Along the way the team recorded several lopsided victories, including blow-outs over Northern Iowa (36-3), Hofstra (33-3), Princeton (45-0), Seton Hall (37-2), Nebraska (30-9), Michigan (29-6), Purdue (31-6), Michigan State (32-3), Penn State (37-3) and Wisconsin (33-6). In addition, Minnesota also garnered wins over North Dakota State, Boise State, Indiana and Illinois. They even beat Iowa twice, a feat which a few years earlier would have been unheard of. The lone blemish on the team's record was an early-season home dual meet loss to Oklahoma State, which saw several of the Gophers' top stars out from injuries. The Gophers rebounded to win 14-straight dual meets to end the regular season though, including a 20-12 revenge victory over those same Oklahoma State Cowboys in the title meet of the National Duals.

All season long different members of the squad stepped up big-time as the team persevered through some tough times. When Owen Elzen went down with a knee injury, true freshman Eli Ross came in and got it done. When Elzen returned, torn ACL and all, he sucked it up and posted a 30-3 overall record, capturing third place at both the Big Tens and NCAAs. It was leadership by example all the way around and a real team effort that pulled them through.

Minnesota then dominated at the conference's dual meet tournament with an amazing 8-0 campaign in Big Ten competitions. Then, at the Big Ten Championships, sophomore Jared Lawrence (149 lbs.) and redshirt freshman Garrett Lowney (Hwt.) won individual titles to lead Minnesota to a 24-point team victory over both Illinois and Iowa. With all 10 wrestlers placing in the top seven at the conference tourney, Minnesota amazingly advanced its entire line-up to the national tournament in Iowa City.

There, the Gophers competed as a team and got the job done. In fact, not one Gopher grappler became a finalist — marking the first time in the 71-year history of the national tournament that the winning team won the team title without one. The U of M got a full-team effort to garner an NCAA-record 10 All-Americans and 138.5 points to capture the school's first ever wrestling crown. (Iowa finished second in the team race with 125.5 points, followed by Oklahoma State with 115.5 points, Oklahoma 93.5 points and Illinois with 89.0 points.) With the team title, the Gophers unseated the six-time defending champs from Iowa.

All 10 Gophers finished in the top eight, earning All-American status. Three finished in third place (Leroy Vega, Owen Elzen and Garrett Lowney), three in fourth (Luke Becker, Brad Pike and Jacob Volkmann), one in fifth (Damion Hahn), one in sixth (Jared Lawrence) and two in eighth (Brett Lawrence and Chad Erikson).

With the big win the Gophers signified the proverbial "passing of the torch" from Iowa to Minnesota. How sweet it was. The media was all over it and wrestling was finally getting its props.

"I had written down three goals for the 2001 season," said Robinson of that dream season. "The first was to beat Iowa, in Iowa City, one of the toughest venus to compete at in the entire sports world. I mean Iowa had multiple national championships over the years and was like 136-5 or something ridiculous in duals at Carver Hawkeye Arena. So, our chances to win were very remote. But, we went down there and somehow pulled it off. It was amazing. The second was to have 10 All-Americans and the third was to win the Big 10 as well as the national championship. Those were our team goals and I knew that they were going to be tough. I knew we couldn't win with individuals but I knew that collectively, as a team, we could do it. That became our rallying cry for the year and really drove us that season. I remember too that we also spent a ton of time training for the third day of the national tournament, which was notoriously the toughest day. It is the day when guys are just beat up and tired and want to go home. For many, their dreams have been broken and they know they don't have a chance to be an individual champion."

"Then, amazingly, it all came down to that third day. We had six guys in the semifinals that night and incredibly, they all got beat. To top it all off, Garrett Lowney, our heavyweight who was a bronze medalist in the Olympics, wound up losing a coin flip in overtime and lost the match. So, we had no finalists. But we went back and regrouped and came out that third day determined. We had a lot of leadership on that squad with guys like Hartung, Kraft, Eggum and Morgan, and we knew we still had a chance. We calculated the points and figured it out. We were still in it and we knew that this was going to be our day. This is what we had trained for and we were going to do it. I can still remember going to weigh-in with Hartung out in the van with the radio blared to the tune of 'Who Let the Dogs Out?' and that was just a great memory of how that day started. It went back and forth that day and it came down to the finals when Owen Elzen, Damion Hahn and Garrett Lowney all pinned their guys within like three minutes of each other to seal it. When it was over it took us a while to realize what had happened. We won, and it was an amazing experience to see it all come together like that. I will never forget it."

Coach J

Since taking over the program 21 years ago, head coach J Robinson has built one of the strongest and most respected wrestling programs in the nation. Originally from California, Robinson grew up loving the sport of wrestling. He went on to wrestle at Oklahoma State University and from there wrestled internationally, competing on two World teams — placing fourth in 1970 and fifth in 1971. Robinson also represented his country in the 1972 Olympic Games as a member of Team U.S.A. In all, Robinson captured four national wrestling titles during his amateur career, two in freestyle and two in Greco-Roman.

After graduating Robinson began his coaching career at Oklahoma State as a graduate assistant before moving on to serve as a captain in the U.S. Army from 1969-72. He served a tour with the First Cavalry Division in Vietnam and upon returning home joined Iowa's staff as a graduate assistant. He was later promoted to assistant in 1976. He would serve as an assistant coach at the University of Iowa from 1976-84, helping to lead the Hawks to seven NCAA and eight Big Ten crowns. In addition, he served as an interim head coach during the 1984 Big Ten and NCAA championship season as well. From there, Robinson was offered the head coaching position at Minnesota, and he has been in Gold Country ever since.

In his first season, the Gophers finished the year without winning a single Big Ten dual match. In 1999 Minnesota went undefeated in conference duals and won the Big Ten title, breaking Iowa's 25-year conference title winning streak. Today, Coach Robinson is a three-time national champion (2001, 2002 and 2007). A phenomenal coach, he has built this program from the ground up. Currently the winningest active coach in the Big Ten , Robinson has compiled an amazing overall record of 318-103-3 with the Gophers, including a 113-51-2 record against Big Ten competition. During his tenure in Gold Country, he has led Minnesota to six Big Ten titles and 15 top-three league finishes. He has led the Gophers to top-four conference finishes in 17 of his 21 seasons, including placing in the top three at the Big Ten Championships each of the last 11 years. In addition, Robinson has coached 41 different wrestlers to a total of 85 All-America honors, while also leading 23 different wrestlers to 35 Big Ten individual titles. Further, he has also coached eight Gophers to 11 NCAA individual titles.

TEAM CHAMPIONS

Robinson has also coached at the national and international levels, serving as an assistant coach on four consecutive U.S. Olympic squads from 1976 to 1988, and then as the head coach for the U.S. at the 1983 Pan American Games. Among his many awards and honors, he was named as the 1998 and 2001 Dan Gable Coach of the Year, and the 2001 National Wrestling Coaches Association Coach of the Year. The six-time Big Ten Coach of the Year was inducted into National Wrestling Hall of Fame in 2005 as well.

A brilliant tactician and teacher, Robinson's teams are consistently nationally ranked because he knows how to recruit and attract the top talent from around the world to his program. As a result, he has emerged as one of the top college coaches (in any sport) in the nation. In addition to coaching, Robinson also owns the very successful "J Robinson Summer Camps," which have been training athletes of all ages to achieve their goals since 1978.

What Does it Mean to Coach the Gophers?
"One of the nicest things about winning a national title is that you can share your achievements with the entire state. The feeling of joy of being No. 1 is a great thing and I am just really happy that I was able to bring that to the people. We did it together and it is all of ours to share. That is a great thing. So being a Gopher is a great, great thing for me. I have a lot of pride in being a part of this program and a part of this university. Being a part of building this tradition has just been a wonderful experience. I also want to add, however, that I am just a part of the process. In fact, when we won that first national championship we had NCAA champion watches made. We then sent one to everyone who had coached in the program from years past. We all were a part of that and we wanted to let everyone share in the achievement. A lot of people believed and gave huge parts of themselves to get where we

are today. It wasn't just one guy. So, I am just the keeper of the flame for a while until it starts to grow and burn. Then, I will need to pass that torch to the next guys, who are ready to make that flame even bigger and brighter. It's a great family and I am honored to be a part of it."

On Winning it Again in 2002:
"It was a little different to win that second one. We came in ranked No. 1 and were in the drivers seat, so everyone wanted to knock us off. But we persevered and made it two in a row and that was special in its own way. We proved to everyone that we belong here and it really validated that we were for real. It was also important for us as a team for everyone to know that we weren't just a one-hit wonder. It was a real statement for our program and it felt really good. It was a different kind of satisfaction, but a tremendous satisfaction nevertheless."

On the Future:
"We have a target on us now and everyone wants to knock us off. That makes us want it even more though. I think our guys know that we aren't here to defend our titles, rather, we know that we have to go out and win it again. We just have to work harder than everybody else and stay on top. We can only take it a year at a time though and keep building on what we are doing. Our goals into the future are to be aggressive, dominate our opponents and have fun. As long as we can control those things, we will be just fine. We also feel like we are carrying the torch for our sport as a whole too. I mean if we can get 20,000 fans into the Xcel Energy Center, then that sends a powerful message across the country that this sport is growing and can be marketed just like the other major sports on campus. We hope to have other programs duplicate our formula for success and grow the sport into the next generation, that is what this is all about."

On Life:
"Coming to Minnesota when they weren't very good to begin with and then going through that whole process to get to where we are now, is what it is all about. The journey is what this has all been about and it has been a great ride, that is for sure. I mean you wake up every morning to try and get to the top of the mountain, and for me it was sweet to finally get there on my own."

Gopher Tombstone:
"I am just one of a bunch of guys who came here with a dream and made it happen."

Since winning the 1999 national heavyweight championship, Brock "The Rock" Lesnar has gone on to superstardom in the worlds of both professional wrestling and ultimate fighting.

2001 RUNNER-UP: KOREY STRINGER

Vikings Pro Bowl tackle *KOREY STRINGER* tragically dies from complications brought on by heat stroke during the team's training camp in Mankato on August 1, 2001. The former Ohio State star was a first round draft pick of the Vikings in 1995 and played for the purple for his entire six year NFL career. The Vikings retired his No. 77 jersey during the 2001 NFL season, an emotional year which resulted in a 5-11 record.

HONORABLE MENTION: SHANNON MILLER

The University of Minnesota-Duluth Lady Bulldogs win their first of three straight NCAA hockey national championships, beating St. Lawrence University, 4-2. Maria Rooth was named as the MVP, while Brittny Ralph and Tuula Puputti were named to the All-Tourney team. UMD, which won its second straight WCHA Playoff title that year as well, was led by coach *SHANNON MILLER*. As of 2008, Miller has amassed an overall record of 234-61-25 and has led the Bulldogs to seven NCAA playoff appearances, five NCAA Frozen Four berths and four NCAA titles (2001, 2002, 2003 & 2008). Miller has also enjoyed tremendous success coaching on the international stage with Team Canada, guiding the squad to a sliver medal at the 1998 Winter Olympics. Further, in 2003 she was named as the American Hockey Coaches Association Coach of the Year.

JORDAN LEOPOLD
The Hockey Gophers Win it All

The 2002 Gopher Hockey season was pure magic. And, for the Maroon and Gold faithful who had waited so patiently since Herbie Brooks' boys brought home the hardware all the way back in 1979, it was oh so sweet. The leader of this club was Jordan Leopold, an offensive minded defenseman who patrolled the Mariucci blue line with authority that year.

The Gophers opened their season by beating hated North Dakota in the annual Hall of Fame Game at the newly christened Englestad Arena in Grand Forks. There, they quieted the Sioux faithful with a 7-5 victory. From there Minnesota went on to sweep upstart Bemidji State, followed by another sweep of Colgate, which resulted in a combined two-game score of 17-0. Goalie Adam Hauser was playing well early on, while Leopold, Johnny Pohl, Troy Riddle, Paul Martin and Jeff Taffe were all finding the net as well.

Minnesota then went on to rough up Michigan Tech, MSU, Mankato, Minnesota-Duluth, Michigan and Michigan State, sweeping Mankato and Duluth while allowing just one tie each from Tech and Michigan State. They then ran into a road block on November 30th, when St. Cloud upset them, 3-2, at Mariucci Arena for their first loss of the year. They managed a tie that next night in St. Cloud as the Gophers quickly saw who was going to give them trouble that season.

After a tough split with Denver, Minnesota went on to beat Ferris State at the Mariucci Classic, 3-2. They then crushed Providence, 6-1, only to split a tight one with North Dakota at home. They managed a split with Wisconsin on the road, and then won one and tied on up in Anchorage. Denver was next as they came in and stole one at Mariucci Arena. They split yet another series that next weekend up in Duluth but came back to sweep UND in Grand Forks. Colorado College managed a split of their own at Mariucci Arena in mid-February, only to see the Gophers rebound and sweep the cheese-heads that next weekend. From there the Gophers rolled, sweeping St. Cloud State in a home-and-home series, which led up to the first round of the WCHA playoffs.

First up for Minnesota was North Dakota, and the Gophers responded by crushing the Sioux, 7-2, in Game One, and 4-3, in overtime, in Game Two. St. Cloud State was next in the semifinals at the Xcel Energy Center, and with a 4-1 win, the Gophers advanced to the Finals. Denver then came in and knocked off the Gophers to claim the WCHA Final Five crown, winning 5-2.

It wouldn't matter though, as the team had earned a first round NCAA playoff bye. That next week they headed to the West Regional quarterfinals in Ann Arbor, Mich., where, they wound up beating Colorado College, 4-2. Colorado College got on the board first but just three minutes later the Gophers responded as Johnny Pohl found Grant Potulny in front of the net for a sweet one-timer that beat CC goalie Jeff Sanger. Minnesota then took the lead in the second on a power-play goal from Nick Angell. Moments later, Jeff Taffe got in the action as he took a pass from Dan Welch and slid the puck under Sanger's arm to give Minnesota a 3-1 lead. Colorado College pulled to within one late in the second, but Minnesota sealed it in the third on Pohl's short-handed breakaway that made it 4-2. The lead held up as Hauser stopped 33 shots in net to get the big "W."

With that, the Gophers were finally back in the Frozen Four. Sure, they were no strangers to the pinnacle of March Madness, but it had been nearly a quarter century since they had won it all. Things were looking good for the Gophers this time around though. That's because the Frozen Four was being held at the posh Xcel Energy Center in St. Paul, right in their very own backyard. West Seventh Street was overflowing with maroon and gold that afternoon as a record crowd of 19,234 showed up at the X to watch the team do battle in the opening semifinal round against Michigan.

The Gophers drew first blood in this one when Jeff Taffe, who was forechecking in to the offensive zone, deflected a clearing attempt towards the net. There, Grant Potulny grabbed the deflection and, while on his knees, flipped it past Michigan goaltender Josh Blackburn to make it 1-0 midway through the first period.

Minnesota then made it 2-0 at the 4:33 mark of the second period when Potulny netted his second tally of the evening — this one coming on the power play. Potulny redirected a Jordan Leopold slapper from the point to beat Blackburn through the five-hole on this one as Johnny Pohl gathered his second assist of the evening as well. Hauser played tough through this point and particularly stood on his head with just over 30 seconds to go in the second when he made a leaping glove save across the crease to stop Jed Ortmeyer's scoring bid.

The third period was eerily similar to the previous two in that the Gophers wound up tallying an early goal. This time it was junior Jeff Taffe, scoring his team-best 34th of the season on a thrilling breakaway just over a minute into it. Taffe took a sweet pass from his Hastings High School teammate, Dan Welch, to burn up the ice and deposit the puck between Blackburn's legs on a backhander. It was now 3-0 and things were looking promising.

But, as in all good stories, this one too would have its share of drama. The Wolverines were not about to lie down and they roared back midway through the third, finally scoring at the 13:55 mark on a shorthanded goal by J.J. Swistak, which beat Hauser through the five hole. Then, with just under a minute and a half to go in the game, Michigan, playing with six skaters and their goalie pulled, made it 3-2 when Ortmeyer beat Hauser on a tough angled shot from the goal line that somehow snuck through his pads.

The tension was thick in the X at this point as the Gophers then hung on for their dear lives to stop the Wolverines in the games' final moments. Hauser, who stopped 25 of 27 shots that night, came up huge in the last minute and when the buzzer finally blew, the Maroon and Gold suddenly found themselves back in their first title game since 1989. (Ironically, that game was also held in St. Paul, at the Civic Center.)

The Finals would go down as one of the greatest ever as Minnesota took the ice that next night against the University of Maine. The Gophers opened the scoring at 7:18 of the first period on the power play. A streaking Keith Ballard slammed home a beautiful one-timer from Troy Riddle that beat Maine goalie Matt Yeats through the five-hole and lit the lamp.

The Black Bears rallied to tie it up at the 4:47 mark of the second period, however, when Michael Schutte scored on a power play goal that saw Adam Hauser get screened big-time in front of the net. The Gophers jumped back on top less than a minute later though on an awesome wrister by Johnny Pohl which beat Yeats up high, top-shelf. And, with that timely 27th goal of the season, Pohl was able to clinch the national point-scoring race, pulling ahead of New Hampshire's Darren Haydar with 77 points.

Maine tied it up early in the third though as Schutte tallied his second goal of the game, this one coming on a one-timer from the point which beat Hauser low to the glove side. With everything tied up at two apiece, the action was fierce. Things stayed that way for another 14 minutes or so, when Robert Liscak banked a floater off of Hauser's leg pad from behind the net with under five minutes to go to give the Black Bears their first lead of the game. It was a crushing goal.

Coach Don Lucia's Gophers, which had played conservatively throughout the third period, now rallied fiercely in the game's final moments. Maine hung in there though and it appeared to be all but over.

Lucia finally pulled Hauser with 58 seconds remaining in the game and put an extra attacker out on the ice. Then, in one of the greatest goals in Gopher history, Matt Koalska tied it up with 54 seconds on the clock to knot the game at three apiece and send the home crowd into hysterics. Johnny Pohl, who won the face-off in the Maine zone, dropped the bouncing puck back to Troy Riddle. Riddle then deflected it over to Koalska in the high slot, where he proceeded to pound home a low liner between Yeats' legs.

So, it was now off to overtime, where the collective breath of every Minnesota hockey fan was held in the balance. The other two times that the Gophers had lost NCAA championship overtime games were back in 1954, when John Mariucci's club was upset by RPI, and then again in 1989, when Wooger's club was beaten by Harvard on those very same hallowed grounds on the corner of Kellogg and West Seventh in St. Paul. This one, however, was not going to have the same outcome.

In the extra session the two teams battled mercilessly up and down the ice for nearly 17 agonizing minutes. The fans were beside themselves as the tension mounted with every face-off. Then, at the 16:58 mark of overtime, history was made when North Dakota native Grant Potulny, the Maroon and Gold's lone non-Minnesotan on the roster, ended it all in dramatic fashion. Here's how it went down: Maine, playing on the short side of a controversial power-play for tripping, was trying to ice the puck out of their own end. A face-off in the Black Bear's zone then wound up going right to Jordan Leopold at the point. Leo then shot the puck into traffic in front of the net with the rebound bouncing to Pohl. Pohl then slid it to Potulny, who shot the puck under Yeats' leg pads for the thrill of a lifetime. Minnesota had won the game, 4-3.

Absolute bedlam erupted not only at the Xcel Energy Center, but throughout Minnesota as the fans rejoiced. That 23-year-old monkey was now off their backs and the Gophers were NCAA champions for the fourth time in history. The team, coaches and staff stormed the ice and celebrated amidst a sea of sticks, gloves and helmets, which now littered the rink. Minnesota was finally back on top of the hockey world and it felt damn good.

"That was one of the most exciting games I have ever been a part of and it will go down as a classic," said Leopold, whose 47 points were tops in the nation for defenseman that year. "It was just an amazing moment for everybody that has been involved in Gopher Hockey and it is certainly something that I will never forget. All the emotion that came out on the ice following that incredible ending was indescribable. To be out there with my teammates and friends was so special. It was really a day I will always look back on and cherish forever."

Leo

Jordan Leopold grew up in Golden Valley and went on to graduate from Armstrong High School, where he earned all-conference honors in both hockey and baseball. After spending his senior season with the U.S. National Under-18 Team in Ann Arbor, Mich., he came home to wear the Maroon and Gold sweater that he had always dreamed of as a little kid.

As a Gopher, Leopold was among the very best ever to lace

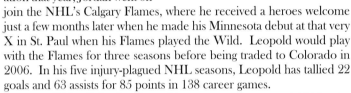

em' up at Mariucci Arena. By the time if was all said and done, he had become a two-time All-American, earned All-WCHA and WCHA Defensive Player of the Year honors, and to round out a perfect career, was named as the 2002 Hobey Baker Memorial Award Winner — emblematic of the nation's top collegiate player. (Previous U of M Hobey Baker winners included Neal Broten in 1981, Robb Stauber in 1988 and Brian Bonin in 1996.) In 164 career games at Minnesota, Leopold registered 45 goals and 99 assists for 144 points.

Following his graduation that year, Jordan went on to join the NHL's Calgary Flames, where he received a heroes welcome just a few months later when he made his Minnesota debut at that very X in St. Paul when his Flames played the Wild. Leopold would play with the Flames for three seasons before being traded to Colorado in 2006. In his five injury-plagued NHL seasons, Leopold has tallied 22 goals and 63 assists for 85 points in 138 career games.

All in all, Jordan Leopold was one of those special kids who comes along just once in a great while. It was not just his ability to find the back of the net that made him so special though. Jordan led by example, epitomized class and helped to resurrect a program that was recently on the verge of slumping towards mediocrity. He is also as humble as he is talented, a quality that has endeared him to the Golden Gopher faithful. No one has patrolled the blue-line like him before and no one will be able to match his exploits in the future. He is a one of a kind player who has certainly made Minnesota proud.

"It's been so much fun being at the U of M and I have just had a great time here," he said following the season. "I grew up watching the Gophers and dreamt of one day playing for them, so it has been a real life dream-come-true for me. Now, to be able to win a national championship was just the perfect ending to a perfect college experience. I will always be grateful to the coaching staff for giving me the chance to play there. Overall, being a Gopher meant everything to me and it always will. I really don't know what my life would be like without it to tell you the truth. The Minnesota fans are so awesome and I have just been very lucky to have been able to play here."

Gopher Tombstone:

"I want to be remembered as a champion, period. That was my goal when I first got here and I finally got to experience it four years later. It was an honor to help rebuild that program and I hope that title will be the first of many, many more. My teammates and I went through a lot, but we came together under a new coaching staff and got it done."

2002 RUNNER-UP: TORII HUNTER

The Twins win the American League Central Division crown with a record of 94-67. From there, the Twins went on to beat the Oakland Athletics in the AL Divisional Series, three games to two. Their luck ran out after that, however, as the team then lost to the Anaheim Angels, four games to one, in the American League Championship Series. One of the stars of the team that year was All-Star center fielder *TORII HUNTER,* who hit a team-high 29 home runs, 94 RBI and posted a .289 batting average. What makes the story of the 2002 Cinderella Twins even more amazing is the fact that the team was nearly contracted during the off-season.

HONORABLE MENTION: PHIL HOUSLEY

1) The U.S. Olympic hockey team wins a silver medal at the 2002 Winter Games in Salt Lake City, losing to Canada, 5-2, in the Finals. One of the stars of the team was South St. Paul native *PHIL HOUSLEY,* who scored five points in six games — including the semifinal game-winner over Russia. Housley played in the NHL for 20 seasons, retiring in 2003 as the top-scoring U.S. born player ever, with 1,232 points in 1,495 NHL games.

2) The *PGA CHAMPIONSHIP* his held at Hazeltine International Golf Club in Chaska, where Rich Beem shoots a 4-under 68 to beat the world's No. 1 player, Tiger Woods, for a one-stroke victory.

The 2002-03 Minnesota Wild made history in the "State of Hockey," taking us all on a magical ride we had not seen the likes of since 1991, when the North Stars made it all the way to the Stanley Cup Finals. The Wild established club records for wins and points that season, with 42 and 92, respectively, finishing third in the Northwest Division and sixth overall in the Western Conference. Further, the team once again sold out all 41 home games at the Xcel Energy Center, as the fans kept coming in droves to see their beloved squad in action. Minnesota made history right out of the gates by winning its first ever opening night game, beating Boston, 5-1, at the X. The team would play well that year and finish the season strong, making history on March 23rd when they beat Detroit, 4-0, to secure their first ever Stanley Cup playoff birth.

With that, the team headed west to face the Colorado Avalanche in the first round of the playoffs. The Avs had just won the Stanley Cup in 2001 and were the odds-on favorites to win it again this year. The Wild had other ideas, however, and opened the quarterfinals in Denver with a huge 4-2 win. The team jumped out to a 3-0 lead in the second period on goals from Filip Kuba, Gaborik and Wes Walz, and then held on behind Dwayne Roloson's 39 saves in net. The Avs rallied in the third, but Andrew Brunette iced it on a late unassisted goal. Colorado roared back to win Game Two the next night, 3-2, despite goals by Walz and Brunette.

The series headed back to St. Paul for Game Three and the fans were ready. It was the first time Minnesota had seen playoff hockey since the early '90s and the entire state had seemingly jumped on the bandwagon. Unfortunately, however, the team got blanked, 3-0, in front of a record crowd of 19,354 at the X. Avs Goalie Patrick Roy was the hero in this one, turning away all 18 shots he faced to post his NHL playoff record 23rd shut-out. Game Four wasn't much better, as the Wild lost yet again, 3-1. Joe Sakic scored a pair of goals for Colorado, while Gaborik tallied the lone goal for Minnesota in the loss.

With a commanding 3-1 series advantage, the Avs were now set to close out the Wild back home at the Pepsi Center in the Mile High City. Facing elimination, the Wild went with Manny Fernandez in net to shake things up. It worked. The team jumped out to 3-0 second period lead on goals by Willie Mitchell, Filip Kuba and Pascal Dupuis, and held on for a 3-2 victory to force a Game Six back in Minnesota. There, the Wild battled the Avs to a 2-2 tie on goals by Gaborik and Richard Park, to force overtime. Park would be the hero in this one when he notched the game-winning goal at 4:22 of the extra session. What ensued next was utter pandemonium in the X as the fans erupted in celebration.

Game Seven would be back in Denver and there, Minnesota would make even more history. The two teams battled to yet another 2-2 tie in regulation, forcing sudden death overtime. Peter Forsberg had put the Avs up 1-0 in the second period, only to see Dupuis answer on a power-play goal to even it up. Colorado went up 2-1 at 13:15 of the third on Sakik's series-leading sixth goal, but then saw the momentum swing the other away when Gaborik scored the equalizer just two minutes later. From there, the two teams went back and forth into the extra session. Finally, at the 3:25 mark of overtime, Andrew Brunette skated in and beat Patrick Roy on a fabulous deke in front of the net to score the biggest goal in franchise history. The stunned Colorado players couldn't believe their eyes,

while the Cinderella Wild piled onto Manny Fernandez out at center ice in pure ecstasy. Minnesota had become just the eighth NHL team in history to come back from a 3-1 deficit to win a series.

Next up for the Wild were the Vancouver Canucks in the Western Conference Semifinals. The team opened the series on the road at GM Place and wound up losing a heart-breaker in Game One, 4-3, in overtime. Wes Walz scored twice in the loss, while Minnesota native Trent Klatt netted the game-winner in OT for the Canucks. The team rallied to take Game Two, however, 3-2, behind goals from Gaborik, Zholtok and Walz. Games Three and Four were back in Minnesota and both proved to be heart-breakers for the Wild faithful. Game Three saw Vancouver score three power-play goals to win 3-2, while Game Four saw the Wild lose by the same score in overtime. Gaborik scored both Minnesota goals in regulation, while Canucks forward Brent Sopel slipped the game-winner past Fernandez for Vancouver at the 15:52 mark of the extra session to give his team the win.

Down three games to one, the Wild were about to make even more history as the series headed back to the west coast. There, with Dwayne Roloson now in net, Minnesota staved off elimination thanks to five second period goals by Cliff Ronning, Marian Gaborik, Jason Marshall, Andrew Brunette and Wes Walz, to win the game, 7-2. Game Six was back at the X and Minnesota won convincingly, 5-1. Rollie played solid between the pipes, while the Wild got a pair of goals from Andrew Brunette, and one each from Lubomir Sekeras, Darby Hendrickson and Antti Laaksonen to force a Game Seven back north of the border.

There, Minnesota battled back from a 2-0 second period deficit on goals from Pascal Dupuis — a magical shot which he whacked out of mid-air and into the net, and Wes Walz, to even it up at 2-2 midway through the third period. Then, with just under six minutes to play, Darby Hendrickson beat netminder Dan Cloutier on a slap-shot for the game-winning goal to give the Wild its first-ever trip to the Western Conference Finals. Dupuis added an insurance goal late to ice it as the team went on to win the game by the final score of 4-2, silencing the sell-out crowd at GM Place. With the win, the Wild became the first team in NHL history to come back from a 3-1 deficit twice in the same post-season, and also became only the second club ever to win two Game Sevens on the road in the same playoff year.

With their playoff beards in full bloom, the Wild then faced the Mighty Ducks of Anaheim in the 2003 Western Conference Finals. Game One, which was played at the Xcel Center, was brutal. The team got shut-out, 1-0, thanks to the brilliant netminding of Ducks goalie J.S. Giguere, who turned away all 39 shots he faced in goal. Game Two was even worse as Giguere simply dominated, shutting out the Wild yet again, this time by the final of 2-0. Incredibly, he did it for a third straight time in Game Three out in Anaheim at Arrowhead Pond, winning this one, 4-0. The Wild players were devastated. The NHL hadn't seen goaltending like this in decades. He was the hottest player in hockey and there was nothing Minnesota could do about it.

They did manage to get a puck past him in Game Four, but it was too little too late as the Ducks went on to win the game, 2-1, on a pair of goals from Adam Oates to sweep the series. The magical ride was over. Andrew Brunette netted the Wild's lone goal of the series, while Manny Fernandez stopped 26 of 28 shots that came his way. Giguere, who posted a 4-0 mark in the series, turned aside 122 of 123 shots faced and recorded a 212:43 shut-out streak. The numbers were simply incredible.

It was a tough loss, but in no way did it overshadow the amazing season that the team had put together. They would finish the year with a 42-29-10-1 overall mark, good for a franchise record 95 points. In addition, Jacques Lemaire was named NHL Coach of the Year, becoming just the fifth coach in league history to win Jack Adams Award twice. The young franchise had taken a giant leap that season and truly took the hockey world by storm. To make it to the final four in such a short amount of time was unheard of, making the accomplishment even that much more special for Minnesota sports fans.

Gabby

Marian Gaborik was born on February 14, 1982 in Trencin, Slovakia. Gaborik grew up loving hockey and played in the Slovak major league as a teenager. At just 19, the speedy winger made the leap to the NHL where he was selected as the third overall pick of the 2000 NHL Entry Draft by the expansion Wild. As a rookie, Gaborik wasted little time in making a name for himself, tallying 18 goals and 18 assists for 36 points. He made a giant leap in his sophomore campaign, notching a whopping 67 points en route to leading the team to its first ever playoff appearance. Gabby went through a rough patch in 2003 and 2004, getting bogged down with injuries and contract issues that limited his ice time. He played overseas in Slovakia during the 2004 NHL lock-out season, and then struggled through the 2005-06 season with a nagging groin injury that limited him to just 65 games. He did manage, however, to play on the Slovakian Olympic team that year. The groin injury would rear its ugly head again in 2006, putting him on the shelf for nearly two and a half months.

One of the highlights of Gaborik's career came on December 20, 2007, when he scored six points against the New York Rangers with five goals and an assist. In all, he would tally 83 points that year and lead the team back to the post-season for the second straight season. Over his illustrious seven-year NHL career, Gaborik has tallied 206 goals and 208 assists for 414 career points in 485 games. His rare combination of speed, strength and vision make him one of the game's brightest stars. As one of the game's elite playmakers, Gaborik is widely regarded as one of the most electrifying players in hockey. The two-time NHL All Star is also considered to be one of the fastest players in the history of the game as well.

On the Fans:

"The fans here in Minnesota, they are the best. I can't thank them enough for all of their support. The Wild have had a sold out building since day one and that has always meant a lot to me. Our fans have been with us through the good times as well as through the bad times, and they are extremely loyal to their team. When I see them out there when I come out onto the ice, it just makes me want to work as hard as I can. The Xcel Center is a big home-ice advantage for us. The fans are so loud in there and so supportive of us. They are very smart too. They really understand what is going on and get behind us at just the right times to give us the lift that we sometimes need. Overall, our fans are unbelievable and their support for us is huge. They have shown me so much support over the years and I just can't tell them enough how much I appreciate that."

What Does it Mean To Be a Member of the Wild?

"Being the team's No. 1 overall pick back in 2000 has meant a lot to me. The organization has been very loyal and committed to me over the years and has shown me a lot of respect. The Wild have been the only team that I have ever played for in the NHL and I feel very fortu-

nate to be a part of such a first class organization. It is crazy to think that I have been on the team longer than anybody else, since the very beginning. I have seen a lot of teammates come and go over the years. Playing for Jacques (Lemaire) has been great too. He has been my only coach in the NHL and I have a lot of respect for him. He understands the game so well and is very respected by the players. He has won a lot of Stanley Cups, so he has a lot of credibility with us. His coaching style is unique and he is very demanding, but that is why he is so successful. Without him this team would not be where it is right now, that is for sure. It is only a matter of time before he finally wins a Stanley Cup here in Minnesota. He is a tremendous teacher."

On Living in Minnesota:

"Overall, I just really enjoy working and living in Minnesota. I have been here for eight years now, so I guess I am a Minnesotan too. I love living here, it is a beautiful place. I live in downtown Minneapolis and have a lot of fun here. The people are very nice and friendly to me, which I really appreciate. Maybe if it wasn't quite as cold in the winter, that would be my only wish. Other than that, it is great. I have also really gotten a taste for just how much hockey is a part of the culture here. I will never forget the first time I saw the high school tournament and how they were selling out games at the Xcel Center. That kind of stuff doesn't happen back in Slovakia, so that is pretty neat. All of it, from the youth levels to girls hockey, it is all fantastic. I love it. What a fantastic place Minnesota is for hockey, at all levels. I am just happy to be a small part of it. It truly is the state of hockey."

Wild Tombstone:

"You know, when it is all said and done for me, I would just like to be remembered as a hard working player who did his best to help his team win. I hope that people will think of me as someone who was exciting to watch and who was a good teammate. It has been a great experience to be here in Minnesota and I am grateful for the opportunity. I don't take anything for granted. Most of all I want to be remembered as a winner. My hope is that I can one day win a Stanley Cup for the fans of Minnesota. That would be a real dream come true."

2003 RUNNER-UP: PAUL MARTIN

The hockey Gophers become the first team in more than 30 years to win back-to-back NCAA national championships. Don Lucia's squad finished with a 28-8-9 overall record in 2003, winning the WCHA Playoff title before advancing on to the Frozen Four in Albany, NY. There, after beating Mercyhurst and Ferris State in the playoffs, the Gophers topped Michigan, 3-2, in overtime, on freshman sensation Thomas Vanek's game-winner. Minnesota then went on to crush New Hampshire in the Finals, 5-1, scoring four unanswered goals in the third period. Leading the way was All-American defenseman *PAUL MARTIN*, who scored 39 points that season and 97 overall in Gold Country before going on to play in the NHL with the New Jersey Devils.

HONORABLE MENTION: JENNY POTTER

The University of Minnesota-Duluth Lady Bulldogs (playing on their home ice at the DECC) edge Harvard in double overtime, 4-3, behind Nora Tallus' thrilling game-winner, to win their third straight NCAA national championship. (UMD beat Brown in 2002.) Leading the way was two-time All-American *JENNY POTTER*, a four-time Kazmaier Award (nation's top player) finalist who is UMD's all-time leading scorer with 265 career points. Potter is also a three-time Olympian, having won gold in 1998, silver in 2002 and bronze in 2006.

HONORABLE MENTION: LAWRENCE MARONEY

The 10-3 Gophers defeat the Oregon Ducks in the Sun Bowl, 31-30, in El Paso, TX, behind running back *LAWRENCE MARONEY'S* 131 yards and a touchdown. Maroney, who ran for over 4,500 all-purpose yards and 30+ TDs at the U, would go on to be selected in the first round of the NFL Draft by New England.

Fresh off of their epic Sweet-16 run in 2003, the Lady Gophers made history in 2004, going 25-9 under head coach Pam Borton and advancing all the way to the NCAA Final Four. Led by senior All-American guard Lindsay Whalen, the team started out with an amazing 15-0 record. Minnesota then dropped three straight in January to Purdue, Penn State and Michigan State, before winning five of its next seven games. They ultimately finished at 9-7 (6th) in the Big Ten, and were especially tough at the Barn, going 13-2 at home. Record crowds of more than 14,000 rabid U of M fans were now showing up regularly at the Barn to watch their beloved Gophers. It was unlike anything Minnesota sports fans had ever seen. They just knew that they were on the verge of something special.

With that, the seventh-seeded Gophers got an invitation to the NCAA's Big Dance and opened at home in the first round against UCLA. There, Whalen showed why she was regarded as one of the top guards in the nation, scoring 31 points and leading the Maroon and Gold to an impressive 92-81 victory over the Bruins. What made the feat even more impressive was the fact that she had just returned to action from missing the previous five weeks of the season with a broken hand. Center Janel McCarville was dominant in the low post as well, scoring 19 points and hauling in 17 rebounds. In addition, Shannon Schonrock added 15 points while Kadidja Andersson chipped in with 14 of her own.

Next up was Kansas State, which Minnesota easily defeated, 80-61, to advance on to the Sweet-16. Whalen and McCarville each had 15 points apiece in this one, while Bolden added 14 for good measure. From there, the Gophers squared off against Boston College at the NCAA Tournament Mideast Region Semifinal in Norfolk, Va. Janel McCarville, or "Shaq" as she was affectionately called, dominated in this one, garnering her seventh consecutive double-double of the season with 25 points and 15 rebounds. Up by two at half-time, Whalen paced Minnesota with 13 second half points and 10 assists as the team cruised to a 76-63 victory. With the big win, the Gophers advanced on to the Elite Eight for the first time in program history. Standing in their way, however, was No. 1-ranked Duke. Minnesota came out of the gates ready to go in this one and got 27 points from Whalen and 20 points and 18 rebounds from McCarville to upset the top-seeded Blue Devils, 82-75. After several lead changes early in the game, Whalen's three-pointer with 13:53 left in the half gave the Gophers the lead for good. For her effort, Whalen would be named as the NCAA Mideast Region MVP. McCarville got into foul trouble early and had to take a seat, but her teammates stepped it up and held on for the big win.

Coach Pam Borton's Cinderella Gophers now headed to New Orleans to do battle with perennial NCAA powerhouse Connecticut in the NCAA Final Four. Hordes of Gopher fans made the trek to the "Big Easy" to support their gals and to be a witness to history. Playing in the second game of the day, the night game, all eyes were on Minnesota. U-Conn, the defending national champions, showed no mercy from the opening tap, however, jumping out to an 11-point lead in the first half. With their nerves settled, Minnesota's defense came around in the final minutes of the first half as they were able to cut the deficit to 37-29. The Huskies executed their game plan to perfection, which involved shutting down Janel McCarville. McCarville scored 10 points in the opening frame, but managed only

three rebounds. With the steady chant of "Believe," from their loyal fans, the Gophers played some inspired ball in the second half. Led by Bolden's three-pointer and Whalen's lay-up, Minnesota quickly cut the lead to just four points. The Huskies answered right back though, with a six-point surge that extended the lead back to 11. Back and forth it went, with the Gophers rattling off nine unanswered points, seven of them by McCarville alone, to make it 46-44 with just over 12 minutes on the clock.

Connecticut's All-American guard Diana Taurasi answered by drilling a big three pointer that sparked a nine point lead. Down but not out, the Gophers rallied behind Jamie Broback's big three pointer with under eight minutes to go. Kelly Roysland then drove in for a tough lay-up with just under six minutes to go and just like that, the Gophers were within three at 58-55. With the momentum clearly on their side, Minnesota got key steals on the next three U-Conn possessions, but sadly could not convert on them. They had decent shots in all three tries, but could not get a lucky bounce to save their lives. With just over two minutes to go, Whalen drove through the lane for a tough lay-up, but was visibly shaken when no foul was called. Connecticut weathered the Gopher storm and stood strong for the last two minutes of the game, never relinquishing their five point lead. They added four straight free-throws and shut down the Gophers down the stretch, holding on for a 67-58 victory. It was a sad ending to an otherwise brilliant season that caught the imagination of the entire Gopher Nation. When it was all said and done, McCarville led the Gophers with 18 points and seven rebounds, while Whalen added 11 points, seven assists and six rebounds in what would prove to be her final game ever as a Gopher.

The Pride of Hutch

The oldest of five children, Lindsay Whalen was born on May 9, 1982, in Hutchinson, Minn. At Hutchinson High School Whalen starred in basketball, tennis and track — earning All-Missota honors in each sport. The hardcourt was her passion, however, and it was there that the four-time all-conference and four-time all-state (honorable mention) selection led her Tigers to three consecutive conference championships. From there, Whalen went on to fulfill her childhood dream of playing for the University of Minnesota. In fact, she would become the first three time All-American and four time team MVP in Gopher history. The speedy guard wasted little time in making a name for herself in Gold Country, averaging 17 points per game as a freshman and instantly becoming a huge fan favorite. The 2002 Big Ten Player of the Year would go on to earn All-Big Ten honors in 2002 and 2003, followed by academic and athletic All-American honors as well.

When it was all said and done, Whalen had rewritten the record books on campus, ending up as the school's all-time leading scorer (male or female), with 2,285 career points — good for 20.3 points per game and ranking fifth all-time in the Big Ten Conference. She scored in double figures in 103 of 108 games in her college career, including 20 or more points 44 times. Among her many honors and accolades, in 2004 Whalen was the first woman to be named as the Minneapolis Star Tribune's Sportsperson of the Year, beating out Twins' Cy Young Award winner Johan Santana and NBA MVP Kevin Garnett. She was even the first athlete in U of M history to have her own bobble-head doll. Further, on January 3, 2005, her No. 13 jersey was retired by the University on what was officially declared as "Lindsay Whalen Day" in Minnesota. Whalen will forever be remembered as a savior who helped transform the women's basketball program from obscurity to national prominence. Her impact was remarkable and her legacy will always be that of a hometown champion.

Whalen graduated from the University of Minnesota in 2004 with a degree in sports management and then went on to play professionally in the WNBA. She was selected the first round of the 2004 WNBA Draft (4th overall) by the Connecticut Sun. In so doing, she had become the highest drafted WNBA player ever from the Big Ten Conference. (Her teammate Janel McCarville would surpass her the following year when she was selected No. 1 overall by the Charlotte

Sting.) Legions of Minnesota basketball fans were hoping that some how, some way, the Minnesota Lynx could find a way to draft the hometown hero. They tied, making an unsuccessful pre-draft trade with the Seattle Storm to acquire the 6th pick in the draft, but Connecticut swooped in and picked Whalen before Minnesota had a chance. Connecticut was quite familiar with her, after all, having just seen her a few months earlier in the NCAA Final Four against the U-Conn Lady Huskies. Lindsay quickly won over the Connecticut fans with her energy, attitude and talent. She would lead the Sun to the WNBA Finals in her first and second seasons in the league, even playing injured throughout the team's 2005 playoff run. She worked hard and evolved into an elite point guard, even earning All-Star accolades along the way. In July of 2008, during a game against Houston, Whalen dished to Barbara Turner for a three-pointer. In so doing, she became the team's all-time assists leader, with 738.

Lindsay continues to play for the Sun as of 2008, while also playing for an elite team in Prague, Czech Republic, during the off-season. She and her husband, former Gopher golfer Ben Greve, who were married in 2007, live in Connecticut and Minnesota.

What Does it Mean For You To Be a Gopher?

"It meant the world to me. Growing up I dreamed of playing for the Gophers. So, when it finally happened, it was a real dream come true for me. To get recruited and earn a scholarship to play there was so cool. I will never forget the day I found out that I had been accepted and that it was official. It was amazing. The entire experience was just so wonderful. Williams Arena is such a special place. I love the Gophers and will always wear the Maroon and Gold proudly."

On That Magical 2004 Season:

"What an incredible season that was. I remember it like it was yesterday. From the pre-game talks to watching film to team meals, it was so much fun. For me personally though, it was really an emotional roller coaster. I had broken my hand pretty badly that season and was forced to watch a lot of the action from the bench. That was tough. I wasn't even sure I was going to be able to play again that season. When I finally did come back though, it was like I was possessed. I couldn't wait to get back out on the court. It was a big relief to finally get back out there and I think I was able to kind of get the momentum going for us a little bit. It was a big boost for everyone. We just took off from there. We finished out the season strong and then got our invitation to play in the NCAA Tournament. I remember how excited everyone was when we got the news. We just had a really fun team that year. I would

have to say that it was by far my favorite season with the Gophers. All of us girls got along well and we genuinely enjoyed playing with each other. Our team chemistry was amazing. I was blessed to be on a team with such great people. We worked hard and had a common goal, which was probably why we had so much success. We just came together and bought into what our coaches wanted us to do. Everyone stepped up that year and it was magical. I would have loved to have won the national title, but it was a wonderful experience getting to the Final Four and being able to represent my school and my community in such a positive way. We knew that Connecticut was going to be tough, and they proved to be everything we thought that they would be."

"You know, we had just gone to the Sweet-16 the year before, but making it to the Final Four was big-time. I remember losing to Texas in the 2003 tournament and thinking about how badly I wanted to get even further the following season. I don't think any of us imagined that we would make it as far as we did though. It was almost surreal as I look back on it. I am extremely proud of our accomplishments that season, I have so many great memories. It was just an amazing experience, I wouldn't trade it for the world. I hope that what we did will help the program to grow and prosper in the coming years, that is the most important thing. We had always had a good program in Minnesota, but that team really put us on the map as one of the elite teams in the country. Women's basketball fans from around the country stood up and took notice that year that there were other good programs outside of Connecticut and Tennessee. I just hope we can continue to recruit strong, positive young women from throughout Minnesota and beyond. That is what this is all about. We have to all do our part to keep this thing going, bigger and better, year in and year out."

On the Minnesota Fans:

"First and foremost, just thanks for all your support. Our fans are awesome. They were there for us no matter what and we really appreciated that. Hopefully our run to the tournament in 2004 not only entertained our current fans, but also created a whole bunch of new ones as well. We all felt a sense of responsibility to help grow the game and to get more and more young girls playing basketball, so hopefully we accomplished that in doing what we did."

Gopher Tombstone:

"I just want to be remembered as someone who was a good teammate, who worked hard, was reliable and could always be counted on to do her best for her team."

2004 RUNNER-UP: FLIP SAUNDERS

Led by league MVP Kevin Garnett, the 58-24 Timberwolves beat Denver and Sacramento to advance on to the NBA's Western Conference Finals. There, they wound up losing to the Los Angeles Lakers, four games to two, to end the season. Steering the ship for the T-Wolves was coach *FLIP SAUNDERS*, a former Gopher guard who guided the team for 10 seasons, from 1995-2005. Saunders later took over as the head coach in Detroit and has a career record of 587-396.

HONORABLE MENTION: LAURA HALLDORSON

The Lady Gophers win their first ever NCAA women's hockey national championship. Led by coach *LAURA HALLDORSON*, the U of M dominated in 2003-04, winning their third WCHA title with an overall record of 30-2-2. Behind All-Americans Krissy Wendell and Natalie Darwitz, Minnesota went on to beat Dartmouth in the Frozen Four semifinals, 5-1, followed by Harvard, 6-2, in the Finals. Halldorson coached the Gophers for 11 seasons before retiring in 2007 with a career record of 278-67-22.

HONORABLE MENTION: MARION BARBER III

The 2004 football Gophers finish with a 7-5 record and go on to beat Alabama, 20-16, to win the Music City Bowl in Nashville, Tenn. Leading the way is running back *MARION BARBER III*, who went on to get selected in the first round of the NFL draft by Dallas. Barber, whose father also played for the Gophers, racked up over 4,500 all-purpose yards and 30+ TDs in Gold Country. He is currently an NFL Pro Bowler.

For the second straight year in a row, coach Laura Halldorson's Lady Gophers beat Harvard University in the Frozen Four to win the NCAA National Championship. Minnesota's quest to defended its crown started at the WCHA Championships at Ridder Arena, where Krissy Wendell notched the overtime game-winner over Wisconsin to lay claim to the conference crown. From there, the Gophers hosted an NCAA Regional game against Providence College. Down 1-0 early, the Gophers rallied with six unanswered goals to beat the Friars, 6-1, to advance on to the Frozen Four in Durham, N.H. Bobbi Ross and Kelly Stephens both scored a pair of goals in that one, while Becky Wacker and Erica McKenzie each tallied one apiece.

There, Minnesota went on to score five goals in the first period and cruised past Dartmouth in the opening semifinal round of the Frozen Four, 7-1. Natalie Darwitz set a record by scoring just 13 seconds into the game and the Gophers never looked back in this one. Darwitz scored again less than two minutes later and Wendell got into the act shortly after that. Wall and Stephens also scored in that first frame, while Wendell added her second goal of the game in the third, followed by an empty netter by Janelle Philipczyk with about a minute to go to seal the deal. With that, the Gophers found themselves back in the NCAA Finals against Harvard. They had beaten the Crimsen to win the title the year before, 6-2, and they knew that the Ivy Leaguers were going to be gunning for them. It was going to be a rematch of epic proportions between college hockey's two biggest heavyweights.

This one was all about Natalie Darwitz, who figured in all four Gopher goals and wound up ending the season with an NCAA-record 114 points. The game started out slow, however, for the Maroon and Gold. In fact, the Gophers did not get a shot on goal until nearly six minutes had passed. They got on the board first though, when Wendell put back Darwitz's rebound out front to make it 1-0 late in the first period. The Crimson quickly tied it less than a minute into the second period, only to see Lyndsay Wall's slap-shot put the Gophers back up 2-1 about seven minutes later. Harvard tied it up again at 10:33 on a power-play goal, but Ashley Albrecht put Minnesota back on top yet again about eight minutes after that on a slap-shot of her own that beat Harvard goalie Ali Boe. Harvard would tie it up for the third and last time midway through the third period on yet another power-play goal. In fact, it was Wendell, of all people, who was called for a checking penalty with 7:32 remaining in the third period, which allowed Harvard defender Caitlin Cahow to go five-hole on Gopher goalie Jody Horak just over a minute later. With the game tied at three apiece the game seemed destined for overtime. However, with just over a minute to go in the game, Darwitz took over. Kelly Stephens came in on Boe and fired a shot, only to have Darwitz pound home the rebound out front. The goal, which proved to be the game-winner, made it 4-3 at the

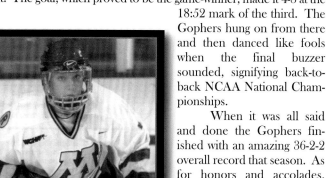

18:52 mark of the third. The Gophers hung on from there and then danced like fools when the final buzzer sounded, signifying back-to-back NCAA National Championships.

When it was all said and done the Gophers finished with an amazing 36-2-2 overall record that season. As for honors and accolades, once again it all started and stopped with Krissy Wendell and Natalie Darwitz, who had proven themselves to be the best of the very best. While both were one of the three finalists for the prestigious Patty Kazmaier Award, emblematic of the nation's top collegiate

player, it was Wendell who actually wound up finally bringing home the hardware. No matter. They were both clearly the best Division I women's hockey players in the country. As for the numbers: Darwitz wound up with 42 goals and 72 assists for an NCAA record 114 points, while Wendell tallied 43 goals and 61 assists for 104 of her own. Meanwhile, Darwitz, Wendell and Lyndsay Wall were each named as First Team All-Americans, while Goalie Jody Horak earned second team honors. The trio were also named to the All-WCHA first team, while Horak and Kelly Stephens earned second team honors. Stephens, who tallied an impressive 76 points of her own, was understandably over-shadowed by her two linemates. No worries, it will go down as the greatest line in the history of women's college hockey.

Krissy Wendell

Krissy Wendell grew up in Brooklyn Park, as, well, just one of the guys. That's right, Krissy was never afraid to compete against the top athletes, even if that meant playing alongside the boys. In fact, she attributes much of her success in athletics to the fact that the guys accepted her and let her play with them. Not only did she succeed on her youth boys hockey teams, she also starred with the fellas out on diamond as well. Back in 1994 she even played catcher on the boy's baseball team that made it all the way to the Little League World Series — becoming just the fifth girl in America ever to do so. Krissy went on to star at Park Center High School, where, as a junior, she became the first high school player (boy or girl) in the nation to score 100 goals in a season, when she tallied 109. She posted 110 her senior year just for good measure. Oh, and by the way, she accomplished all of that as a defenseman! Incredible. In all, she tallied an insane 335 points in just 62 games, en route to leading her Park Center Pirates to the 2000 Girls High School State Championship. For her efforts, she was named as the recipient of the coveted Ms. Hockey award that same year. Hockey wasn't her only gig either. Krissy was also a two-time all-state catcher on her school's softball team, batting .500 as the team's clean-up hitter.

Krissy then went on to play for Team USA as a member of the 2002 U.S. Women's Olympic team, where she won a silver medal in Salt Lake City, Utah. From there, the most highly recruited freshmen, maybe in women's college hockey history, opted to stay put and attend the University of Minnesota. As a Gopher, Krissy simply dominated the college hockey landscape. Alongside her partner in crime, Natalie Darwitz, she lit up goaltenders from Bemidji to Boston, en route to leading her squad to a pair of back-to-back national championships in 2004 and 2005.

When it was all said and done, the two-time first-team All-American had rewritten the record books during her illustrious career in Gold Country. Despite playing only three seasons, she finished second in career scoring with 237 points; second in career goals with 106; second in career assists with 131; third in career plus/minus with +156; and just to show that she was no sissy... she finished third in career penalty minutes with 153. Equally as impressive, Krissy graduated in just three years with a degree in Communications. The six-time U.S. Women's National Team member won a silver medal at the 2002 Winter Games in Salt Lake City and then served as the team captain at the 2006 Winter Games in Turin, Italy, where the U.S. defeated Finland for the bronze medal.

As for the future, she had her first child in 2008 with husband Johnny Pohl, a former Gopher hockey star who played in the NHL with the Toronto Maple Leafs in 2008, and has every intention of representing Team USA at her third Winter Games — this time in 2010 in Vancouver. She will undoubtedly give new meaning to the term "hockey mom" when she hits the ice for Team USA.

What Does it Mean For You To Be a Gopher?

"Being a Gopher meant everything to me. It was a real dream come true for me and something I had looked forward to ever since I was a little kid. Just to have that opportunity is something that I will always be very grateful for. My big brother, Erik, was a Gopher from 1999-

2002 and I saw what a great experience he had there. I will never forget seeing him with his jersey on with the name 'WENDELL' on the back. It looked so cool and I knew that someday I wanted one of my own. So, for me to follow in his footsteps and keep it all going was just awesome. We all grew up watching the team and then to finally put on that Maroon and Gold jersey was truly an amazing feeling."

On Winning the Two National Championships?

"Everything about my experience with the Gophers was tremendous, especially winning the two national championships. They were so awesome. What else can I say? To be able to share those memories with 20 of your closest friends, your sisters, is something you will never forget. The entire experience of being at the University of Minnesota was wonderful, but to win the national championships — that was just icing on the cake. We worked so hard to achieve them and when they became a reality it was just indescribable. The first title was really exciting because we had gone through so much that year. We had a bunch of highs and a bunch of lows, but came together in the end when it all mattered. When we won it and got to throw our gloves in the air and pile on top of each other out on the ice, that was just the most amazing feeling in the world. Then, to win it again, what a thrill."

Gopher Tombstone:

"When it's all said and done, I would hope to be remembered as a winner; as a competitor; and somebody who worked hard both on and off the ice. That is what it is all about."

Natalie Darwitz

In a word, Natalie Darwitz is a phenom. As a 6th grader in Eagan she was voted as the captain of the boys peewee A team, where she led the squad in scoring. The next year she was asked to try out for the new varsity girls team. How would she handle the transition from playing with 12 year-olds to high school seniors? By most accounts she did pretty well, scoring a mere 90 goals and 32 assists for 122 points, en route to leading her Eagan Wildcats to the state title game. From there, Natalie, who also starred on the softball diamond, simply dominated girls hockey in Minnesota, seemingly scoring at will. When it was all said and done she had netted 312 goals and 175 assists for an incredible 487 points in just 102 career games. Amazing. Then, in 1999, at the age of just 15, Natalie was invited to try out for, and made, the U.S. Women's National Team. Natalie spent her junior and senior seasons of high school playing for Team USA. Then, after playing on the U.S. National team, she made the 2002 U.S. Women's Olympic team, where she won a silver medal in Salt Lake City.

Darwitz next got to fulfill a childhood dream when she accepted a scholarship to play at the University of Minnesota. As a Gopher, she simply dominated. By the time the smoke had cleared, the two-time first-team All-American had rewritten the record books during her illustrious tenure in Gold Country. Despite playing only 99 games in three seasons, the All-WCHA Academic selection finished first in career scoring with 246 points; first in career assists with 144; and third in career goals with 102. The six-time U.S. Women's National Team member represented the United States at the 2002 and

2006 Winter Games in Salt Lake City and Turin, Italy, where she won silver and bronze medals for Team USA. As for the future? In 2008 she was hired to serve as an assistant coach for the Gopher women's hockey team. However, Darwitz is expected to take a leave of absence in 2010 to play on her third Olympic team at the Winter Games in Vancouver.

What Did it Mean For You To Be a Gopher?

"Being a Gopher meant so much to me. It was a huge honor. Like a lot of kids in Minnesota, I grew up watching the Gophers every Friday and Saturday night on TV. Watching guys like Mike Crowley and Casey Hankinson just made me want to play there so badly. I mean at that point in my life I had been playing on boys teams and figured that since there was no Gopher women's team, that I could become the first girl ever to play with the boys. It was a dream of mine that seemed so real at the time. Then, when they got the women's program, it was so amazing to be a part of that. I had dreamed of wearing that big 'M' on my chest and when it finally happened it was almost indescribable. I am so lucky and proud to have been given the opportunity to play there and for that I will forever be grateful. The fans have treated me so warmly over the years and I couldn't even begin to thank them for what they have done for me."

On Winning the Two National Championships?

"Winning the two national championships were among the greatest experiences of my life. To be a part of that, twice, is something I will never forget. Winning that first one was my first championship at any level of hockey for me, so to throw off my gloves and pile on the goalie after that final buzzer meant so much. That was such a big highlight for me in my career. We had such great teams those two years. I was just fortunate to play alongside some great players from very diverse backgrounds, and we all came together under a solid coaching staff. All of the players genuinely liked each other too. No, we weren't all best friends, but we all got along and we all respected each other. We played for each other though and that is why we had so much success."

Gopher Tombstone:

"You know, hopefully my accomplishments, such as playing in the Olympics and helping my teams win a pair of national championships will go a long way in growing the women's tradition at the U of M into what the men's tradition has become over the past 100 years. If I had a small part in that success, then that would truly be an amazing legacy."

2005 RUNNER-UP: VINCENT GRIER

The basketball Gophers finish with a 21-11 record and make it back to the NCAA Tournament, only to lose to Iowa State in the first round, 64-53, in Charlotte, NC. The team came on strong at the end of the season by beating Ohio State, Iowa, Purdue and Penn State, followed by Indiana in the Big 10 Tournament to secure their spot in the Big Dance. Leading the way for Minnesota against Iowa State was forward **VINCENT GRIER**, who scored 14 points and hauled in nine rebounds in the loss. Grier averaged 17.9 points, 5.6 rebounds and 2.0 steals per game that season, good for All-Big 10 honors. After leading the team in scoring for two consecutive seasons, Grier was signed by the 2006 NBA champion Miami Heat.

HONORABLE MENTION: RYAN POTULNY

The 28-15-1 hockey Gophers advance on to the NCAA Frozen Four, only to lose to rival North Dakota in the semifinals, 4-3. Minnesota got hot at the end of the season and, despite losing a pair to Colorado College in the WCHA Playoffs, earned an invitation to the Tourney. There, after beating both Maine and Cornell in overtime, the team clawed its way back to the Frozen Four. The star of the team was Grand Forks native **RYAN POTULNY**, who tallied 24 goals and 17 assists for 41 points that season. The crafty centerman would go on to sore 63 points in 2006, good for All-America honors, before signing with the NHL's Philadelphia Flyers.

Led by catcher Joe Mauer and first baseman Justin Morneau, the Minnesota Twins were the feel-good story of Major League Baseball in 2006. When it was all said and done, the Twins finished the regular season with a 96-66 record, good for first place in the American League Central Division. How they won the title though, was the real story. This one came down to the wire... literally, as the team won the division on not only the last day of the season, but on the last play.

The Twins organization was dealt a major blow that off-season when Hall of Famer Kirby Puckett passed away. With heavy hearts, the team played uninspired baseball for the first half of the season. The squad was just 25-33 by the end of the first week of June, and it was about at this time that the team decided to discard some dead weight and bring in some new blood. They needed to shake things up. So, ut were Kyle Lohse, Tony Batista and Juan Castro, and in were a handful of new faces, including Jason Bartlett and Nick Punto. Another new one was rookie pitcher Francisco Liriano, who joined the starting rotation in mid-May. Liriano was viewed by many in baseball circles as a can't miss phenom. He pitched his way into the All-Star game, but unfortunately was sidelined shortly thereafter with serious elbow problems that would ultimately force him to miss the entire 2007 season to recover from reconstructive Tommy John Surgery. He finished the season, however, with a 12-3 record and an impressive ERA of 2.16.

Shortly after their house cleaning the Twins went on to win nine of their next ten games to get back to .500. June was Twins month in the bigs, as Mauer was named as the American League's Player of the Month, Johan Santana was named Pitcher of the Month, and Francisco Liriano was named as Rookie of the Month — marking the first-ever single-team sweep of MLB's monthly awards. One of the big factors in their success that season was the fact that they dominated in interleague play. In fact, their 16-2 record was tops in the Majors. The Twins played great baseball in the second half of the season and leading the charge were Morneau and Mauer. Mauer, who would win the American League batting crown with a .347 average, became was the first catcher in history to lead the Majors in hitting. Morneau, meanwhile, finished the season with 34 home runs, 130 RBIs, and a .321 average. For his efforts, he would be named as the American League MVP.

Another reason for the team's success in the second half was what became known as the "Piranha Effect." You see, sandwiched in between Mauer, Morneau, Torii Hunter and Michael Cuddyer (who also hit 24 homers and drove in 109 runs), were a bunch of smaller, speedier players who knew how to get on base from the top and bottom of the order. Once there, they would wreak havoc and make things happen. The "Piranhas," which included the likes of Jason Tyner, Jason Bartlett, Luis Castillo and Nick Punto, hit for average, not power, which drove opposing managers nuts. In fact, they were given their nickname by Chicago White Sox manager Ozzie Guillén that season, after nearly driving him insane out on the base paths.

As for the pitching that season, it was solid — from the starters to the bullpen. Leading the charge, as usual, was Johan Santana, who won 19 games that season and laid claim to his second Cy Young award in three years. The team's rotation out of the gates included Santana, Brad Radke, Carlos Silva, Kyle Lohse and Scott Baker. Joe Nathan was also solid, posting 36 saves in his role as the team's closer.

Despite the fact that the team was 10 games out of first place at the All-Star break, they didn't give up and kept the heat on the Central-leading Tigers. They eventually secured a playoff berth in an 8-1 win over Kansas City on September 25th, but desperately wanted to win the division in order to gain a home field advantage in the post-season. With that, it all came down to the last day of the regular season. Tied for first place, Detroit led the season series tie-breaker with Minnesota, which would have meant the Twins would have to settle for the wild card if they finished deadlocked.

The Twins, who had just lost the first two games of their final three-game series of the year to the White Sox, took care of business by beating Chicago in Game Three, the last game of the year, by the final score of 5-1. Following the game, thousands of fans decided to hang around to watch the finale of the Detroit vs. Kansas City game on the Dome's scoreboard. Wanting to be a part of the action, the players all decided to hang out in the dug-out, rather than in the clubhouse, to watch as well. Nobody gave the 100-game-losers from Kansas City much of a shot of beating the league-leaders from Mo-Town, but that is exactly what they did — upsetting Detroit in a 10-inning thriller to give the Twins the division crown on the last play of the regular season. The Twins players then all ran out onto the field as their adoring fans went nuts, capsulizing a truly amazing ending to a miraculous season. The feat was even a Major League record for being the latest in a season that a team had moved into first place for the first time all season.

From there, the Twins went on to host the Oakland Athletics in the American League Divisional Series Playoffs. The Tigers, meanwhile, played New York as the wild card. Minnesota opened the series at home against the underdog A's with Johan Santana. Oakland's Barry Zito out-dueled the league's top pitcher, however, and Frank Thomas hit a pair of home runs to give the A's a shocking Game One victory. Rondell White hit a dinger for the Twins, but they were unable to get a rally going late and ended up losing the game by the final score of 3-2. Game Two had the Twins down 2-0 in the sixth, only to see them answer with back-to-back home runs from Michael Cuddyer and Justin Morneau to tie it up. Oakland's Mark Kotsay hit a hard line drive to center field that next inning, however, that hand-cuffed Torii Hunter and resulted in a two-run inside-the-park home run. They would go on to win the game, 5-2, and take a commanding 2-0 lead in the series. With the momentum on their side, the A's pounced in Game Three, crushing the Twins, 8-3, in Oakland. Morneau and Hunter each homered, but it was too little too late as the A's cruised to an easy victory.

Manager Ron Gardenhire's Twins played sound, fundamental baseball that year, complete with clutch hitting and solid defense that resulted in a Major League best team average of .287, and a second place finish in the American League with a .986 fielding percentage. Regardless, it was a tough loss to an otherwise unforgettable season that was truly one for the ages. Most importantly, however, and perhaps lost in this entire magical season was the fact that after more than a decade of lobbying, the Twins finally got the legislative approval necessary to move forward on building a new outdoor ballpark in Minneapolis that would be open for business in 2010. Hallelujah!

As for Mauer and Morneau, the "M&M Boys" (This was the nickname the New York media tabbed to Yankees' sluggers Mickey Mantle and Roger Maris back in the early 1960s.), the former roommates and best pals are hometown heroes who have certainly made Minnesota proud.

Joe Mauer *(To read Joe's bio, refer back to his foreword on Pg. 8)*

Justin Morneau
Justin Morneau was born on May 15, 1981 in New Westminster, BC, a suburb of Vancouver. His father, George, a hitting coach for several area softball and baseball teams, once played pro hockey and even attended a Minnesota North Stars training camp back in the early 1970s. Justin graduated from New Westminster Secondary School in 1999, where he starred in baseball and hockey. Turning down offers to turn pro as a goaltender in hockey, as well as several college baseball schol-

arships, Morneau was selected by the Twins in the 3rd round of the 1999 MLB amateur entry draft. The powerful first baseman would go on to spend the next six seasons playing in the minor leagues, including stints with the Canadian National team in 2001, as well as on the 2002 and 2004 All-Star Futures Games, playing for the World teams.

Morneau made his Major League debut in Minnesota on June 10, 2003, but spent most of the season with the Triple A Rochester Red Wings. Then, in 2004, the Twins dealt veteran first baseman Doug Mientkiewicz to Boston to make room for him on the roster. He appeared in 61 games for the Twins that season, hitting 19 home runs while committing just three errors. He struggled in 2005 with a variety of off-season ailments and then had to overcome a serious bean-ball incident in April. He persevered though and paced the team with 74 RBIs and 22 homers. After representing Canada in the World Baseball Classic that off-season, he had his breakout year in 2006. On August 9, Morneau became the first Twin since 1987 to hit 30 homers in a single season and finished the year hitting .321 with 34 homers and a league-leading 130 RBIs. For his effort, he was named as the American League's MVP, beating out Yankee Derek Jeter.

Morneau kept it going in 2007, earning Player of the Month honors in May en route to being named to his first All-Star Game. Morneau had his first career three home run game on July 6, against the Chicago White Sox, and finished the year with 31 dingers and 111 RBIs. That off-season he made history by signing a six year contract worth $80 million, the largest and longest deal in Twins history. He made even more history in 2008 when he edged out Ranger's slugger Josh Hamilton at the All-Star Game Home Run Derby at Yankee Stadium in New York.

What Does it Mean For You To Be a Twin?

"I love it. There is such a great baseball tradition here in Minnesota and I feel very lucky to be a small part of it. There have been two World Series titles, a handful of Hall of Famers and a whole bunch of great people who have been a part of this organization. The first thing that I thought of when I was drafted by the Twins was Kirby Puckett, who was a such an amazing player and person. There have also been a lot of great first basemen here too, like Kent Hrbek, who is someone I really looked up to growing up."

On Winning the MVP in 2006:

"That was such an amazing season that we had. What a turnaround. We were chasing, chasing, chasing the entire season. Then, when we finally caught them on the last day, it was so special. It is something I will never forget as long as I live. To win the pennant like that, in such a dramatic fashion, was just historic. Sitting in the Dome with 40,000 fans on that last day in the dug-out, watching the game — it was incredible. To see Kansas City come from behind to win, it was crazy. The crowd went nuts when they won it, it was surreal. I still get goose bumps thinking about it. What a run. We didn't finish out the post-season the way we wanted to, of course, but it was a great year nonetheless. Winning the MVP was pretty special too. For me though, it was all about the team. Sure, it is an individual award, but there was no way I could have won it without all of my teammates. I mean there was no way I

would have won the MVP had we not made the playoffs, so it was all about the team in my eyes. Look at the guys hitting around me too, with Joe (Mauer) hitting in front of me in the line-up to protect me. We both had career years that season. We just came together at the right time. It was incredible."

On the Minnesota Fans:

"We have such great fans here, we really do. They are so knowledgeable about the game and so supportive of us, no matter how we are playing. As players, we appreciate that so much. We have a great home-field advantage because of our fans and that gives us a lot of confidence when we are at home. It is a lot of fun to play in front of them too, because they appreciate everything we do. They make it fun to come to the park and that is why we try to win for them. I just hope I can repay all of their generosity by one day giving them a World Series title."

On Living in Minnesota:

"I love it here in Minnesota. If I could play here for my whole career, then that would make me very happy. Living here is great, it is not that much different from where I grew up in Vancouver. People in both places are really friendly and active, and they definitely cherish their free time, especially in the Summer. Overall, it is just a great place. Plus, I get to follow hockey, which means the world to me. When I am not rooting for my Vancouver Canucks, I am definitely a Wild fan. I am friends with a lot of the players and enjoy hanging out with those guys. I wish I could get back out on the ice and lace em' up every now and then, but they won't let me do that kind of stuff anymore. Oh well, I guess I will have to wait until I retire to get my fixx."

On the New Stadium:

"I would just like to say thank you to all of the people who worked so hard and for so long to help get it done. I am so excited to play in there when it opens in 2010, it is going to be amazing. Most importantly, it is so positive for the future of baseball in Minnesota. We were all a little unsure of our futures a few years ago, with regards to contraction, so it is nice to not have to worry about all of that stuff anymore."

Twins Tombstone:

"Hopefully I will be remembered as a World Series champion. That is the only goal I really have for myself and the only thing that matters. I want so badly to be able to help make that dream a reality for the fans here in Minnesota."

2006 RUNNER-UP: JOHAN SANTANA

The Twins finish the season with a 96-66 record and win the Central Division. Leading the way for Minnesota was All-Star pitcher **JOHAN SANTANA**, who went 19-6 that year with a 2.77 ERA. For his efforts, the Venezuelan native was named as the American League's Cy Young Award winner. It would be the second Cy Young of his young career. Santana would pitch in Minnesota for eight seasons before being traded to the New York Mets in 2008 for several players and prospects. One of the most dominating pitchers in baseball, his 101-51 career record, along with his 3.20 ERA and 1,500+ strike-outs, make him a lock for the Hall of Fame.

HONORABLE MENTION: TIM HERRON

Wayzata golfer **TIM HERRON** beats Richard Johnson in a playoff to win the Bank of America Colonial Tournament with a 12-under 268. For his efforts, Herron cracks the top 50 of the Official World Golf Rankings. "Lumpy," as he is affectionately known on the Tour, grew up in Wayzata before going on to play golf at the University of New Mexico. He played on the 1993 U.S. Walker Cup (amateur) team before turning professional later that year. His first win on the PGA Tour was the 1996 Honda Classic, followed by the Texas Open in 1997, and the Bay Hill Invitational in 1999. Herron continued to play consistently after that, but had to wait seven years before claiming his fourth PGA Tour title, the 2006 Colonial.

2007

ADRIAN PETERSON
The Viking's Draft a Rookie Phenom

The 2007 Minnesota Vikings posted an 8-8 record under second year head coach Brad Childress, improving on their 6-10 campaign of 2006. There were two keys to the team's success that season, both of which garnered No. 1 NFL rankings. The first was the team's defense, which finished ranked No. 1 against the run thanks in large part to the efforts of Pro Bowl tackles Kevin Williams and Pat Williams. Secondly was the team's running offense, which also ranked No. 1 thanks in large part to the efforts of rookie phenom Adrian Peterson, who wasted little time in becoming the face of this storied franchise.

The team kicked off its off-season festivities on April 28, when Oklahoma running back Adrian Peterson was selected by the Vikings with the seventh overall pick in the first round of the 2007 NFL Draft. The first running back selected in that year's draft, Peterson fell to the Vikes over concern of a broken collarbone he had suffered that season. He would go on to sign a five-year, $40.5 million contract a few months later — leaving fans of the purple feeling optimistic yet cautious about paying that much cash to a player with that serious of an injury.

With high hopes, Minnesota opened the season with an impressive 24-3 win over Atlanta. In addition to a pair of interception returns for touchdowns by both tackle Kevin Williams and cornerback Antoine Winfield, Peterson proved to be the real deal when he scored on a dramatic 60-yard touchdown pass from quarterback Tarvaris Jackson. The team suffered a tough 20-17 overtime loss in Week Two to Detroit, followed by a 13-10 defeat by Kansas City — despite Peterson's 11-yard touchdown run that put the team up 7-0 in the first quarter. The 1-2 squad then came home to the Dome to face the Green Bay Packers. There, with Jackson on the shelf, quarterback Kelly Holcomb was unable to rally the team to victory, as the cheese heads beat the purple, 23-16. This game was all about Pack quarterback Brett Favre, however, who threw career TD pass No. 421 to Greg Jennings in the first quarter, surpassing Dan Marino in the NFL record books for the most career touchdown passes. As for Peterson, who ran for 112 yards on the ground, he very quietly became the team's first rookie running back since Chuck Foreman to rack up 100-yard games in his first three starts. For his efforts, Peterson was named as the NFL Offensive Rookie of the Month. Minnesota would then limp into its bye week at just 1-3.

After some much-needed time off, the team came back strong in beating rival Chicago in Week Six, 34-31. Peterson blew up in this one, rushing for a pair of touchdowns and a whopping 224 yards on just 20 carries. (He also set an NFL rookie record with 361 all-purpose yards in a single game as well.) Tied late, Minnesota won it in dramatic fashion on kicker Ryan Longwell's 55-yard field goal. The team was unable to carry the momentum into Week Seven, however, as they were upended by Dallas, 24-14, at Texas Stadium, despite Peterson's 20-yard TD run. The next game didn't prove to be much better either, as the Vikes lost this time to Philly, 23-16. With veteran back-up quarterback Kelly Holcomb in for Jackson, who had suffered a thumb injury, the team rallied late but could only muster a trio of Ryan Longwell field goals down the stretch. Week Nine was all about Peterson, who set an NFL single game record (previously held by Jamal Lewis since 2003) with 296 rushing yards, to go along with three touchdowns, as they beat San Diego, 35-17. The accomplishment thrust the rookie into the national limelight after that, with seemingly everybody wanting to know just who in the heck this kid was.

From there, Minnesota was humiliated by Green Bay, 34-0, at Lambeau Field. To make matters worse, Peterson left the game after injuring his right knee. The 3-6 Vikings rallied, however, and went on a roll that saw them win five straight games. First up were the Daunte Culpepper-led Oakland Raiders, which they beat 29-22 at the Dome behind running back Chester Taylor's three touchdowns. Week 12 saw Minnesota dismantle the eventual Super Bowl champion New York Giants, 41-17, on the road at Giant's Stadium. In what most Vikings fans felt was justifiable revenge (for the 2001 NFC Championship game debacle which saw New York embarrass Minnesota, 41-0), the team came out and scored early and often. Jackson hooked up with Sidney Rice on a 60-yard TD pass to open the festivities, which was followed by a Darren Sharper interception return for a touchdown. After Taylor scored on an eight-yarder, the Vikings blew it wide open on a pair of defensive touchdowns from safety Dwight Smith (a 93 yard interception return) and linebacker Chad Greenway (a 37 yard interception return).

Peterson returned to action in Week 13 against Detroit, scoring a pair of touchdowns on 116 yards rushing. The highlight of this one, however, was rookie Aundrae Allison's record 103 yard kickoff return for a touchdown to seal the 42-10 victory. With the win, the team improved to 6-6 and suddenly found itself in the post-season mix. Kevin Williams got it started the following week in San Francisco when he returned an interception 18 yards for a touchdown in the first quarter. Jackson connected with Robert Ferguson on a 19-yard TD pass in the second, followed by Chester Taylor's thrilling 84-yard touchdown scamper in the third to seal the deal, 27-7. After being held to a career-low three yards rushing on 14 carries, Adrian Peterson redeemed himself the following week on Monday Night Football, where he rushed for 78 yards and a pair of touchdowns as the Vikings beat the Bears, 20-13. Peterson's two scores came in dramatic fashion, late in the game, to cap a thrilling rally in front of 64,000 screaming fans at the Dome.

The Vikings hosted the Washington Redskins at home the following week, knowing that if they won they would clinch a playoff berth. The Redskins jumped out to a 22-0 lead at halftime in this one and then held on to win the game, 32-21. Jackson threw one touchdown and rushed for two more to mount a rally, but it was too little too late. So, at 8-7, the purple needed to not only now win the following week in Denver to secure a post-season dance card, they also needed some help from some other teams. With that, Minnesota headed west in what would prove to be a do-or-die scenario.

There, the Vikings jumped out to a quick 3-0 lead on a Ryan Longwell 22 yd field goal, only to see the Broncos score 19 unanswered points — highlighted by a penalty in their own end zone which resulted in a safety. Jackson sparked a thrilling fourth quarter rally, however, and wound up tossing a pair of touchdowns to Bobby Wade, to go along with a pair of two-point conversion runs, to tie it up and send it to overtime. But, at 14:08 of sudden-death, Broncos kicker Jason Elam put the final nail in the coffin when he connected on a 30-yard field goal to end the game and the season for the purple. Ironically, Minnesota won the coin toss and wound up with the ball first. But, on the second play of the drive, Jackson fumbled when he was hit by Alvin McKinley at the Denver 30 yard line. Elam came straight off the bench to kick the game-winner, and just like that it was lights out for Minnesota, 22-19.

"A.P. — A.D."
Translation: "Adrian Peterson — All Day"

Adrian Peterson was born on March 21, 1985 in Palestine, Texas. The son of a college basketball player father (Idaho State University) and a track star mother (University of Houston), Adrian Peterson competed in track and field, basketball, and football at Palestine High School. The National High School Football Player of the Year, Peterson went on to star on the gridiron for the University of Oklahoma, where he rewrote the record books. As a freshman in 2004, Peterson earned

All-American honors en route to setting the NCAA freshman rushing record with 1,925 yards. For his efforts, he finished second in the Heisman Trophy voting to USC quarterback Matt Leinart. After suffering a serious ankle injury as a sophomore, Peterson broke his collar bone during his junior year – ultimately forcing him to sit out for much of the season. He returned for the Sooners' final game, however, against Boise State in the 2007 Fiesta Bowl, where he scampered for 77 yards and a touchdown. Opting to skip his senior year, Peterson declared himself eligible for the 2007 NFL Draft. He would finish his illustrious career at OSU with 4,045 rushing yards, just 74 yards shy of passing Billy Sims as the school's all-time leading rusher.

Peterson, arguably the most talented player in college football that year, was then selected by the Vikings with the seventh overall pick in the first round of the 2007 NFL Draft. When it was all said and done, Peterson finished in second place in rushing yards with 1,341 (San Diego's LaDanian Tomlinson narrowly beat him) and was named as the 2007 NFL Offensive Rookie of the Year. From there, Peterson joined seven other Vikings in Honolulu to play in the Pro Bowl. (The other Vikings included: fullback Tony Richardson, guard Steve Hutchinson, safety Darren Sharper, center Matt Birk, and defensive tackles Kevin Williams and Pat Williams.) There, he rushed for 129 yards and a pair of touchdowns, racking up the second highest rushing total in Pro Bowl history – good for MVP honors – as his NFC squad beat the AFC, 42-30.

Known for his unique upright running style, Peterson possesses that oh-so-rare combination of speed, size, strength, agility and vision. He is a playmaker, a difference-maker who loves to dish out punishment to would-be tacklers and make them pay every time they try to bring him down. He is a force to be reckoned with to be sure. A budding superstar, Peterson has become a beloved sports figure not only in Minnesota, but around the world – where fans have embraced him as possibly one of the best ever. Adrian has one daughter, Adeja, and currently resides in Eden Prairie.

On Winning the Rookie of the Year Award:
"Winning the Rookie of the Year award was pretty special. It meant a lot to me. I went through a lot of adversity leading up to the draft. All of the experts were saying this and that about me and about my broken collar bone. There was a real negative vibe going on and it was tough. That criticism drove me though and made me want to succeed even more. Fortunately, it all worked out and I was rewarded for all my hard work. I couldn't have won it without my teammates though, no way. It is an individual award, but you can't win it alone. My offensive line was amazing and they really took care of me. So many people contributed to me winning it, so I would have to thank my teammates first and foremost."

On that Magical 2007 Rookie Season:
"Just to be a part of the team meant a lot to me. My teammates embraced me and made me feel right at home from the moment I got here. The season was memorable for me in many ways, especially winning the Rookie of the Year award. But, we didn't make the playoffs and that definitely stung. We came on strong at the end. It was tough.

Our offense came together and our defense came together, we just couldn't get over that last hurdle. We have a young team and hopefully we can all take the experience that we gained and apply it to the next season. I think we all feel like we are on the verge of something very special here. I just hope we can stay healthy and play up to our potential. If that happens, then the sky is the limit for us."

On Minnesota:
"I love Minnesota, this is my new home. I am getting used to the cold weather too, it is an adjustment for sure. Being from the south, I had no idea just how cold it could actually get. That's why I try to run so fast, to stay warm up here! Really though, living here is great and everybody has made me feel very welcome. I hope to live here for many, many years to come."

On the Fans:
"I just want to tell them thank you for all of the support that they have given me. We have such great fans up here and they really get behind us out there. The Dome gets so loud when they are into it and that helps us out on the field a great deal. We feed on that excitement and it makes us want to work harder for them. It is almost like a college atmosphere in there, which makes it a lot of fun for us. I know it is a cliché, but they are like the 12th man and that really does make a difference for us. Our fans are die-hards and they have waited a long, long time for a Super Bowl championship. My mindset is all about bringing a whole bunch of Super Bowl trophies back to Minnesota and I am going to do everything in my power to make that happen. That is my ultimate goal and something that I strive for everyday."

What Does it Mean For You To Be a Viking?
"It means everything to me. I am so proud to be able to call myself a Viking. There is so much history here, from the Purple People Eaters to Randy Moss and Daunte Culpepper. Growing up in Texas as a Cowboys fan, I knew about the rivalry between Minnesota and Dallas. The Vikings organization is just so first class and they have treated me so well. I couldn't think of a better place to be. So far so good, I couldn't be happier being a Minnesota Viking."

Vikings Tombstone:
"When it is all said and done, I just want to be known as a player who tried his best and was a good teammate. Most importantly though, I hope to be remembered as a champion. That is what it is all about."

2007 RUNNER-UP: PIERRE MARC BOUCHARD

The Wild finish the season with a 48-26-8 mark, good for a franchise record 104 points. From there, the team went on to face Anaheim in the first round of the Stanley Cup Playoffs, where they ultimately lost to the Ducks, four games to one. After losing Games One, Two and Three, 2-1, 3-2 and 2-1, respectively, the Wild fought back to take Game Four back at the Xcel Center, 4-1. Winger *PIERRE-MARC BOUCHARD* got the equalizer in this one, with Marian Gaborik, Brian Rolston and Mark Parrish each tallying as well. The game nearly got out of hand in the final minutes when Anaheim's Brad May sucker-punched Wild defenseman Kim Johnsson from behind, sending him to the ice and out of the series. Tensions were high for Game Five, but the Ducks played tough defense and won it, 4-1, to take the series. One of the stars of the team was Bouchard, who tallied 57 points that season. In five seasons with the Wild, Bouchard has tallied 221 points in 354 career games.

HONORABLE MENTION: COLE KONRAD

The Gopher wrestling team wins the Big 10 and NCAA national championship, its third in seven years. Leading the charge is two-time heavyweight national champ *COLE KONRAD*, who finished his collegiate career with a 155-13 record. The Appleton, Wis., native also holds the team record for consecutive wins with 76.

2008

MARK PARRISH
The Wild Win the Northwest Division Crown

The 2008 Minnesota Wild made history in the "State of Hockey," winning their first ever Northwest Division title with a record of 44-28-10 and finishing third in the Western Conference with 98 points, behind San Jose and Detroit. One of the stars of the team was Bloomington native and hometown hero Mark Parrish, who, despite having to deal with several major injuries that season, tallied 30 points in 66 games and played a pivotal role as one of the team's captains and leaders, both on and off the ice.

The team started out on fire, going 7-0-1, and didn't lose a game until three weeks into the season. Goalie Niklas Backstrom was playing outstanding in net, having allowed a league-low 11 goals thus far. They came back to earth shortly thereafter, however, and lost five straight due in large part to the fact that the team's three stars, Backstrom, Pavol Demitra and Marian Gaborik, were all are battling various injuries. Gaborik's groin injury was the most worrisome of the bunch, but he was finally able to return to the lineup by Week Seven. Demitra, meanwhile, was on the shelf for much longer, missing 13 of 15 games. His impact was felt too, as the team went 5-9-1 without him on the ice.

Minnesota won four straight over Nashville, Phoenix, St. Louis and Vancouver in late November and were able to catapult to the top of the Northwest Division. They slumped a bit and coach Jacques Lemaire called out his skilled players for not working hard enough. The wake-up called worked, as the team went on to win eight of its next 11 games. One of the highlights of the season came on December 20, when Marian Gaborik scored five goals in a 6–3 win over the New York Rangers at the X. The squad went 7-4-1 in January, highlighted by a stretch of three straight wins over Detroit, Chicago and red-hot Phoenix. Another historic event took place about this time as well, when it was announced that Bob Naegele, the team's principal owner since the team's inception, would be selling his stake in the team to Craig Leipold. Leipold, who had previously owned the Nashville Predators, would be joined by General Partner Phillip Falcone, a Hibbing native and former high school hockey player.

The team played solid hockey throughout February, registering points in nine of 11 games, and sitting atop the Northwest Division for much of the stretch. Then, just before the trade deadline, the team pulled off a very controversial transaction in which they brought in Chris Simon, a longtime enforcer whose career has been tarnished with no less than eight suspensions, including the longest in NHL history. With tough guys Todd Fedoruk and Derek Boogaard already on the roster, it was clear that the team was toughening up for the stretch run. They knew that Anaheim had won the Stanley Cup the year before with grit and toughness, and they figured that if they were going to have to face them in the playoffs, then they had better be prepared. Meanwhile,

the player that most Wild fans were hoping for, All-Star Peter Forsberg, wound up signing with Colorado. The move to get Simon and then pass on Forsberg would be heavily scrutinized in the media.

Down the stretch the Wild continued to play up and down, as the division leader board continued to shuffle on what seemed to be a nightly basis. The team went through a tough stretch in early March, going winless in four of six shoot-outs, while surrendering their first-place Northwest lead. They bounced back though and played inspired hockey down the stretch. In fact, they only lost four games

in the entire month of March, and wound up winning four of their final five games against Edmonton, Vancouver, Colorado and Calgary. The clincher came against rival Calgary on April 3, where the Wild won its first Northwest Division title with a 3-1 victory over the Flames at Xcel Energy Center. The big win also marked the 500th regular season victory in Jacques Lemaire's illustrious coaching career. Three nights later the team finished up the regular season with a 4-3 shoot-out loss at Colorado. In so doing, the Wild had secured the Western Conference's No. 3 seed and would have the home ice advantage in the first round of 2008 Stanley Cup Playoffs. Ironically, their opponents would be those same Avalanche who had just beaten them in the season finale.

The Wild, which had made the post-season in 2007 for the second time in team history, but were eliminated by the eventual Stanley Cup Champion Anaheim Ducks in the opening round, were determined to get out of the first round and deep into the playoffs. Game One took place at the X on April 9th. There, the Avs jumped out to a 2-0 lead, despite the fact that the Wild had outshot them 20-7 after two periods. Mikko Koivu and Todd Fedoruk each scored goals 3:21 apart within the first seven minutes of the third period to tie it up, but that was as close as Colorado goalie Jose Theodore was going to allow it to get. The game went to overtime, where Ruslan Salei's point shot deflected off a skate and right to Joe Sakic, who put it past Backstrom for the game-winner.

Minnesota came back to take Game Two in dramatic fashion. Peter Forsberg's late first-period goal held up until Demitra's power-play goal early in the third made it 1-1. Koivu's fluttering slap-shot made it 2-1 late, only to see the Avs tie it up with just 43 seconds to go in regulation on Milan Hejduk's power-play goal. Both teams played tough in overtime, until Keith Carney's point shot ended it late in the extra session to give the Wild a thrilling 3-2 win.

Tied at one game apiece, the series now moved west to Denver. Former Wild winger Andrew Brunette opened the scoring in the first. Mikko Koivu's third goal of the series then tied it up at 1-1 midway through the third. Rolston put Minnesota up 2-1 on his sixth career short-handed goal, only to see Sakic tally the equalizer on a back-hander into an open net with Brunette laying on top of Backstrom. The score remained tied for the next five minutes and then into overtime, for the third straight game. The Wild dominated the extra session, but couldn't get anything past Theodore, who denied both Demitra and Gaborik on great scoring chances. They finally won it, however, when Rolston beat out an icing call that resulted in Pierre-Marc Bouchard's thrilling overtime winner.

Down two games to one, the Avs came out smoking in Game Four, winning the penalty-fest with ease, 5-1. The series then shifted back to Minnesota for Game Five, where the sell-out crowd at the X was ready for battle. The team got a boost when defenseman Nick Schultz returned to the ice less than two weeks after undergoing an emergency appendectomy. The Wild played solid in this one, but it all came down to one factor: Jose Theodore. Playoff hockey is all about hot goaltending, and just like Anaheim's J.S. Giguere had single-handedly beaten the Wild the year before, Theodore was playing like a one-man wrecking crew. The Wild would outshoot the Avalanche 40-17 in this one, getting goals from Pierre-Marc Bouchard and Brian Rolston, but still lost, 3-2, on Paul Stastny's game-winner late in the third.

Game Six was back in Colorado and unfortunately for Wild fans, it would not result in a happy ending. Down 1-0 early on Ben Guite's first-period short-handed breakaway goal, Aaron Voros, who hadn't scored since late December, tied the score 36 seconds into the second period on Marian Gaborik's first point of the series. Gabby, who scored a record 42 goals and 83 points for the Wild that season, was neutralized by the Avs defense all series long. Minnesota would take over from there, out-shooting the Avs 10-2, but Theodore was a wall and refused to surrender the go-ahead goal. Midway through the second Mikko Koivu turned over the puck in the neutral-zone, which resulted in Ryan Smyth scoring what would prove to be the eventual game-winner. Up 2-1, Theodore hung on down the stretch as the Avs eliminated the Wild, four games to two. It was a sad ending to an otherwise great season.

Fully eight years into their existence, the Wild have still sold out every single one of their home games at the Xcel Energy Center, proving that St. Paul truly is "Hockey Town USA."

The Pride of Bloomington

Mark Parrish was born on February 2, 1977 in Bloomington, and went on to star Bloomington Jefferson High School, where he led his Jaguars to back-to-back state titles in 1993 and 1994. From there, the crafty winger headed to St. Cloud State University, where he tallied 72 points in just two seasons with the Huskies before making the leap to play in the NHL. Originally drafted by the Colorado Avalanche in the third round of the 1996 NHL Entry Draft, Parrish went on to play with the Florida Panthers, New York Islanders and Los Angeles Kings before signing with the Wild in 2006. Parrish signed a five-year deal with Minnesota worth more than $13 million, but had his contract bought out after only two seasons, ultimately becoming a salary cap casualty. The speedy winger scored 35 goals and 34 assists in his two seasons in Minnesota, despite suffering several injuries that kept him on the shelf for much of that time. In his 10 seasons in the NHL, Parrish has scored 208 goals and 164 assists for 372 points in 660 career games. Known for being a clutch player who is never afraid to crash the net, Parrish also has 37 career game-winning goals as well. In addition, he is extremely philanthropic with his time and money, as evidenced by the success of his charitable foundation "21 for Kids," which gives back to numerous hockey and civic causes not only around the state of Minnesota, but around the country.

On Coming Home to Minnesota:

"For me to be able to come home and play for the Wild was really a dream come true. I felt so lucky and blessed. I grew up playing hockey on the ponds of Bloomington pretending to be Neal Broten and Dino Ciccarelli, imagining myself scoring the game-winning goal to win the Stanley Cup for the North Stars. So, for me to be able to play for my hometown team, that was really something special. I had to pinch myself every now and then, I really did. Just to be a part of Minnesota hockey is such an honor. I have such a great respect for the game and how it is played here. The traditions that we have all built up over the years are what it is all about and I am humbled to be able to say that I have played a small part in that."

On the Fans:

"To the Wild fans all I can say is thank you from the bottom of my heart. After playing in Florida, New York and L.A., to finally get the chance to come home and play in front of such unbelievable fans meant the world to me. The fans here truly get it and really understand the game at a high level. The atmosphere at the Xcel Center is incredible and the fans in there just make us want to work as hard as we can for them. I will never forget the first time I stepped onto the ice there for my first home game. I was so nervous and so excited, it was just exhilarating. I literally couldn't stop my legs from shaking, it was a feeling I cannot even describe. I don't think my skates even touched the ice on

my first shift, I was so pumped up. I remember scoring my first goal, getting my first hat trick against Chicago, and then winning Game Four of our playoff series against Anaheim in 2006. Winning that game was just intense, I don't think I have ever been in a louder arena in my entire life."

On the 2008 Season:

"The 2008 season was fantastic. We were all very proud to win our first ever title. It was a big deal for the players, it really was. It is our first banner and every time I see it hanging over the ice, I will look back and remember how sweet that was. We came up short in the end though and we were obviously very disappointed. For me, personally, it was tough at times because I had some bad injuries to deal with all year. I had two concussions and had to deal with some pretty serious injures to my back, foot and hip. I was a mess! Everybody has to deal with injuries at this level, but it seemed like I just couldn't stay healthy. I stayed positive and came back strong in the second half though. I felt good about helping the team finish the season strong too. Winning the Northwest Division was one of our main goals and fortunately we were able to achieve that."

On the Future:

"As for my future, I am optimistic that I will be able to play in this league for a very long time. My dream of one day winning a Stanley Cup is still alive and is something I will continue to work hard for, wherever I am. As for the fans here in Minnesota, I can't say thanks enough for all of your support. I appreciate it so much. You made me feel so welcome and supported me so much. I will never forget that. To be able to come home to Minnesota and play for my hometown team was truly a dream come true for me. It was surreal, truly amazing. This is a fantastic organization and I just want to thank them for the opportunity. Sadly, it didn't work out, but that is just business. Now it is just water under the bridge. My time here was absolutely awesome though and I have nothing but love for the 'State of Hockey.' My wife and I are from here and this is where we intend to live and raise our family. So, I will always be a Wild fan and root for them proudly."

Husky and Wild Tombstones:

"As for my legacy, I would hope to be remembered as a hard working player who was willing to do whatever it took to help his team win. That is what it is all about in my eyes. I am certainly not the best player out there, but I pride myself in being not only a hard worker but also a good teammate who can be counted on."

2008 RUNNER-UP: JONTE FLOWERS

Winona State wins its second NCAA Division II National championship in three years. The Warriors took the crown after defeating Augusta State University (GA), 87-76, in the championship game of the NCAA Division II Elite Eight Tournament held in Springfield, Mass. Winona, which won its first title in 2006 over Virginia Union, 73-61, narrowly lost in the final seconds to Barton College (NC) in the Finals in 2007. The star of the team during this amazing stretch was **JONTE FLOWERS**, who helped the Warriors set a Division II record for consecutive wins with 57, and were 97-3 in his last 100 games. The Madison, Wis., native teamed up with John Smith, the Player of the Year in 2008, to create a Division II basketball dynasty.

HONORABLE MENTION: KIM MARTIN

The University of Minnesota-Duluth Lady Bulldogs win their fourth NCAA national championship in eight years. The Bulldogs won the title by blanking Wisconsin, 4-0, at the 2008 Frozen Four, which was held in Duluth at the DECC. UMD, which notched a school record 34 wins that year, also won the WCHA regular season and WCHA Final Face-Off titles as well. The team was anchored by All-American goaltender **KIM MARTIN**, the Tournament's Most Outstanding Player who set a trio of single-season records that year with wins (31), saves (843) and save percentage (.943.) For her efforts, the sophomore from Stockholm, Sweden, was named as a top-three finalist for the Patty Kazmaier Award — emblematic of the nation's top player.

BRONKO NAGURSKI

(Even though the Bronk played back in the '30s and '40s, you simply can't write a book about the history of Minnesota sports without somehow including him. It's a respect thing...)

The legend of Bronko Nagurski began back in 1926, when then-Gopher Coach Clarence "Doc" Spears was on a recruiting trip up in northern Minnesota. As the story goes, one day while driving through International Falls, Spears saw a hulking young man plowing a field — without a horse. When the curious Spears stopped to ask for directions, instead of using his finger, the kid just lifted the enormous plow and pointed with it! No, it wasn't Paul Bunyan... it was Bronko Nagurski.

Bronislau Nagurski was born Nov. 3, 1908, on the Canadian side of Rainy Lake in Rainy River, Ontario. At the age of four, his family moved to International Falls, just a slap-shot away on the other side of the U.S. border. His nickname supposedly came about when his first-grade teacher, after not being able to understand his mother's thick Ukrainian accent, called the youngster "Bronko," and the name stuck.

He grew up loving all sports, but, amazingly, in his two years of prep football at International Falls High School, his sophomore and junior years, he never played on a team that won a game. In fact, he even transferred to neighboring Bemidji High School for his senior year, because he was upset when his principal canceled the team's trip to a district tournament when a couple of other players required some disciplining. There, the transfer student was ruled ineligible to play football, but he did manage to play basketball and run track. It was hardly the kind of a prep career that would have attracted college recruiters, even in those days.

Following high school, the "Bronk" headed south, to wear the Maroon and Gold at the University of Minnesota. (In reality, he met Doc Spears while he was up north fishing, and convinced him to come to the University.) Once there, Spears' greatest dilemma quickly became deciding where to play his new star. Then he finally figured it out — he would play him everywhere. And that's exactly what he did. Bronko would go on to play tackle, fullback, defensive end, offensive end, linebacker and he even passed the ball as a quarterback from time to time as well.

He was a massive man for his time, measuring six-feet-two and weighing in at 235 pounds. He had giant hands, donned a size-19 neck and could even run a 10.3 100-yard dash. He literally became the fullback no one could tackle and the tackle no runner could escape. As a sophomore, Bronko first got noticed by the national press when he forced and recovered a late-game fumble against a heavily favored Notre Dame team, which led to a game-tying Gopher touchdown. During his junior year, wearing a steel plate to protect a couple of broken vertebrae, he almost single-handedly defeated Wisconsin when, in addition to intercepting three passes and making numerous touchdown-saving tackles, he forced a fumble and ran it in for the game-winning score.

So talented was the powerful Nagurski that he would go on to earn All-America honors at three different positions. Sportswriters decided after his senior season in 1929 that he was the best fullback and tackle in the nation, making him the only player in college football history ever to be named a first-team consensus All-American at two different positions in the same season. Incredibly, he was even named as a defensive end on a few other All-America teams. Over his illustrious three year career in Gold Country, the Gophers lost a total of just four games, and none of them by more than two points.

In the fall of 1930, Bronko graduated and became *THE* "Monster of the Midway," literally, when he signed on with the NFL's Chicago Bears for the then-pricey, Depression-era sum of $5,000. The Bronk went on to reach superstar status in the Windy City, where he would lead the team to three NFL championships during his eight-year gridiron tenure.

It was also in Chicago where the bruising fullback's exploits soon took on legendary proportions. Papa Bear Halas, the team's owner, recalled a game against Washington at Wrigley Field, where Nagurski barreled up the middle, sent two linebackers flying in different directions, trampled two defensive backs, ran through the end-zone and bounced off the goal-post, finally bulldozing into the brick wall that bordered the dug-out used by the Chicago Cubs — even cracking it. "That last guy hit me awful hard...", the dazed Nagurski would say upon reaching the sidelines.

One tall tale had him falling out of bounds during a game once, and toppling a policeman's horse standing along the sideline. Another had the Bronk missing a wild tackle and shearing the fender off a Model-T Ford that was parked near the sidelines.

As a runner, Nagurski didn't bother with dazzle and finesse, and as a lineman he never bothered to learn great technique. Instead, he simply used his brute strength to overpower his opponents. In other words, he was about as subtle as a Mack Truck. When he ran, he simply tucked the ball under his arm, lowered his giant shoulders, and charged full speed ahead — ramming through anything in his way.

"I was OK, I guess," Bronko said years later. "I wasn't pretty, but I did all right. Our teams won most of the time, so that was good. I know I'd love to do it all over again. I never enjoyed anything as much as I did playing football. I felt like it was something I was born to do."

Bronko wasn't the only star running back on the team though, as future Hall of Famer Red Grange was also in the Bears' backfield as well. In fact, Bronko even took over in that same Bears backfield for another future Hall of Famer, former Duluth Eskimo great, Ernie Nevers. "Halas stockpiled backs and he believed in spreading it around," Nagurski told Sports Illustrated in 1984. "Plus, he wanted to keep me fresh for defense, where I'd put in a full afternoon."

"I have said it a thousand times, Nagurski was the greatest player I ever saw, and I saw a lot of them in my lifetime," Red Grange would later say. "Running into him was like getting an electric shock. If you tried to tackle him anywhere above the ankles, you were liable to get killed."

Overall, Nagurski was a clutch player who did whatever it took to get his team a victory. He threw the winning touchdown pass in the 1932 playoff game against the Portsmouth Spartans, and that next season he led the Bears to another NFL championship when he tossed a pair of touchdown passes in Chicago's 23-21 victory over the New York Giants. Nobody could quite figure out how to stop him, although Detroit Lions owner G.A. Richards had one idea.

"Here's a check for $10,000, Nagurski" quipped Richards, "not to play for the Lions, but just to quit and get the hell out of the league. You're ruining my team!"

In 1937, Nagurski, still upset about his salary being decreased throughout the 1930s from $5,000 to $4,500 in 1931, and down to $3,700 by 1932, decided to retire, and pursue a career in pro wrestling. The Bronk had gotten into wrestling a few years earlier, but found it tough to juggle both careers. In one three-week stretch that year, he played in five Bears games and wrestled in eight cities: Portland. Vancouver, Seattle, Phoenix, L.A., Oakland, Salt Lake City and Philadelphia. Life in the ring was not as glamorous as he had hoped, but it was a living.

"I wrestled guys like Jim Londos, Strangler Lewis and others," said Bronko. "But they weren't in their prime then. I never liked wrestling. At that time, there wasn't a lot of money in it. And it was a sport where you worked every night and traveled a lot. I had a family at the time and didn't want to be away from home. But we were just getting out of the Depression in those days and we needed the money. The promoters told me I would make a million in no time. But it didn't happen."

Then, in 1943, because of player shortages caused by World War II, the Bears issued an S.O.S. to Nagurski to return for one final season. He agreed, and fittingly, at the age of 35, even scored the game-winning touchdown of the NFL title game against the Washington Redskins. He hung em' up for good after that season though, finishing his amazing NFL career with 242 points scored on 4,301 yards rushing. The six-time All-Pro also averaged nearly five yards per carry, a remarkable feat.

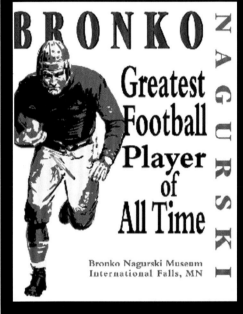

"My greatest thrill in football was the day Bronko announced his retirement," said Green Bay Hall of Fame fullback Clarke Hinkle. "There's no question he was the most bruising fullback football has ever seen. I know, because I've still got the bruises!"

After wrestling professionally for more than a dozen years — a career he would later call "degrading," Nagurski returned to International Falls with his wife Eileen to raise their six children. (One of his boys, Bronko, Jr., played football at Notre Dame and later in the CFL.) There, quietly and unassumingly, he became the most famous gas station owner in America. He could finally live in peace and privacy, and enjoy the fruits of his labor. He loved the outdoors, and was an avid hunter and fisherman. He even liked the cold weather.

"We don't have summer," Bronko once explained of his beloved hometown, "just a season in the middle of the year when the sledding is poor."

He would later do some endorsements, including a couple of $50 deals for promoting Wheaties and Camel Cigarettes — which included a carton of smokes a week. "I bought Kools and gave the Camels away," he later said jokingly.

Tragically, on Jan. 7, 1990, Bronko died at the age of 81. His awards and honors are many and include being named as a charter member of both the Pro Football and College Football Halls of Fame, as well as being elected to the Football Writers Association of America's All-Time team. In 1995 that same group also voted to have his name attached to college football's Defensive Player of the Year award, called the "Nagurski Trophy."

In 1979 his No. 72 was retired by the U of M, and Sports Illustrated later named Bronko as Minnesota's Greatest Athlete of the 20th Century. In addition, in 1992, International Falls honored its most famous son by opening the "Bronko Nagurski Museum," the only museum in America dedicated to a single player. That same year the Gophers' practice facility was renamed as the Gibson-Nagurski Football Complex, after Bronk and his Gopher teammate, 1928 All-American guard George Gibson. Perhaps the biggest honor came years ago though, when his old high school renamed themselves as the International Falls "Broncos" in his memory.

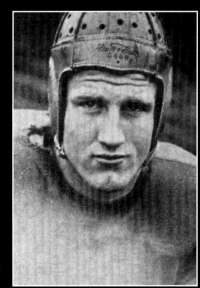

Legendary Notre Dame Coach Knute Rockne called him "the only football player I ever saw who could have played every position," and George Halas said he was "the greatest fullback who ever lived. He was absolutely unstoppable."

Bronko Nagurski was larger than life, and his size 22 Super Bowl ring, the biggest ever made, was proof. Perhaps no name has become more synonymous in the history of the sport than his. Nothing says leather helmets and high-top cleats louder than Bronko Nagurski. With his barrel chest and tree trunk legs, he became one of America's most colorful all-time characters and greatest sports heroes.

Perhaps Grantland Rice, once the most respected football authority in the nation, summed him up best when he was asked to select an all-time All-Star team.

"That's easy," said Rice. "I'd pick 11 Bronko Nagurski's. I honestly don't think it would be a contest. The 11 Nagurski's would mop-up. It would be something close to murder and massacre. For the Bronk could star at any position on the field — with 228 pounds of authority to back him up."

BIBLIOGRAPHY

1. *Ross Bernstein: Hundreds of personal interviews and also various bits of information from each of his more than 40 books about sports history.
2. "Fifty Years – Fifty Heroes: A Celebration of Minnesota Sports," by Ross Bernstein
3. "Hubert H. Humphrey Metrodome Souvenir Book," compiled by Dave Mona. & MSP Publications, Inc.
4. Minnesota Sports Almanac, by Joel A. Rippel. MN Historical Soc. Press, 2006
5. "Gold Glory": by Richard Rainbolt: Ralph Turtinen Publishing, 1972
6. "The 100 Greatest Pitchers of All Time": Barnes & Noble Press
7. "The Harmon Killebrew Story": by Hal Butler: Juliann Messner Publishing
8. Star Tribune Article by Curt Brown - March 11, 1993 (An Investment of 26 Years Yields Nothing But Memories)
9. Minnesota Almanacs - various throughout 1970s
10. "The Official National Hockey League 75th Anniversary Commemorative Book": by Dan Diamond, NHL Publications, 1991.
11. "A Thinking Man's Guide to Pro Hockey": by Eskenazi, Gerald, E. P. Dutton, 1972.
12. "The Hockey Encyclopedia": by Fischler, Stan, and Shirley Fischler, Macmillan, 1983.
13. "NHL The World of Professional Hockey": by Jay Greenberg, On Frarik, and Gary Ronberg, Rutledge Press, 1981.
14. "The Pictorial History of Hockey" by Joe Romain and Dan Diamond, Gallery Books, 1987.
15. "The Sporting News Hockey Guide & Register" :1984-85, 1986-87, 1989-90.
16. "Season Review": ESPN Sports Almanac by Jerry Trecker, Total Sports Pub., 1983.
17. "NFL Football" by Ron Smith, Collins Publishers, NFL Properties, 1995
18. "Unstoppable": The Story of George Mikan, the First NBA Superstar: by George Mikan and Joseph Oberle, published by Masters Press, Indianapolis, 1997.
19. "The Kid From Cuba" by James Terzian, Doubleday Press
20. "Twenty Five Seasons": The First Quarter Century With the Minnesota Twins by Dave Mona and Dave Jarzyna: Mona Publications
21. "Rod Carew": by Marshall Burchard: Longman Canada, Ltd., 1978
22. "Sid!" The Sports Legends, the Inside Scoops, and the Close Personal Friends: by Sid Hartman and Patrick Reusse - Voyager Press, 1997
23. "Good Timing": The Paul Molitor story, by Stuart Broomer: ECW Press
24. The Winfield Foundation publication
25. Sports Illustrated: article on the Minnesota Twins, May 22, 1997
26. "Kirby Puckett": by Bob Italia: Abdo and Daughters, 1992
27. "Season of Dreams": by Tom Kelly and Ted Robinson: Voyageur Press
28. "Kent Hrbek": by Jerry Carpenter & Steve Dimeglio: Abdo and Daughters, 1988
29. Star Tribune article: Kirby Puckett Weekend, May 23, 1997
30. Star Tribune article: 1987 Twins, Aug. 8, 1997
31. Star Tribune article: "Broten Lived Out a Dream" by Dan Barriero: Oct. 16, 1996
32. The U.S. Hockey Hall of Fame Handbook
33. Pioneer Press: Dick Siebert article: "A molder of Champions," by Charley Walters
34. Pioneer Press: Dick Siebert article: "Siebert Built 'U' Baseball" by Charley Hallman
35. Sun Times: Kevin McHale article: "He's Just Warming Up," by Phil Hersh
36. University of Minnesota Sports News: Chuck Mencel article: "Making His Mark Through Effort and Intelligence," by Len Levine
37. Press: Dick Siebert article: "From the Majors to Minnesota," by Jim Ramsburg
38. High Minnesota State High School Hockey Tournament Media Guide, 1997
39. "Tony-O," the Trials and Triumphs of Tony Oliva, by Bob Fowler: Hawthorne Books
40. "One Goal - A Chronicle of the 1980 US Olympic Hockey Team": by John Powers and Art Kaminsky: Harper Row, 1984
41. The US Olympic Hockey Guide -1996
42. "Players of Cooperstown": Publishing International
43. "Tarkenton" by Jim Klobuchar and Fran Tarkenton: Harper Publishing, 1976
44. "Winfield" - A Player's Life, by Dave Winfield with Tom Parker: WW Nortan, 1988
45. "Gagliardi of St John's": The Coach, the Man, the Legend: by Don Riley and John Gagliardi: R. Turtinen Publishing
46. Saint John's University Football Media Guide, 1996
47. Star Tribune: North Stars article by Curt Brown - March 11, 1993
48. Star Tribune: "An Investment of 26 Years Yields Nothing But Memories" - 1981
49. "Frank Viola": by Jerry Carpenter And Steve Dimeglio: Abdo and Daughters, 1988
50. Links Magazine - "Heroes of American Golf" March 1995, by Pamela Emory
51. Sports Illustrated: "Ready or Not" article on Kevin Garnett, June 25, 1995
52. Dayton's Challenge Official Souvenir Program, 1997: (Lehman article, by Ken Cohen)
53. North Stars Media Guides (various 1970s - 1990s)
54. "Before the Dome," by David Anderson: Nodin Press, 1993
55. Twins Magazine: "Home for Good" - Terry Steinbach article by Jim Bohem, July 1997
56. Twins Magazine: "Baseball Pioneers" article by Mark Engebretson, July 1997
57. Sports Illustrated Article on Terry Steinbach, "Cold Sweet Home" (1-27-97)
58. "Basketball Stars," by Nick Dolin, Chris Dolin & David Check: Black Dog and Leventhal Publishes, 1997
59. College Hockey Magazine: "Don Roberts Bids Farewell to Gustavus," by Jim Rueda - Free Lance Writer for the Mankato Free Press
60. Mpls. St. Paul Magazine, Aug. 1997 "North to the Pole" - Ann Bancroft Article
61. "Greg LeMond's Complete Book of Cycling," by Greg LeMond and Kent Gordis: G.P. Putnam Publishing, 1987
62. "On to Nicollet," by Stew Thornley, Nodin Press, 1988
63. "Basketball's Original Dynasty," by Stew Thornley, Nodin Press, 1989
64. "The Christian Story": Christian Brothers, Inc. Press Release Information
65. "Rashad," by Ahmad Rashad with Peter Bodo: Viking Press, 1988
66. "Minnesota Trivia," by Laurel Winter: Rutledge Hill Press, 1990
67. "Minnesota Awesome Almanac," by Jean Blashfield: B&B Publishing, 1993
68. The University of Minnesota Duluth Hockey Media Guide, 1997
69. "Gopher Sketchbook," by Al Papas, Jr.: Nodin Press, 1990
70. "NCAA Championships": The Official 2001 National Collegiate Championships Records
71. The Phoenix Coyotes Media Guide: 1997
72. "Kirby Puckett, I Love This Game": by Kirby Puckett: Harper Collins, 1993

74. The U.S. Olympic Committee, Olympian Report, 2008
75. Various Minnesota State High School League Programs, all sports, 1948-2008
76. Star Tribune, "Randle becomes $32.5 million man" - article by Don Banks: Feb. 2, 1998
77. Minnesota Daily: article on Tom Lehman, Jan. 19, 1995
78. Grandmas Marathon Race Program, 1997
81. The Star Tribune Minnesota Sports Hall of Fame insert publication
82. Star Tribune: article on Grandma's Marathon: 6/97
83. Star Tribune: article on Kirby Puckett: May 23, 1997
84. Article: "Nicollet Park, Home of the Millers," by Dave Mona
85. "Lexington Park: Campy, The Duke, The Babe, and Oh, That Coliseum!," By Patrick Reusse
86. Sports Illustrated: "Home at Last," by Peter King: March 2, 1998
87. Jill Trenary biography press release: IMG
88. Star Tribune: articles on Gopher Baseball, June 15-17, 1956
89. Fran Tarkenton press releases: Washington Speakers Bureau
90. "Hockey": The Illustrated History, by Dan Diamond
91. Sports Illustrated: North Stars article, May 25, 1981
92. Sports Illustrated: North Stars article, June 1, 1981
93. "One Hundred Years of Hockey": by Brian McFarlane
94. "The Official NHL Stanley Cup Centennial ," by Dan Diamond
95. Minnesota Twins - 1978 Yearbook
96. "Can You Name That Team?" by David Biesel
97. Tribune: Various articles from Janet Karvonen, March 16-22, 1978
98. Pioneer Press: Various articles from Janet Karvonen, March 16-22, 1978
99. Janet Karvonen Basketball Camp Brochure
100. Tribune: Vikings article, Jan. 13, 1976
101. Sports Illustrated, Fran Tarkenton article, Jan 5, 1976
102. Tribune: Tarkenton article , Dec 29, 1975
103. Star Tribune: Bud Grant article, Jan 7, 1986
104. Star Tribune: Bud Grant article, Jan 28, 1984
105. Tribune: Kevin McHale article, March 20, 1980
106. Tribune: Chuck Mencel article, Feb 21, 1955
107. Star Tribune: Rickey Foggie article, Dec 22, 1985
108. Tribune: Mariucci article, March 13-14, 1984
109. University of Minnesota "Gopher" Year Books: 1954, 1955, 1956
110. Star Tribune: Gopher Hockey article, April 1-2, 1989
111. Links Letter: Patty Berg article, Feb. 1997
112. Country Club Golfer: July 1977, Feb. 1980
113. Golf Course Management: Dec. 1985, March 1986
114. The Senior Golfer: June 1988
115. The Memorial: May 1988
116. Fairway: Patty Berg article and interview 1989
117. Minnesota Golfer: Spring 1993
118. Links Magazine: March 1995
119. Duluth News Tribune and Herald: UMD Hockey article, March 25, 1984
120. The Sporting News: UMD Hockey article - April 2, 1984
121. Sports Illustrated: Rod Carew Cover Story article, July 16, 1977
122. "The Autumn Warrior," by Mike Wilkinson, 1992
123. Ivory Tower: "The Coach Behind the Comeback," by Peter Vanderpoel, 1953
124. Ambassador Magazine: "Leveling the Playing Field," by Curt Brown, July, 1996
125. Minnesota Monthly Magazine: "Bent but Not Broken," by Paul Levy, August 1996
126. Star Tribune: article on Alan Page - "Mindworks" by Misti Snow, May 25, 1993
127. Minneapolis Star: "Twice Down for Nine Count - St. John's Rallied" - Dec. 16, 1963
128. St. Cloud Times: John Gagliardi article - Nov. 4, 1963
129. Minneapolis Tribune: Gagliardi article - Nov. 29, 1963
130. "The Vikings: The First Fifteen Years," Minnesota Vikings Publications
131. "Obsession: Bill Musselman's Relentless Quest to Beat the Best "- by Heller: Bonus Books
132. Twins Yearbook: 30th Anniversary Edition - 1991
133. Article: "Year by Year with the Minnesota Twins": by Bill Morlock and Rick Little
134. Article: "How the Vikings Came to Be": by Jim Klobuchar
135. "Hockey Chicago Style": by Paul Greenland: Sagamore Pub.
136. "No Time for Losing," by Fran Tarkenton: Revell Publishing, 1967
137. "Purple Hearts and Golden Memories," by Jim Klobuchar: Quality Sports Pub, 1995
138. Sports Illustrated Vikings article: "In on a Win and a Prayer," - Jan. 5, 1976
139. Sports Illustrated Twins article: "The Best of the Worst," - Aug. 30, 1982
140. Sports Illustrated: Vikings article: Jan. 13, 1976
141. Various Wikipedia Articles and Features online
142. "Minnesota Twins" - Professional Sports Teams Histories
143. "Minnesota Timberwolves" - Professional Sports Teams Histories
144. "Dallas Stars" - Professional Team Histories
145. "Minnesota Vikings"- Professional Team Histories
146. Minneapolis Lakers Media Guides/Game-day programs (various)
147. The Minnesota Fighting Saints Media Guides (various)
148. The Minnesota Wild Media Guides (various)
149. The Minnesota Vikings Media Guides (various)
150. The Minnesota Twins Media Guides (various)
151. The Minnesota North Stars Media Guides (various)
152. The Minnesota Timberwolves Media Guides (various)
153. The Minnesota Kicks Media Guides (various)
154. The Minnesota Strikers Media Guides (various)
155. University of Minnesota Men's Athletics Media Guides: Football, Basketball, Hockey, Baseball, Track & Field, Golf, Swimming & Diving, Wrestling, Gymnastics and Tennis
156. University of Minnesota Women's Athletics Media Guides: Basketball, Volleyball, Track & Field, Golf, Swimming & Diving, Soccer, Gymnastics, Softball and Tennis
157: Various media guides: MIAC, NSIC, NCC
158. Star Tribune, "Randle becomes $32.5 million man" - article by Don Banks: Feb. 2, 1998
159. "75 Memorable Moments in Minnesota Sports History," by Joel A. Rippel, MHSP, 2003